W9-ASA-992

Ralph McGill, Reporter

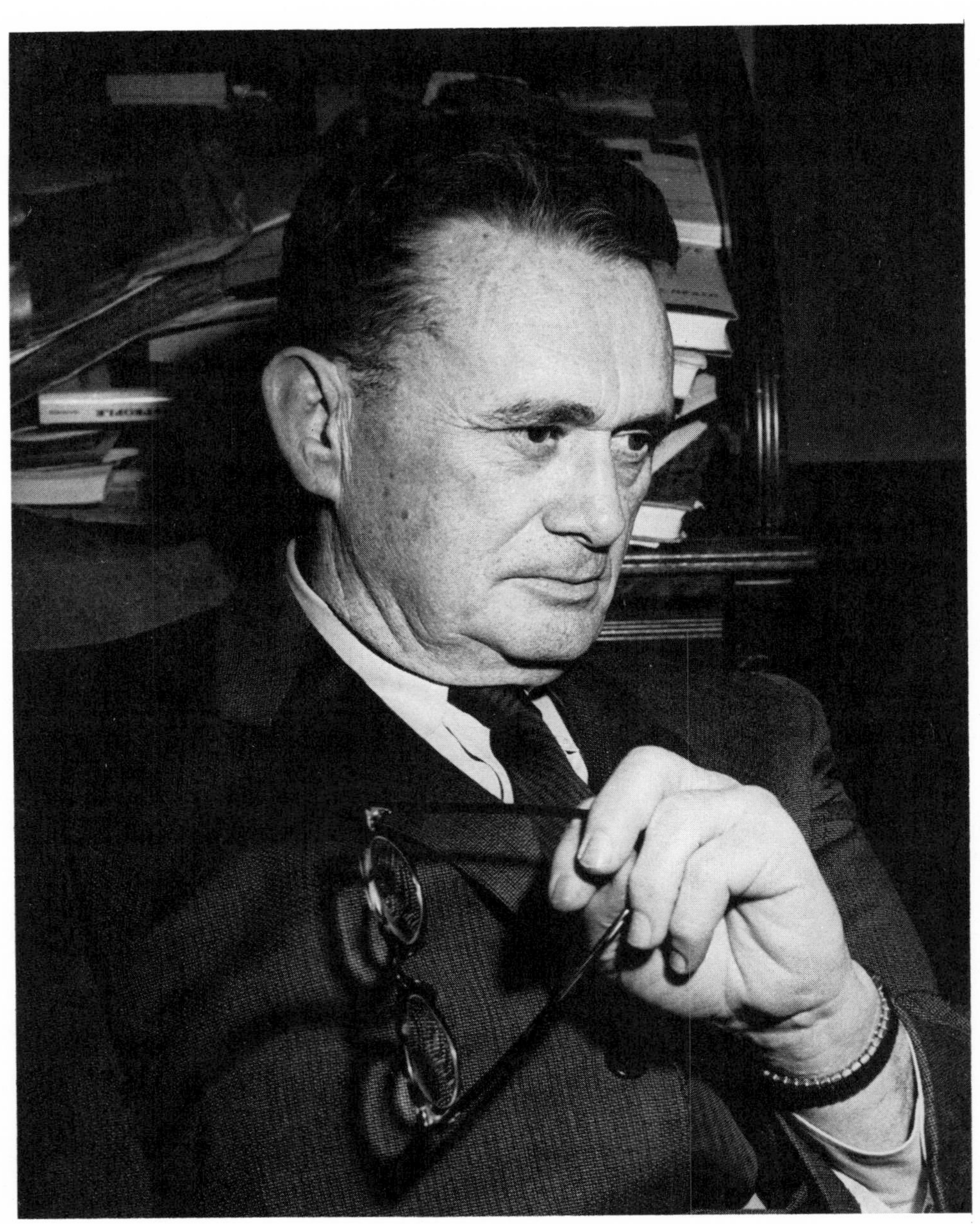

Ralph McGill

Ralph McGill, Reporter

by HAROLD H. MARTIN

AN ATLANTIC MONTHLY PRESS BOOK
Little, Brown and Company — Boston — Toronto

FIRST EDITION

T 06/73

Library of Congress Cataloging in Publication Data

Martin, Harold H
Ralph McGill, reporter.

"An Atlantic Monthly Press book."
1. McGill, Ralph Emerson, 1898-1969.
PN4874.M37M37 070.5'092'4 [B] 72-13478
ISBN 0-316-54772-7

ATLANTIC–LITTLE, BROWN BOOKS
ARE PUBLISHED BY
LITTLE, BROWN AND COMPANY
IN ASSOCIATION WITH
THE ATLANTIC MONTHLY PRESS

Published simultaneously in Canada
by Little, Brown & Company (Canada) Limited

PRINTED IN THE UNITED STATES OF AMERICA

To Grace Lundy and Gene Patterson,
who meant much to him — and to me

. . . and with grateful appreciation to the friends and colleagues of Ralph McGill around the world who so generously shared with me their memories of him. Many of them are named in this book, but there are others whom I would particularly like to thank: Al G. Smith, Ann Equen, James Townsend, Luanne Nance, Earl Mann, Louise Suggs, and the members of Ralph's family, who added greatly to my understanding of him as a private person. Without the wisdom and experience of Edward Weeks, and his unerring judgment to guide me, I would have been lost — and without the services of Susan Rigell and Mrs. Dixon Preston, the book could not have been put together at all. Both are former secretaries to Ralph McGill, and out of their devotion to him they endured the agony of transcribing my handwritten hieroglyphics into readable typescript. I acknowledge, too, a deep debt to David Estes, curator of Special Collections of the Woodruff Memorial Library at Emory University, where the McGill papers are kept, and to Professor Thomas H. English. Their counsel, and the deft help of the amiable and competent "den mothers" of the Special Collections staff, Mesdames Gillespie, Stearns, Beischer, and Matthews, made light my burdens.

Introduction

RALPH McGILL was a man of high courage, of vast good humor, and of an almost antic wit — a huge and vital and merry man with a gargantuan appetite for food and drink and friendship. He had a zest for life that never diminished in all his seventy-one years, and he plunged to meet each new challenge with a headlong drive. Despite the gusto with which he tasted each new experience, however, there was in him a special anguish, a gnawing self-doubt, a dissatisfaction with himself and the world around him. Making and keeping new friends, working without letup, traveling incessantly, and toward the end, a happy second marriage, helped him to beat back the darkness of the spirit. But always it was there — "the eternal note of sadness . . ."

On his desk in his office he kept a tattered old paperback book of poems, the book he and his colleagues on the *Constitution* used to read aloud from, sitting in his office in the late afternoon after his column had gone to the composing room and he was relaxed and easy, waiting for his wife to come and pick him up and drive him home. It was also the book he would slip into his pocket on Saturday at noon, when we would go across the street and down an alley to a delicatessen run by an earnest old Russian émigré named Max Muldawer, whom McGill always addressed as the "last of the great innkeepers." Max, who loved McGill, would bustle about in a great flurry, setting up a card table with a red-checked cloth upon it in the basement kitchen amid the barrels and bags of beans and sugar and the huge cans of fruit and vegetables. Then, putting on a clean apron, he would rush up and down the narrow stairs, bringing a platter of meat and cheese and bottles of red wine.

The stains of the wine and the food are still on the book, and it now is falling apart. But somehow, more than all the other mementos of McGill — the honorary degrees with their proud citations, the medals and the certificates bearing witness to his virtues from presidents and popes and ballet dancers and editors and prime ministers — this battered old book of verse still evokes the warmest memories of the man. The dog-eared pages show which were his favorites, the poems he liked to read aloud with husky-voiced, croaking eloquence, or listen to, eyes closed, lips moving silently to the familiar words.

They were, for the most part, poems which appealed to the brooding melancholy strain he attributed to his Welsh ancestry, and in which he took a sort of somber pride. Matthew Arnold's "Dover Beach" and Edward Arlington Robinson's "Mr. Flood's Party" were two of his favorites.

After his first wife died and Ralph was going home to an empty house, he remarked, "I am acquainted with Mr. Flood, and I have walked his path. But, thank God, I found out that a book is a better antidote for loneliness than booze. Otherwise, I would be in a hell of a shape now."

Always, in time of trouble, he would come back to the philosophy which sustained him, his faith in man's power to hang on, to endure, to survive, and in the words of William Faulkner's magnificent evocation of the human spirit as he accepted the Nobel Prize, "not merely to survive, but to prevail."

Carl Sandburg's lines from "The People Will Live On" gave him reassurance: "Man will win," wrote Sandburg, "brother may yet line up with brother, this old anvil laughs at many broken hammers. . . ." This was McGill in his last years, the old anvil, dented and scarred, but still standing up under the pounding of the hammers, still holding firmly the faith that man at last will win, that in time, no matter how dim the prospect might seem, brother will line up with brother. Through patience, through compassion, through love and understanding, through stubbornly holding fast to a dream without faltering, he managed to put down the doubts and fears that haunted him, and to make of his life, at last, a triumphant affirmation.

Sandburg, who was his friend, once said of him that he was a "paradoxical blend of holiness and humor," and it is true that he was a good man in the highest sense. But he was no saint, and he did not expect to find saintly attributes in others. He was, as other men, a mixture of warring traits. Like Sandburg's Lincoln, he could be "as hard as rock, as soft as drifting fog." He was the kindest and most considerate of men. At the same time he could be a fierce and unrelenting antagonist. In his early days as editor, before he learned to quell a turbulent and rebellious spirit, his inner tensions would sometimes burst forth in tirades of unprovoked anger against his closest friends — to be followed by profound remorse and abject apology. He was, in short, a human being, capable of both love and envy, jealousy and generosity, intolerance and magnanimity, high purpose and shabby compromise.

Sandburg once wrote him: "Sometime there will be a hummer of a biography about you . . ." a book which the poet suggested should be titled *Ralph McGill, By God: Ancient and Modern Prophet.* This does not claim to be that book. But if, in the chapters that follow, he does come through to those who never knew him as a tremendously warmhearted, loving, angry, sometimes wrongheaded, stubborn and exasperating man — an Old Testament prophet touched with the grace of tenderness and humor — then I will be satisfied.

HAROLD H. MARTIN

Atlanta, Georgia

Ralph McGill, Reporter

1

BENEATH a rumpled, almost bucolic, exterior, Ralph Emerson McGill was an urbane and cosmopolitan man. At the same time he was proud to have it known that he was country born and that his ancestors' roots ran far and deep into the rural earth of Scotland, Ireland, Wales, and the state it was often his whim to call "Tenn-O-See." He was like Dante, in that "to him all the world is native country, just as the sea is to the fish."

McGill's birthplace, to which he returned so often in his writing, was an old farming community in East Tennessee called Igou's Ferry some thirty miles north of Chattanooga on the Tennessee River. On the foggy February morning in 1898 when Ralph came feebly into the world — a baby so weak he was given little chance to live — it was a hardscrabble corn, mule and hay farm on which his parents, Benjamin Franklin McGill and his wife, Mary Lou, managed to make a meager living. Both the house in which he was born and the fields his father plowed have long since drowned in one of the lakes of the Tennessee Valley Authority.

Because his mother's people, the Clifts, had lived on adjoining lands for generations, there were kin and neighbors in plenty. It was, though, like many a farmstead of those days, a place remote from the amenities of urban living. The nearest post office and trading center was ten miles away, along a dirt road, the little grimy coal-mining town of Soddy. An equal distance in the opposite direction was an even more unpretentious hamlet called Daisy.

In later years, McGill, with his insatiable curiosity, looked into the region's history, trying to find out how Soddy got its name. In 1770, he found, a man named William Soddor had settled in the quiet, little valley in the foothills of the Great Smokies. It was a place where the grass grew deep and clear springs flowed, the Indians were reasonably amiable, and around Soddor's Trading Post a settlement soon grew up. The name "Soddy" or "Soddy's" was a pioneer's abbreviation.

Eighteen years later, after the Revolution, a group of Welsh arrived. Miners by instinct, they soon uncovered the coal deposits and began to produce coke in crude ovens. As a boy, McGill, riding home in a buggy from the town at dusk, would see the flares from the coke ovens lurid against the darkening sky, and later, when he read Dante's *Inferno,* he had no trouble visualizing what the flames of hell looked and smelled like.

In 1822 came another inrush of settlers, Scotch-Irish Presbyterians, bearing the names of McGill and Wallace and McCree. They were farmers who moved on west, past the little mining town, to the rich bottomlands beside the river, where, with an admixture of the Welsh miners, they became the ancestors of Ralph McGill. Dour Calvinists all, their first act, once their rough cabins had been built, was to erect a church. The meeting to organize the Presbytery and name the elders was held under a huge oak tree, hard by a fine, deep spring which the families of Clift and McCree jointly shared.

In later years, this spring was upon land owned by one of McGill's half-dozen uncles, who rigged up an ingenious device for bringing up water without excessive labor. From the house high on the hill above the spring, a bucket was let down on a wire trolley, dipped in the spring, and carefully pulled back up again through an avenue cut through the trees. It was the daily task of small boys in the family to operate this contraption, and one of Ralph's earliest memories is that of being highly praised, while on a visit to his uncle's house, for pulling up a bucket of water without spilling more than a quarter of it.

In 1960, in a letter to Ralph de Toledano of *Newsweek*, he wrote:

> . . . on our farm, children and old people were riches. There were things for them to do. A farmer with children didn't have to hire much labor. The old people looked after the children and did such jobs as mending and putting on buttons, darning socks, etc. I remember my grandmother actually worked a loom, and I can see her yet, a great pile of clothing beside her. She would be busy repairing it, or putting on buttons. Today this sort of

thing doesn't work any longer. I am by background conservative, but I am convinced there must be legislation and organizations to care for the problem of the old people and the children, as that problem is created by our industrial civilization. . . . We simply cannot escape it.

McGill's rural background colored his life and thought. He was fond of using the country phrases. When he was talking to young reporters, urging them to write more simply, he would say, "You have got to put the fodder down where the mules can get at it." His days on the farm gave him more than a city man's sense of the changing seasons, of the great rhythms of the earth's turning. Occasionally he would try to recapture in his column the memories of his boyhood:

You could walk out on my grandmother's porch and see the pasture sloping off to the bottom cornfields with the willows, that smell of peppermint early in the morning mists, growing thick along the banks of the river.

In the morning the mists would float up into the pastures or hover above the tops of the corn, wandering maverick clouds, until the sun came up to set them on fire and burn them up in an exploding glory of iridescence.

You could stand there and look at it and the hills far beyond the distant bottoms on the other side of the river. In the early morning you could sometimes hear the voice of a hound running a rabbit and now and then there would come riding the wind the sound of a man's voice shouting at something across the river, or a plow-hand singing in the covering rows of green.

I can see it yet as plain as ever and I can remember, too, the mystery of it at night, with fireflies in the pasture and the corn. . . .

One night, riding home late in a buggy from the small town at the foot of the mountains to the farm ten miles away by the river, there was a scream in the hills not far from the road. I remember my father pulling up the horse:

"Whoa, boy, whoa there," as the horse attempted to run off one side of the road and then began to rear and plunge against the reins.

"A painter," he said, using the hill term for panther, "always sounds like a child screaming."

That night stayed with me for years.

As a speaker McGill would draw from his boyhood details to touch the special interests of his audience, as when in addressing the Hybrid

Corn section of the American Seed Association, he told these highly scientific technicians:

> I grew up with the taste of fried mush for breakfast and mush and milk at Sunday night suppers. I still like to crumble cold cornbread into a bowl of milk and eat it as a cereal. . . . As a young boy I have ridden a horse to the mill with a sack of corn in front of me. I remember yet the nut-sweet smell of the mill, the warm feel of the stones and of the meal itself as it fell into the bin. I have plowed corn, first "busting middles," and then graduating with pride to the advanced step of plowing around corn with a double shovel plow. . . .

The nation, he went on, was founded on corn, the hard flint corn his father grew. It wore down the teeth of a mule, he said, but it gave the pioneer the strength to push on to the Pacific shore.

Much of Ralph's farm lore centered around mules. He had quite a streak of mulishness in his own makeup, which is why, perhaps, he always looked upon them as being superior to horses, which he considered flighty and untrustworthy. A mule, he would point out, practiced the art of the possible. It would not lunge and strain against too heavy a load. It would give its utmost, but it would not let itself be driven beyond its strength. Nor would it ever commit the utterly idiotic act of rushing back into a blazing stable, seeking security, as would a horse.

McGill's actual sojourn on the farm was brief, but his richest and most memorable experiences came to him as he returned there in the summers. The land his father tilled was shared in joint ownership with a half-dozen brothers and sisters; it had been plowed by McGills for nearly three-quarters of a century, and in 1899, Benjamin Franklin McGill decided that, so far as he was concerned, this was long enough.

When Ralph was one year old, his father sold his share in the farm to his brothers and moved to Soddy, ten miles away. The decision was partially because of Ralph's frail health; in Soddy he would be closer to the town's physician, Dr. Richard Walker, who had attended Mary Lou McGill at her lying-in, and to the outrage of the Presbyterian uncles and aunts, had suggested for the baby the name of the Unitarian and transcendentalist philosopher, Ralph Waldo Emerson. As McGill commented later, somewhere along the way the Waldo got lost.

But in Soddy, the baby's health did not improve. He remained puling, subject to hideous nightmares, until he was old enough to start school. Long afterward, as if speaking of someone else, he described the agony of those seizures: Lying there in the dark, hot and sick, with the room feeling strange and unfamiliar in the darkness, he would see the terror coming. It always was a whirling blur, small and far away as the stars. It could just be seen, whirling so fast it looked like a ghostly spinning top with white circles about it. And it came toward him. . . . He knew that if it ever struck him, it would engulf him in its whirling and take him away. . . . But always, just before it reached him, he would cry out, and the terror would vanish. There would be a sound of steps and of hurrying, and lights and voices. . . . Then he would sleep again, going to sleep eagerly, knowing the terror would not come again that night.

In 1949, after he had sold a story on southern cooking to the *Saturday Evening Post,* the editors requested some autobiographical background. "I was, as they said in those days, a sickly child," McGill replied. "I was not expected to live long. I suffered from an inability to assimilate my food, a fact which causes much merriment in my small circle now, where I am regarded as having assimilated too much food." McGill at that writing weighed two hundred twenty pounds; as a sportswriter, he had weighed nearly two hundred forty, and wrestlers, line coaches, and other noted trenchermen had looked with awe upon his prowess at the table.

But there was no hint of robustness in the scrawny child who toddled about after his mother in the little house on unpaved Ducktown Row in Soddy.

His mother he remembered as a person both merry and brave, a free spirit undaunted by any hardship or misfortune, and she was much in his thoughts as long as she lived. No matter where he might be wandering across the world when his birthday came, he would send her a telegram thanking her for giving him the gift of life. On her birthday, as well as on Valentine's Day, Easter, and any special occasion, he would telegraph his affections. Even the memory of her whims and crotchetiness gave him pleasure. Her father had been a wandering journalist, a man of wit and charm but an irresponsible ne'er-do-well who abandoned her and her mother when she was a child. She was determined to bind her own family together in closer bonds, and one way was to have young Ralph and his three sisters ready to greet their father when he came home from work: she would call them from play and make them scrub their hands and faces and change into clean clothes. "No father," she would say, "wants to hug a dirty child or kiss a dirty face."

McGill always felt himself closer to his mother than his dour, Calvinistic father, but to him also he reached out in love, sending him, when he traveled, awkwardly affectionate letters. For a brief time in Soddy, Benjamin Franklin McGill worked in the coal mines, coming home black-faced and weary. He would wash up and then, taking his young son on his lap, he would patiently point out words and letters to him, teaching him to read. Then he left the mines and began commuting daily by train to Chattanooga, where he worked as a clerk in a small heating and roofing firm. Each night on coming home, the routine was the same. He would take down whatever book was handy — the family Bible, a volume of Presbyterian sermons, a farm publication, an almanac — and seat young Ralph on his lap and begin the reading lessons.

It was not until his father died that Ralph comprehended the deeper meaning of this. "He was not only teaching me to read," he said. "He was teaching me that all man's knowledge of things past, and all his hopes for what is to come, lie in books."

It was a lesson well learned, for Ralph was reading two years before he went to school. He read omnivorously all his life — in maturity, fourteen or fifteen newspapers a day, two or three books a week.

When the boy was six his father moved the family to Chattanooga and for the next decade Ralph revisited the family farm only on the summer holidays. Ill health still dogged him in the new neighborhood, and too puny to go to school, he stayed at home with his mother, spending much of his day in the kitchen. From her he learned the rudiments of cooking, and in later life it became his hobby. (Many years afterward, when the *Constitution* erected a new building, he asked for and got a small electric kitchen, built just off his office. There, on rainy days, he would cook simple lunches for his editorial staff.)

Slowly, without medication, his health began to improve. He was eight when he started his formal education in the old, square, red-brick

Fourth District School of Highland Park and by the time he was twelve he had grown to be a stringy, healthy, small boy with the appetite of a crocodile. He was also a member in good standing of the Central Presbyterian Church Sunday School and of the Highland Park gang, a typical small tribe demonstrating what anthropologists later would call the Territorial Imperative by throwing rocks at boys from other sections who attempted to invade the Highlanders' home grounds. Athletic contests were sandlot affairs, which sometimes degenerated into gang fights.

An aging ballplayer named "Buttermilk" Meek, who caught for Chattanooga in the Sally League, had given Ralph an authentic pair of baseball socks; his rivals were so envious that they would chase him home, throwing rocks and shouting insults.

Early in his school days, Ralph became a commuter to the Carnegie Library, only two miles from his home. First on foot, later on his bike, he made the round trip in the afternoon, taking out a book, sampling it overnight, and turning it in when finished. He began with the Henty books, the Rover Boys and Frank Merriwell, but soon moved on to *Treasure Island, Ivanhoe, Robinson Crusoe, Vanity Fair, David Copperfield, The Deerslayer,* books which left their mark.

"I got from them and from my Welsh and Scottish ancestry too much sentiment; an ability to weep at sad movies and over many pieces of poetry, or passages in books and at grief generally, a mixture of naïveté and reality, a belief in loyalty and a liking for causes. Also the bitter fact that high ideals, devotion to duty, and honor are not in themselves passports to victory."

The story of the Confederacy and its great war leaders fascinated him, and he read everything he could lay hands on about Robert E. Lee, Stonewall Jackson, and Nathan Bedford Forrest. He was attracted by the Indian legends, and gradually discovered that the land around Chattanooga was itself a book of Indian and Confederate history and that every rain turned a new page, bringing to light artifacts left by an aboriginal people, commingled with the debris of the Civil War battlefields.

Chattanooga, which in Indian language meant "where the mountains look at each other," had been a hunting ground and tribal meeting place for Creek Indians, and their burial mounds were thick along the riverbanks. In the Civil War, bloody battles had been fought here — Chickamauga, Lookout Mountain, and Missionary Ridge — and the land was thickly strewn, if one knew where to look, with the arrowheads and pottery of the Indians, the minié balls, belt buckles, canteens, and rusty gunlocks of the Union and Confederate armies.

Ralph was a zealous relic hunter, and his room in the little white clapboard home on Kirby Avenue was cluttered with artifacts, which worried his mother, a tidy person, who took pride in keeping a clean house. The family had now grown to six, with the arrival of three younger sisters, Bessie Flo, Lucille, and Sarah, and when a visitor arrived for overnight — and there was always a great coming and going of kin from the country — Ralph was moved to a cot in his parents' room and the guest was bedded down among the minié balls and the arrowheads. There was also a large sign on his wall which his mother feared might offend a sensitive visitor. It read: "If You Expect to Rate as a Gentleman, Don't Expectorate on the Floor."

McGill's collection could not match that of his close friend, Charles Peacock, who had among his relics the complete skeleton of a Creek Indian, a stone pipe, and a horse pistol that had last been fired during the Seminole wars. Peacock kept a detailed diary of his grammar-school days, and there are frequent references in it to "Gillum," McGill's nickname in those days.

Highlights of the Peacock diary, in which the author and McGill felt a shared excitement, included the visit of the first airplane to Chattanooga in May of 1912; the arrival of Buffalo Bill's Circus, with Indians, in 1913; and in that same summer the reunion of the Confederate *and* Union veterans, at which both boys served as guides.

Like East Tennessee in the Civil War, McGill's own family became a house divided. Though some of his mother's people had been Democrats and Rebels, others were Republicans and strong Unionists. One of his forebears, in fact, had wreaked great havoc, even though inadvertently, upon the Confederates.

McGill's great-grandfather, Colonel William Clift, a prosperous Welshman rich in mines and steamboats, proved his loyalty to the Union by organizing and commanding a group of volunteers designated as the 8th Tennessee Infantry, a small but doughty band armed with shotguns, squirrel rifles, knives and pepper-pot pistols. Their heaviest piece of ordnance was a homemade cannon, fashioned from a large cylinder which had once been part of the driving machinery of the *Black Hawk*, one of Colonel Clift's steamboats, which they loaded with black powder, rocks and fragments of metal. Unhappily, in their first engagement, McGill's great-grandsire and his men were surrounded and attacked, and their cannon captured, though the colonel himself managed to escape. The Confederates, members of the 7th Alabama, returned in triumph to Chattanooga, where the cannon was put on display as a prize of war. There somebody discovered it was loaded, touched it off, and it exploded, killing or wounding a number of Rebel bystanders. The colonel, who had a habit of clearing his throat nervously, was later told of the accident. "Humph, humph!" he grunted. "That's what I loaded it for."

At the end of the school year in Chattanooga, Ralph went back to the old home place on the river to spend the summer with his grandmother Wallace, whom he called Mammy, and to pitch hay and plow corn for his uncles. The fresh air, sun and exercise were the tonic which eventually filled him out and built up his strength.

Up to now, McGill had taken his frequent illnesses as he had taken the piano lessons his parents required of him — with Calvinist stoicism, as a visitation from a wrathful god upon a small boy for whatever unknown sins he had committed. When he was sixteen, though, a siege of illness really scared him. His younger sister, Bessie Flo, had come down with scarlet fever, and during her illness he had sat just outside the door of her room, reading aloud to her. This precaution was not sufficient. On the day the quarantine was lifted after Bessie Flo's recovery, Ralph came home from school early, shiny-eyed and flushed. He felt so hot, he said, he had stopped to take a swim in the McCallie pool. It was a cool day in May. His mother looked at him. "Get in the bed," she said.

All his life thereafter McGill vividly remembered that bout with fever in which he lay for days delirious and close to death.

The scarlet-fever attack spoiled for that summer a trip he and Peacock had long planned — a journey to the McGill farm at Igou's Landing to open up the Indian mounds which dotted the bottomlands there.

Next summer, however, they made it. Lugging a borrowed tent and camping gear, they headed upriver on a chuffing steamboat called the *Joe Wheeler*. Years later, McGill wrote:

> I can see her yet and smell her cargo. I recall the roustabouts, with their chanting work songs. I remember the food, served on the thick, heavy china, the many vegetables, the ham, fried round steak, and chicken on the table — and the mystery and skill of the landings at night . . . the powerful searchlights with moths whirling in their beams, the shouts of the mate, the gangplank pushed into the muddy bank. . . . That was living.

Camping in the woods along the river, they dug for two weeks in the old burial mounds — and found nothing but a few shards of pottery. When the time came to go home, they trudged wearily down to the riverbank, hoping to hail the *Joe Wheeler* on its morning run downstream. Their supplies had run out, and for two days they had been living mainly off watermelons pilfered from a nearby farmer's patch. Peacock, who later was to become a Boy Scout executive, was made nervous by this. McGill was reassuring. "Don't worry, Charles," he said. "We'll be careful to bury the rinds."

For a day and a night and a morning, unable to sleep for fear the boat would pass without seeing their signal, they kept a red-eyed watch. Finally, a hungry McGill, in a borrowed rowboat, set out across the river to where a party of pleasure fishermen from Chattanooga was anchored. Two meals and a long sleep later, the boys were home.

Ralph, in his Chattanooga boyhood, went with his parents to the Sunday services at the Central Presbyterian Church. Restless by nature, with a questioning mind, he found the sermons soporific, but his attendance there was opportune. The pastor of the church, Dr. Thomas H. McCallie, was brother to the founders of McCallie, a new preparatory school located on the slopes of Missionary Ridge. Together they persuaded his parents that the boy would be good material for the Presbyterian institution. The cost of a private school was a problem, but his father borrowed the money for his tuition, and Ralph himself, soon after his matriculation, found a small source of walking-around money by writing themes for classmates who were lazy or lacked literary ability. His mother, seeing this silver on his dresser, suspected that he had taken up crap shooting.

McGill's entry into McCallie and Charles Peacock's enrollment at Chattanooga City High, McCallie's bitter athletic rival, did not dilute their friendship. In Ralph's first football game for McCallie, Chattanooga trampled them, 47–7. In his diary, Peacock put down this fact, then added loyally, "Gillum played good."

McGill continued to play with great effectiveness for the four years he was at McCallie. In 1916, he was captain of the team, made all-city guard, and helped wipe out the memories of defeat four years earlier by leading his team to victory over City High, 48–0. One touchdown he made himself by grabbing up a fumble and running fifty-five yards. The memories of his football days never left him. On a journey back for Homecoming in 1949, he leaned against a fence, watching the junior teams of McCallie and Darlington. The next day he wrote:

> I could feel myself out there again. I could hear the panting breath and the rasp of canvas pants, the gasped-out exclamations. I could feel again that wonderful spirit of comradeship, of sharing in a common effort for a cause which for us was solemn and great.

McGill as a McCallie student also was stagestruck, his interests beginning to focus on the glamorous world of Broadway. In 1912, the year Ralph put on his first long pants, he tore the swatches out of a tailor's book displaying gentlemen's fashions for 1911 and began to fill its pages with pictures of bosomy actresses. His prize exhibit was a collection of colored pictures of famous female stars, including Laurette Taylor and Alla Nazimova.

There is little doubt that, if McGill had not had a voice somewhat reminiscent of an asthmatic bullfrog, he would have chosen the stage rather than journalism as a career. Often in later years he recalled his early yearnings:

> I remember my agony in the school plays. I was going to be a great actor then and, to tell the truth, almost went trouping with Fritz Leiber's Shakespearean company after he left Robert Mantell and formed his own company. It was a wrench for me, because I all but worshiped Mantell. He used to say he was my cousin because there was a McGill in his ancestry. But

Leiber told me the truth, namely, that my voice did not have the dramatic range to enable me to go far. So I have played in plays like *What Happened to Jones?*, *Brown of Harvard*, and *A College Town*, and so on.

But back to my agony. I was a shy and self-conscious boy, and in the plays when I had to kiss a girl I nearly died. It had to be really done the night of the real play.

Always, in his memories of Chattanooga, McGill expressed his special love for a brilliant, vivacious, black-eyed Jewish girl and his devotion to her family. They had met on his fifteenth birthday — she was a little past fourteen — at an interschool debate on the subject of Panama Canal toll charges. He was representing McCallie and she Girls' Preparatory School, and at the social hour which followed the debate, a spark of friendship began to glow between Rebecca Mathis, later Rebecca Mathis Gershon, and Ralph McGill that never dimmed.

McGill, in his shyness, began to keep a diary of his own, writing craftily in his prep-school German, which he hoped would serve as code, his thoughts about "*das Schöne Mädchen Reb*." As a mysterious cipher it was effective. McGill's German was so bad that forty years later, German scholars trying to translate it could hardly make out what he was trying to say. It did come through, however, that there was in the beginning the warm glow of first love. "I went to Reb's tonight. She gave me a flower. Her father gave me a book. There is a boy in Atlanta. I am afraid I am not as strong as he. Help me, ye gods."

Night after night, his diary reported his visits to Reb's. Then slowly the truth began to dawn. The gods were not being helpful. The book and not the flower was to be his fate.

The summer passed. She had been gone much of the time, visiting in Atlanta. He wrote, and she replied, but the wait for her letters seemed long. Finally, a September diary entry had the chill of first frost in it: "I went to Reb's and found out I am, what? I do not know. I believe that we are only friends."

He was right. They were "only friends," but it was a friendship born of the mind and spirit, a sharing of attitudes and philosophies, and it would endure long after the first sweet sickness of young love was over. Half a lifetime later, on the flyleaf of a copy of his book *The South and the Southerner*, McGill wrote:

"For Reb, who will, I hope, read in the lines which begin on page 54 some of the love I have had for her and hers across a long span of years."

In the book he had written:

> In our school plays and literary club discussions we enlisted the cooperation of the young ladies from the downtown Girls' Preparatory School.
>
> One of the GPS girls was Rebecca Mathis. Through her a new sort of world opened up for one but lately come from an upriver farm. For all my enthusiasm, I was painfully shy. The Mathis family saw this, and when I came calling on their daughter, which was as often as I could, they took me in and made me welcome. Thereby was I introduced to music, paintings, books and a culture older than mine. More, even than that, I was a part of conversations about issues, international and domestic. They listened to me and did not smile at my naïveté or the immaturity of my conclusions. The Mathis family gave me something I would not have found anywhere else in Chattanooga — an awareness of international events and of forces which were involved in them. Well before the First World War was declared I knew it might come. They were a very real inspiration to me, broadening the horizons of my mind and making me see and understand beyond the provincialism of Chattanooga.

There is no doubt that out of this experience grew McGill's later knowledge and sympathetic understanding of the Jews as a people, their yearnings for a homeland, their pride, their anger, their faith, and their agony. Throughout his career this sympathetic interest manifested itself in many trips to Israel to tell the story of the new state being born in ancient Palestine.

For more than half a century the friendship between Ralph and Reb Gershon endured. During the years of his loneliness after the death of his first wife, he would go to her house for dinner — and, going out to the kitchen, he would put on an apron and cook the meal himself. On the Saturday night before he died, he and his wife Mary Lynn dined at Reb's house. He arrived, Reb remembers, like Benjamin Franklin with his bread loaves, clasping a bottle of wine under each arm.

That evening as they talked, she was reminded that as a boy he had a funny habit of pulling at his hair when he talked, and the more interested he became, the more he would do this. He was doing it still on this night of their last dinner together. And she remembers thinking how little basic change the years had made in him since the night they had said good-bye in Chattanooga, he to go on to Vanderbilt, she to Smith, and neither ever to go home again. She had, over the years, watched

> . . . that slender, gangling, supershy youth develop into an internationally renowned editor, a man beloved and hated according to the advocacies of the reader. But always he remained unspoiled by any praise or position, the same rare blending of thundering execration and gentleness, of shyness and self-assurance, force and sensitivity, humility and quiet pride.

2

McGill graduated from McCallie in 1917, bearing rather more honors than the average graduate. He had won the Orator's Gold Medal of the Daniel Webster Literary Society, was editor of the school paper, served as captain of the football team, was a leader in the Boy Scouts, and despite his confessed nervousness, had been proclaimed the school's best actor for his performance in the title role of *What Happened to Jones?*. He had published in the school's literary magazine — of which he was also editor — a number of short stories, tales of adventure mostly, based on the poems of Robert W. Service. In one, a tale of the South Pacific called "Death Chant of the Su Li Priests," he had, without self-consciousness, given his hero the name of "Gim McRath," a man "tall, stalwart and bronzed by the tropical sun."

What satisfaction he might have felt in his achievements at McCallie was overwhelmed by the eagerness with which he looked forward to his enrollment at Vanderbilt that fall.

That excitement never diminished. Out of regard for an uncle he liked and wished to emulate, he went to Vanderbilt to learn medicine. But the fascination of putting down words on paper soon overwhelmed his theoretical interest in doctoring — though all his life he read voraciously of medical news and would prescribe for ailing friends with assurance. He kept in his desk a huge bottle of some sort of analgesic pills which he called "The Big Fix" and recommended for everything from the sniffles to a hangover.

His decision to abandon medicine was influenced by two great teachers. Dr. Edward Mims demonstrated in his classroom that there was nothing sissy in loving poetry and reading it aloud. Dr. Edwin Reinke, in biology, awakened Ralph's mind to the clear, cold discipline of science. For a while, he wavered. Then the search for the hidden meanings in Browning's poems won out over the search in the biology lab for the five kidneys of a dissected earthworm. When McGill, on a biology test, answered all the questions in rhyming couplets, both he and Dr. Reinke knew that literature, in some form or another, had triumphed. There would be no Ralph Emerson McGill, M.D.

Whatever he learned in college — and outside the classes of those two professors and the football field there was precious little — it had far less impact on his thinking than the wisdom that had come to him from other sources. Once, in a moment of self-analysis, he wrote:

> Coming from an old "Blue Stocking" Presbyterian family which, in my grandmother's time, allowed no cooking on Sundays, except breakfast coffee, I always have had an immense interest in things religious. The hot breath of Calvin always is on my neck, and remorse and sorrow, hot and cold flashes of "conscience" follow my every dereliction.
>
> Nevertheless, from my mother, who is one of the few real Christians I know, I early learned not to be afraid and not to hate or fear or dislike other persons because of their beliefs, even members of the Republican party. This made it very easy for me to get along despite a great shyness and self-consciousness. Persons always have been persons to me, during and since childhood. It did not occur to me to think of or identify a person by his religion. I honestly do not believe I have ever thought of a person as a Catholic or a Jew or a nonbeliever, but always as a person possessing the same sort of human reactions as I. A Negro's color sets him apart, but I have never understood hatred for him or discrimination of him and certainly I have always regarded a Negro as a person and therefore entitled to be so treated. This did not make it necessary to be either a "nigger lover" or anti-Negro. It involved none of the social equality argument. I simply regard him as a person entitled to complete justice and economic opportunity. All this has been entirely natural to me, southern born, southern educated, with no trace of outside influence.

Early in 1918, out of a fervent admiration for Woodrow Wilson and a profound belief that democracy was at stake, McGill dropped out of college, joined the Marine Corps, and was shipped straightway to Parris Island. Ralph, from the start, was a gung-ho marine who gave his uttermost to the corps. He washed and washed again his khakis, trying to give them the faded, "salty" look of an old-timer. He clipped off the tops of his leggings to shorten them, for this was supposed to be the mark of a veteran. Many years later, he said:

> The greatest compliment I ever had was one day shortly before I finished recruit training. We had been put through the manual of arms for the benefit of the visiting officer who was inspecting the training. By that time I had my khakis faded, my leggings were short, my old campaign hat had the proper disreputable look, and I was really slapping that rifle hard on every move. At one of the pauses the drill instructor left the visiting officer and walked directly to me. My heart went way down in my shoes. He said to me. "Have you ever served in the marines before?" "No, sir," I said. "The officer thought maybe you had," he said, and walked away.
>
> It was a great moment.

McGill's saltiness as a marine boot, plus the fact that he had had a high school education and part of a year in college, kept him on this side for higher training. While the other recruits went off to France, he and a handful of qualified marines were enrolled in noncom school. They were still there when the armistice was signed. On his return to Vanderbilt, McGill was given temporary command of an ROTC company. At his first formation, he attempted to imitate the look and manner of his old DI. Striding up and down, glowering at his troops, he announced that he was responsible for their training and intended to see to it, and if there were any among them who thought they could whip him, let them step one pace forward. Since about half the company were ex-soldiers, some of whom had been in combat, a number immediately stepped out of ranks. Faced with this unexpected challenge, McGill thought quickly.

"COMPAN-EE — DIS-MISSED," he bellowed.

Vanderbilt, in the years after World War I, was a place of ferment, full of talk and new ideas about books and plays and poetry. A young member of the English faculty named John Crowe Ransom began to attract to himself a small group, calling themselves the Fugitives, who rejected Dr. Edward Mims's opinion that there had been no worthwhile poetry written since Browning died. They wrote poems, plays and novels, gathered in the evenings to read their works aloud to each other, and several of them went on to make names for themselves in literature. Among them were novelist Robert Penn Warren and poets

Allen Tate, Ransom, Donald Davidson and Merrill Moore, a sonneteer, later to become a noted psychiatrist.

McGill, who was playing football and acting with the drama unit, was a little too robustious to be a full-fledged Fugitive, but he shared their interests. Three or four evenings a week, he and two or three other admirers of belles lettres would gather at the home of Professor Stanley Johnson of the English Department to read aloud the plays of Shaw, Ibsen and O'Neill, recite the verse of contemporary poets such as Edward Arlington Robinson, and to talk about the novels of Sinclair Lewis, Ellen Glasgow and Willa Cather. Henry Mencken, McGill recalled, "was our knight in shining armor who each month slew the dragons of dullness in the pulpits in Washington, the governor's office, the legislature and the seats of the mighty generally."

Ralph made an occasional spasmodic effort to qualify for entry into the inner sanctum of the Fugitives — the poet's circle — but for all his Welsh heritage, his verse was not quite good enough. A sample has been preserved for posterity by his roommate, Brainard Cheney, who found it in McGill's typewriter one morning after a night of drinking.

I am scared and so I run breathlessly
And sop my bread of pain and fear
Into the gravy that is God . . .

At that, he had given up and gone to bed.

Once convinced that poetry was not his métier, McGill turned to the more congenial craft of journalism. He became a columnist on the *Hustler*, the student newspaper, a founder of and contributor to the *Jade*, a magazine of humor, and a part-time cub on the *Nashville Banner*, taking the Southern League baseball play-by-play over a direct line from the ball park and functioning thereafter as a copy boy until far into the night.

At one time or another, he waited on tables, ran a campus laundry route, and stoked furnaces as others have done before him. But in his last year as a student, his finances improved. He served as unofficial assistant to an elder brother in the fraternity of Sigma Chi who was conducting some fruitful experiments in chemistry. A graduate student with access to the laboratory alcohol supplies, he would chop up dried peaches and apricots, stew the organic acids out of them, allow the residue to ferment, then distill it into a brandy. Fortified with pure alcohol, this made an extremely potable drink, far smoother than the white lightning, colored and flavored with cherry juice, which was the usual campus drink during Prohibition. The proof could be adjusted according to the tastes of the purchaser — 60, 70 or whatever.

McGill, through his social and journalistic connections, would take orders at ten dollars a quart from fraternities and other groups who were planning social gatherings, and in his last year he made enough to buy himself a new suit. The graduate student prospered even more, earning enough to buy a Franklin automobile. Though Ralph, in later years, was to say that "the hot breath of Calvin was always a blowtorch on the seat of the pants of my immortal soul," his role as a scofflaw in Prohibition days never seemed to perturb him.

His departure from Vanderbilt shortly before he was to graduate in 1922 came at the end of a long period of declining interest in any subjects except football, which he played for three years as varsity guard with an amazing effectiveness for a man weighing only one hundred fifty-two pounds, and journalism, which he tackled with equal vigor. It was his column in the *Hustler*, in fact, that brought about his downfall as a student. His insatiable curiosity had led him to dig up the will of a bachelor professor who had left a bequest of some twenty thousand dollars to the university with the provision it be used to build a student lounge. No such facility had ever been provided, and McGill, in his column, accused the administration of embezzlement. This caused him to be suspended, and soon the suspension became permanent.

What fired him was a prank directed not at the administration but at a social organization whose pomposity he felt needed deflating. McGill's fraternity, Sigma Chi, was the great rival of Beta Theta Pi, and each tried to outdo the other in the elegance of its dinner dances held at the Hermitage Hotel. The Betas had sent out engraved invitations for their ball, stipulating that gentlemen should wear white tie and tails, and the guest list was limited to those considered to be the most socially acceptable. This offended McGill's sense of democracy. Through a friend and fellow Sigma Chi whose family owned the local printing company, he got access to the copper plate from which the invitations had been engraved, printed an extra batch, and flooded the campus with them. Some were still left over, and these were distributed to the town's bootleggers and the madams and girls of the bawdy houses in what was euphemistically called the "restricted district."

So outrageous a flaunting of the mores of the community could not be overlooked, and as soon as his guilt was discovered, McGill, who was bored with his studies anyway, became a full-time journalist. In years to come he was to receive honorary degrees from the nation's most prestigious institutions, but he never received any kind of diploma from the university he always looked upon as his alma mater.

As a beginning reporter on the *Nashville Banner*, McGill was perhaps the most willing cub who ever sat down at a typewriter in a city room with his hat on. Brainard Cheney, with whom Ralph still roomed on the Vanderbilt campus — the university, after kicking him out of school, made no protest at his continuing to live in a dormitory — later joined him at the *Banner* and remembers him when he was at the peak of his career there:

> Looking back now, on that bright and distant time, it seems to me its glamour for us came out of the romance of journalism — the then new notion of Bohemianism, and our own youth. The corn liquor that we drank had something to do with it, too. There was much chanting by those of us who affected a literary posture of Baudelaire's "Be drunken — on wine, love or art" — and to me the embodiment of that commitment, the ebullient and prodigious spirit of that time, was McGill himself.
>
> He was a freshet of good humor, his ebullience only exceeded by his appetite for work. He regularly and cheerfully took outside assignments, theater and concert reviews, interviews with late-arriving bigwigs, anything, late or early, that would make a piece for the paper.

McGill went to work full-time on the *Banner* in 1922. He left in 1929. In those seven years he turned out to be a reporter of fabulous versatility — a political writer who could cover with zest the pistol-toting strife of that rough-handed day; a sportswriter who wrote with acumen, humor and authority on everything from football to fox hunting; and a general-assignment reporter who could make a reader weep with his description of a mountain hunter called Floyd Collins, trapped and dying in a cave.

The Collins story brought him his first national recognition as a reporter, but in after years he was to remember it with some bitterness, for it brought him into his first unhappy contact with a species he had not encountered before — a female reporter. She had come down from New York to cover the Collins story, and McGill soon learned to hate her, which was unlike him.

It was a dirty story as far as working conditions went. It was winter. There were no accommodations save one small hotel at Horse Cave, Ky. The cave where Collins had got himself caught was six or eight miles out in the country along a narrow, slippery dirt road. It froze at night and thawed by day. It was miserable and cold and there was no decent food or drink. The native whiskey was known as "Coroner's Delight," being white and sour and likely to explode in one's pockets and drive the pieces of bottle into one's hide.

It was a bizarre story at best, with politics in it and the National Guard on duty and barbed wire stretched here and there. Reporters hated it and they came, finally, to dislike poor Collins, dead down there like a rat in a trap, as the source of their misery. They hated the adjutant general and they hated the troops and they hated one and all concerned.

The fellow in charge was a mean, condescending person who liked to shove reporters around, and the one girl reporter on the scene, Tamara, went for him . . . for stories. She was, as I recall, no particular vision of delight. But she didn't take snuff and she didn't have four gold teeth, or if she did they weren't where they showed. Most of the immediate females did back there in the hills. And she was the only one around the cave site where they dug for Collins.

She got the stories. The soldier boy saw to that. Every day Tamara had the story of the day and our own offices were wiring the rest of us asking "How come?"

Every man there, when Tamara and the soldier boy went riding out to some neighboring tavern, would announce frightful plans to push Tamara into the deep ravine or maybe run her down with a car.

In the end we did get rid of Tamara and the plot was fairly diabolical. Some very mean person persuaded a Horse Cave girl to telephone the soldier boy's wife in Louisville and say she was Tamara and she loved him dearly and would she please divorce him because she loved only him with a pure love that could not be denied.

The next evening the night accommodation chuffed up and deposited a lady who wanted to locate her soldier boy. The fact that she located him with Tamara as they sat at a table with two glasses of Coroner's Delight and ginger ale between them was just a coincidence. But it helped matters not at all.

Tamara went away from there and so did the soldier boy and after that it was merely dull.

For all his pique with Tamara, McGill, as Cheney remembers him, was a man of unaffected graciousness. McGill and Cheney often collaborated on stories, one of which brought them both a certain amount of local fame. A young woman cashier at a downtown ice cream parlor had taken her life because her lover, a gambler by trade, had abandoned her and gone to Miami. Cheney found among her effects a letter pitifully setting forth her loneliness but had not been permitted to tell the story in full because the secretary to one of the *Banner*'s officials — a sentimental young lady known as "Snooks" — felt this would be an invasion of the dead girl's privacy.

The next day, her lover, returning from Miami, had gone to the undertaking parlor where the body lay and there shot himself to death over her casket. The undertaker had immediately called McGill. There was a reason for this. McGill's managing editor, an irascible old man named Marmaduke B. Morton, a disciple of Henry Watterson, had told McGill when he first came to work — emphasizing his point by poking him in the chest with the stem of a corncob pipe — "Get to know those undertakers, boy. Train those undertakers so they will call you when an important corpse comes in." Then, more quietly, so the society editors would not hear, "Get to know the madams, too. They know when a big-time crook comes to town."

McGill had assiduously carried out these instructions and was well known to both the madams and the morticians.

The repentant gambler's suicide added, of course, a new dimension to the story, which McGill made the most of, including the headline that streamed across the top of the front page of the Sunday *Banner*. It was the distraught lover's last words as he held the pistol to his temple: "She killed herself for me. I'll be with her in two minutes."

This was Victorian journalism, with a Victorian aftermath. There was a house of prostitution about a block away from the *Banner* office, and when Cheney and McGill dropped by that Sunday afternoon to buy the girls a drink, they were still in tears over McGill's story. "He was," said Cheney, "the hero of the hour."

McGill's memories of his days as a *Banner* reporter revolve around the police beat. Nashville had a tough side and in covering it there was fierce competition between Ralph and his friend Tommy Little on the rival *Tennessean*. A police lieutenant in charge of a murder investigation tantalized them by telling them he had just received important information by phone which would break the case wide open. He refused to divulge what he had been told, admitting only that he had taken some notes which he had torn up after committing the facts to memory. McGill and Little left for their offices to write an early edition story, and as soon as they parted, McGill doubled back to the police station where he gave a Negro trusty who was serving as janitor a dollar to slip in quietly and bring out the lieutenant's wastebasket. He then patiently pieced together all the paper that had the lieutenant's handwriting on it. Finally he came up with a note bearing the names of two men in Dickson, Tennessee, a town about forty miles from Nashville. McGill was familiar with Dickson.

"It so happened," he recalled, "that Dickson was an old stomping ground of mine at that time. I was much in love with a young lady there upon whom I called frequently, but who had the intelligence to marry somebody else. I also had a close friend at Dickson with whom I had roomed in college, and in whose kennels I kept my foxhounds—foxhounds being, at the moment, a hobby of mine." He called his fox-hunting friend, gave him the two names he had deciphered from the torn-up notes, and told him what questions to ask. In a few hours, he had a story which was given big play in the Sunday paper, to the great chagrin of Tommy Little.

On another occasion, McGill's enterprise earned him a bruised sacroiliac. The railway mail clerks had formed a union and gone on strike, holding secret meetings from which the press was barred. McGill somehow obtained the password, which was "I am a stranger here," and for two days was able to give full reports in the *Banner* on what the union was up to. On the third day, he showed up at the door and announced blithely, "I am a stranger here," and two very tough-looking characters said, "You sure as hell are, buddy, and we've been looking for you."

Whereupon, they kicked him down the stairway.

McGill's affection for foxhounds and fox hunters was real. He became an eager student of the bloodlines of the various breeds — the Trigg, the Walker, the Redbone, the Bluetick and the July — doing his research at the convivial gatherings of the fox-hunting fancy. One of his favorite stories was of the traveling salesman, new to the territory, who had taken a room at an old hotel in Dickson where a group of fox hunters had foregathered. Finding himself unable to rest because of the, to him, hideous moaning noise, accompanied by shouts and laughter, which came from a room across the courtyard, he threw up his window, stuck his head out, and bellowed, "What in the hell do you-all think you are doing over there?" There was a moment of silence. Then a voice came back, in a tone of pained surprise, "Why, we're drinking liquor and blowing fox horns. What in the hell did you think we was doing?"

In his last five years on the *Nashville Banner* McGill was officially the sports editor, but in practice his sports column roamed wherever his fancy led him. "The Nashville of those days," he recalled nearly thirty years later, "was a great newspaper town, especially for police reporters and political writers. What other town ever framed the governor of the state, put him drunk in bed at a sporting house, and then raided it, taking him down to the station in a Black Maria?

"In what other city could a young and aesthetic reporter lie in the gutter under the wheels of a wagon loaded with watermelons in the old square while the bullets of two feuding political factions sang and ricocheted off the old stone buildings?"

Prohibition, McGill remembered, turned Nashville into a little Chicago, taking an "almost pastoral underworld" and peopling it with men and women who became more vicious and ugly as the tide of quick profits kept flooding in: "I have never known whiskey to do anything but harm, but as an impressionable youngster dedicated to being a newspaper reporter to match anything fiction had turned out, I saw Prohibition in the raw. And whatever the flaws in legal control, they are relatively small compared with the corrosive evil of Prohibition. . . . But Nashville in its grip was something for an eager-eyed youngster to see, from behind the scenes as out front — the hustlers, the gamblers, the moonshine runners — the town's tough guys, the big shots with power in the grand jury rooms — in time the trained undertakers got them all."

To his sports reporting McGill brought the same humor, drama, and pity for the underdog with which he wrote of the bawds and bravos who inhabited Nashville's tough district to which, for its many shootings, he gave the name of the "Western Front."

The dead hand of the schools of journalism, with their rules about putting the whole story into a who-what-why-when-where lead, did not apply to sports writing. The sportswriter could just cut loose and McGill could do this better than most. One who knew it was Ed Danforth, gravel-voiced and leather-faced sports editor of the *Atlanta Georgian*, a man of humor and sentiment with a high regard for the nuances of the language. Early in the spring of 1929, he called McGill in Nashville, told him in confidence that he soon would be leaving W. R. Hearst's *Georgian* for Clark Howell's *Constitution*, and asked him if he would come to Atlanta to serve as his assistant. McGill was thirty-one and had for a long time been Nashville's top reporter. At the moment, he was weary from covering a long, drawn-out murder trial. He told Danforth "yes" so quickly it was only after he hung up that he realized that he had not asked what his pay would be.

A few weeks later, on April 2, 1929, he stepped off the L & N day coach at Atlanta's Union Station. A rotund man with a curly forelock, his great girth made him appear shorter than his five feet ten inches. He wore a green-striped suit that was slightly shiny in the seat, and he carried two suitcases, one containing his other suit, the other full of books.

The old, red-brick *Constitution* building was only a block away, and within an hour he was at work.

Not long thereafter, Robert Sherrod, later to become editor of the *Saturday Evening Post* but then a cub on the *Constitution*, wrote in his diary:

Ralph McGill, 31, came here four months ago from *Nashville Banner* where he was sports editor. Best writer on the paper. Fine person. Well liked. Offered $150 a week at *Georgian,* it is said, but refused. Came here for $75. [Actually, it was $90, soon to be reduced by a ten percent depression pay cut.]

Sportswriters then, as now, followed the teams, and in their travels a sort of jealous camaraderie grew up among them. Frequently, on dull days, they would write about each other. A revealing vignette of Ralph, just before he moved to Atlanta, came from the typewriter of his friendly rival, O. B. Keeler, the famous golf writer on the *Atlanta Journal.* McGill had visited Keeler's office in his absence and left a note. He had evidently been in one of his dark, Welsh moods, for he had written: "I have come all the way from Nashville today to find one to suffer with, and someone who understands the art of giving up. I will return tomorrow for just five minutes of suffering."

Keeler replied in his column, "Ralph, I am here. At the freestyle or catch-as-catch-can, I will undertake a suffering match with or against anybody in the world — even though I don't yet know what you want to suffer a duet about."

McGill, Keeler went on, surprised him by expressing a need for suffering at all. Surely his outlook on life was "too calm and well-tempered a texture to be ruffled by the crimes and misdemeanors of ball clubs." (McGill was in town, with the Nashville Vols, who were not doing well in the Southern League.) Keeler went on:

> Mr. McGill has always reminded me of a Buddha . . . calm, reflective, placid and comfortable, and above everything else, giving the impression he knew what it was all about and that it didn't matter a — well, it didn't make much difference. If I did not love Mr. McGill so much, I would be envious of him. I would rather have his placid and contemplative nature than a rain check for the new Jerusalem. . . .
>
> Mr. McGill is an admirable example to his fellow sportswriters in the South and elsewhere. The contemplative habit of thought does at least two things for him. His work is always smooth and craftsmanlike: it has the impress of the trained writing man. . . . Mr. McGill, good at all games, is particularly good at the game of life, which he seems to understand better than most. He doesn't take it too seriously, and he writes of it in a mode delightfully whimsical.

In the last column he wrote for the *Nashville Banner* Ralph made a sentimental recap of the things he remembered best in the nearly eight years that had passed since Vanderbilt had kicked him out a "very rattled young man." Many of his recollections were of sports, of famous figures he had seen and interviewed in Nashville. Mrs. Fiske he remembered in a revival of *The Rivals;* Fritz Kreisler had shown him his violin; Will Rogers had bummed a cigarette from him; Strangler Lewis had applied a headlock to him in a room at the Heritage Hotel. He remembered Paderewski playing the "Marche Militaire," and the bar a block long at Tijuana, Mexico, and the bartender who looked like John L. Sullivan. He recalled the small boys following Babe Ruth around at Sulphur Dell, and he remembered the Ku Klux Klan marching in hoods and robes through the streets of the little town of Franklin, Tennessee.

He recalled the face of a mother saying good-bye to a son who was to be electrocuted the next morning, the mourning of the women at the mouth of a burning coal mine where sons and husbands were trapped below . . . the moaning of a woman who had drunk carbolic acid, as she lay dying on the floor of the police patrol car that was taking her to a hospital.

He closed with a paragraph of tribute to Signor Domenick Petrucelli, an Italian restaurateur who shared McGill's love for old wine and pasta and Caruso records, and who had named in his honor a highly caloric dish made of meatballs and spaghetti called "Chili Mack."

"I commend Signor Petrucelli's food," he wrote. "It is excellent. Mainly because all he does is shout the order to the kitchen; the food is supervised by Mrs. Domenick. . . ."

Danforth had been more clairvoyant than he knew when he said in his introductory column that Ralph McGill's addition to the *Constitution* sports staff was the most important move the paper had made. Ralph was on his way. And for nearly forty years, the paper, the town, and the South he loved and lectured and chastised and tried to lead out of its old ways, all were moved and shaken and changed because of him.

3

McGill came to the *Constitution* as assistant sports editor in the spring of 1929, sleeping for the first months on a fold-down bed in the living room of Ed and Betty Danforth's small apartment, and arising early each morning to demonstrate that he was, indeed, as Danforth had once described him, the world's outstanding waffle cook.

It was his only domestic attribute. The shyness around girls which Reb Gershon had noted in him as a prep-school swain persisted into his thirties, and he frequently told his family and bachelor friend Brainard Cheney that "It will be a cold day in July when they get me to the altar." This seemed borne out when, after very nearly becoming engaged to a young lady described in Nashville as a "Belle Meade type" — meaning that she was wellborn, socially proper of speech and manner, and well-to-do — they suddenly stopped going together. Years later in a letter to his son urging him not to devote too much time to card games, he threw light on why the romance fell through. "I liked books, she liked bridge," he wrote young Ralph. "She never could teach me to play so she gave me up as a bad job. I was glad, for not long after I met your mother."

The girl who did make a more lasting impression on him in the summer of 1928 was Mary Elizabeth Leonard, the red-haired, freckled daughter of a McMinnville, Tennessee, dentist. Ebullient, happy-go-lucky, sometimes raucous but always kind, Miss Leonard when they met had just been released from two years in a tuberculosis sanitarium. Eager to make up for all the happy times she had missed while in the hospital, she plunged headlong into life with a gusto that both dismayed and fascinated McGill. Not long after they met, a football train from

Nashville was to pass through Chattanooga en route to Atlanta. McGill phoned his mother asking her to meet him at the Chattanooga station; there was a friend, he said, he would like for her to meet. Sensing that something was afoot, his mother bought a new dress and went, coming home to tell her daughter Bessie: "I have just met your new sister-in-law."

Bessie gasped in astonishment, "Did Ralph tell you he was married?"

"No," said Mrs. McGill, "but I could tell by looking at him he soon will be."

In early September 1929, McGill was back in Nashville for the wedding. Danforth was his best man, and Betty Danforth was Miss Leonard's matron of honor. The *Chattanooga Times,* in announcing the nuptials, headlined "Creator of the Gink Yields to Cupid," in reference to the fact that McGill, while in Nashville, had written and syndicated a column of folksy humor called "I'm the Gink."

Mary Elizabeth, known to her friends as "Red" and to Ralph as "Pet," cared neither for books nor bridge. She liked her kitchen and her herb garden and her friends and her church. She was warm, impulsive, generous, kind of heart, and full of laughter, but with a barbed wit that could quickly put down the pompous. "We both," McGill wrote to a friend, "seem to have married wives who have the power to unsettle staid persons such as we. Perhaps it is for the best."

As time would show, she possessed a shining courage, a gallantry that was to carry her through many years of illness, the death of children, and the loneliness of staying at home to keep her house and raise their only son while McGill was away for weeks on his travels for the paper.

There was no hint, though, of the coming trials on this bright September afternoon. The newlyweds, the Danforths, and an usher or two boarded the day coach for Atlanta and the tiny little apartment on a tree-shaded side street that was to be the McGills' first home. There was no honeymoon trip, then nor soon thereafter. Less than two months after they were married, the stock market crashed, and the Great Depression began. McGill, who had come to Atlanta for a salary of ninety dollars a week, took three ten-percent pay cuts in quick succession. Sometimes there was little pay in cash at all — a few dollars, perhaps, to cover the rent. The rest was in vouchers, good at the grocery stores.

Through the late 1920s and well into the depression, sports was a religion whose pantheon was made up of the great champions, Dempsey, the Four Horsemen of Notre Dame, Bill Tilden, Bobby Jones, and Babe Ruth. The sportswriters were the high priests of this cult, employing in their writing the most absurd hyperbole. A team that held the opponent at its own goal line was inevitably likened to those who fought at Thermopylae, and any backfield that gained more than one hundred sixteen yards running was, in the South, of course, likened to Jeb Stuart's cavalry. McGill, if he chose, could write this florid, breathless prose though usually his style had a pace and rhythm that was all his own.

To make ends meet, McGill was forced to employ this skill with words on outside writing. Happily, soon after his arrival in Atlanta he had met and become good friends with Robert W. Woodruff, president of the Coca-Cola Company, and he would now and then be called upon to do a piece for the *Red Barrel,* the company house organ, for a five-hundred-dollar fee.

One assignment holding out the promise of a thousand dollars fell through, to his great disappointment. In 1931, when his finances were at an extremely low ebb, he had gone up to cover the William Stribling-Max Schmeling heavyweight championship fight at Cleveland, Ohio. He went up to Stribling's camp a month before the battle, ostensibly to bring to Georgians a detailed daily account of the training of their favorite prizefighting son, but also to prepare, with the aid of Ma and Pa Stribling and Strib himself, a quick "Life of Young Stribling," commissioned by a press syndicate. The day before the fight, McGill, perspiring profusely in the summer heat, had finished his fourteenth chapter and was so sure of the triumphant ending that he had wired Mary Elizabeth to come up to see the fight.

The biography expired on the night of July 4. Stribling lost the fight. McGill lost the thousand dollars, and sportswriter James E. Doyle, of the *Cleveland Plain Dealer,* who walked away from the stadium with him that night, described him, in fake southern accents, as being "the saddest and maddest fat man you-all eva did see," who had to be restrained from throwing his typewriter into a pond.

Always, McGill's writing style had a certain distinction, a poetic touch. It is highly unlikely that any other sportswriter, on his way to

New York to cover the fight between Max Baer and Primo Carnera, looked out the window of his plane at daybreak and wrote:

> And then suddenly there was dawn. The fields became lighted. The houses took on outline. Day was breaking. I thought of one of Oscar Wilde's poems and that line which reads: "And the dawn, on silver-sandaled feet, crept down the street like a frightened girl." The dawn came to the world like that.

The next night at ringside he saw Carnera fall and rise, and fall again, blinded by his own blood, under the battering fists of Max Baer, until the referee stopped the slaughter. The man who saw the beauty of a dawn could also see, and describe, sheer, wanton brutality in the ring. He wrote of Carnera:

> It was a bewildered Italian giant who found all his science gone before this man who hurt him and then laughed at him. Baer was the clown tonight, and a snarling wolf, too.
>
> He tore at Carnera . . . the bloodlust in his face. He could have put Carnera away in the fifth. He had him out, sliding along the ropes, about to fall, and instead of boring in, he stopped and put down those killer hands with the bloodstained gloves and laughed that bloody smile. The white rubber mouthpiece, like the inside of a fish's throat, added to the ferocity. He was a bloody horror.

As Carnera, in the eleventh round, went down twice, "booming on the boards," McGill wrote:

> I thought then of the line from Kipling's poem of the slaying of Hans, the blue-eyed Dane, who "came down like cattle drop across the fist-banged boards." Carnera tonight was like a felled ox. The ring was a shambles with his blood. . . .

McGill went back to Carnera's dressing room after the fight. "He was pathetic to me. I felt sorry for him as he sat there a thousand miles from home, with no real friends about him."

Alan J. Gould, AP sports director during the Golden Decade, recalls one incredible golfing feat at which McGill was one of only three reporters present. It was, Gould recalls, the 1935 Masters Tournament at Augusta, before radio or TV had brought that event into the nation's living rooms. But the AP had been experimenting in electronic sports reporting and for this event had equipped its sports staff with short-wave radio equipment. McGill, ever curious, was fascinated by this novelty and was sticking close to AP's Ken Gregory, who was using it. This, wrote Gould, was the climactic scene:

Craig Wood, the tall, blond and handsome shotmaker from New York, who had lost the first Masters crown by a stroke the year before to Horton Smith, had finished with 282 — three strokes in front — and appeared assured of his first major triumph. So confident of the outcome were sportswriters that most of them wrote their lead stories, and tournament officials prepared for ceremonies in Wood's honor. Only one player on the course had even a remote chance of catching the leader; he was the veteran Gene Sarazen, one of the toughest of all competitors, but he had only four holes to go and was three strokes down to Wood, who had finished these holes in even par, 5–3–4–4. The gap looked insurmountable, the gallery wandered back to the club house, and only a corporal's guard of friends and sportswriters escorted the chunky Connecticut "Squire," including the AP's field captain, Ken Gregory, Paul Gallico of the *New York Daily News*, and — of course — Ralph McGill.

McGill would always remember that hot afternoon, trudging along in the wake of Gene Sarazen. Sarazen, whom he called the "Little Sardine," was his friend, and he wanted to be there at the end to cheer him up after coming so close.

Sarazen had fired his tee shot on the 520-yard 15th hole. Right this minute, I can remember him as he came trudging down the fairway, serene and hot.

I stood around, waiting for my man to die.

Sarazen came up and studied the ball. He squinted at the green and then set himself. No thunder rolled and no sense of drama invaded our little group.

The ball got up. I shaded my eyes and looked. It was a good shot with just the hint of a curve in it as it screamed along, bending in toward the green.

Then I saw it hit and slow up and go running toward the green. I knew then it was a great shot and the excitement caught at me and not until it was all over did I know I had been holding my breath.

The ball went straight for the flag cup, slowed up, and dropped in.

Gene Sarazen had got a two on a par five hole.

Our little gallery let up a yell and the Little Sardine stood there looking stunned and then he turned and grinned strongly. There was never any false modesty about the character from Connecticut.

That was the greatest shot I ever saw. It was played under pressure. It was lucky, sure, but then don't forget he was shooting for what he got. He had not quit.

That was history, but the toughest part was yet to go. The finish was three tough holes. Sarazen had to finish them in par to tie Craig Wood.

That looked impossible. He had just had a great explosion of luck and skill. In one magnificent effort he had put himself back in the game.

I saw him do 16 in par and then I left him. I was just as confident then he would shoot par or better as if I had read it in the book of destiny. I went back to the clubhouse to see what was happening there.

What was happening was the best human interest story of the day. Craig Wood was on his honeymoon. Up on the gallery, all by herself, there was his beautiful young bride. She was walking up and down, staring out there at the great crowd which had rushed out to see the Little Sardine finish.

"He can't do it, he can't do it," she was saying. It sounded like a prayer, the way she said it. So, I went away and left her alone there with her prayer and never asked the questions I had in mind. I knew what the Sardine was going to do and it would not make her happy.

He did it, too, canning his putt on the 18th for a 282 and a tie with Craig Wood. . . .

The next day they played it off and the Little Sardine casually and calmly won the 36-hole play-off — and the check — by a five-stroke margin.

Golf rates after baseball and football in my liking for games, but I would have to turn to golf for my greatest play and thrill. The double eagle and the finish by Gene Sarazen in the Masters of 1935.

There were, of course, perquisites the sportswriters enjoyed that were unknown to other reporters. The Georgia Tech team, when invited to the Rose Bowl, for example, took along not only the writers but their families. In January 1931, McGill and Mary Elizabeth went to California with Tech, and Ralph, with a country boy's wide-eyed zest, wrote to his parents in Chattanooga from the elegant Huntington Hotel in Pasadena:

Dear Dad and Mam,

Just a line to let you know we are having a swell time. It was funny being here at Christmas with the sun shining hot and oranges growing about.

Every night we go out and pull a few oranges and eat them before going to bed.

I've thought of you all every day and wish we could all be here together for a trip. We are staying, eight of us, in a cottage which rents for a mere $3,500 for the winter season.

The flowers here are beautiful and the landscapes are awfully pretty. Pasadena is the city of millionaires and it looks it.

Yesterday Mary Elizabeth and I went to the MGM studios — just us two — I had a letter there. They had us to lunch and showed us everything. We saw Jean Harlow and Robert Montgomery and Wallace Beery and Ricardo Cortez and William Powell — we went to Robert Montgomery's dressing room and talked with him for thirty minutes. Mary Elizabeth nearly had a fit. We had our picture made with Nat Pendleton, who makes comedy, and with William Powell. . . .

To his delight, McGill learned from Clark Howell, Sr., owner and publisher of the *Constitution,* that he would not be expected to devote himself exclusively to sports. Mr. Howell, known as "Papa" Howell to the staff, was a short, dignified man with a fair round belly and a big, squarish head full of political savvy. He remembered that McGill had gained considerable fame in Tennessee for his coverage of the fiercely polemic gang wars that passed for political debate in that state during the late twenties, and he was happy for McGill to make use of these same talents in Georgia.

In the summer of 1936, he called McGill into his office for a friendly chat. Young Senator Richard Russell, he told McGill, was defending his seat against Eugene Talmadge, and for some reason, his campaign had not caught fire. Would McGill like to join Russell's campaign cavalcade, travel with him a few days, and write about him?

"Just straight factual reporting, Ralph," he told McGill, "nothing exaggerated. Nothing fancy."

McGill's first story from the field, carried on the front page of the *Constitution,* began:

ROYSTON, GA.: Senator Richard Brevard Russell lighted the watchfires of democracy on a thousand hills here yesterday before a great concourse of people gathered from five counties to hear him. This was no mere great crowd. This was a vast crowd. . . . It shouted its approval as Senator Russell stood foursquare for the Democratic party. This was no demagogue speaking but an honored citizen of the state, giving an account of his stewardship. He definitely pinned Governor Talmadge to the Republican party. . . .

Before he came back into the office a week later, McGill's perfervid prose had convinced the *Constitution* readership that Dick Russell not only could set watch fires of democracy blazing on hilltops, he was a man with the oratorical powers of a Demosthenes, the clear, logical mind of Solomon, the wisdom of Socrates, the probity of George Washington, and the guts of a polar bear. In McGill's word pictures, he became Bayard and Lancelot, and Galahad and El Cid, and any other hero of history or mythology that popped into McGill's mind. It was, of course, press-box prose, the hyperbole of the sportswriter applied to political reporting. But it got Dick Russell's campaign off the ground, and it set his opponent, Eugene Talmadge, to screaming in impotent rage and buying full-page ads in newspapers to denounce McGill.

He was somewhat nervous when he returned to the office, feeling that he may have laid it on a little too thick. He remembered sitting at his typewriter in his glassed-in cubicle in a corner of the *Constitution* city room, putting a sports column together, when he saw "Papa" Howell come out of the men's room, buttoning his trousers and bowing a polite greeting to the society editor as was his custom at that time of morning. He put his head into McGill's glass cage: "Just what I wanted, Ralphie," he said. "You hit just the right note."

It was the beginning, for McGill and Russell, of a mutual respect that lasted for years, until the great battle over civil rights and the Supreme Court's school decision brought on an estrangement that neither man sought to reconcile. With Russell filibustering in defense of the racial patterns of the past, and McGill plunging doggedly into an unknown future, there was no longer a common ground on which they could meet.

The Russell series marked McGill's entry into Georgia politics as a commentator and shaper of political thought, who would leave his mark upon the state long after he was gone. This was also the beginning of his curious relationship with Eugene Talmadge, a man whose Neanderthal politics McGill despised, and who in turn held all that McGill stood for in loathing. Curiously, though, there grew up between the two men a certain grudging admiration. Talmadge once asked McGill to write his biography, saying that he already had a title that would be sure to sell a lot of books — *The Life of Eugene Talmadge, by his Enemy, Ralph McGill.*

4

McGill's settling-in at Atlanta was a time of trial and testing: personally and professionally he was being molded and tempered for the years that lay ahead. It was a period of financial struggle and of personal grief, brought on by the death of two babies and by the beginning of Mary Elizabeth's long illness; and it was almost as if he sought to lessen his own sorrows by beginning to take upon himself the burdens of a region and the troubles of a race.

It was a period of groping for a road to follow, and of insomnia: "Out of these crawling hours when sleep will not come," he wrote, "one comes to know that chief among the virtues are stubbornness and humility . . . that we are all involved in mankind with a degree of responsibility that increases with man's increase."

More than any other writer of his region, he realized that under the gray misery of the depression there was the surge of a new tide running, a push toward change, the murmuring of many voices of discontent. The curtain was going up on the tremendous drama of the South in transition; its old dependence on cotton and tobacco and the day labor of black men and women was coming to an end. Not even the beginning of the end of segregation was yet in sight, but in many small and subtle ways the South had begun to say farewell to its overromanticized past. In the fierce struggle to break out of the grip of the depression, the spirit of man, whether black or white, was being freed of its bondage, and something in McGill's nature told him that this was a story that he must follow.

So, while continuing to write his sports column, "Break O' Day," every morning in the *Constitution*, he began to travel about the state with economists and political scientists and agricultural experts from the universities. Their travel was financed, in large degree, by government funds, and the basic purpose was political — to interpret the New Deal and its aims and goals to those its agencies hoped to help.

To McGill there was no difficulty in making this transition from observer to spokesman for a cause. He loved politics. Though his father was Republican, his mother had been a strong Democrat, and he himself at the age of fourteen had been converted to the Democratic party by reading the speeches of Woodrow Wilson. He was now an unabashed admirer of Franklin D. Roosevelt. He had visited the President at Warm Springs and had listened raptly as Mr. Roosevelt described Georgia as an "unfinished state" — its growth cut short by the Civil War and the tortured aftermath. He had heard, and believed, as Roosevelt predicted that out of the depression would come a new and more prosperous Georgia, and he was determined to become an instrument of that progress.

In this determination he had the full support of the owners of the *Constitution*. The man who had founded the paper in 1868, Colonel Carey W. Styles — "a man of fire and dreams," as McGill once called him — was a staunch Democrat and the Howell family had continued that commitment. Nor were the state politicians against McGill when he spoke with warm approval of PWA and NRA and the virtue of Lespedeza as a cover crop, though they would oppose him violently when he spoke in favor of labor unions or civil rights legislation. Criticism also came from the well-to-do businessmen who read his column every morning, and who called him "Mack" and drank with him and sang with him and swapped tales of sports heroes of the past when they met. But it annoyed a great many of them when McGill wrote of politics and economics and they let him know it. One of them, a textile tycoon, said to him: "Ralph, I read you every morning, but what in the hell do you think you know about the Smoot-Hawley Tariff?"

One of the more enduring of the McGill anecdotes has to do with a drinking scene, this one on a train bearing the Georgia delegation to the 1936 Democratic convention in Chicago. The bar was set up in the baggage car. The delegates, state politicians closely allied to the textile industry, began giving McGill a hard time about his admiration for Franklin D. Roosevelt. Finally, McGill, who had drunk copiously of beer, could take no more. Head lowered like an old bull in the ring, swaying rather more than the movement of the train warranted, he glowered at his tormentors. "Piz on the lot of you," he said thickly, and proceeded to try to do so. "He had them running and hollering and climbing up the stacks of baggage," a witness recalled.

The criticism of his political friends stung, for he was not yet possessed of that tough hide that was to protect him in the future. But he winced and plowed ahead — riding one hundred fifty miles with his college-professor friends to talk at a forum in a country schoolhouse, riding back that night, hoarse and weary and trying to catch a nap in the back of the car.

In his farm articles, he wrote of the lonely chimneys in the abandoned fields, the old houses falling in, and he took his readers into these empty houses and let them hear the ghostly voices speaking there. "They stand," he said, "like tombstones marking something that has died. . . . A hope, a dream, an effort of sweat and toil." He told how that dream had died: "The boll weevil came. . . . It war'nt any use anymore. . . . The land wore out. You couldn't get a half bale to the acre. . . . It was sharecroppin' without no share." And finally, the ending, the man saying to his wife at last, "Get the young-uns ready. We are leaving. . . ."

And they left for Akron and Detroit and the industrial cities of the North, carrying with them their ignorance, their anger and their hope.

Behind them, they left dying communities, supported only by little cotton mills, their worn machinery capable of making only the roughest duck or drill, paying wages so low for hours so long that the unions moved in and the strikes began. This was in the twenties, in Georgia, where the depression came with the weevil, long before the market crash and the industrial collapse of the thirties.

The Negro's civil rights were not an issue in this time of economic disaster. All the black man could expect if he were hungry was a job, no matter how rough and dirty, at any wage, no matter how low. Even his more militant leaders were bold enough to ask for only this — that in the great pump-priming public works projects, a few paved roads, sidewalks, sewer and water lines, and electric lights be extended into the Negro sections, which were still as black as night, and as deep in mud and dust as a city slum.

McGill's main concern, then, was for the economic well-being of the farmer, whatever his color. At the crossroads schoolhouses and before the civic clubs in the little towns and from the backs of flatbed trucks in the courthouse squares, he preached his hopeful sermons, telling how even thousands of years ago a Roman writer named Virgil had known about rotating crops and cover crops and the building of pastures. He haunted the Agricultural Experiment Stations, and he urged the farmers to listen to their county agent. He also urged the county agent to get out and do his job where it was needed, instead of sitting in his office at the county seat. He himself practiced what he preached. He walked the fields with the farmers, and one of the most appealing pictures of him shows him — a big, fat man in white shirt and suspenders and a city man's dusty shoes — squeezing through a pole fence with a camera dangling from his neck.

"The earth is the Lord's, and the fullness thereof," he told his deeply religious audiences. "But it is man who must save the earth's substance." He salted his talks with humor. He told them of the preacher who looked around him at the green fields and full barns and pastures in which fat cattle grazed and said to the farmer whose sweat and toil had gone into this, "You've got mighty rich land here, Brother Johnson. The Lord surely has been good to you." And the farmer said, "Yes, He has. But you ought to see what shape the place was in when the Lord had it all to Himself." Poor soil, McGill said, had caused more souls to be lost than the works of the devil.

Though McGill could preach soil conservation and crop rotation with the zeal of an evangelist, he found it necessary to take a more cautious stand on other matters of profound interest to his region. The New Deal's Farm Security Administration, in its efforts to improve the plight of the small farmer, had the support of all "except the big landowners, who also own the small-town banks and the gins and the stores," he wrote. But its interest in the workingman, the wages he earned and the hours he worked, was a subject of greater controversy. The unions, which moved South in the depression to attempt to organize the textile mills, were greeted with suspicion by the workers themselves and with hostility by the mill owners.

McGill felt little sympathy for the textile, timber, turpentine and rock-quarry barons who, almost in tears, testified before federal wage-hour panels that a thirty-five-cents-an-hour minimum wage would force them into bankruptcy. At the same time, he could not give himself wholeheartedly to labor's cause, as represented by the CIO and by the AF of L's United Textile Workers, for he found their tactics blundering, their methods inept, and many of their leaders unworthy of the workingman's trust.

One outstanding exception whom McGill not only admired greatly but held in deep affection was Miss Lucy Randolph Mason, a Virginia aristocrat who was a highly effective labor organizer. Gentle of speech and manner, the daughter of a well-loved Episcopal minister in Richmond who numbered among her ancestors and close kin three signers of the Declaration of Independence, Chief Justice John Marshall, and Robert E. Lee, Miss Lucy served the CIO at a time when, according to McGill, hired evangelists were going about the South thundering that the people must choose between God and the CIO. Many a small-town sheriff, prepared to jail any CIO organizer who came into his bailiwick, was startled into swallowing his chewing tobacco when the organizer who showed up turned out to be a small gray-haired lady in her middle fifties, with a little white-trimmed black hat sitting primly on her head, wearing immaculate white gloves.

Bankers, who were the bosses of the small towns in those days, were equally disconcerted when she came into their offices and began to lecture them sternly, but in ladylike tones, for permitting workers in their towns to toil for five dollars a week and for condoning the beating and jailing of the union organizer who came in to rectify these wrongs.

Miss Mason, in her role as labor's spokesman and advocate, was what McGill was later to become in the field of race relations — a symbol of the conscience of the South. In the great struggle of the thirties between industry and the unions, though, it was she who was the more firmly convinced of the virtue of her cause.

"I cannot be a good crusader," McGill said, "because I have been cursed all my life with being able to see both sides of things. . . . It must be very pleasant to see only one side of things, and therefore, to be furiously anti- or pro-labor. . . . But I have never been able to do it. . . ."

To McGill, "the mental gyrations of the NAM, the CIO and the AF of L frequently were equally disturbing and inconsistent," and he liked being free to say so. To him also, the wage and hour laws could only palliate a deeper economic sickness. The South, he argued, had been willfully held in economic subjugation by discriminating freight rates and tariffs which insured that "it could never compete with northern industry." It was one of the penalties of losing the Civil War. Wage-hour laws, though desperately needed, could not solve the basic problems until these discriminations were removed. Now, he saw even these protections of the workingman swept away.

Memories of his father coming home from the mines, black with coal dust and sagging with weariness (the Soddy mines, John L. Lewis once told him, were among the worst in the nation before the unions came), plus his own natural compassion, made him sympathetic toward the cause of all who worked with their hands, and he deplored their exploitation from any source. To him, therefore, the saddest event in a dreary time was the effect upon the South of the Supreme Court decision in 1935 which outlawed the NRA: the tragic exploitation of miserable men and women which followed the death by court order of the famed and execrated Blue Eagle. Years later in the book written in his maturity, *The South and the Southerner*, he termed it "one of the most shameful stories in the South's economic history." States and communities, in their desperate struggle to attract industry, literally sold into a form of serfdom their labor force, presenting their people as being "white Anglo-Saxons," and therefore, by implication, impervious to the blandishment of the unions.

Unprotected by any form of wage or hour regulations, those who were hired into a new factory built by the community to lure an industry were made the victims of a managerial checkoff system as brutal as any the unions had devised. From their meager wage was taken every week a percentage, sometimes as much as six percent, which went to the municipality to pay for the factory buildings.

To McGill, this was an outrage, and so were the means used of hiring labor. "Always," he wrote, "the local committee passed on each applicant to be sure the right sort of contented, compliant Anglo-Saxons were hired."

Contented or not, hunger, the desperate need to work, had made them compliant. The human tragedy, said McGill, could not be expressed in words or pictures: "One had to see them, the listless men and women, dozens of them for every job . . . shabby and gaunt, their feet sometimes wrapped in guano sacks. Illiterate, ill fed, sick of hookworm or worse, they waited patiently, hopefully. It made a person's throat taste salty to see them, already degraded, being pushed down a bit deeper. . . ."

This was not the Georgia of the future, he wrote, this was regression, the sorry paternalism of an older day. "New mills are coming," he wrote, "new methods are running toward us. All around the earth there is movement and change — but still there are those who cry: 'Let's go back. Let's cling to the old ways.' "

Stubbornly, patiently, he called upon Georgians to recognize that the old days were over and would never return, that cotton was leaving the South and the time when men's lives were locked into the economics of cotton, either in the fields or in the mills, could never come back again. With husky eloquence in his speeches, and in his special articles in the paper, he pleaded with his fellow Georgians to see this change, and accept it, and move on.

The thirties saw the beginning of McGill's interest in international politics. On a brief stopover in Havana with the Tech team, he had sensed that revolution was brewing in Cuba, and in 1933 he went down to see what was happening. Bombs were exploding in the streets, dictator Gerardo Machado's soldiers were brutally putting down all protests, political prisoners were being cast to the sharks from the old prison fort in the harbor, and the hungry and homeless were sleeping on the once beautiful Malecón.

McGill went directly to the top — to United States Ambassador Sumner Welles for briefing, and then to an interview with the dictator himself. He found the old man in his sandbagged castle, with guards armed with machine guns at the door of the room where Machado waited, "A gross old man, heavy with fat, who spoke in platitudes about how his people loved him."

McGill had seen no evidence of that love. He had seen, instead, young students who had come to his room to strip off their shirts, showing him their backs scarred by whips. He had visited in the home of a prominent Cuban whose cellar contained kegs not only of fine wine, but of TNT for the making of bombs. As he walked through the park on his way to the interview, he saw dramatic evidence of revolutionary protest. A young man dressed in his best suit, clasping a bunch of red hibiscus in one hand, went into the park before the police and shot himself through the head with a pistol. In his interview, McGill remembered, the old man's face was dull and stolid, but his eyes shifted restlessly. "He knew the jig was up."

McGill came away to write that Machado the Butcher was finished; he could not last; and this estimate was true. In a few weeks the old man had fled the country by plane. Behind a succession of powerless presidents, Fulgencio Batista, an army sergeant, "a remarkable man of good common sense who came from the ranks of the cane cutters," as McGill characterized him, was running the government.

In the chaos and confusion which followed the exile of Machado, Ambassador Welles came in for some harsh criticism. To McGill, Welles had "stood like a man in a time of danger," and he wrote to President Roosevelt, defending Welles's actions and decisions as being wise and proper under the circumstances, a gesture for which Welles sent a gracious note of thanks. This became a habit of McGill's — whenever on an overseas assignment he ran into a diplomat or a wire-service bureau chief or a military man or company employee who seemed to be doing a good job, he not only said so in the paper, he dropped a personal letter to the man's boss.

Eighteen months after Machado's departure, McGill, along with twenty-five other American newspapermen, returned to Cuba for another look. They went at the invitation of the Cuban Tourist Bureau, and as part of their ceremonial duties, they laid a wreath at the statue of José Martí, the father of Cuban liberty. When the American journalists were asked to name one of their number to speak of the martyr, it was McGill who stood up in the old square, in a rumpled seersucker suit, his tousled hair blowing in the hot wind, paying an impromptu tribute to the great Cuban revolutionary who "had fought the Spaniards for eighteen years with sword and pen and eloquence before they finally killed him."

His column out of Havana told of his deep emotion as he stood in the old square, talking of the hero who had raised the cry of Cuban freedom until we finally had heard and heeded it. Then, with that change of mood that was characteristic of him, he went on in the next paragraph to describe, with gusto, a visit to a nightclub called the Sans Souci, which had "a great patio, shaded by mangrove trees, through which the moonlight fell in beauty."

McGill, throughout his life, was rare in his praise of nightclubs, and avoided them when he could. This one, though, intrigued him, for its mood was not rowdy and raucous like that of nightclubs in the States, which he felt were evil places, the by-product of the greater evil of Prohibition:

> There was a great crowd at the Sans Souci, and as it was not the tourist season, most of them were Cuban. The only unseemly noise came from one lone American who was very potted indeed and kept yelling "Whoopee" as each number opened in the program of dances. The Cubans, who have a bar on every corner do not get potted. I do not understand these things, but they are true.

This was his way of kicking the dead carcass of Prohibition. The Volstead Act had been repealed two years before, but Georgians were still wary of all ardent spirits except those made by their own moonshiners, and their preachers and bootleggers both were determined the state should remain forever dry. This course McGill looked upon as purest hypocrisy and subterfuge.

The special stories he filed at the *Constitution* reported what by now most Cubans had come to realize. The president, in the twenty-four-million-dollar Palace of Government that Machado had built, might bear the name of any politico. But the man behind the president, keeping peace and order in Cuba, was the once lowly Sergeant Batista, "that genius of a man," McGill wrote, "born in a thatched hut, educated briefly in a Quaker mission, who came on the scene unheralded."

It is not, of course, given to any prophet to be infallible, and McGill, by instinct, felt a rapport with any revolutionary who would overthrow a ruthless dictator. His articles on Batista were sympathetic and approving. Nearly a quarter-century later, after Batista had followed Machado down the bloody road to dictatorship and exile, McGill was back in Cuba again, writing with sympathy and approval of Fidel Castro, for whom at first he had high hopes.

Ralph's memories of his first reporting job in a foreign land, even so close a neighbor as Cuba, never left him. During his visit there, three bold American airmen, one in a land plane, two piloting frail gliders, brought the first international "sky train" into Havana from the United States. Before the capitol, a crowd of forty thousand gathered to watch the gliders float down to a landing on the broad avenue, the historic Paseo de Martí.

"The gliders came in, trembling a bit, but true," McGill wrote. "The first one swept in, dipped suddenly as if it were to nose down, and then flattened out and slid on its wooden skids to a landing. Then came the other, and the swelling cheers of the forty thousand people echoed off the old palace across the way."

McGill fought his way through the crowd to shake hands with the pilots. Then, to clear the square, the policemen began to rap their clubs noisily against their own boot heels, instead of against the skulls of the people, which McGill noted as an improvement since Machado's day. The crowd moved, and then came the first crashing notes of "The Star-Spangled Banner," in honor of the American pilots who had brought the gliders in.

Wrote McGill:

> I came to attention and stood there getting a great thrill from hearing my country's anthem played in another land by a foreign band. And I thought of what the two nations meant to each other and of the tie that binds them. And I looked at the two flags flying together on the balcony of the capitol. They looked good there.

5

McGill came home from Cuba to learn from Mary Elizabeth the happy news that, after nearly six years of hoping and waiting, a baby at last was on the way. To pad out the family income, which was still anemic from three depression-induced pay cuts, she had gone to work that summer at Rich's, an Atlanta department store, as director of the personal shopper service. "A sort of public relations job, as I get it," McGill wrote to a friend. It did require a certain amount of bustling about the store, and the nagging backaches, results of a kidney ailment from which she had suffered since she was a child, seemed to become worse under the strain of the new job. She said nothing of this to Ralph, though, whom she had begun to call Pappy in anticipation of the coming event, and he went joyfully off each autumn weekend, following the football teams.

As fall deepened into winter, the pains worsened. A few weeks before Christmas, intermittent chills and fever came with the pain, and as a precaution, her doctors put her in the hospital. There, gay and blithe and full of laughter and jokes, she wrote her Christmas cards and wrapped her presents and concealed from all but her doctors the pain that was by now becoming more than she could bear.

In January a little girl was born prematurely and within thirty-six hours had died. With McGill carrying the tiny casket in his hands to the open grave in West View Cemetery, the graveside prayers were read under a gray and wintry sky on a day of bitter cold. Only a handful of old friends was there — the Danforths and Evans Joseph, who had been an usher in the wedding, and Julia James, later Julia Crawford, the tiny cook and maid and housekeeper who was to be friend and nurse and counselor to the McGills in all the coming years.

Now, in this time of trouble, other good friends stepped in to help. Three years earlier, in the winter of 1933, Ralph had gone down to Albany, Georgia, to cover the Southern Amateur Field Trials. There he had met Thomas Caldecott Chubb and his wife Caroline. Chubb, a Yale graduate and onetime ship news reporter for the *New York Times*, had given up journalism for more lofty literary pursuits. He was now spending his winters at the family plantation, Springwood, a hunting preserve near Thomasville, where he raised bird dogs, shot quail and turkeys, and wrote verse and scholarly biographies of picaresque characters of the Italian Renaissance.

McGill had arrived late in the field that morning, and so had Chubb, who had come to the trial bringing a handsome but still untested young pointer named Springwood Spider. The dogs had been put down before they arrived and had long since gone, with the gallery trailing after, and there was no way to find them. So they waited and talked about bird dogs and poetry and the writer's lonely trade, and McGill, who needed a column for the next morning's paper, sat down on a beer crate and "interviewed" Springwood Spider and took his picture. That afternoon, in the races for the young dogs, Springwood Spider did very well, even though, as McGill remembered, Chubb, who was handling him, was so nervous he could hardly fire the pistol to flush the birds and prove his dog steady to shot and wing. The Spider finished second in this, his first time in competition, and that night, in Chubb's room at the Albany Hotel, he thumped his tail amiably on the floor as McGill and Chubb drank to his health in white corn whiskey and predicted great things for him.

Their confidence was not misplaced. The Spider did go on to make a great field-trial dog, finally, though on one occasion he disgraced himself. He was running in the finals of the All-Age Stakes, with the championship in his paw, so to speak, when he started up a herd of half-grown shoats, ran one down, and killed it. He was standing there by the body of the dead pig when the judges came up, "a mingled look of fear and pride in his topaz eyes," McGill reported later.

The friendship formed at this chance meeting — "We were introduced by a bird dog," Chubb would say — grew and flourished. Each year as field-trial time approached, Chubb would write McGill, asking him to bring Mary Elizabeth and come to Springwood to shoot wild turkeys before the bird-dog trials opened at Albany. But each year some sports event — a Rose Bowl game or a winter golf tournament somewhere — had intervened. This year, though, Chubb's invitation came as a godsend. McGill was steeped in deepest gloom, remembering the cold gray winter morning and the tiny casket and the open grave. They were at Springwood for ten days, and afterward McGill wrote to Chubb:

> The visit to Springwood is altogether the finest I ever had, combining, as it did, rest and peace and the smell of woodsmoke and the trees and the fields . . . and providing, as it did, the greatest thrill I ever had, when the two turkeys came crashing down . . . and the grand talks before and after dinner — well, it was just perfect. I often lean back here, tired and dispirited, and think back on Springwood and feel refreshed, mentally and spiritually. I remember the dogs and picture them in my mind. I wish I could see the pups and Spider and Roma, my sweetheart. [Chubb, while in Rome doing research for a book on the life of a notorious Venetian roué and political fixer, to be called *Aretino, Scourge of Princes*, had bought an Italian bird dog, Spumoni Roma, which McGill said looked like a cross between a pointer, an airedale, and a chrysanthemum.]

The thrill of seeing the turkeys go down was one that McGill was to treasure all his life, and he described it often in later years, his eyes lighting up as he told how they came, low against the pine trees just at dusk, two hens flying together. And he remembered how the engraving looked on the barrel of the beautiful English-made shotgun that Chubb had loaned him, and how it felt against his cheek and shoulder as he brought the first turkey into his sights and fired, and the turkey went down at sixty yards, and he swung the muzzle to find the other and dropped it at forty yards. It was remarkable shooting for a man who had never fired at a turkey before, and McGill was looked upon with awe by all who witnessed it. Until, a little later, a magnificent gobbler came rocketing by, and McGill banged away with both barrels and never ruffled a feather.

For Mary Elizabeth, Springwood was a place of peace and rest and recovery, too. But her thoughts were at home. Before she had left the hospital the doctors had told her it could be dangerous — perhaps fatal — for her to try to have another baby. But both she and Ralph desperately wanted a child and the decision was made to adopt a little girl if the adoption agency could find one that had been born about the same time as the baby that had died. They came home from Springwood to get the happy news. A baby was coming up for adoption which would be born about the same time Mary Elizabeth's baby would have been if it had gone full-term. Within two months the baby had arrived and was ready for adoption — a tiny but healthy black-haired, black-eyed girl. They named her Virginia Colvin McGill for Mary Elizabeth's doctor, and nicknamed her Miss Virginia, and took her to their hearts.

The change in McGill was remarkable. He came out of the dark mood that had held him and began to look forward to a summer of action. The Georgia Tech Naval Unit had asked him to come along on their Caribbean cruise, and when that was over, there would be the fine donnybrook of a presidential political campaign, with the *Constitution* firing all its guns in support of the Three R's — Roosevelt, Russell, and a dapper little gubernatorial candidate named Eurith Dickinson Rivers.

In the spring of 1936, the old pains began coming back stronger than ever, and Mary Elizabeth McGill went back to the hospital with a kidney infection that sent her fever up to 105 degrees, where it stayed for five days. When, finally, the doctors could operate, they found a kidney so wrecked by stones and so terribly abscessed that it had to be removed. Two days after the operation, she came down with post-operative pneumonia, and for all of a long weekend, from Saturday to Monday morning, she was given only a fighting chance to live.

McGill was half out of his mind with worry, but his old boss, Ed Danforth, and his wife, Betty, got him and took him to their home. During the crisis when Mary Elizabeth was most ill, they drove him around town all Sunday night, going back by Emory Hospital every hour to check on her condition. Then the miracle happened and as they stopped by at dawn, they found her sitting up in bed, a ribbon in her hair, her fever gone, calling for her baby.

Mary Elizabeth came home thin and frail and with a drain in her side, but feeling chipper. A week later, McGill left for his cruise with the Georgia Tech Naval Unit. He was on a destroyer and the seas were rough. "I needed an old sailor of your experience to comfort me," he wrote to Chubb. He came back to find all well at home. Mary Elizabeth was feeling frisky, the baby under control and showing unmistakable signs of cutting a tooth.

In the political races all the *Constitution* candidates — Rivers, Russell and Roosevelt — seemed sure to triumph over the forces of darkness as represented by Thomas Dewey, "Ol' Gene" Talmadge, and a gaggle of candidates opposing Ed Rivers. Ralph's finances, though strained, were looking up. The *Red Barrel,* the Coca-Cola Company house organ, had bought a story from him about Margaret Mitchell, who was his friend, and how she had come to write *Gone With the Wind.* They had paid him five hundred dollars for it. And he sold an amplified version of it to the *New York Times* — it all helped to pay the doctors.

So with a lighter heart than he had known for months, he plunged with gusto into the football season. On a bright afternoon in November Ralph came to the stadium in New Orleans early, as was his habit, to write the lead story of the Tulane-Georgia game for the Sunday edition. He sent the first half play-by-play, described the marching bands and the beauty of the majorettes, and added a colorful twist by noting that the carrier pigeon that was carrying film to the *New Orleans Picayune* office had circled the scoreboard twice before departing, as if to make sure that Georgia, the underdog, actually was in the lead.

In the middle of the third quarter, with Tulane driving hard toward the goal, the operator who was tapping out McGill's copy on his Morse key suddenly stopped and bent his ear close to the Prince Albert tobacco can he used as a resonator, listened, and frowned, as he passed to McGill in the row behind him a message from Atlanta telling that Clark Howell, Sr. — "Papa" Howell, his boss, mentor and friend — had died that morning.

Ralph sat there a moment, staring straight ahead. Then, slowly, he pulled the running story out of his typewriter and cranked in a clean sheet of copy paper, and his thick, square hands hovered for a moment over the keyboard and then, with two fingers, slowly at first, then faster, he began to write. And this is how it began:

> When he left us and passed over to the other side, all the golden trumpets sounded for him. . . . He was a stalwart warrior and a happy one. He loved a fight. He gloried in a great one. He was a truly great man . . .

who never lost the human touch, the understanding heart and mind. It has been said of another man who died that if all those for whom he had done a deed of loving-kindness were to bring a single flower, he would sleep beneath a wilderness of flowers. . . . It was so of him. . . .

On without a break for nearly two thousand words.

The game ended. Georgia, the underdog, had won. McGill handed to the operator the last take of his two-column tribute to Clark Howell, spun a clean sheet of paper into the typewriter, glanced at the scoreboard, and resumed his story of the game.

The eulogy went into a thousand scrapbooks, and it brought to mind something that Coach William A. Alexander of Georgia Tech once said: "If you want to live in the memory of your fellowmen, arrange for old, fat, sentimental McGill to write your obituary."

The passing of "Papa" Howell meant no immediate change in McGill's status. As Clark Howell, Jr., called "The Major," took over as publisher and editor, McGill remained bound to the cycle of the sports seasons — baseball in the spring and summer, football in the fall, basketball, which did not excite him, in the winter, and at the turn of the year, the field trials at Albany, which he always referred to as "All-benny."

In many ways, the running of the dogs was the highlight of his year. Dog men are great storytellers, and great liars in a harmless way, and the camaraderie of the evenings in the New Albany Hotel much appealed to the convivial McGill. In his daily column, and in a special dog column called "Kennel Barks and Yelps," which he wrote for the Sunday paper, McGill gave wide circulation to such tales as that of the mule that had been trained to point quail, and of the Texas champion that had retrieved a skunk.

The trials were run in the open country, and this stirred McGill, who had an eye for the beauty of the tawny landscape, the hills and the trees and the golden grasses ruffled by the wind. The field-trial galleries delighted him, too, made up as they were of all sorts and conditions of men and women, riding on fine horses and nags and mules and ponies, and in Hoover carts, buggies, surreys and farm wagons with plank seats. Strung out across country, following the dogs, they looked to McGill like stragglers from Robert E. Lee's old Army of Northern Virginia.

Above all else he thrilled to the sight of the working dog, wide ranging, casting left and right at the quiet signal of his handler, all fierce energy running wild and free and coming to a sudden frozen halt as sensitive nostrils picked up the scent of birds, and training and instinct took over in what was to McGill "the drama of absolute stillness after furious action."

"There is the old, old thrill as you come up and see him there," he wrote. "It is a picture that makes the pulses pound. There are other pictures that take the breath away — the surf on a wild cold day and ships under sail and ducks in flight. But the sight of a great bird dog on point is the greatest of them all."

Always, in his writing of dogs, he came back to that quality of endurance which he inordinately admired both in dogs and men. "The bird dog," he wrote, "is no groomed and pampered pet. He will run all day through rough country, and he will come in flecked with his own blood, for he runs with his tongue out, and it is cruelly slashed by briars. There is no quit in him." In his column in the Sunday paper, McGill once wondered why such a foppish dog as the poodle should have been judged "Best in Show" at Westminster. This so outraged the poodle fanciers that Tom Chubb had to get him off the hook by writing for him a scholarly guest column on the history of the poodle as a hunting dog.

McGill, out of his profound admiration for anybody who could put a poem together, would suggest ideas to Tom Chubb which he believed Chubb, if he set his mind to it, could turn into epic verse. The story of Leopold Hazzard, a onetime slave whom McGill had once interviewed while on a visit to Butlers Island on the Georgia coast, was one that McGill felt should be told in verse. Hazzard, as a small boy, had been the personal servant of Fannie Kemble, the great British actress who had lived briefly at Butlers Island as wife of the owner, Pierce Butler. She hated the life around her, and wrote of it so bitterly that her writing, both in England and America, gave great impetus to the Abolitionist cause. The old man still lived, and through him, McGill believed, a sensitive poet could tell the whole story of slave and master and of what slavery had done, and what the memory of it was still doing, to destroy the South.

Chubb, in his turn, urged McGill to write magazine pieces, and offered ideas for them. One was to expand the story that McGill had written about Peggy Mitchell and her book into a longer piece that would include all the "new women" of the South, not only writers of novels but others who were rapidly dispelling the myth of the southern lady as a swooning creature with a swanlike neck. If McGill did such an article, Chubb would pass it on to his friends, the editors of the *North American Review*. This old magazine did not pay much, but to be published in it carried prestige.

McGill responded eagerly. "I'd like very much to make the magazine," he wrote to Chubb. "I never tried for one before." Working at home at night, he wrote the article and sent it to Tom Chubb, who felt it might be a little long but forwarded it to the magazine. After several weeks, it came back. The editors thought the beginning was lively and good. The rest needed rewriting. McGill tried again. This time, the delay was even longer. Finally, six months after the first submission, back it came. Part of it had been to the printers and had been set in type before an editor changed his mind and pulled it out.

This near-miss left McGill profoundly discouraged. He wrote Chubb, thanking him for his help and adding: "I'm tired. I haven't been sleeping well, and I've decided I can't write a line and will never be able to do anything but this newspaper drivel."

McGill, it turned out, was more morose than need be. What he called his "newspaper drivel" had attracted attention far beyond the readership of the *Constitution*. The Julius Rosenwald Fund at that time was actively pursuing in the Atlanta area its endeavor to improve rural education in the South and to provide fellowships for young southerners, teachers and journalists, both black and white, who showed promise of making their voices heard. McGill's friends at Emory had brought to the attention of the fund's recruiters his stories of rural Georgia and its needs, and he was asked to apply. With his usual pessimism, he gave himself no chance. "It is all fantastic and impossible, and I know the odds are against me. But I feel good about being asked even if I don't get it," he wrote to Chubb.

He got it. When his application came up, there was hardly any discussion. One member of the selection board was Mark Ethridge, famous liberal editor of the Macon, Georgia, *Telegraph*, and later of the *Louisville Courier-Journal*, who had read McGill's farm stories.

"It was the feeling of the board, and certainly mine," he said, "that McGill was far too intelligent and too socially conscious to be a mere sports editor. If the cycle of sports writing could be broken, Ralph would come into his own."

The grant totaled seventeen hundred dollars. Not much, even in the depression, but with half pay from the *Constitution,* it meant that he and Mary Elizabeth could spend six months traveling and studying in the British Isles and Europe.

On the day that Georgia Tech and the University of Georgia met in the football game that divides all Georgians into two fiercely partisan camps, he sailed from New York to write of farms and farm cooperatives in the Scandinavian countries, and of farm tenure in Ireland. The cycle at last had been broken, a trumpet had blown for him, and doors were opening on the world that would never close again.

The Rosenwald Fellowship, he said in retrospect, was one of the luckiest things that ever happened to him, and the most valuable. To a critic who felt that, by accepting the Rosenwald money, he had somehow betrayed the South, he wrote: "There is no one thing that has helped me so much as this award. It enabled me to travel in Europe, to broaden my perspective, to shake off the narrow provincialism which still holds so many of us captive."

He went off with a blithe heart. Mary Elizabeth, over her illness now, was feeling fine and was happy to be going with him. The baby, nearly two years old and thriving, was sent to Chattanooga to be cared for by his mother.

In one hundred ninety-three days of travel, more than two hundred columns and articles poured from McGill's typewriter. New scenes, new sounds, new people and new places always excited him. Humor, sentiment, a sense of history and of drama marked his Scandinavian columns, and those he wrote on unscheduled side trips to London, Berlin and Vienna had in them the apprehension of inevitable tragedy.

He began his Scandinavian travels by steeping himself in Danish history. A thousand years before Christ's birth, he learned, men were tilling fields in Denmark. Five hundred years after that event, the Viking ships set sail to conquer England and all North Europe. Once the historic background was firmly fixed in his mind, he began to do the same kind of people-to-people reporting he had done in Georgia. He walked the fields with the Danish farmers and looked at their crops and livestock. He went to dairies to observe the making of butter and cheese and to factories where pigs were transformed into hams and bacon. He sat in classes at the folk schools and slept in their dormitories, and he had tea with the faculties of the great universities.

Everywhere he went, he compared what he was seeing with what he knew of Georgia. The population of the two was about the same. Both had fought, and lost, a bloody war in the decade of the 1860s. Both, in the beginning, had tilled their soil with bondsmen — the Danes with serfs bound to the land, Georgia with black slaves. Somehow, from these similar beginnings, Denmark had made the greater progress. There was almost no illiteracy there and little farm tenantry and no tide of migration from the farm to the cities. In Denmark, good food, good housing, and good clothing were cheap and only luxuries were dear. In Georgia, nearly a third of the population was undernourished, poorly clothed, and poorly housed.

Why these differences? To McGill, the answers were obvious. In the early 1920s, when the Danes began to break up the vast entailed estates by compensating the great landlords for the acres taken, the onetime tenant became a landowner. Once the land was his, he took pride in its fertility and used every means to improve it. The black slave had gained his freedom, but he had remained a tenant, a landless man.

Denmark's system of universal education helped prepare the landowner for his new responsibilities. The folk schools wiped out illiteracy, making it possible for every man to read and learn and follow the teachings of the great agricultural universities. And crowning these were the market co-ops, giving to the individual farmer the tremendous buying and selling power of the group. These were particularly impressive to McGill, who remembered the Georgia farmer trying to peddle his baskets of beans and peaches and okra and "roas'nears" house to house in the little Georgia towns.

"Only a dreamer," McGill concluded, "would come back to America and say, 'This is the system for us.' " Denmark's system, transplanted whole, he pointed out, would not work in Georgia, where the tractor was rapidly turning the little farm into an unprofitable economic unit.

But there were many things we could learn from the Danes, about education of farm populations, about tenure and care of the land and diversification of crops and the power of the co-ops.

"They are much like us," he wrote, "in their love of the land, in their family life, in their love for their children. Even their fighters are like ours. They favor the slashing, headlong attack. They do not box like the British."

While he was working on his Danish articles, he began to feel restless: his reporter's instinct told him to move on — not to Norway and Sweden — he could come back there later to fulfill his obligation under the fellowship — but to Germany, where news was breaking that had nothing to do with farms.

In mid-February, he and Mary Elizabeth said good-bye to their friends in Copenhagen and flew to Berlin. At daybreak on February 18, they were awakened in their hotel room by the tramp of booted feet, the sounds of harsh commands in German, and the voices of Germans singing a new and boastful song: "Today the Fatherland, tomorrow the world."

Dressing hastily, McGill went down to the street. Years later, he still could vividly remember the scene. All the streets leading past the burned-out Reichstag to the opera house, where Hitler was to speak, were hung with flags and banners and lined with soldiers in steel helmets, armed with rifles. He took up position just behind a special guard of SS troops. Each man was sworn to defend Adolf Hitler with his life if need be, and in token of this vow, they were allowed to wear on the cuffs of their uniform Hitler's name stitched in black silk. Each was at least six feet tall, a handsome, well-turned-out company of men. They looked grim and harsh as they marched up stamping, wheeled, and fell into line, every third man facing toward the crowd.

"Then they stood at ease and took off their steel helmets and mopped their sweaty brows and looked like what they were," McGill remembered. "Boys. Just boys."

The friendly fat man with the camera around his neck seemed harmless enough, and he had no trouble striking up a conversation with the young troopers — he in his rough German, they in the few words of English they had picked up from American movies.

"When they found out I knew a couple of German folk songs, they were much impressed," he said. "We got along handsomely."

He found a street hawker working in the crowd and bought cakes and candies and brought them back to the soldiers, and they seemed pleased. They posed for pictures willingly, and one of them, whose English was better than the others, told McGill that at the moment Der Führer passed, he would move closer to his partner to clear a space between them through which McGill could snap a picture.

McGill asked a few questions about Hitler, and immediately it was plain to him that these men were fiercely, fanatically loyal. The taller one said, "We are pledged to die for him," and the others listening said, "*Ja, ja.*"

Finally, far up the street he heard the sound of thousands of voices screaming, "*Heil, heil, heil.*" The limousines began to flash past, bearing the lesser notables, and over his shoulder, out of the corner of his mouth, the tall soldier would name them as they came. Goebbels, the propagandist who had arranged this vast display of flags and banners . . . Goering, huge and grim, his chest a billboard of medals.

And then the roar grew deafening and there was Hitler. In a gray field marshall's uniform and overcoat, he was standing in the rear of a car, his hand raised in salute. If he heard the thundering cheers or saw the startled, round-faced babies thrust suddenly above the crowd in their parents' hands, he gave no sign.

He was there for a moment, then swiftly gone, and McGill, staring, trying intently to read what was on the face of the man, forgot his camera.

What he saw there in the set, unsmiling face, and heard later in the harsh, arrogant voice as, for three hours, Hitler harangued the world from the Kroll Opera House, lingered in McGill's memory as long as he lived.

"Here was an evil evangelist with something in his voice which thrilled men. Even one hostile to him could feel the power of it, and see its effect on the men who listened," he wrote.

McGill watched as Hitler departed, this time seated in the front seat of the car, his overcoat pulled up under his ears, his right arm in salute. His face was still a mask.

He watched the young troopers march away, feeling for them now not sympathy, but a sense of pity.

He went on to England then, to sit in the visitors' gallery in the House of Commons and listen to the great debates on which the fate of the world was hanging. With a sure sense of what his readers back home could absorb, he started off by comparing Britain's Parliament with the Georgia legislature, concluding: "You will hear more knowledge expressed in a brace of minutes on the House of Commons floor than in a brace of hours in the average state legislature. But the methods are about the same. The British dress theirs up in the regalia of tradition and better order. There is no banging of gavels. When the speaker speaks, and he does not raise his voice, there is instant silence." He heard Churchill there, denouncing the policy of appeasement of Prime Minister Chamberlain.

Hitler's triumph, McGill wrote, was made at Versailles. The great men gathered there to write the treaty attempted to wring too much from the victory. They forgot the cause for which men died. They thought too much of ore and oil and ships and rivers and gold and trade. "The German war machine," he wrote, "is back again, in a more deadly form than before. The dead of that war did not die in vain. Some of our statesmen have lived in vain."

Then his conscience drove him back to the Scandinavian countries to complete his survey. He wrote about the ski jumpers in Norway, rugged men who made football look like a finishing-school sport. He discovered that Norwegian seal hunters liked to exaggerate as much as the owners of bird dogs back home. He went to look at the Viking ships, "beautiful as poems," which the Norwegians had dug from the muck of their fjords. They were almost perfectly preserved, and in his mind's eye, he saw them, and could make his readers see them, propelled by thick-muscled oarsmen, bearing fur-clad fighting men to Vinland, their shields gleaming black and yellow in the pale sun of the North Sea. He pushed on to Sweden, where he was able to report that every barber shop in Stockholm was the one where Greta Garbo had worked as a lather girl.

His series on Denmark had dealt largely with farming. In Norway and Sweden, his interest centered largely on politics. His conclusions: nowhere in the North Country was there sympathy for Moscow. Nowhere was there sympathy for fascism. "The North Countries are democratic in mind and institution," he wrote. He examined their social legislation and found that, in the Scandinavian countries, many of Mr. Roosevelt's controversial New Deal reforms had long been in use.

As a break from the heavier tasks, he moved on to France, where he wrote two columns remembered for many years thereafter by his readers. One was in the form of a letter to an old pal named Charlie, a veteran of the AEF in World War I, who had asked him to look up a little French girl named Charmaine. She was cute as a speckled pup and no bigger than a minute, Charlie had told McGill, and when he had leave in Paris, he used to go on picnics with her in the Bois de Boulogne.

"Well, Charlie," McGill wrote, "I did just what you asked me to. I walked right down the Rue St. Honoré until I found that door . . .":

> And the lady who came to the door was Charmaine all right, but she was more like a mastiff than a speckled pup, and as for being about as big as a minute — well, Charlie, she's about twenty minutes now. And she had a hard time remembering which one was you. We had to look up some old snapshots. . . .

The next day's column — in a complete change of mood — was the story of a trip to the old battlefields of World War I:

> We rode out of Paris down the road which lies between fields where men were plowing, and through villages and narrow streets and came at last to the old stone bridge across the Marne. . . . There is no more peaceful spot on earth today. . . . Yet it was along this road and over the river there came the strangest army in all the history of armies . . . the army of 40,000 men who rode into battle in the taxicabs of Paris and saved their city.

He went on to Château-Thierry and had lunch at a sidewalk café where workingmen were eating soup and meat and cheese and drinking red wine and laughing. There was a little museum there, unattended, and on the wall in dusty cases were many pictures of young

Americans who had died in battle at this place. One of them was a young man named Edward Frank Graham of Rochester, New York, and with his picture was a letter he had written to his parents shortly before he was killed: "This trouble is not a thing to be finished in five years, or a decade, or a generation. The effort to rule the world by force and barbarism may go on for one hundred years, and the battle must begin now."

A few weeks later in Vienna, McGill again remembered what the young American had written two decades before. In London, after much string-pulling, he had finally gotten permission to enter Austria. He had met two Viennese refugees, Jews who had fled the coming Nazi terror, and in his head he was carrying messages to their relatives still trapped in Austria — messages that gave directions as to where certain papers could be found that must be burned before they fell into Nazi hands. He found the family, a lawyer and his aged mother, in a fine old house that already had been pillaged by the Nazis. The mother was eighty years old, but Hitler's troops had come and pulled her out of bed, had taken the paintings and much of the old and beautiful furniture, and had sealed the silver service and other valuables with orders that they not be used. The son could not practice his profession or even go on the street or he would be put to work sweeping the streets or polishing automobiles. McGill's visit was an event. "It makes us feel good to have a visitor," the son had said. "It makes us feel there is, after all, a little liberty left in the world."

The next day McGill went for tea with a second family. The husband, a cultured man, a patron of the arts, had fought for Austria with distinction in the First World War. He, too, was a lawyer and had been forbidden to practice. There was present also a woman who was a Christian, happily married to a Jewish husband for fifteen years. She had been ordered to get a divorce under penalty of losing her Austrian citizenship. She had refused. Their small son had come home that day singing a new song he had learned at school:

Wie Schön ist Eisen.
Wie Schön ist Stahl.
Wie Schön ist der Jud am
härterphal.

They translated for McGill:

How beautiful is iron.
How beautiful is steel.
How beautiful is a Jew at a
stake of torture.

"I sat there in their house," McGill wrote, "with the lights on by day because the curtains were drawn, and tried to believe that this was the world of 1938 — that it was not a dream. I had read the Nazis' very effective propaganda that such things were not true. But I was seeing them."

Two days later in the gloom of early morning in his hotel room in the center of Vienna, he heard again the tramp of booted feet. It was the day before the plebiscite, which would show the world that the people of Austria supported the Nazi take-over. With his camera at the ready, he moved through the morning streets, where thousands were already assembling, to the West Station, where Hitler was to arrive. It was slow going through the crowds and the propaganda towers with their lettered sides proclaiming "*Ein Volk, Ein Reich, Ein Führer.*" "The street seemed to drip red," he wrote. "Great red tongues of flags whipped in the wind. Tremendous banners with the black swastikas hung over the street. There was a barbaric, almost oriental splendor about it. Pylons everywhere bore the message, 'One people, one land, one leader.' "

Then Hitler came, standing in a car. "The crowd seemed to explode with sound, completely hysterical, mad, fanatical, loud. I saw wet eyes, blazing eyes, mouths that frothed as they screamed, '*Sieg Heil, Sieg Heil, Sieg Heil.*' "

This time McGill did not forget his camera. As he reached to unsnap the cover of its case, a rough hand grabbed his wrist. A trooper, hard-faced and unsmiling, pulled him aside, peered into the case, examined his credentials, and lectured him strongly. "*Nein!*" It was verboten to take pictures; only the official photographers were permitted. McGill, playing the role of innocent tourist, pretended not to understand. The trooper waved him on. At a trot, he cut across a park to where he could intercept the procession again as it approached the Imperial Hotel, which was Hitler's destination. It took him an hour and a half to work his way for half a block to a position in front of the hotel. All around him, massed thousands were chanting, "We-would-our-leader-see, we-would-our-leader-see." There was a stirring at a window, and as he raised the camera to focus on the balcony where Hitler was expected to appear, strong hands grabbed him again, and two men in plainclothes hustled him out of the crowd. They opened his camera and confiscated his film. They noted that his passport identified him as a newspaperman. Did this not mean that he was a journalist?

"I did not feel it was the time or the place," McGill said later, "to give them the classic definition of a journalist — as one who carries a cane and borrows money from newspapermen." Again he pleaded a tourist's ignorance, and a hostile crowd which had begun to gather drifted away.

Now came the most dramatic moment of the day. At high noon all sound was hushed, all motion stopped, as loudspeakers announced the beginning of the "holy moment" when Austria and Germany would symbolically reunite. McGill, watching warily for cops, climbed to the pedestal of a pylon and looked about. Around him, two hundred thousand people stood absolutely motionless, arms upthrust in the fascist salute. For two interminable minutes they stood and then came a barked command and again great roaring shouts, *Sieg Heil, Ein Volk, Ein Reich, Ein Führer.* There was a roaring in the sky, and a wave of Hitler's black bombing planes swept over — a salute to Austria that was also a grim warning to the world. Behind them came transport planes, loosing upon the crowd below millions of pieces of paper bearing the one word, *Ja.*

The vote was not until the next day, but the deed was done.

The crowd began to disperse. McGill climbed down from his pylon and started toward his hotel. (Mary Elizabeth, ill, had stayed in London.) It was cold, and he turned in at a restaurant, found a table, and sat down, weary of body and sick at heart.

The waiter came up and lifted his arm in the fascist salute.

"Heil, Hitler," he said.

"Coffee," said McGill.

McGill's venture into Austria during the Hitler plebiscite was a sort of journey on the road to Damascus. There, for the first time, he saw all rights guaranteed in a written, published constitution disappear because the will of the people to maintain them had disappeared. And yet he could understand why this had happened. Germany and Austria had known hunger and sickness and unemployment in the years after the first war. Adolf Hitler, a grim ex-soldier, had given them, in the promise of a new and united race, the first new gleam of hope. What he had witnessed, McGill wrote in the last of his series on Hitler's putsch, "should be a lesson to the democracies to check up and see to their own houses. Are there seeds of terror and horror and despair being nourished there for some strong man to harvest?"

Then, McGill seemed to turn almost eagerly to lighter things. Back in England, he wrote about the boat races on the Thames and the racing at Aintree, the boxing matches and the coconut shies. "Out of patriotism," he explained, he did a column about a fan dancer imported from America to entertain the British. He interviewed her and gave her the coconuts he had won at the coconut shy. "Hoorah for the red, white and blue," he wrote. "American fan dancers über alles." He did a fine, emotional piece about a rugger match at Twickenham between England and Scotland which seventy-five thousand people witnessed. The hawkers did not sell pennants, he noticed, but heather and red roses, and he bought a bit of heather for himself and the lady who was traveling with him. To his vast surprise, the band played "Dixie," and "Marching through Georgia." "The best I could do for the latter was one muted boo," he said.

In serious articles, he wrote of England getting ready for war, of the rooms in the houses that the people were trying to gasproof with curtains and seals at the windows, and of the gas masks for the babies. Papa and Mama, he said ironically, would have to have their monograms on their gas masks to identify them, like napkin rings, but this would not be necessary for the baby. Its mask would be the smallest one. . . . And he ended on the foreboding note: "What a war the next one is going to be!"

With Mary Elizabeth feeling better, they moved on to Ireland. In Dublin, he tested and found wise the theory of his old friend, Colonel Tillinghast L'Hommedieu Huston from Dover Hall, Georgia — that the best way to see a country and to learn the character of its people is to observe the passing throng from the front window of a nice, warm pub.

It was in such a place that McGill learned of the strongest man in the world, who lived in the neighborhood of Castlefinn in the county of Donegal. "He can," wrote McGill, "take himself by the ear with his right hand and lift himself off of the ground. There are not many men who can do this."

A trip to Donegal was not on his itinerary, but something in him told him he must go there. From a stone cottage in Castlefinn, where he had gone to rest, he rode out to find the strong man, who turned out not to be at home. His journey, though, was not entirely wasted, for it was made on a bicycle to the giggly delight of the colleens watching from the doorways of the thatched houses along the way.

To McGill, whose ancestors had sailed from Ireland in 1741 — one of his great-great-grandfathers was born at sea — everything he saw there was a delight:

> It is a country much misunderstood, but one of the loveliest on earth. Ireland does not seem part of anything else. You may sail to the five hundred islands that are Denmark and feel a part of the world. You may go to Norway, or Sweden or France or Germany, and feel "in" things. The island that is England does not seem to be an island, but when the ship puts you down at Dublin, you feel you're far away from the rest of the world. And when you come inland to a small village or a farm and walk the lanes and look at the hedges of hawthorne and furze, you feel positive you are in "The Other Country." It is in the sounds of Ireland, the sheep and the bells, and the sight of the ruins and the people themselves. . . . It is in the very air, in the winds and the fields and the flowers of Ireland, this mysticism and this feeling of a land apart.

In a stone cottage in the little village of Castlefinn, with ducks waddling in the yard and a pet lamb butting against the back door, McGill labored to finish his Rosenwald chores, the work interrupted by his trips to Berlin and Vienna. It was no simple task. "Something happens to a man in Ireland," he said. "It is not laziness. It is contemplation and it does the inner man much good to sit and contemplate."

Putting aside for the moment his memories of Vienna and Berlin, his increasing sureness that soon an unimaginable terror would be unleashed upon the world, he stayed for two weeks in the little village, sitting for hours on an old stone fence overlooking the river Finn, playing with the lamb, and letting the quietness and beauty around him, the dreamy atmosphere of Ireland, sink into his soul.

For a while his writing took on the lilt and cadence of Irish speech, and the memory of those he met stayed in his mind. He remembered the gatekeeper at the Punchestown Races, where, burdened with an overcoat not needed because of the sun, he said, as he reached for his ticket, "I've got too much in my hands."

"Sure and now, that's a fact," said the gatekeeper with a grin, "but it would be much worse if you had nothing at all."

Coming out from the races, he ran into another old woman, this one selling flowers, and when he shook his head, she said, "It is not every day ye can buy beauty." "So I bought some flowers," he wrote, "being a sucker for such sayings."

He wrote of football also, passing on the Irish claim that they were playing the game at least two thousand years ago. "When there was no ball handy," said McGill, "they used the skull of a Roman or a Briton, the Irish of those days not being particular in such matters."

Finally, there was the ship waiting that would take him home, and he knew, though others didn't, that the sports stories he had written on this trip would be the last he would ever write as a sports reporter. He was going home to write on things that were broader and deeper than athletic games. In his pocket was a letter from Clark Howell of the *Constitution.* It had come to him in London, and it spoke of what might happen on his return. "My thought is," wrote Major Howell, "that you would disassociate yourself from the sports department and become editorial director, at the same time handling a daily column on the editorial page."

Again, doors were opening for him on a wider world.

6

McGill, a sentimental man, had left Atlanta misty-eyed when friends brought a brass band to the train to see him off. He came "dangerously near to bawling" when he found on his return an even larger throng waiting to welcome him. Only one person was missing, his adopted daughter, Miss Virginia, who had not yet come home from Chattanooga. In his pocket was a letter to her that he had written on his last night in Vienna. It told her of all he had seen that day — the flags and the people shouting and the evil man called Hitler, and in it he told her of Victor Hugo saying of Napoleon that God at last had grown bored with him. He planned to keep it for her until she was twenty-one years old, when they would read it together.

Ten days after his return, the *Constitution* announced his new assignment. He was to be given the title of executive editor, which meant that McGill, who as sports editor could not bring himself to fire, or even strongly rebuke, an incompetent colleague, would have complete charge of the news, sports and society departments. He would also write a daily column for the editorial page — "on any subject which he sees fit" — but that page would be under the direction of Associate Editor Ralph T. Jones, a dry and bloodless Englishman who had long been the *Constitution*'s chief editorial writer.

His last "Break O' Day" column appeared on the sports page on a Friday — June 18, 1938. It was a graceful farewell to sixteen years of sports reporting.

On the following Monday he appeared on the editorial page with a new column heading, "One Word More." His first column was a reminiscence of a day in Vienna and a curiously carved statue he had seen there. It was a statue of Augustin, hero of the song beloved by German beer-hall bands — "Ach, du Lieber, Augustin" — the verses of which in English can be roughly translated, "Oh, you dear Augustin, all is gone. Money is gone, property is gone, everything is gone."

This Augustin, McGill explained, was a strolling minstrel, a street singer who, during the Great Plague in Vienna, had called at too many taverns on his rounds. He had fallen drunk into the gutter, and taken for dead, he had been transported to the outskirts of the city and tossed into a ditch with others dead of the plague. The next morning when he woke up, he immediately made his way back to the city, playing his pipes and singing his songs. And all Vienna, thinking Augustin had returned from the dead, took heart and the plague began to lose its grip. Thus Augustin became a symbol of survival, McGill wrote. And so long as his statue stood and his story was remembered, not even the Nazi terror could destroy the soul of Vienna.

Sharing the *Constitution*'s editorial page with McGill were columnists Joseph Alsop and Robert Kintner, concentrating on national affairs; Pierre van Paassen with his "Window on the World" of international politics; Westbrook Pegler working the misanthrope beat; George Sokolsky writing on labor; and Robert Quillen producing a daily ration of homespun philosophy. To this varied company McGill added his unflagging interest in everything that human beings did, said, or thought about from politics to poker, from bookkeeping to the ballet.

His column on bees was based on his own experience of raising them in his backyard, and it brought him an invitation to speak to a local garden club. It was not a success.

"I began," Ralph recalled, "by saying that the social system of the bee was not unlike our own. The female bee, called the queen, is a bit fat, has to be waited on all the time, and the male bees work themselves to death keeping her in the style to which she is accustomed. . . . Noting that this bit of levity was not exactly rolling them in the aisles, I quickly turned to the subject of pollination."

McGill took over as executive editor at the beginning of a political year in Georgia, with former Governor Eugene Talmadge running for the Senate seat held by Walter F. George, a distinguished conservative whom President Roosevelt was seeking to purge in favor of a pleasant but unimpressive United States district attorney named Lawrence Camp.

McGill was a great admirer of FDR. But he also admired Senator

George. So he handled this ticklish situation with the political dexterity which was to serve him well. He wrote that President Roosevelt had every right to try to purge a senator who was not in entire sympathy with his program, but that fortunately, this was not Italy or Germany and Roosevelt was not a dictator. So the people of Georgia could go right ahead and vote for George if they wanted to. And this he urged them to do, for he was afraid that if too many heeded Roosevelt and voted for Camp, this might mean that Talmadge would be the nominee.

Georgians heeded this warning and sent George back to the Senate, and Roosevelt took the rebuke with good grace. But Talmadge was not pleased, and two years later, in a race for governor, he rawhided McGill mercilessly from the stump. He called him "Rosenwald Ralph" and displayed the checks which the state had paid McGill during a brief, ill-advised tenure as state athletic director. In order that he would not forget to attack McGill, Talmadge carried with him a claque known as "The Tree-Climbing Haggards," a one-gallus family who would perch on the limbs of trees around the speaker's stand and holler, "Tell 'em about ole Ralph McGill, Gene." Talmadge would holler back, "I'm acomin' to that." He always saved McGill and the check-waving until the last, knowing it was a crowd-pleaser.

McGill actually expressed surprise at Talmadge's violent reaction. He thought that he had dealt most gently with Talmadge in the Senate race, pointing out that a thread of logic ran through his platform, even though it did contain fatal weaknesses. Actually, he said, the fact that Talmadge had any program at all was an improvement over his past performances, which were based on sheer demagoguery.

McGill then turned his attention to the Ku Klux Klan. "We can't do much pointing of the accusing finger at Adolf Hitler or Ill Doochey for trying to give their people an exaggerated idea of the supremacy of their blood," he wrote. "We have the Klan.

"It takes real daffiness to join the Klan and pay ten dollars for a bedsheet and a hood and go around speaking of Brother Kligrapp and Brother Dragon and Brother Kleagle. Yes sir, I think that is even more ridiculous than the stuff that Adolf Hitler and Ill Doochey give their people.

"The Klan breeds crime and intolerance and bigotry and never a single good thing."

Naturally, the Klan was angered by this, and robed and masked, they paraded before the *Constitution* office carrying signs which denounced McGill. Informers the FBI had planted in the Klan passed the word to McGill that the Klan in Kloncave assembled had debated whether or not some of the boys should catch him and "touch him up a little."

Whatever concern McGill might have felt about this threat — and if he felt any, he gave no sign of it — was overshadowed by a far deeper worry. The year before at Christmas he and Mary Elizabeth had been in Denmark. This Christmas they were determined to make up to Miss Virginia the holiday they had missed. Shortly before Christmas, though, she became mysteriously ill. Tests showed that she was allergic to a number of foods, including fish and chicken and anything with wheat in it.

It was, well into the summer of the following year before the allergies were brought under control. Then she came down with scarlet fever, with the house quarantined, and McGill recalled that he had caught scarlet fever by sitting just outside the bedroom door and reading to his little sister as she lay ill in her bed. Now he was immune. So, every night when he came home, he would sit by Miss Virginia's bed, and read to her from a new book he had bought for her that day. Sometimes, in his harsh, unmusical voice, he would sing to her.

Eventually the quarantine lifted, and Miss Virginia, her black eyes huge in her pale face, went out in the sun to play. Somehow she fell and hurt her knee; it did not heal as it should; there were more tests, and finally, the microscope told the hard truth. Miss Virginia had leukemia. So began for McGill an agonizing period, the memory of which never left him. For six months, the doctors battled to save her, trying every new and experimental technique known.

"The doctor has not given up fighting," McGill wrote his friend Tom Chubb in early November. "They have given her an experimental-type transfusion which lasted for almost twenty-four hours, the constant flow of new blood at the rate of sixteen drops per minute . . . a most arduous thing. . . . They gave her a really tremendous amount of blood and had to keep a doctor in constant attendance, taking the pulse and blood pressure every few minutes. We do not yet know the result. . . . We are clinging to hope." By early December the results were known. The hope which the doctors held out did not materialize. It was only a matter of time. . . .

This was the winter of the most important event in Atlanta's history since Sherman's visit — the world premiere of the movie version of Margaret Mitchell's *Gone With the Wind.* There were parties every night to which the McGills were asked, only one of which did they attend. The great ball that preceded the premiere with all the stars in attendance was sponsored by the Atlanta Junior League for the support of its charities — one of which was the Henrietta Egleston Hospital, where their baby lay dying.

Those who knew Ralph realized how much of his own private suffering went into these lines in his column before the premiere:

> I wish the Junior League might have an *annual* ball with movie stars in attendance, so that the sound of dancing and of music might resound every year and be translated into bandages and medicines, and the care of nurses and the relief of pain and suffering by little children. The real charities after all are those which touch the lives of the very young, and the old who are helpless and cannot do for themselves.
>
> It is difficult to discuss them without becoming, perhaps, a bit too emotional. Yet we may know that in the years ahead there will be mothers and fathers . . . who will thank God for those merry dancing feet. . . .

The next day, on December 20, at Egleston Hospital, after six long months of suffering, Miss Virginia died. She was five years old.

He was never to forget the tiny, laughing, black-eyed girl and the long agony of her last illness. To the aching sorrow of the baby's death was added his concern for Mary Elizabeth's reaction to it, which took the form not of withdrawal from life, but of an almost reckless gaiety. In retrospect, he wrote to Tom Chubb: "It was a ghastly six months which produced a breakdown for Mary Elizabeth and a near one for me."

To his old friends of sports-writing days, the serious-minded McGill was becoming a stranger. As his interests gradually grew away from theirs, they recalled the good companion, the storyteller, the listener, who had worked and played with such zest. They remembered the antic moods, unpredictably merry or melancholy, that would come over him when he was drinking. He always had something to say when he lifted his glass, they remembered. Such as, "Well, good night all" — as if that one would finish him, which it never did. Or that line he had picked up from some old poet about the bird of time being on the wing, which prompted his toast, "Drink to the bird."

McGill, in his joyful moods, was amiable enough. It was only toward the end of the evening, when some semisober friend would try to take him home, that he would grow truculent and hard to handle. Protesting that he had to go back to the office and work, he would try to stop the car by snatching the keys, kicking the brakes, or by reaching under the dashboard to rip out the wiring. When they got him to his house, he would jump out of the car and run across the street, where he would try to hide behind a tree far too slender to conceal his girth.

In strange cities, when his companions were heading wearily back to the hotel and bed, he would set off alone, exploring. The next morning he would be up and dressed and down to breakfast, looking remarkably fit but proclaiming to heaven that he was dying and apologizing abjectly to all those he had insulted the night before. His hangovers were peculiar. He never suffered from headache, or nausea, or the shakes. He never required a morning drink to steady the nerves. He would, instead, proclaim that things were crawling on him. "I know I must pay the piper," he would moan, "but why does the s.o.b. have to charge me time-and-a-half?"

Haunted by his Calvinist conscience, well aware that the editor of the *Atlanta Constitution* should hold himself under self-discipline, McGill did his best to quell the rantipole spirit which led him into such exhibitions as this. He was not always successful, especially when he felt himself set upon by stuffy and pompous men.

His sympathy, by instinct, went to the underdog, the man hemmed in by the spears. He admired poets and philosophers and other journalists, and doctors and most politicians and anyone in any profession who he thought was earnestly striving to make life better for others. He looked askance at lawyers, and when in their presence was fond of quoting a line from Carl Sandburg: "Why does a hearse horse snicker, hauling a lawyer's bones?" He distrusted most preachers and all but a few businessmen, and in his dark moods he did not bother to conceal these feelings.

This sometimes led to embarrassing moments in Major Howell's office. The major was a man of great patience and forbearance who was well aware of what a treasure he had in McGill. Frequently, though, he was made unhappy when his friends would call him up to tell him that they had been insulted by McGill.

One of Major Howell's friends, an insurance man, civic leader, and heavy advertiser who always inserted his picture in his ads, called him to report a confrontation with McGill.

"I ran into Ralph at the Capital City Club last night," he told the major, "and I asked him if he'd send a photographer to my office on Monday to get a picture of me announcing the kickoff of the fund drive. He called me a narcissistic son-of-a-bitch. What I want to know, Clark, is what does narcissistic mean?"

Among the few rich and powerful men whom McGill did admire greatly — and who greatly admired him — was Robert W. Woodruff, president of the Coca-Cola Company. "He had a lot of guts," said Woodruff. "Sometimes he'd get so wrapped up in his theories he'd go off the deep end. But he wasn't afraid of the devil, and I respected him for this. I had a great affection for him. I told him I thought he could go far in advertising or public relations, but he said no, he only wanted to write for the paper, and I never pressed him."

There is reason to believe that the knowledge that Woodruff would hire him if anything disastrous should happen to him at the *Constitution* gave McGill the courage stubbornly to advocate measures that he knew were anathema to many of the major's influential friends. McGill's opposition to Eugene Talmadge, for example, was offensive to many of Atlanta's fatter cats, for though Talmadge's voting strength came from the boys from the forks of the creek, he actually was the protégé of the bigger bankers and businessmen who saw in him their strongest shield against the extremes of FDR.

Woodruff was one of those whose lack of admiration for Roosevelt was boundless, but the friendship between him and McGill was too strong to be shattered by their political differences. Their lifelong friendship began in the hunting field, as had McGill's friendship with

Tom Chubb. Both he and Woodruff felt the same deep emotion at the sight of a dog on point, the same surge of excitement as the birds got up on thundering wings. Woodruff was a taciturn man, who might feel these things but could not put them into words. McGill could, and over the years, Woodruff's scrapbooks were filled with McGill's prose describing "the beauty of the morning in the bird country with the sun's rays slanting through dark pines to lie in pools of gold on the forest floor," and "the smell of woodsmoke riding on the air like a nostalgic memory from the campfires of long ago." This love of nature was a bond they shared together, and it transcended politics.

Though Woodruff might not be the most articulate of men, he was sensitive to the moods and needs of others. It was his habit on Sunday morning to drop by McGill's house for a brief chat, and in the first months after Miss Virginia's death, it was plain to him that McGill was desperately groping to get his bearings, to find a faith, a certitude, a way out of the darkness of the spirit that threatened to overwhelm him. At Woodruff's urging, he went down to Ichauway, Woodruff's country estate, as he had gone to find peace at Springwood when the first baby had died. There was a blind Negro guitarist there, and the house servants could sing like an angel choir. After dinner they would take their places on the stairway leading down to the living room, and with no light in the room except from the log fire on the hearth, they would sing the old spirituals.

One of these, "Yonder Come Day," had a particularly meaningful message for McGill. He wrote from Ichauway:

> When trouble comes or a great sorrow shakes him, a man wants desperately to find a faith that nothing can shake. I am not sure about anything, but I know that if one is hurt and lonely and desperately hunting something on which to lean, he can do worse than to sit before a log fire listening to these spirituals. The Norsemen, the Greeks, the Christians, the pagans, all had an idea about God. . . . The spirituals express it best.

Not being a theologian, he went on, he could not explain what he meant exactly, but the song "Yonder Come Day" evoked a special meaning: he saw the coming of the first faint light, growing stronger, and then the birds beginning to wake and sing and fly, and then all at once, it is day. So, he implied, the light of faith comes to men out of the depths of darkness and despair:

> I am not a religious man, yet every now and then I get a quick and inadequate glimpse of this thing they call faith. . . . And I am glad then that I was not a preacher or a statesman, but merely a newspaperman who can wonder, and hear faith in a song. For you realize, all of a sudden, that is the way you feel — yonder come day, coming up over the horizon of the night, and when it breaks, it does seem to break into one's soul . . . driving away the darkness, making things better. . . .

Woodruff worried about McGill, and when he felt he was getting "too tensed up and nervous," or drinking too much, he would try to get him down to Ichauway for a week, or out to his ranch at Cody, Wyoming.

Once when McGill "was so tensed up he wasn't fit to live with," Woodruff asked him out to Cody in haying time. McGill, who always liked to stretch his muscles at heavy labor, would get up at daybreak to work in the hayfields. One day when Woodruff's ranch hands were moving some horses from one ranch to another fourteen miles away, McGill volunteered to help, riding one bronc and leading another.

"It's real hard work, riding a bronc over a rough road," Woodruff remembered, "harder than on a trail. You have to keep kicking him, and your ass gets sore."

On top of this, it was snowing, and Woodruff, snug and warm at the ranch house, finally decided he should go out by car to rescue McGill. He caught him about three miles short of his destination.

"I told him to turn the horses over to the other fellows and come on with me and we'd go have a drink," Woodruff said. "He didn't even smile. The snow was spitting in his face and I could tell he was in agony from the riding, but he said, 'No, I've made it this far, and I'm going on if it kills me. Which,' he said, 'the way I feel now, it damn well may.' But he went on and finished. He wouldn't quit."

This stubbornness, this determination to keep on trying, was one of the things Woodruff admired in McGill — particularly his long and finally successful battle to bring his drinking under control.

"He was both high-strung and emotional, and at the same time pragmatic," Woodruff said. "He knew that the most inefficient way to drown your sorrow is with alcohol."

At Ichauway and Cody, McGill used physical work as his therapy, driving himself hard. Once, after a day in the hayfields at Cody, sore of bone and muscle, he wrote:

> How sedentary is man, and how ridiculously he tries to escape from his shell and cram into a few days all the beauty of air and field and dog and bird. How juvenile he is, trying to eat all the honey in the gourd of life in one brief time. But it is glorious, and one may live on the memories of it for a long time.

There was another refuge, different in its appeal as a place of rest and tranquility, a cottage called Endden at Fernandina, Florida, on the dunes overlooking the sea. Owned by a brusque but amiable merchant named Frank Neely, then president of Atlanta's largest department store, and his wife, Rae, a gentle and highly intellectual person who greatly admired McGill, it was during Mary Elizabeth's illness and young Ralph's growing up a summer retreat for the McGill family.

There he did some of his most sensitive and perceptive writing, not to be published anywhere but destined only for Rae Neely's guest book.

A shell, picked up at the sea's edge, could set him brooding:

> Shells make one think . . . certainly nature cannot be all chance . . . chance would not spend so much time on the infinite beauty of shells, making each different. . . . The sand dollar, with its exquisite fine petals flowering in the center could have been as utilitarian without the carefully shaped petals . . . obviously nature is more than evolution. . . .

Lying on his bed at Endden, he listened drowsily to the booming of the surf nine-tenths of a mile away:

> Eternally it rolls and makes its soothing retreating, returning sound in which the sibilants are so flung together they become a hissing, muted roar.
>
> Thought, I believe, is like that. Especially is it true in these times when new dangers, crises and decisions come in on us like a surf. They change

our shorelines, remove or create sandbars, make for tides high and low. . . . But they will never stop coming. . . .

Nobody knew better than McGill that at home and around the world tides were running, both racial and political, that would sweep away old shorelines everywhere.

War and politics kept McGill on the move. He traveled the campaign trail with both presidential candidates, and his experiences with Wendell Willkie, the Republican nominee, provided him with one of his raciest political anecdotes.

He had gone up to Philadelphia to join the Willkie campaign train as it came in from a western tour, only to discover that the train had arrived at one station, while the welcoming committee, with bands and banners, was waiting across town at another. Then each group set out to where the other group was reported to be waiting, thus missing contact again. This fiasco led McGill to inquire of one of the reporters leaving the train just what it was like to travel with the Republican candidate.

"Ralph," the reporter said, "were you ever in a whorehouse on Saturday night when the madam was in jail and the girls were all drunk? Well, that's about the way this thing is organized."

Despite the confusion among the confident young political amateurs surrounding Willkie, McGill came home much impressed with the big, earnest, hoarse-voiced and shaggy man. The Democrats were deriding him as a "simple, barefoot Wall Street lawyer," but McGill saw other virtues in him, and in the last week before the election, he was expressing privately the conviction that Mr. Willkie was going to win. It was one of the few times his political acumen failed him.

As Christmas came around with its sorrowful memories, Ralph and Mary Elizabeth, against the advice of the Atlanta children's agencies, began actively seeking another child for adoption. By early spring of 1941, they had found one, in an orphanage at Macon, Georgia. No baby this time, but a little boy three and a half years old. The McGills bought him a puppy to play with, and toys in great quantity, and a handsome wardrobe of little-boy suits. Unhappily, though, he had been too long neglected, and neither love nor discipline could control him.

He turned out to have the vocabulary of a mule skinner, a complete disregard for the uses of indoor plumbing, and an uncontrollable impulse to smash mirrors and sweep lamps off tables. At the end of a six-month trial period, they regretfully sent him back to the orphanage.

Convinced by this experience that the role of parents would always be denied them, McGill bought a tiny house on two acres of land eight miles out from the office. It was in a residential section, a narrow, one-hundred-twenty-five-foot lot running back nine hundred feet from Piedmont Road, and on it, he soon discovered an unexpected dividend. In some excitement, he wrote to Tom Chubb:

> The back of the lot is rather wild and protected. I have a small garden back there. Sunday I walked back to see what the weeds have done to it. A Chesapeake retriever, untrained, was with me. She blundered into a covey of quail which got up almost under my feet. It was totally unexpected, and I must have leaped a foot in the air, no mean achievement for one of my weight.
>
> I am highly pleased they are there, and I am going to plant some benne for them, hoping they will stay.

However pained Major Howell might have been by his executive editor's occasional brusqueness with his rich and pompous friends, he did not let it blind him to the fact that McGill had an appeal to the *Constitution*'s readers unknown on the paper since the days of his great predecessor, Henry Grady. For three years under Major Howell as editor and publisher, McGill had been working at Grady's old rolltop desk. In 1942 he got the title that went with the office.

He was made editor-in-chief of the *Constitution*, with full responsibility for its editorial policies. At last he had found his unrestricted forum; and the South that, in pain and travail, was coming to birth had found its spokesman.

The governor's race of the following year demonstrated how strong that editorial voice could be. The *Constitution*'s young candidate, Ellis Arnall, to whom McGill was confidant and counselor, trounced the fiery old Negro-baiter, Eugene Talmadge, but McGill, being a political realist, was the first to admit that fate had played a large part in the Talmadge defeat.

On his way to his kickoff barbecue at Moultrie in south Georgia,

Talmadge, pausing briefly in a country privy, was so painfully bitten by a black widow spider he could not make his opening speech. A supporter, Representative "Hellbent" Edwards, did his best as a substitute, but rain drowned out both the oratory and the fires in the barbecue pits. After this unfortunate start, the Talmadge candidacy never got off the ground.

McGill was always an omnivorous reader of biography and history, and one book which taught him that most of what he had read about the South before was bunk was C. Vann Woodward's *Tom Watson: Agrarian Rebel,* the story of Georgia's great Populist leader.

Watson, a strange, tragic mixture of good and evil traits, began as a champion of human brotherhood. He ended as a raging and pathologically vindictive enemy of the Negro, the Catholic and the Jew. His story fascinated McGill, who traveled over the state talking with old Populists who had known Watson and looked upon him as a hero who had died "fighting the sons of bitches of this world." It is not, in fact, too farfetched to say that, in his own career as a rebel against the mores of his time and region, McGill was sustained and encouraged by the support which grass-roots Georgians had given to the ideas put forth by Watson in his earlier, gentler days.

Watson, for example, had preached that racial antagonism makes both races the poorer. So did McGill. Watson spoke out against lynching at a time when such a stand was an implied invitation to violate southern women and a slur on the manhood of the southern male. A generation later, when McGill was calling lynchers yellow rats and pleading for the states to pass their own antilynching laws, the opposition arguments were much the same. Watson spoke to mixed audiences from platforms he shared with black men and women; so did McGill. Watson did not advocate desegregation in the schools, but he did strongly insist that the Negro be granted full political equality and all the rights of citizenship. McGill affirmed in many a column that he believed in the separation of the races in the schools — but that the Negro should be given every right the Constitution of the United States guaranteed to any citizen. Watson fought against the concentration of power, wealth, and privilege in the hands of a few at the expense of the many. McGill, a generation later, did the same.

"Watson," wrote McGill in his *The South and the Southerner*, "attacked prejudice against the Negro fearlessly, and with an honesty never before seen in the political life of the cotton South."

McGill, in his time, spoke out against the bigotry and the prejudice which poisoned the South with a boldness few other southern editors chose to emulate.

And there the parallel ends. Watson, when his political goals were thwarted, turned against all he once stood for. When his political enemies defeated him for Congress by openly buying the votes of black men, he became the living symbol of the southerner's latent fear and hatred of the Negro.

McGill, in his role as editor-teacher, himself changed as times changed, but in the other direction. Patiently, stubbornly, lovingly, even tediously at times, he plodded on, growing a little bolder each year, trying to touch again that chord of reason, fairness, decency and brotherhood that Watson in his early days had found buried deep beneath the southerner's overlay of prejudice.

He began with one small, seemingly unimportant act. On his first day as executive editor, he sent down an order that in the future the *Constitution* would print the word "Negro" with a capital "N" — the first paper in the South, he believed, to afford the Negro even this small dignity. He waited for the reaction, which was mild. Two printers sent word they'd be damned if they would set the word with a capital "N." But they did. Three or four subscribers quit the paper. A half-dozen angry letters came in. But a number of teachers from the all-Negro colleges and universities in Atlanta wrote in to express their appreciation. It was a small thing, but a beginning, and today the columns of the Atlanta papers routinely carry pictures and engagement announcements of Negro brides-to-be.

Another book whose lessons McGill never forgot was Carl Sandburg's great four-volume biography of Abraham Lincoln, *The Prairie Years and the War Years.* The value of using humor to make a point, the knowledge that not too much virtue may be expected from frail, flawed human beings, the flexibility of mind that allowed McGill to shift with the winds of change while always steering generally in what to him seemed the right direction — all of these were supported by his reading of Sandburg's Lincoln.

In the early 40s he found a document which told him how far he could go. It was a study made by novelist Hervey Allen for the War Manpower Commission in 1943, and it dealt with what the southern white man thought of the government's effort to give the Negro greater opportunity in war jobs.

The conclusion was blunt: the dark heritage of Watson in his latter days still cast its shadow over the state. Not even to help the war effort would the southern white man agree to any change in the Negro's status. Fearing above all else an eventual racial fusion, he would strongly oppose any effort whatever to elevate the Negro above his traditional role as domestic servant or common laborer.

Allen had written:

> I am not defending this position. I am simply pointing out that it exists. . . . Looking back over eight or nine decades of history, it would seem that the best that can be done practically to ameliorate this condition is to continue to appeal to the white man for a little more justice, a little more understanding and sympathy. . . .

Somehow, out of his study of Watson, his understanding of Lincoln's patience and gentleness, out of his awareness that there did exist in the South deep fears of amalgamation that must be recognized, and allayed if possible, McGill shaped the policy he would pursue as editor in all matters dealing with race. He never spelled it out in so many words, but its outline was clear in all he said and wrote. He would push on, as steadily as he could, in the direction he instinctively knew the South must go. He would not try to please the extremists of the left, the modern-day abolitionists who could be satisfied with nothing less than sudden and complete equality. Nor would he try to appease the unreconcilables among the southern traditionalists — the hot-eyed men who said "Never" to any change at all. He would continue to attack the Ku Klux Klan and oppose the race-baiting politicians. To these he would grant no quarter.

But quietly, insistently, he would appeal to the best instincts of the progressive southerner, to his sense of justice and fairness, to his tolerance, to his special understanding of the Negro born of the years the races had lived side by side in peace together.

It would not be an evangelical crusade; it would be a dialogue, a calmly rational discussion of black and white relations, directed at the great massed millions of southerners in the middle — those who held allegiance neither to the NAACP nor the Ku Klux Klan. Then, as time moved on and attitudes changed and that which had been unthinkable became commonplace — the races riding together on buses, for example, or eating side by side in restaurants — he would take one small step more, always speaking with quiet reason and always urging only that which he knew it was possible for his readers at that moment to accept. He knew to be effective he "had to put the hay down where the mules could get at it." He knew, too, it had to be a kind of hay they could digest.

In all he wrote, or spoke from the platform, in criticism of his region and its mores, his deep love for the South shone through, the testament of his faith in it, his eagerness to help its citizens "drown in the creek every litter of the bitch called Ignorance, from which prejudice was whelped."

He wrote:

> Let us say to the world, we love this crippled child which is the South; crippled by a war hard fought and lost, crippled by the tariffs and rates you set when you made the laws, crippled by being made a supplier of raw materials to the industrial East. . . . We love her with a passion and pride you will never understand.
>
> But we are fighting for her now. We are fighting to make her well and strong. And we will not much longer be fooled by false prophets of prejudice and fake words and fears. . . .

Only when a sense of outrage overwhelmed him did he break the pattern of reasoned, low-key pleading. When a church was bombed or a school burned or a man taken out and killed by a mob without trial, his voice became harsh and angry, and his words were like fire and heavy hammers. Ancient fears and prejudices could be understood, and even looked upon with some compassion, but there could be no compromise with arson or with murder. "Sometimes," he used to say, "you have to step out in the center of the ring and hit them in the nose."

It is only in this light — of a man of good and decent instincts and stubborn courage speaking with the voice of reason in a violent time — can the McGill who guided the policies of the *Constitution* for thirty years be understood. He pleased some; he angered many, including powerful executives of his own paper. But over the years he accomplished what he set out to do — he persuaded thousands of Georgians and thousands of southerners to listen to what their own hearts told them was just and right in their treatment of the black man, the poor man, and the child.

He was not an integrationist in the way the South understood that fearful word. Eight years before the Supreme Court handed down its school decision, he was writing in his column:

> There will be no mixing of the races in the schools. There will be no racial equality measures, now or later. . . . There is not a newspaper or a thoughtful person in Georgia of either race who believes in or would seek either of these things. . . .

Yet he would go on to say:

> A Negro's color sets him apart, but I have never understood hatred for him or discrimination of him and certainly I have always regarded a Negro as a person . . . entitled to complete justice and economic opportunity. All this has been natural for me, southern born, southern educated, with no trace of outside influence. . . .
>
> Our failure even today to give the Negro equal justice in our courts, to make him safe from police brutality, to give him his due education, on playgrounds, and the usual civic facilities such as paved streets, public health, sewers, and so on, is another example of injustice. Yet whoever protests . . . will bring upon his head a flood of denunciations among which "traitor to Southern traditions" and "nigger lover" are the most frequent.

7

McGill was backstage in the Atlanta Auditorium with the troupe of the touring Ballet Russe when the announcement came that the President's report to the nation on the Pearl Harbor attack would be broadcast to the ballet audience. The troupe had just danced *Swan Lake*, and he was talking to its premiere ballerina, Tamara Toumanova:

> Perspiration stood in little beads about her forehead and along her nose. She had on a dressing gown, an old one, and a towel was thrown about her shoulders. Her makeup that gave the face a masklike appearance still was on. She still managed to look beautiful. . . .
>
> Here was a woman born in a wagon rolling across Siberia, her mother fleeing the Red Revolution of 1919. She was dancing at Shanghai when she was six years old. . . . In Paris as a young girl, she caught the eye of the great Anna Pavlova, who became her friend and teacher.

"I have no country," she told McGill, "and yet, this is my country. All of us feel so deeply what has happened. All of us are so depressed, and so hopeful."

As the announcer's voice came over the loudspeakers in the auditorium, the troupe of dancers gathered on the stage behind the heavy curtain. Some were still in costume from *Swan Lake;* others, dressing for the next dance, the modern *Saratoga*, were wearing jockey costumes. Some wearily stretched out on the bare boards of the stage.

"Before the broadcast began," McGill remembered, "there was a whispering babble, in Russian, French, Polish and American. Here were men and women whose life stories were every bit as colorful as that of Toumanova."

Then the President began to speak, and all was hushed. No one moved, no one spoke. Their painted faces, looking up, were oddly grotesque in the dim light.

McGill wrote:

> I never saw more rapt attention. Here were people of many bloods, still, silent, listening to the voice of Franklin D. Roosevelt proclaiming faith in democracy, denouncing the raw, treacherous ruthlessness of the Axis gangsters. When his voice ceased, and the music of the national anthem came through the curtain, they stood stiffly at attention, ballerinas, clowns, dancers, their faces solemn, strained. . . .

Remembering Toumanova and the dancers, McGill went back to his office and sat down to write. We could be grateful to the Russians who gave us the ballet, he wrote. We could be grateful to them also for another lesson; on the great plains of eastern Russia they were proving that the Germans were not supermen, but soldiers who could freeze and bleed and die like lesser men.

Now, the Japanese had caught us asleep and had sorely hurt us.

"They got the jump," he wrote. "They still have the jump.

"But they aren't supermen either. . . .

"We'll get them. It will take time."

For nearly eighteen months, restless and fretting, McGill attended meetings of the draft board, to which he had been appointed, or sat at his desk, writing of the growing power and resolution of the country at war. He flew to Chicago to be on the Chicago Round Table. He spoke on racial matters there, pointing out that the South was a minority in the nation, long held down by a succession of Republican administrations in a tributary and colonial status. The Negro was a minority in the South. Each had suffered from unfair and unnecessary discrimination, the South as a region, the Negro as a person. It was his first national exposure, with twelve million listening in; he was awed by it and his fumbling for words and inept phrases embarrassed him. "But," he wrote, speaking of his performance, "it is there, and all my tears cannot wash out a word of it."

Finally, there came the chance he'd been waiting for. In mid-July of 1943, bearing a War Department identification card certifying him as a civilian assigned to the military with the "assimilated" rank of second lieutenant, he reported to an inconspicuous hotel in Baltimore. There, under conditions of greatest secrecy, he awaited transportation to London, where he would join a small group of other American editors invited to England by Brendan Bracken, minister of information, to see firsthand how the British were bearing up under the strain of war.

He remembered the pulse-tingling excitement as he moved by night from the hotel to the blacked-out dockside, where the big flying boat lay at anchor; the strong smell of the cold dark cabin; the smell of oil and stale blankets, where forty other passengers, mostly British officers in civvies, huddled in unpadded seats along the walls, their knees rubbing against the bales and boxes of tied-down freight that filled the center of the plane.

Then the big doors slammed shut and the plane began to move, buffeting hard against the black water, with the roar of the engines loud in the metal shell of the cabin, from which all insulation had been removed, and white spume flashing past the portholes. They were moving faster and faster. It was his first takeoff from water, and his breath came shallow and his heartbeat quickened, and then the pounding, jarring, bouncing suddenly stopped, and they were up and flying. Around him in the dark, faces were white and strained, and he wasn't aware that his own look was any different until the man in the next seat asked him, "What the hell are you grinning at?" And McGill told him he was grinning because he was happy. He was on his way to the war at last.

For twelve hours, they flew between the tumbled clouds below and the vast arc of a steel-gray sky that never quite lost all its light in those high latitudes in summer. It was very cold in the plane once they got above the clouds; there were not enough blankets to go around, and he huddled shivering in his G.I. raincoat, taking off his shoes now and then to rub his feet. And he dozed and waked and dozed again, until the pressure on his ears and a different sound in the engines told him they were going down. For a long time they were in cloud; then, suddenly beneath the wing, there were stone houses with thatched roofs, and stone walls enclosing fields of golden Van Gogh–colored grain; water began to pass the portholes again, and they were down, smoothly, on the River Shannon.

They went ashore to a pub that served a breakfast of Limerick bacon and fresh eggs, and he ate heartily of these. Then, under a protective cover of Spitfires, they flew on to Poole, in England, where that night he boarded a blacked-out train for dark, hungry, battered London.

The days of the great blitz were over, the dreadful nights when the German bombers came and went away almost unchallenged. The Spitfires had done their work, the American Forts and the British night bombers were hammering the Reich, and the "great gray elephants of the barrage balloons, whose mahouts all were women," now were defending London. To Americans at home, the war was still far away, even though their sons were fighting around the world. McGill brought it to their breakfast tables and made them hear it, see it, smell it, feel it as the English had endured it for four long years. In his report from England, he wrote:

> All of us at home thrilled to Winston Churchill's voice back in those grim days after Dunkirk when the myth of the superman stood strong. . . . "We will fight him on the beaches, on the streets and in the hills," said the prime minister of Great Britain, in perhaps the greatest of his many great speeches.
>
> Traveling about England now one may see at crossroads and along highways, beside railroads and in the towns, the old and deserted pillboxes. Some are of concrete, hastily and inadequately thrown up. Others are of sandbags.
>
> I suspect that a couple of grenades would have destroyed any one of them had the Germans come in those days. They were not strong or well made.
>
> But there they are.
>
> One sees, too, old rusting barbwire defenses and tank blocks. They were built for the invasion that didn't come. Now they are of no more use. But it is the small pillboxes, or blockhouses, that one sees most. Inside them the British home guards, townspeople and soldiers would have gone with shotguns, with rifles, with a few old guns and there they would have died.
>
> They were not fooling. They meant it when they said they would fight him in the streets, on the beaches and in the hills. They would have done it.

The people he saw that touched him most were the bomber crews — the young Americans taking their flying Fortresses across the Channel day after day, defying the German fighters and braving an incredible eruption of antiaircraft fire.

In the *Times* of London, he found a poem by Noel Coward which said what he in many columns had tried to say about the airmen and their skill and courage. The last verse, addressed to "magnates and contractors, workers and politicians, diners and musicians," went:

Safe in your warm civilian beds,
Count your profits and count your sheep.
Life is passing above your heads,
Just turn over and try to sleep.
Lie in the dark and let them go;
There's one debt you'll forever owe.
Lie in the dark and listen.

"Somehow that poem hit me hard," he wrote. "It said for all the fliers what should be said . . .":

> I wish I could do the same sort of poem for the Forts. I saw them go off, the dew flying off their wings, catching the sun and glowing red and green for one brief moment. I saw them climb and form and move off into the distance toward Germany, their guns ready, faces seen briefly in the windows and in the tail of the Forts.
>
> In London and in coastal cities I have stopped and listened to the Forts going over. Far up, out of sight, they were passing through the sky. . . .
>
> Life was passing above our heads and our lives below were trivial and unimportant. And, I must say, a bit selfish. I then looked up and, corny as this may sound it is still true, said a quick brief prayer for them. . . .
>
> I wish for a lot of things. One thing I wish is that all Americans could see once and hear once the Forts go over. You can't turn over and go to sleep when you hear them. You have to start thinking. And perhaps that is best.

Again and again he spotted those little touches of humor and humanity which added grace notes to the British character. In a graveyard at blitzed Coventry he found a stone in memory of John Parks, who died in 1773. The inscription said, "He was a man of mild disposition, a gladiator by profession," a description which delighted McGill. He also found in Coventry one J. B. Shelton, a carter, or drayman, who was also an authority of world renown on the archaeology of Roman Coventry. The great blitz destroyed his house and sorely wounded his wife.

He carted earth and planted flowers in the rubble of his house, and when he at last was allowed to see his wife in the hospital, his mood was cheerful. Noting her bruised and swollen face, he said, "Well, old girl, I'm glad it was Hitler that blacked both your eyes and not me." She smiled and began to get well.

"These two I will remember," McGill wrote, "the man of mild disposition who was a gladiator by profession and J. B. Shelton, the carter who was an archeologist." Standing in the flower garden he had made in the ruins of his home, Shelton told McGill, "Property is not anything. I dig up what the dead thought was grand and great and permanent. Living is important — if you use it."

"Measured by any standards," wrote McGill, "he is a great and useful man."

Often he told the story of England's courage in the way most meaningful to him — in terms of food:

> The eggs are our big contribution and they aren't bad. You take a tablespoonful of the yellow powder and mix it with water or milk. Then you mash out all the lumps as you stir. . . . You can cut into it some onion tops or maybe some parsley. You put it into the skillet and cook it and there is your morning ration of eggs. There just aren't any fresh eggs. You get about one a month. Maybe. . . . The sausage has only enough meat in it to flavor it. The rest is cereal and soybean flour.
>
> There are no fruit juices, no bananas, no oranges, no lemons. There just aren't any. . . . There are children here who have never seen an orange, a banana or lemon. . . . Today I saw, in one of London's largest food shops, six peaches. Just six. They were from Georgia. They were selling at about fifty cents each. I tried to find out who grew them . . . but that wasn't possible. I wanted to write him a letter about seeing six of his peaches going at fifty cents each. . . .
>
> Shopping for restaurants is quite an art. You find a small restaurant with a good chef. You get to know the two or three waiters. . . . Now I am known to two or three small restaurants. The cashier and head waitress in one of them is in love with a soldier from Georgia named Plunkett. I have let it be known that I am from Georgia and that I admire all persons named Plunkett.
>
> Now and then, when I go in, she whispers that there is a small piece of mutton left for favored customers. . . . It is an art, this business.

More lasting even than his memories of England at war — and more important, it turned out, to his future career — was the friendship that began there between him and two fellow Americans who shared his experiences. Also guests of the British minister of information were two proper Bostonians, Laurence Winship, editor of the *Boston Globe*, and Edward Weeks, editor of *The Atlantic Monthly*.

Years later, when McGill's column at last was syndicated, Winship's *Globe* became his platform in New England and Weeks's *Atlantic* published the first of the autobiographical reminiscences that later were gathered into his revealing book, *The South and the Southerner*.

A picture of McGill at work in wartime England soon came back to the *Constitution* from Winship's typewriter.

"People who know Ralph McGill will understand this story," Winship began. He then described how they had gone to visit Hull, a seaport town that had been heavily bombed many times during the war and shortly before their visit had been bombed again. The probability that Hull would be hit again was so great, in fact, that the old people and young slept below ground, in bomb shelters deep beneath the earth.

The lord mayor was showing them around when they came to the large basement of a schoolhouse, where a great many young people were gathered, singing songs and dancing a romping boomps-a-daisy before they had to go to the dreary, blacked-out concrete shelters for the night. They listened to the singing for a moment, and then the lord mayor suggested they move on, which Weeks and Winship dutifully did. But when they got to the shelter canteen and the aid station, of which the lord mayor was most proud, the "ample figure of the Atlanta editor," Winship reported, "was nowhere to be seen."

He was finally discovered, still back at the schoolhouse with a little girl about nine years old sitting on his lap and carefully spelling out for him the words of a little song called "Doing the Hokey-Pokey," which he solemnly wrote down in his notebook.

It was getting on toward blackout time, and the lord mayor was getting nervous, and McGill looked up and nodded that he would be along in a moment, but now the children had all gathered around and were sitting in a circle at his feet, and he was telling them that he came from America, from the state of Georgia, which is way down at the bottom of the map of the United States, and that he had come over the sea by airplane from the city of Atlanta, where the lady lives who wrote *Gone With the Wind.* Then he told them that he wished all the people in America could see the people of England as he had seen them, bravely carrying on, even though their homes had been destroyed by the bombs.

Then a dock worker with a baby on his shoulder said, "Three cheers for the man from America," and all the children in piping voices said, "Hip, hip, hooray." And the girl at the tinkling old school piano struck up "For He's a Jolly Good Fellow," and McGill, embarrassed, got up and lumbered off to find the lord mayor, with the smaller kids hanging onto his coattails and asking him to stay.

By this time, Weeks and Winship had let it be known that McGill was also from the town where Joel Chandler Harris had lived. So McGill, late that night, found himself dragooned into sitting late in a bomb shelter telling, in Negro dialect, tales of Brer Rabbit and the Tar Baby to the little children.

Up until then, Weeks, a man with a certain grace with words, had been the speechmaker whenever someone had to respond for the three while visiting in various cities. Thereafter, McGill was their spokesman.

Years later, in a letter to "Ted" Weeks, McGill recalled that evening and other highlights of his travels in England, including the evening in Edinburgh when the three of them had watched as the king and queen awarded prizes to the winners of a Scottish cooking contest in which the contestants had done amazing things with oatmeal and potatoes.

McGill had written a column about this, quoting Dr. Samuel Johnson, the lexicographer, who in his dictionary had defined oats as "food for horses in England, food for men in Scotland." To which a Scot had replied that this was no doubt true: "See what fine horses there are in England, and what fine men there are in Scotland."

"Also," McGill told Weeks, "I remember you and Colonel Winship framing me by telling one of the young women in the bomb shelter at Hull that I would be a good one to tell Uncle Remus stories. This does, though, remain one of my favorite memories, of trying to imitate an Uncle Remus dialect, at which I was never good, down in the bowels of Hull."

He was grateful, he told Weeks, for the piece of luck that had brought the three of them together. "In the twenty-three years that have passed since that time," he wrote, "my life has been enriched by the two friends made on that journey.

"To you also," he told Weeks, "I owe the publication of *The South and the Southerner*. . . . I would never have got around to doing it but for your patient prodding and encouragement."

After the English trip, Weeks, Winship and McGill always addressed each other as "Colonel" in their correspondence. The honorific was McGill's idea. During their travels their mail, when forwarded, was addressed in the English style to "Ralph McGill, Esq.," but simply to "Ted Weeks." This seemed an outrage to McGill. "You might think the eminent editor of the *Atlantic* was a prizefighter," he fumed.

As soon as he got home, he had Governor Ellis Arnall of Georgia commission Weeks a lieutenant colonel on his staff. He did the same thing for Winship so that he would not have to salute Weeks.

8

McGill came home from England by sea, on the gray ghost of the Atlantic, the *Queen Mary*, converted to a wartime transport. Also aboard was Winston Churchill, bound for Quebec and his conference with Roosevelt, at which the future conduct of the war was planned. McGill, later, through sources at home and abroad, was able to obtain some slight information as to what these plans were. Not much, but enough to tell him that the columnists and commentators who described the conference as "dull, important, meaningless, a flat failure" were wrong. Enough also to hint to him that the turning point of the war would come sometime in the following summer of 1944; and to him this meant that war, and not politics, would be foremost in the minds of the people in that presidential election year. It would be a quiet political summer, he predicted, and it was. The great cross-channel invasion, the plans for which had been worked out between Churchill and Roosevelt at Quebec, began on June 6. The political conventions came later.

On the eve of the Republican convention, McGill predicted, correctly, that Dewey would be the nominee. He spoke of him as the "petite Mr. Dewey," and forecast his defeat; and even though his heart was not in it, since he looked upon the campaign as no true contest, he did feel it necessary to point out certain flaws in Dewey's candidacy as the campaign went on. Quoting several statements by Dewey which he considered to be less than forthright, he recalled an old derisive jingle which Bob Taylor used to employ against political opponents in Tennessee:

He wiggled in and he wiggled out
And left the people all in doubt
As to whether the worm that made the track
Was going in or coming back.

McGill added hastily that he did not look upon Dewey as a worm, but as a chameleon.

He chanted a litany of Democratic accomplishments, adding that the Democratic party, with the greatest record of service to the people in the history of government, will offer Roosevelt, proudly and with confidence.

His admiration for Roosevelt led him to read into the President's appearance as he approached the fourth-term election a physical strength and soundness which was not there. To all who saw him close up it was plain that his strength was fading swiftly. But at a press conference in Washington, McGill, his partisan loyalty blinding him to the obvious, said he looked about him at some of the journalists who had been writing that the President was ill, and that he was "a tired old man," and discovered that "the wear and tear of the times seems to have treated them even less kindly than Mr. Roosevelt.

"In fact," he said, "the physical condition of some of them was distressing to see." As for Mr. Roosevelt, "he looked good . . . in fact, he looked splendid. He was on his mental toes. He laughed and joked. . . ."

Naturally, McGill pointed out, twelve years of depression and war had left their mark. For months on end, he said of FDR, "he ate when he could, he got no exercise. He slept, they tell me, as little as two or three hours across long stretches of time, until he finally was made ill. But now he is a well man. He is older, as we all are older, but the spirit is not old. . . ."

(Eighteen months later, in Melbourne, Australia, while on a trip around the world, McGill got the word of Roosevelt's death of a massive stroke at the Little White House in Georgia.)

As both the war and the presidential campaign ground on to the inevitable end, McGill's thoughts moved on to the shape of the future. With the end of the war still months away, he began pointing out how absolutely necessary it was that the country start to plan at once for the day when millions of men would be coming home, taking off their uniforms, and looking about them at the country they had defended. And he wrote:

> There will be a lot of new ideas in the minds of the men who come back from this war. If he is from the wrong side of the tracks, he is going to be completely intolerant of any smug attitude about such a position and any restrictive implications. If he came from the slums of a city, he is never going to believe it right or necessary for people to live in them. If from a poor, run-down sharecropper or tenant farm, he is never again going to let his mind accept . . . the grinding poverty. He is going to be intolerant of the economic system that makes it so. . . .
>
> There will be several millions with new ideas about education. They will demand it be more available, more applicable to life. This calls for planning. It calls for jobs. And the administration . . . which fails to provide them will be swept from the political life of the nation.

He was thinking, too, of how to keep peace between nations in the postwar world. The glowering intransigence of Russia toward her allies worried him. He urged the creation of an "Association of Nations" to prevent any aggressor nation from taking over the technological developments which inevitably would come out of the war and preparing a campaign which would be overwhelming in its effects.

He spoke of the technological advances that might well threaten the peace of the world. One, he said, was the splitting of the atom, which rumors from the gossip capitals of Europe said the Germans were about to do. "Any physicist will tell you," he said, "that if any nation should manage to do this and control the vast amount of energy so released . . . it could destroy any other nation because they would have only the choice of annihilation or surrender." He spoke also of new engines, called jets, burning cheap and low-grade fuel, which would far surpass in power any piston engine ever built.

He was speaking out of no special information, only out of his reading and listening and thinking and feeling, his instinctive knowledge of the shape of the future. The United Nations Conference was still nearly a year away; the Manhattan Project was still the darkest of secrets; the dropping of the A-bomb over Hiroshima was more than a year in the future; and the jet aircraft engine was not proved in combat until the Korean War.

McGill had been pleased but not vastly surprised at Roosevelt's victory in the 1944 elections. He had been surprised, and more than a little pleased, when, late in the year, John S. Knight, president of the American Society of Newspaper Editors, named him to a committee of three to travel around the world calling on editors and government information officers, urging that a free flow of uncensored news between all nations be guaranteed by treaty in the postwar years.

It was an exciting and challenging assignment which McGill was happy to accept — until Mary Elizabeth came home from her doctor's office with some exciting news of her own. That weight she had been putting on, she said, was not, as he had libelously suggested, due to her partaking of an occasional beer. She was pregnant, and against her doctor's advice, she was determined to have the baby. If all went well, it would arrive about the time the dogwoods bloomed in April. McGill's first reaction was one of complete incredulity. Both he and Mary Elizabeth understood, or thought they understood, that at the time of her massive kidney operation the doctors had also performed a hysterectomy, to spare her the hazard of pregnancy. For nearly a decade there had been no reason to doubt that this was true.

McGill's next reaction, therefore, was a mixture of joy, hope and deepest concern for Mary Elizabeth's health. He well remembered the first baby that had died and how near death Mary Elizabeth had come. So, as challenging and exciting as the ASNE assignment would be, he would have to turn it down. He could not leave her to go through that again. She had lived with him long enough to know what he was thinking. And she knew her own mind. She was going to have this baby, and he was going wherever his job called him.

Don't be silly, she told him. There was nothing he could accomplish by staying home. Having babies was woman's work, and she and Julia could manage very well without him around, fretting and worrying. Anyway — she counted on her fingers — if he left early in January and traveled fast, he could make it back in time. While he traveled she'd keep him posted. Periodically she would go down to the office and have a photo made standing in profile which she could send him.

On the morning of January 10, 1945, McGill and Wilbur Forrest, assistant editor of the New York *Herald Tribune*, and Dean Carl W. Ackerman of the Columbia Graduate School of Journalism, climbed aboard an Air Transport Command C-47 at LaGuardia Airfield in New York. Before they touched American soil again on the other side of the continent, they would travel nearly fifty thousand miles in their visit to twenty-two countries.

Ralph came back to a London still at war. The V-2 bombs were falling when he arrived, and one of them dropped about a mile from the hotel room which he occupied with Wilbur Forrest. He made note of the fact that the explosion of the warhead was tremendous, rattling the windows, but the more unsettling sound was the long, continued roaring which followed the explosion, the sound the bomb had made in its passage through the atmosphere. Falling to earth at thirty-five hundred miles an hour, it had outrun the sound of its flight. He and Forrest "stood at the windows and in chorus cursed the dirty —— —— Huns." The people of London, he reported, looked gray and tired after five years of war, but when he went out to ride on the buses with them, and to drink bitters in the pubs, and talk to them, he found that: "They still break into song; they still have time for a laugh or a joke. They are still a great, tough, resilient people."

He moved on to Paris, and in a dining room so cold he had to eat with his hat, gloves and overcoat on, he noted that the dessert was *bombe glacée* — the French, in matters of food, liking to do things right no matter what the circumstance. There was no heat in all of Paris, not even in the hospitals, that winter, and their breath froze in the air as they listened to an old man named Albert Bayet tell how it was to run an underground newspaper in Paris at the daily risk of being shot or hanged by the occupying Germans.

He was a tall, thin, old man, slightly bald, with a salt-and-pepper moustache, and he looked like a country editor from any American small town. But ever after that to McGill he was the embodiment of an uncensored press: "Here was the real thing. A man who had daily put his life in balance to publish a small one- or two-page newspaper, with poor ink and bad type on inferior paper. There were ghosts there, too, for a lot of newspapermen had lost their lives because of those little sheets."

They moved out of Paris to join up briefly with Patton's armies, fighting in the hills above Luxembourg. It was a freezing ride in an open jeep, through wrecked villages, along roads pitted with shell craters and lined with the hulls of burned-out tanks and guns. They found the general at his forward headquarters. It was not long after the incident when the general had struck a battle-weary soldier, which the press had fully reported, and they were not sure how Patton would react to their mission, which was to urge that there be no postwar censorship.

"Let the light shine," said General Patton. "It's better that way. It may sting for a while, but not as bad as stuff that's covered up."

McGill understood his reference. Rumors of the slapping could have been magnified into a cause célèbre that might have destroyed Patton. Frank and full revelation had saved a great soldier's career. They moved on to Italy, to call on an American general whose headquarters were near the town of Capua. There an Italian scholar on the general's staff told them about Capua. "It was here that Hannibal wintered his troops," the scholar said. "It was a mistake, for in the spring when they started to move, they couldn't. They all had a social disease. Even the elephants."

McGill solemnly made note of this as they moved on to an audience with His Holiness, Pope Pius XII, who received them "seated at his desk in his ivory-colored robe and skullcap," McGill reported. As they traveled, McGill had been besieged wherever they went by Georgians and Atlantans to the extent that both Forrest and Ackerman had begun to rib him. Even at SHAPE, when they called on General Eisenhower, there had been a Georgia connection. The general's son at Benning, it seems, was courting an Atlanta girl who was the daughter of a friend of the McGills.

"One thing sure," Wilbur Forrest had said as they set out for the Vatican, "the Pope won't have a son who's courting an Atlanta girl."

After the Pope had blessed their St. Christopher medals, he turned to McGill. "Mr. McGill," he said, "I had a nice letter about you from Bishop O'Hara in Atlanta. . . ."

The Greeks delighted him for there was a liveliness in them, a bounce that he had not seen among the Italians or the French. He talked with their leaders and he went to the taverns where the chickens pecked about on the floor between the tables, and he drank retsina with the people. He came back to Atlanta urging all his friends to drink more of this Greek resin-flavored wine. "It is a preservative," he told them. "When an old Greek dies who has been drinking retsina all his life, his stomach is so well preserved, they have to take it out and beat it to death with a stick."

Nowhere else except in Russia did he find anything fit to drink. The fine cognacs of Europe, he reported, had become a secret weapon the Germans had left behind. There was an Egyptian vodka from which a small cloud arose, like a genie, when the stopper was removed from the bottle. In Teheran the cognac "had the aroma of a camel caravan that has just come all the way from the Caspian Sea and finished up on a warm afternoon."

Later, in Chungking, he made the wary acquaintance of what he described as the two most famous beverages in the world — Chungking gin and Chungking vodka. Both were made in the same vat, but the gin was flavored with aloes. When he arrived at the press hostel in Chungking, he found on the bulletin board a notice posted by the navy medical officer. It said: "Gentlemen of the press: As per your request, I have analyzed Chungking gin and vodka. Neither is fit for human consumption. I have just ordered a case."

McGill's most vivid memories of his trip were of the flight over the Elburz Mountains from Teheran to Moscow. Their plane was the military version of the famed DC-3, a C-47 flown by a Russian crew. It was a bucket-seat job with no seat belts, hauling cargo that was not lashed down but had to be held in place by the passengers on takeoff and landing. The pilot took off on cold engines and climbed the ship like a fighter plane while an amiable Russian passenger, sitting on the extra gas tanks placed forward in the cabin, smoked a cigarette. One of the Americans, smelling the fumes of petrol, woke a snoozing sergeant who functioned as a sort of flight steward and nodded toward the smoker sitting on the gas tank.

The sergeant looked and laughed amiably. "Boom!" he said, making a gesture as of something going up and falling back down again. He then went back to sleep.

They stopped first at Baku on the Caspian Sea, and from there, there were steppes deep in snow, and frozen rivers, and finally below, the wrecked buildings of shattered but unconquered Stalingrad. It was for

McGill a moment of great emotion. Here the war had turned, here the German thrust had been beaten back. A city under siege only a year before now was at work again, its factories smoking, turning out war materials even before the roofs had been restored. Here for four days the plane was weathered in, deep snow piling up on the wrecked German tanks and planes and guns around the airport, "their snouts poking up out of the snow like prehistoric monsters."

It was bitter cold, and food was in short supply but good — black bread, butter, cabbage, red caviar and soup. The passengers slept six in a room in the airport barracks, reminding McGill of the old days in country hotels in Tennessee when he went on tour with a political candidate. Braving a wind so strong he had to lean against it to walk, feeling the bite of the twelve-degree cold, he moved about as best he could. Around the airport, he noted, people bombed out in the war lived in sod huts like those of the Nebraska pioneers. There were no hangars, and girl sentries, protected only by their heavy clothing, stood armed guard over the planes. "They stood out all night in that cold and they were there all day," McGill reported. "They were on the job, too. One night before bedtime three of us blundered out for a breath of air and were brought up sharp by a shrill challenge. We knew the young lady was over there in the dark on guard, bayonet on rifle. It was no time for a walk anyway."

Dozing and waking, and dozing again, McGill landed at Moscow to find waiting there old newspaper friends Eddie Gilmore and Daniel DeLuce of the Associated Press, and vodka and cheese and warmth. He was to need the warmth and friendship, for the sessions he and his companions spent with the Soviet journalists were sometimes brusque, the questions thorny.

S. A. Losavosky, vice-commissar of foreign affairs, an old Bolshevik with a beard like Lenin's, was pleasant enough in his greeting, but he got straight to the point in his questioning.

Why, he asked, were many American papers — particularly the Hearst papers and the *Chicago Tribune* — so harshly critical of the Soviet Union when the United States and the Soviets were allied against a common enemy? Why did they use falsehoods to support their criticism? Could the American editors explain this?

A humorous recollection of his childhood flashed through McGill's mind. He recalled that once in Soddy, Tennessee, he had heard an old man reading aloud from a newspaper, and when he finished he had slapped the paper with his hand and said, "May the Lord have mercy on the *Chicago Tribune* for its sins."

Now, incongruously, years later he found himself in a small bare office in Moscow trying to explain the *Tribune*'s sins. "It was not easy," he wrote later in a report in the *Atlantic*. "We tried. Hard. I remember that I was sweating from my effort to be both lucid and honest in explaining that in America you may disagree with, and even hate, what another man says, but will defend his right to say it."

Russian newspapers, Losavosky pointed out, reflected the will and thinking of the Russian people. American newspapers, too, claimed to represent public opinion. Yet, every time Roosevelt ran for President, the people elected him, though most of the press opposed him. How did McGill and his friends explain that?

"We tried to explain that even those newspapers which opposed Mr. Roosevelt gave him generous space, that they often carried daily columns by men and women who supported him, and the people could get enough information to make up their own minds."

McGill admitted that articles critical or fearful of the Soviet Union sometimes appeared in American papers. Unhappily, McGill pointed out, many *Tass* correspondents in the United States sent back to Russia only these critical articles. Thus the Russian people knew nothing of the great mass of favorable comment that appeared in the American papers. It was also true, McGill admitted, that the American people sometimes got a distorted view of what was going on in Russia. The American press had not always sent impartial correspondents to Moscow. A few had come in with chips on their shoulders, determined to see nothing but evil in the Soviet system. A few others came in seeking some sensational story that would give them a temporary bit of fame.

He visited the offices of *Pravda* and *Izvestia* and at both was sharply questioned as to how much control advertisers exerted on the American press (The Russian papers carried no advertising save for brief notices from theaters and the opera announcing what was playing.) McGill admitted cautiously that there were one or two American papers, perhaps, which allowed the advertisers to shape their editorial policy, but that in the great bulk of the American press the advertiser was interested only in the pulling power of his ad. He couldn't care less about the paper's politics. He also tried to convince the Russians that many newspaper readers felt the same way. They wanted the news and were unmoved by editorial arguments.

McGill came away from Moscow feeling that some good had been accomplished. His committee's plea for a free flow of news between countries after the war had met with tentative agreement by Losavosky. Surely, the Russian had said, if the United States and Russia could get together on common ground to fight Germany and could find a common ground on which to build a new system of international security, they should find no difficulty in reaching agreement on an international flow of information.

The cross fire of questioning had its effect on McGill, and ever after his Russian visit he was inclined to look with a more critical, albeit a still loving, eye on the whims and vagaries of his admittedly flawed profession.

Though honored often by journalism schools, McGill was never one greatly to honor them, though he strongly supported the Nieman Fellowships. A young reporter would be well advised, he felt, to study history and economics and to read omnivorously on a variety of subjects rather than to seek a formal education in journalism.

The clamor for a "free press" sometimes bored him. To him a free press meant not only the right to publish what the editor or the owner believed in, but the obligation to give voice to ideas and attitudes that were anathema to them. Unless the newspaper reader knows that his local paper follows this policy, McGill argued, he will not be impressed with any high-flown oratory about freedom of the press. He may continue to take the paper because he likes the comics or the sports page, but he will not be blind to its duplicity. "The publisher and the editor, seeing the circulation figures, may think all is well," he wrote, "but if they get around to asking the man in the street, they may be shocked to hear him say, 'A free press? Don't make me laugh. It stinks.' "

McGill's bruising encounter with the Soviet journalists was modified in great degree by his fascination with Moscow and its people. He tramped the streets, peered into shops and stores, and talked through his interpreter to casual passersby. He came out of Russia feeling great respect for "the brave, enduring Russian peasant," and less sympathy than ever for those Americans of the "let's-show-Russia-we-can-be-tough" school. "I like the Russians very much, admire them, and respect the great job they have done. I do not like the one-party system. . . . I do not condone the loss of freedom of speech and of the press. . . . But I do think Russia has made great strides forward for her people, and no amount of criticism can alter this fact."

This summing-up reflected McGill's deepening sense of liberal democracy, his abandoning of all parochialism. The trip proved to be, for all its hardships, a memorable one, both to him and his readers. In all the great cities he met the men he admired most, the skilled professionals of the journalist's calling. He drank with them, ate with them, and argued with them, despite language barriers, in that camaraderie which specialists in any profession feel. As he neared his journey's end, he had become truly a part of all that he had met; it would be forever impossible thereafter for him to be other than a cosmopolite, a fish at home in any waters, a citizen of the world, and a brother to all its peoples.

Though the column he was sending back never openly revealed his worry, as the long weeks passed and Mary Elizabeth's time grew nearer, he began to feel a restless urge to push on toward home. It had begun to trouble him first in Cairo, in the museum where the gold and jewels taken from the tomb of Tutankhamen had been laid out. "I do a lot of things which seem dumb to me at the time," he wrote, "but I can never escape them. I had this feeling coming out of the museum at Cairo. I was feeling deeply and genuinely sorry for a youngster who died some three thousand years ago."

He had gone there, he said, because he was "a tourist at heart and a sucker for museums." And he had looked at all the treasures, the gold and the jewelry:

> But, I think it was one tiny little object or so which got me. He was a wistful-looking youngster, was Tutankhamen, and his wistfulness shows through all the statues they made of him, especially in the gold mask of him they put about his face wrapped in the many windings of the mummy.
>
> But it was not this. It was a small toy of his sister's and a small paint box

she had used that had been put into his tomb with him. There, in all the fantastic magnificence of tremendous wealth and regal glory, were these two little toys. He had been such a good brother that his sister put them in there with all the gold and jewels, and there they are today, after three thousand years. . . .

I think it was that which got me and made me feel a sort of personal friendship for this youngster dead three thousand years in the darkness of the great tomb in the Valley of the Kings at Luxor on the Nile. . . .

This mood of sadness, of regret for a child long dead grew into a brooding melancholia that stayed with him for the rest of the trip as he moved on to Russia and back to Teheran, waiting there restlessly for the weather to clear and the planes to come which would carry him on to China and India and Australia, where at last he could turn for home.

He went into China over the Hump, flying from Calcutta to Chungking, feeling as the plane began to roll down the runway in the boiling heat the same old thrill he had felt on his first flight twenty-seven years before. He was frightened on takeoff and landing, "but," he said, "it is a pleasure-creating, minor sort of fear." He flew the Hump twice, in and out of China, going in by day, coming out by night, seeing close below the wings the jagged peaks of the tortured Himalayas under a coppery moon. But his big moment came when, in Chungking, he saw a pair of Georgia mules walk sedately out of an airplane that had flown across the Hump. "I felt like hugging them," he wrote.

It was April when they came out of Chungking, and McGill, knowing that Mary Elizabeth's time was drawing near and fearful that he would not get home for her lying-in, was beginning to show signs of strain. Though he had immediately established a rapport with Wilbur Forrest, he and Dean Ackerman of the Columbia University School of Journalism rubbed each other the wrong way. McGill, though usually the most amiable of men, could form strong dislikes on whim, and Dean Ackerman's professional and pedantic manner seemed to annoy him from the start.

McGill, who had the constitution of a rhinoceros, was anxious to press on. Dean Ackerman, older and more fragile, was often ill, delaying the trip briefly while he gathered his strength, or remaining behind while Forrest and McGill pushed on. By the time they had reached

Chungking and were ready to turn for home, the nerves of both men were raw and their tempers on edge.

After a joint interview with Chiang Kai-shek, Ackerman came away announcing that he felt he had been in the presence of deity. McGill, to whom Chiang was merely another warlord taking refuge under the wing of the United States military, exploded in outrage at what he considered Ackerman's naïveté. Harsh words were passed and there was little warmth thereafter between McGill and the dean. Years later, in a letter to Chester Bowles, then ambassador to India, McGill related the incident with Ackerman in explaining why he thought that his articles written on a journey to India would have no chance of winning the Pulitzer Prize. Any personal confrontation always worried him, and this run-in with Ackerman made him feel so unhappy that he went out and got morosely drunk on Chungking gin, which made him feel even worse.

Finally the job was over. At 4:27 on the morning of April 25, 1945, at Brisbane, Australia, McGill climbed aboard a Liberator bomber converted to hauling passengers and freight to begin the long, slow trudge across the Pacific, bound for home. A half an hour earlier, at Emory University Hospital in Atlanta, Mary Elizabeth had felt the first strong pains of labor.

It was a slow, seemingly endless journey. The old plane set down first at Nouméa, in New Caledonia, before plodding on to Fiji, and from Fiji they went on to Canton Island, gaining a day as they crossed the date line. They took off from Canton for Christmas Island just before dawn, and landed at Christmas in a rainstorm, with McGill pacing the floor of the local Hotel de Gink like a father in the waiting room of a hospital maternity ward. At last, late in the afternoon of the second day, they landed at Hickam Field, Honolulu. There another omnipresent Georgian, Frank Wells, a young naval officer, handed him a message. It was from Jack Tarver, a sharp-tongued associate on the *Constitution*, and it said: "Baby boy, weight six pounds seven ounces, born Caesarian, 8:42 A.M., Wednesday, April 25. Looks like you but is healthy."

He slept that night his first unbroken sleep in weeks, and took off the next day for San Francisco. He kept on flying until he reached

Atlanta and his first meeting with Ralph Emerson McGill, Jr., around whom his life thereafter was unashamedly to revolve.

Julia Crawford, tiny and brisk, loyally holding things together at the house while McGill was gone, greeted him with an admonition as he walked in, putting his bags down wearily. "I will tell you what I told Miss Red," she said. "We is getting too old for this here foolishness."

9

THE birth of a son after sixteen years of childless marriage left McGill dazed with joy. Becoming a father at forty-seven, he told a friend, was an awesome responsibility. It made him feel like the legendary old hen with one chick, and he knew that he would have to watch himself to keep from fussing over the boy and spoiling him. "I hope," he wrote Tom Chubb, "to bring him up to love books and dogs and the hunting field, and if he should feel the urge to write a poem now and then, that will be all right with me. None of these things ever brought me any material gain, but life would have been barren without them."

It also occurred to him that now that he was a father, he should try to quell the restlessness that had always held him in its grip, a heritage, he believed, from a footloose grandsire who had also been a journalist. For six months or so he held firmly to this resolve, riding the bus to town in the morning and riding it home at night, happy at the thought of playing with the child. He would lie on the floor and let the little fellow bounce happily upon his ample stomach; he read to him long before he could understand, and he walked out at night to show him the stars. On Sundays he would perch him on his shoulder and take him out to hear the quail whistle, always talking to him seriously, man-to-man with no baby talk.

Daily, though, despite his great joy in his son, McGill became more restless, particularly when some wandering journalist he had known in Cairo, in Moscow, or in Chungking (where there was a Mr. Mo whom Ralph had taught to lift his glass and toast, "To hell with the Republicans") would come through and they would sit long at the bar. He would wake up the next morning red-eyed and remorseful, with the urge welling up in him to go and see firsthand what was happening out there in the world, now that the war was ended and our occupation armies were taking over in the rubble of the wrecked nations. The press wires were chattering ominously of new wars brewing in Palestine, and of Russia, with its captured German scientists, pressing on toward the development of its own atomic bomb, and Ralph, in his dark mood, would write that "fear runs through our thinking like mice through an attic. The black wing of fear brushes us all. That is the reason there is so much trouble and petulance in this period of peace."

McGill's personal petulance was reflected in an uncharacteristic sharpness of tongue. Every few weeks he'd go up to Washington to touch base with friends who might know what Harry Truman was up to. Once, coming back on the train, he sat in the diner across from a young naval officer who had very strong opinions about nearly everything and was sounding off about them. He began by denouncing the British for the way they had treated the Indians, and he felt lend-lease to Russia had been a big mistake. None of which annoyed McGill too much since the young man was entitled to his opinion. Then the young man called the waiter, and the waiter, who was old and kidney-footed, moved slowly; and the young man made some remark about "niggers" and went on to say that, even though he was a Yankee from Connecticut, he felt that the South was going to have trouble with the "damned niggers."

This was rudeness, and more than McGill could stand, so, very quietly, without raising his voice, he tore the young naval officer to pieces. Addressing him as "sir," he said that he had been studying his ribbons and that he noted among them a singular absence of battle stars, or anything to indicate that the young man had been in any theater where there had been any action. In short, he told the young man, "you are a dining-car hero and a phony."

Then he rose and went back to his car, where, later, a couple of marines whose ribbons did indicate they had seen a great deal of action stopped briefly. "We heard you tell off the hero, Jack," they said. "It did us good."

By this time, McGill was feeling a little ashamed of himself.

"I'm just a fool," he said. "An old frustrated fool."

It was plain to those who knew him that McGill was going through a traumatic period, trying to decide which should have ultimate dominion over his life — his family or his profession? On the one hand was his boy, whom he yearned to guide and shape throughout his formative years, on the other hand was his own need to go wherever the news led him, anywhere, anytime.

Deskbound by day, homebound by night, he brooded and fretted and tried to soothe his restlessness by burying himself in the old familiar things — Benét's *John Brown's Body,* and the King James Version of the Bible, and Thoreau, and whatever poetry came to hand. In memories of his boyhood he tried to shut out the thorny problems of the postwar world, and he wrote nostalgic pieces about fox hunting, hog killing, and the time when, out of admiration for George Bernard Shaw, he gave up eating meat and became a vegetarian, ending up with dysentery.

And then the letter came from the Overseas News Agency, signed by Herbert Bayard Swope:

> Dear Ralph McGill:
>
> There is no newspaperman in America with a finer sense of fairness than you; there is none freer from motivation; there is none, because of your independence, whose words would carry further than yours. These reasons prompt the Overseas News Agency to ask if you would do the real story of Palestine. It has not been done. . . .
>
> We should expect to pay all your expenses and an honorarium and give the series wide exploitation. How about it?

That was the fire bell. Five days later, Swope was writing McGill to tell him how pleased he was that he was willing to go. "You will be under the same instructions that used to be given to me as a staff member of the old *New York World,*" wrote Swope. "The instructions are that there ain't no instructions, except to get the story."

He left in January 1946, this time carrying with him another letter, written by William Benton, assistant secretary of state for public and cultural affairs, and addressed to all American chiefs of mission, telling them he would be gathering information on the effectiveness and needs of the United States Information Agency in central Europe and the Near East, and his findings might be used in the State Department's budget hearings before the Appropriations Committee. It was the first of many such missions that McGill was to carry out for State, or some other government agency over the years.

He began his reports on Palestine from Nuremberg, where under the bright, hot lights the Nazi war criminals were on trial. There was "Goering with his porcine features, his shrewd and greedy eyes. Hess's strained masklike countenance; stolid Schacht; dapper von Ribbentrop." How in God's name, he asked himself, did this ordinary bunch ever rise so high that they threatened the world?

He listened to the witnesses in horror; "agony and terror rolled into the ears until they drowned the senses. Death seemed to be trying death. . . ."

He moved on to the DP camps and saw the people the war had driven from their homes. They had been physically displaced, but far more important, they had been spiritually displaced as well. They could not go back again to the homelands they had known. There were Jews from France and Hungary, Poland, Austria and Holland, whose families had lived in these countries for five hundred years. They had never thought of themselves as being other than nationals of these countries. McGill had gone on this trip believing that every effort should be made to repatriate the displaced Jews, to send them back to their native countries so that they could take up life there as before.

> It is with equal sincerity that I write that I was wrong. People who are not survivors or who have not seen these survivors cannot know how haunted by the past are these people, how untenable life would be if they were forced to go back. . . . The German sickness (anti-Semitism) . . . remains in the minds of Europeans like mustard gas in old shell holes . . . after a battle has ended.

McGill from then on was a convinced and confirmed Zionist. It was not only the old who wanted a quiet place to go and die, or the middle-aged who wanted a place where they could "belong," he wrote. "There were young and militant Jews of all nations who were willing to die for such a place. If there had not been a Palestine," he concluded, "it would have been necessary to create one."

He moved on then to Cairo to get the Arab point of view. He found the Egyptians charming and good hosts, as he had remembered them — and eager to talk of the Arab League and the new dream of Arab nationalism. In the beginning, McGill discovered, this had been a concept mainly of the Christian Arabs of Lebanon, and it envisioned an Arab world of freedom from foreign restraints and of racial and religious freedom. It had, unhappily, abandoned these civilized creeds for a stern Pan-Islam movement.

"The movement is reactionary," he wrote. "It is right out of the medieval era in concept and plans for execution. It is hostile to everything western, especially to the Christian West." It was completely hostile also to any plan to open Palestine to Jewish immigration.

McGill went on to Palestine to see the Jewish people working there on the farms, in the factories, in the laboratories. His conclusions: "The land is there, the time is now, for a Jewish home in Palestine.

"If allowed to live and grow, this movement of the Jewish DPs to Palestine," he wrote, "could become the basis for a great renaissance of learning, of modern farming and industry to improve and lift the standards of all the Middle East. There is room in Palestine for all the Jews who would want to come there — without crowding out a single Arab."

The point that seemed to shape his thinking on the Israel-Arab question, so that it became impossible for him to entertain any sympathy for the Arab who might feel himself crowded or displaced, was the fact that during the war the "Arab nations were the eager aids and agents of the Axis powers."

"What claim does the Arab have," he asked, "on a world which gave enormously of its lives, blood and treasure to insure freedom and human dignity? Nothing at all," he concluded.

His solution — "To open up Palestine to immigration by the homeless ones of Europe . . . to be mandated to the United Nations as a Jewish national home within which the Arab should have every right and privilege accorded others . . . and this must be done now."

In his visit to the Nuremberg trials, McGill had used field glasses, even though he was in the courtroom and very near, so that the faces of the men on trial — "the plucked peacocks of Nazidom" — were so enlarged that their eyes, when they turned toward him, seemed to be staring directly into his own. On the screens where the pictures of the death camps were displayed, McGill watched "with horrid fascination the crawling, convulsive movements of a pile of dying bodies, the dead stacked high like so much grotesque cordwood." It was the German leaders who had ordered these things, out of some dread sickness in them; but it had been the German people who carried them out. It was the German people who had committed little atrocities of their own. "It was they," he wrote, "who kicked the crutches from the hands of wounded American airmen, hobbling from one railroad station to the other through the streets of Frankfurt."

Now, in Frankfurt, he saw old men and women, blue with cold and clothed in rags, pulling through the streets crude little carts loaded with wood or coal they had dug from the cellars of their blasted houses. And no matter how he tried, he could not feel sorry for them.

The children, though, were different. When he looked at them, you could tell he was thinking of his own small son at home — warm and strong and well fed:

> You see them, the little ones, and you wonder what in God's name is ahead for them. You know they are getting no milk or cod-liver oil. You know, too, when the Germans had occupied France and other countries, they ruthlessly starved the people, and the children. So you try to harden your heart. But you cannot. You take your own slim share of chocolate or candy and give it to the kids. It is a gesture. It helps not at all, really. But you do it. You go along, wanting to weep for them.

He walked the streets of the blasted German towns, and the starved, pinched faces, the red chapped legs of the children filled him with sorrow. On a Sunday afternoon, along with three other journalists, he went to Heidelberg, the old university town, untouched by Allied bombs. Like any tourists, they went to the cellar of the old castle where there is the huge wine barrel that holds sixty thousand gallons and has a dance floor on top. There were four little German girls there, and McGill and his friends asked them if they would pose for a picture in front of the great barrel.

They were cute, as only little girls can be, but there was something special about one of them. When she smiled, she reminded Ralph of a girl he had been fond of when he was a young reporter covering foxhound trials in Dickson, Tennessee. He asked for her name, and she wrote it for him, in the careful script of a ten-year-old: "Else Bender, Heidelberg, Rohrbach, Am heiligenhaus 12." When he left Germany, he did not forget her. He wrote, asking for sizes, and when she answered, he asked Mary Elizabeth to find all the things for her a little girl would need — skirts and sweaters, stockings and saddle shoes.

The next year, on another assignment with the army, he went back to Germany. Through the military, he had passed word of his coming again to Heidelberg. He found the little girls, and the mothers of three of them, waiting for him on the schoolhouse steps. Else, he discovered, had no mother, but lived with her grandmother, who was old. They all began to grin and make little bobbing bows as McGill left his jeep and walked toward them with his German-speaking guide and interpreter. Now children and grown-ups were coming from everywhere, and McGill, with gestures and in halting German, motioned for the children to get into the jeep. They climbed in, squealing with delight, for none had ever ridden in a car before. With the mothers, he climbed into a battered sedan and followed them to Else's house.

It was an old house on a narrow street in the poor workmen's section of the town. But it was clean and the old grandmother, McGill saw at once, was a magnificent person.

He had brought with him a musette bag packed full with chocolate bars along with some sewing needles and two spools of thread, vitamin tablets, bars of soap, chewing gum, cigarettes and coffee beans, which were more precious than pfennigs when it came to buying food and coal. He also had four little bracelets he had bought with cigarettes a few days before.

He tried to divide everything as evenly as possible, but by now people from the street were climbing up the narrow stairs and the little three-room flat was bedlam. So he fled with the four children and the guide in the jeep, and they traveled around the city, stopping to have their pictures made together and to buy four packages of fruit and figs. (The next day the children were so sick from the unaccustomed food they could not go to school.) He asked many questions before he departed, but his driver-interpreter could not understand too well the dialect the children spoke.

Three days later he went again to Heidelberg, this time bringing a young lady, an officer of the occupation army who spoke fluent German. For this visit he had scrounged from army friends three loaves of white bread, two cans of milk, a pound of sugar and a carton of cigarettes.

He had also checked with army intelligence and he now knew something of Else's story. He was not helping Nazis. Her parents and grandparents had been poor working folk, too humble to belong to the Nazi party. All five of the old grandmother's sons had been drafted into the Wehrmacht, and three of them, inclulding Else's father, had been killed.

Each year thereafter until he died McGill continued to send money, clothes and food to the people he had come to think of as "my loved ones in Heidelberg." Else grew up, married a young soccer player and metal worker named Heinrich Volkwein (McGill, like a nervous father, had an investigation made to see if he was worthy). To this union was born young Ralph Emerson Volkwein, who, McGill on a visit noted, had a reporter's inquiring mind. He had taken his godson and namesake to witness a great pageant commemorating the nine-hundredth anniversary of the Cathedral of Speyer at Heidelberg. As the magnificent processional passed by, young Volkwein, then three and a half, announced from his godfather's shoulder: "I knew there was one Santa Claus; where did all those others come from?"

It seemed as if, by his kindness to Else and her children, McGill was trying to make amends for all the pale-faced, starving children he had seen in Germany in the years just after the war. "It breaks my heart and makes me afraid to see the children and us doing so little for them. It was our responsibility," he wrote in an editorial, "that the children of postwar Germany should not grow up to become the monsters their parents had become after growing up in a defeated Germany after World War I."

He had done, in person, and on a minute scale, what he was pleading for his country to do.

"I was not helping Nazis," he said. "I was helping, in a slight way, just a few of those who are almost never 'helped' in any country. And I know there are at least four little girls, now grown to womanhood, who never wish for war, or hate America, or Americans. They aren't many, but they are four. . . ."

McGill came home from Palestine and Germany in time to fight, and lose, his last great battle with his longtime political antagonist, Eugene Talmadge. On a steamy night in mid-July of 1946, he sat in his office in the ancient red-brick *Constitution* building, watching the primary returns pour in that told him that the old Tom Watson political poison still was potent enough to set the fires of hatred burning. Other issues being equal, the candidate who shouted "nigger" loudest would be elected governor of Georgia.

Up until then, McGill had hoped, had even prophesied, that the race issue would lose its power to terrify. Millions of young white southerners during the war had rubbed shoulders with people of darker skin and had come to know them as human beings. In the last years of the war, the Negro and white man had fought together side by side, and the Negro, when not set apart in a segregated unit, had proved to be a first-class fighting man.

The issue, however, was not dead, only sleeping. A Supreme Court decision outlawing the Democratic white primary, by which Georgia had effectively disfranchised its Negro voters, had aroused all the old fears, and candidate Talmadge had made haste to fan the flames.

With McGill in his office on election night, sharing his feeling of anger and despair, was Ellis Gibbs Arnall, the outgoing governor, a young and progressive politician who, four years before, with McGill's support and a certain assist from fate, had soundly trounced Talmadge. Now the old Wild Man from Sugar Creek, sounding his war cry of white supremacy, was headed for the statehouse again.

Though the *Constitution*'s candidate, businessman James Carmichael, was leading by some ten thousand popular votes, Georgia's peculiar electoral system, which weighted the balloting heavily in favor of the rural areas, was giving Talmadge a resounding victory in county unit votes.

McGill and Arnall were brooding darkly over this sad fact when a copyboy stuck his head in the door with an announcement that caused them both to sit bolt upright, their eyebrows lifted in alarm. Governor Talmadge, the copyboy hissed, was coming down the hall. Governor Arnall jumped up to leave, but it was too late. There in the doorway, wearing a rumpled seersucker suit and the malevolent glare which for him passed as a benign expression, stood Eugene Talmadge, his black forelock dangling over one eye, his steel-trap jaw snapped shut around a cold cigar.

"Ralph," he said, removing the cigar, "I give you a good whuppin' this time, didn't I?" He reached across McGill's desk to shake his hand.

McGill, startled, stood up to shake and motioned Talmadge to a chair. He sat down, ignoring Governor Arnall, who sat nearby as if poised for flight. Talmadge was in an expansive mood. If he felt any rancor toward McGill for having called him a mudslinging demagogue still raising the old, stale issue of race, he gave no sign. If he felt embarrassed at having called McGill "Rosenwald Ralph," charging him with being a tool of the eastern interests and a traitor to his southern heritage, he made no apologies. He had come, it seemed, merely for an amiable chat, and he talked nostalgically about old campaigns — for governor and for the Senate — in which he and McGill had crossed swords before. Finally he took notice of Arnall. "I'll tell you another thing," he said, pointing with his cigar. "This little fellow here wouldna beat me the last time if that black widow spider hadna bit me on the balls."

He rose to leave. At the door he paused a moment. "This has been a rough 'un, Ralph," he said. "The way I feel now, it took about fifteen years off my life."

His words were prophetic. Before the year was out, he was dead.

After he left the office on this election night, McGill turned to his typewriter. He did not mention Talmadge's visit. He wrote of the election and his reaction to it:

> Since I was in there with my coat off swinging as hard as I could, it is but natural, I suppose, there are those who wonder how the results of the primary of July 17 affected me.
>
> I do not mean those characters with mean, festering little minds who call up to say obscene things, but those on the other side who were in there swinging, too. They won. And they would like to know how it went with me.
>
> It went hard.
>
> It made me feel pretty sick.
>
> It was a bitter pill to swallow. . . .
>
> I don't like to lose. I don't guess anyone does. Losing goes awfully hard with me. But I was on the losing side. I did all I could. It wasn't enough. And that's how I felt. I hope that covers it.

Mr. Eugene Talmadge said he wants to be a good governor. . . .

I hope he will be. I won't do anything in opposition to that platform. . . .

I would be less than honest if I did not say, in this recapitulation, that I believe the issue which gave Mr. Talmadge his victory was presented in a manner which deceived the people.

There never was any deep, dark racial plot. There was no one advocating, or wanting to advocate, mixing races. There would not have been any attempt to mix the races in schools, to propose any equality save equality of opportunity, education and equality before the law.

Nevertheless, many normally commonsense persons, largely in south Georgia, where most of the Negro population is, were afraid. . . .

It was the last time he was to write of Talmadge as an adversary. The old man, he noted when he was in his office, had looked tired and ill. On December 21 in Piedmont Hospital, he died of cancer. His last interview, given from his hospital bed, was with his old enemy, McGill, and it was McGill who wrote his obituary.

There was not a flattering word in it, nor one that could be interpreted as approving Talmadge's tactics or his beliefs. Yet the overall tone was sympathetic.

"Eugene Talmadge had no middle name, yet it might well have been Ishmael. Certainly there were times when, like Ishmael, his hand was against every man, and every man's hand was against him. . . ."

McGill then recounted the victories and defeats of the man who gloried in the title of the "Wild Man from Sugar Creek." And far down in the story there was one sentence which may help explain why McGill could harbor a secret admiration for the roaring old demagogue: "He was something of a political miracle," McGill wrote, "in that the defeats never hurt him, but seemed instead to give him more political resiliency."

That resiliency, that ability to endure, was a quality McGill much admired in a man, whether friend or foe.

He himself had it, in full measure.

The death of Governor-elect Eugene Talmadge before his inauguration threw Georgia politics into a ludicrous muddle in which, for a time, three men laid claim to the governor's office.

M. E. Thompson, the lieutenant governor-elect, assumed that he was the legal successor. The Talmadge faction, knowing that Old Gene was nearing death and wishing to keep the governorship in the family, had sponsored a write-in vote in the November general election for Herman Talmadge, the governor's son. Followers of James Carmichael, who had finished with 314,421 popular votes to 305,777 for Talmadge, did the same thing for their man. The public, unused to voting in a general election, turned out in minuscule numbers to cast 775 write-ins for Herman Talmadge and 669 for James Carmichael. On the basis of this victory, Talmadge claimed the governorship, and the General Assembly, reluctant to offend a Talmadge, named him to the office after his father's death the following month. Not satisfied that the legislature had this power, Governor Arnall, who by law could not succeed himself, announced that he would not vacate the office until the State Supreme Court had ruled on the issue. The court ruled in favor of Thompson, who was duly sworn in for a two-year term.

Throughout this period of legal and political maneuvering, McGill showed a strangely detached, nonpartisan attitude. If he had any preference, he seemed to lean to Herman Talmadge. He praised the political acumen of Roy Harris, who had masterminded Talmadge's write-in campaign and had supported his cause in the legislature. He also later expressed the view that the House of Representatives was closer than any other agency to the will of the people. And he deplored the "pious whooping" of those who looked upon Harris's write-in gambit as shady politics.

Actually, McGill's curious political stance in the matter of the three governors caused a rift within his own staff that greatly troubled him. Some three years before, he had hired off the *Macon News* a sharp, young editor and political columnist named Jack Tarver — a bespectacled, innocent-looking young man whose nature it was ever to say — and write — the cutting rather than the kindly thing.

Together they had fought the battle against Talmadge-ism with an evangelist's conviction that they were doing the Lord's work. Tarver, who was McGill's right hand on the editorial staff, was familiar with his good friend's tendency to change the set of his sails slightly when he felt that a new tack was desirable.

"He was always saying, 'Mr. Tarver, I am like Mr. Lincoln in that it is my policy to have no policy,' or he would quote whoever it was that said 'a foolish consistency is the hobgoblin of little minds,' " Tarver remembered. "And I would usually go along with him, though sometimes when we'd shift from one editorial stand to another one hundred eighty degrees opposite in the space of a week, it would nearly run me crazy."

Tarver was unhappy with McGill's bedside interview, which he felt tended to canonize the elder Talmadge, even though he knew that it was McGill's pity for an old, sick man that motivated it. When it appeared, though, that he was going to turn against M. E. Thompson to favor Herman Talmadge's candidacy for governor, that was too much.

"I was ready to quit," Tarver remembers. "The idea of Herman just sort of inheriting the governorship was anathema to me. I went into McGill's office, and I got so worked up I got to crying, and I said, 'Look, dammit, just take me off editorials. I'll make up the page, but I don't want to write any more editorials.'

"Then *he* got to crying and said no, dammit, if I felt that way, we'd come out for M. E. Thompson. And I said no, I wasn't that much for Thompson, but I couldn't stand the idea of supporting Herman after fighting him all these years."

McGill had no way of knowing it then, but by mollifying Tarver and persuading him not to quit, he in all likelihood insured his own survival as the *Constitution*'s editor and his continuing development as the South's leading liberal journalist. For it would be Tarver who would risk his own career to "steady the soapbox" for McGill in the rough years that were to come. On many occasions his abrasive wit was to wound McGill, but their friendship would endure.

Tarver was one of those rare newspapermen whose journalistic genius lay as much on the business side as in the editorial. He soon was to be taken off the editorial page by Major Howell, not for his own sins but for his talents. The major, caught up in a wave of enthusiasm just after the war, had moved his paper out of its ratty old building into a fine new edifice. He had also purchased a TV station. As a result of these new and heavier expenses, the *Constitution*, which had been making fifty to sixty thousand dollars a month, began losing some one hundred to one hundred fifty thousand dollars. Tarver, who as a youth had owned and operated his own weekly newspaper in Lyons and Vidalia, Georgia, was called off his editorial duties and given the task of getting the *Constitution* back in the black. Within a few months he was showing a thin but definite profit of fourteen thousand dollars.

"We had turned the son-of-a-bitch around," said Tarver. "I was never so surprised in my life."

His brief sojourn in the red, and the heavy expenses attendant upon the new and expanded operation, caused Major Howell grave concern. This did not escape the attention of Governor James M. Cox of Ohio, who in 1939 had bought the *Constitution*'s afternoon rivals, the *Atlanta Journal* and the *Georgian*, and merged them into one highly successful paper.

In 1949, rumors began to drift through the office that Cox was now dickering for the *Constitution.* McGill, who was packing to leave on a trip for Europe, made worried inquiry of the major if this was so. The major was reassuring. If any sort of a deal was made, he said, it would be a merger only of the mechanical departments. The papers would remain autonomous. Not long after McGill's departure, the major called Tarver in and told him the story. He had sold the *Constitution* outright for 37½ percent of the preferred stock in a new corporation to be called Atlanta Newspapers, Inc. Within two years, he could sell this stock for roughly four million dollars, or he could convert it into common, as he thought best. Meantime, he would retain the title of publisher of the *Constitution* and would be there in his office every day.

Tarver was not a man who had to have things spelled out for him. It was clear that Governor Cox, a grand old liberal who once had run for President with young Franklin D. Roosevelt as his running mate, now owned the *Constitution.* But the man who would be calling the signals was George C. Biggers, a gruff and hard-nosed ex-advertising salesman whose interest in newspapers, other than as a medium for ads, hardly extended beyond the sports pages.

Tarver went home and tried to phone McGill. Finally he found him, in a little hotel in London. He told him what had happened — and it was far more, he made clear, than any mere merger of the mechanical departments.

There was silence at the other end. Finally, across two thousand miles of empty sea and sky came McGill's despairing cry.

"Ohhhhh shit!"

McGill's anguish, which he sought to drown in the nearest pub, and

Tarver's misgivings, which he sought to assuage by sending out feelers to various publishers in other cities, proved to be without foundation. Within a few days after McGill's return home, the governor, in Miami, sent the company plane for him and Tarver. They talked a long time, and it was a comforting conversation to two men unsure of their jobs.

Back in their hotel room, McGill threw himself upon the bed, heaved a great sigh, and said:

"Well, Mr. Tarver, all of our *old* troubles are over."

10

The Supreme Court ruling which destroyed the Democratic white primary in 1946 not only gave the ailing Eugene Talmadge the issue for his last campaign, it also breathed new life into the almost moribund Ku Klux Klan.

In the closing years of the forties, therefore, McGill found himself locked in fierce contention with the reviving Klan. His interest in it had first been aroused in the early twenties when he saw a Klan parade wind its way through the little town of Jackson, Tennessee. Under the profane urging of his managing editor, old man Marmaduke B. Morton, he had studied what history he could find of the Klan of the 1860s, whose memory was so revered in southern hearts. He found that it soon had degenerated into a masked mob and that its founder, General Nathan Bedford Forrest, had disbanded it. Later, out of curiosity, he had made a study of the Klan of the twenties, which at its peak had some four million members and had "ruled with intimidation, terror and murder" in such widely separated states as Indiana and Louisiana.

Curiously, the man who had organized this powerful political force was a pompous old fraud who was more a figure of fun than of evil. His name was William Joseph Simmons, a promoter of lodges and secret orders which had for their main purpose the sale of group insurance.

"Doc Simmons," as McGill described him in *The South and the Southerner*, "was a pious, prissy-walking big man, heavily burdened with lodge emblems. Mint and cloves wrestled mightily with the bourbon on his breath, and his britches were rump-sprung from sitting much in the wooden chairs of lodge halls, rural church pews, and high-backed pulpit chairs."

The title "Doc" he had worn since he had failed his courses as a medical student, and he was also known as "Colonel," a title conferred on him as a former leader of a uniformed drill team of the Woodmen of the World.

Inspired by a vision of robed horsemen riding across a night sky after seeing the historic motion picture, *The Birth of a Nation,* he determined to revive the ancient glories of the old Klan in the form of a secret order that would combine a mumbo-jumbo ritual with burial insurance.

"It was," McGill wrote, "the best and only idea the old man ever had, but he didn't know how to bring it to pass. Unfortunately for the country, he fell into the clutches of a man who did — a sharp-witted advertising man and promoter named E. Y. Clarke."

Clarke, McGill recalled, used old Doc as a front, putting into his hitherto vaporous speeches a wonderful flow of image-making phrases praising God, Christ, brotherly love, patriotism, morality, Americanism and the purity of womanhood. The motivating element which Clarke introduced into the Klan was embodied in the third paragraph of the Klan ritual, in which "we avow the distinction between the races of mankind as same has been decreed by the Creator, and we shall ever be true in the faithful maintenance of White Supremacy and will strenuously oppose any compromise thereof in any and all things."

Without this, the Klan was just another secret order. With it, the Negro could be made the scapegoat for all the nation's fears and angers.

"The political and social climate at this moment was ripe for such teaching," said McGill in *The South and the Southerner.* "America was disillusioned by the war. Isolationism, 'America for Americans' was in the air . . . hysteria about Reds, the depression of 1920–21, rural discontent, unemployment, strikes . . . the race riots in eastern cities — all these created a perfect soil for the Klan development."

Under Clarke's sharp management, the revived Klan flourished, becoming such a power in the politics of many states that it could elect governors, senators, congressmen and judges; it controlled police chiefs, sheriffs and mayors.

But in the thirties, the Klan dwindled, its membership falling to a few thousand. In an act of hilarious irony, the Catholic Church, so long a Klan target, bought the Klan headquarters in Atlanta and turned it into a rectory. In an act of Christian forgiveness, which McGill had suggested, the Catholic bishop, Gerald P. O'Hara, invited Imperial Wizard Evans to attend the dedication of the new cathedral which was erected next door to the rectory. The wizard attended, "his face beaming like a Halloween pumpkin, as High Mass was said before him," McGill reported.

Now, nearly ten years later, the Klan was stirring, and again, the climate was right. In the aftermath of another war, another anti-Communist hysteria was sweeping the land. The religious issue was less important. Taking its place was a states'-rights issue, agitated by a new breed of southern politicians, calling themselves Dixiecrats, which gave aid and comfort to those of the Klan mentality who had no trouble equating states' rights with white supremacy.

McGill had been writing, as he had written all along, that the Klan was a sucker trap, bringing in poor, deluded, ignorant men who were willing to pay a ten-dollar entrance fee to be told that they and they alone were the defenders of the sanctity of womanhood and the supremacy of the white race. He felt sorry for these men. But, he added, the Klan was also infiltrated by "sadists as wicked and cruel as any who ever toiled for Adolf Hitler . . . rascals and ruffians of the worst sort . . . who enjoy beating and torturing other persons, a fact which sometimes surprises Klan officials themselves. Cops who like to beat up prisoners inevitably are enthusiastic members, and Klan organizations still corrupt police, sheriff's offices and rural juries in those communities where they are allowed to get a foothold."

McGill, in calling for legislation unmasking the Klan, pointed out that no law could unmask what was in the malignant hearts and twisted minds of the more psychopathic Klansmen who made up the lynch mobs. (A dreadful massacre of four Negroes in Walton County, Georgia, shortly after the election in 1946 was never attributed to the Klan but was obviously a product of the racial fears aroused in the contest for governor.) But being unable to hide their faces would drive out the fearful, "the little cowardly men who are the eager helpers of the brutes within the Klan."

McGill's statement as to the viciousness of some Klan members was not based on guesswork. For a number of years he had spies planted within the Klan who attended Klavern meetings and gave him detailed reports on who was present and what was said.

McGill not only dealt the Klan heavy blows, he backed up the small-town editors who had the courage to oppose the Klan in their own areas. In a letter to Mrs. Amelia Knoedler, editor of the *Unadilla Observer*, he wrote to say "how much I admire and respect your courage in the manner in which you handled the Klan episode in your city. [The Klan had burned a cross in front of the home of Unadilla's only Jewish citizen.] It was a shameful incident and I am sure your stand will have a wholesome effect. . . ."

Later, when the Klan again showed its hand there by causing a Negro church to cancel its Easter observance because it had invited white ministers to attend, McGill let Mrs. Knoedler know she was not alone. In a column titled "The Yellow Rats of Unadilla," he wrote:

> This rat-souled gang has set itself up as being more powerful than the meaning of Christ. The Klan is antichurch and it always has been, despite its cynical and depraved use of the cross. Men who set it in flames violate every Christian concept. The Klan is un-American and always has been, despite its use of the flag, and its hypocritical protests.
>
> The Klan is not powerful in Georgia or the South. It is powerful only in communities where law enforcement isn't willing to kick it in the teeth . . . where the people are uselessly afraid of a few small-souled, evil wretches.

Eugene Methvin, later to become a Washington editor of the *Reader's Digest* but then working on the family newspaper in Vienna, Georgia, well remembers McGill's help in time of the Klan troubles in south Georgia.

"You felt like a young second lieutenant out there, ambushed and surrounded, when all of a sudden the *Constitution* hits town with Pappy's column in it. It was like a barrage of one hundred fifty-five howitzer shells had landed, blasting the enemy to bits. . . ."

Actually, McGill wrote, the Klan of the forties was spiritually good for the South. It forced the South to make decisions it might otherwise have postponed — decisions having to do with the ideas of human dignity, of freedom, of human and civil rights.

> It has forced the South to decide what it thinks about Klan philosophy. The answer is plain. . . . There are local acts of stupidity and violence and worse, but they may be almost accurately predicted ahead of time. They appear where conditions, economic or social, are conducive to violence. Such places grow fewer as their economy improves . . . where industry and jobs and wages have come, racial tensions have lessened and the Klan's climate faded.

The climate which spurred a revival of the KKK also gave birth to a similar organization called the Columbians. This was a neo-Nazi outfit whose central motivation was hatred of the Jews and whose members wore armbands bearing the drunken thunderbolt design once worn by Hitler's Elite Guard. They were fair game for McGill, who attacked them with scorn, contempt and bitter humor. He accused them of starting "a cut-rate war in the hate racket by charging three dollars for a membership instead of the ten dollars charged by the Klan."

McGill, as he had done with the Klan, was able to infiltrate the Columbians with informers, and thereby kept fairly well abreast of their activities. On one occasion he learned there had been a debate in a Columbian meeting as to whether they should take McGill out and hang him or merely waylay him some night and give him a slugging. The vote was in favor of the beating. He reported this in his column, adding, "always grateful for small favors, I appreciate this. It is a small concession. But it will do."

The rank-and-file Columbians, wearing brown shirts and armbands, used to march and drill and salute each other without attempting to conceal their purpose, which was to take over as a police force when the Columbians' idea finally prevailed. Their leaders were a man named Homer Loomis, born on Park Avenue, the son of a wealthy Wall Street lawyer and for two years a student at Princeton, and his second in command, Emory Burke, an Alabamian, born of poor parents, who, during the war, was an open and avowed supporter of Adolf Hitler. Their purpose, openly admitted, was to exterminate the Jews and the idle rich, and to send the Negroes back to Africa.

Though Governor Talmadge might welcome Klan support, he had no sympathy for the Columbians. In the first place, McGill said, he was never anti-Jewish. He had no wish to exterminate the rich, idle or otherwise, for many men of property were his quiet supporters. And with farm labor as short as it was in postwar Georgia, he had no idea of depriving the state of hoe hands by sending the Negroes back to Africa.

Though the Columbians promised to be "forty times worse than Hitler," their anti-Jewish campaign made little progress in Atlanta. Their main activity, therefore, centered on intimidating Negroes, whom the brownshirts would rough up occasionally for no cause. They also were involved in an anti-Negro scheme involving housing, in alliance with a group of shady real estate vendors which McGill named "Punks, Inc."

A Negro family, desperate for housing, would be sold a home in a white neighborhood, being assured there would be no trouble. When the family moved in, the brownshirts would appear, wearing the thunderbolt emblems and marching up and down with the hard Hitler stare, "like the clean-cut bully boys of the 1938 newsreels." The Negroes, terrified, would hide in the house, afraid to go on the streets. The real estate man would reappear. If they didn't like the neighborhood, he'd say, he'd be glad to buy the house back from them. They would sell for a price much less than they had paid. The Columbians and "Punks, Inc.," McGill charged, would split the profits.

The Columbians didn't last long. The Atlanta police soon grew tired of having the brownshirts take over the police functions. One afternoon a Negro man and his wife with the Anglo-Saxon name of Mr. and Mrs. Frank Jones arrived on shabby Garibaldi Street, a deteriorating white slum, bringing with them a truckload of poor furniture and high hopes. Before they could unload their household goods, the brownshirts arrived and began to swagger up and down. The police, acting on an anonymous tip, came soon after, led by a mild-mannered chief of police named M. A. Hornsby, a Sunday school teacher, and a tough captain of detectives named Buck Weaver. McGill tells the story:

Chief Hornsby walked up to the nearest Columbian, a former prizefighter and wrestler, and asked:

"What are you doing here?"

"Protecting the white people."

"What business is that of yours?"

"The police won't do it. The people asked us to help them."

The two men stared at each other hard. Finally Buck Weaver blurted: "Who's going to police this town, Chief, us or them?"

"Us," the chief said, using language that would have dismayed his Sunday school class. "Take 'em down."

The brownshirts were arrested. One of them had with him his sixteen-month-old daughter. She was wearing the brown uniform with the armband with the thunderbolt patch on the shoulder.

Then the chief turned to the frightened Negroes. "Move on in the house," he said.

With his capacity to see some good in nearly everything, McGill felt that the Columbians, like the Klan, had served a purpose. They had exposed the real threat — "the existence of poor, inarticulate and uneducated people with legitimate grievances and no agency or persons to whom to go; the growing pressure on the southern Negro who still is at the end of the line in housing, education, health and plain simple justice.

"Until something is done about all this, there will always be, not only in Georgia but the whole country, fields for the hate racketeers to harvest."

McGill's statement to Tarver about their "old" troubles being over reflected the feeling of unease that had begun to haunt him during the *Constitution*'s last days as an independent newspaper. Major Clark Howell, the paper's owner, was an easygoing man who liked to give his editors their head, and in the main, he remained calm in face of the fact that McGill was becoming more and more, as one politician described him, a "known liberal." Certain of his business office executives, however, were concerned about some of McGill's statements and actions. For example, McGill in 1944 had joined with thirteen other distinguished southerners to found the Southern Regional Council. This was a fact-finding organization which brought together both black and white clergymen, business and professional men, labor leaders and educators, in the hope that they could sort out and identify problems affecting the races in the South and begin a dialogue which might lead to some sensible solutions to them. It was still functioning decades later, quietly working behind the scenes to bring about the equality of opportunity guaranteed to the Negro under the Constitution, with special emphasis on his voting rights.

In its early days McGill found it necessary to defend the council strongly against charges that it was Communist-inspired, or that it advocated a mixing of the races in the schools — which, in its beginning, it did not. The fact that so obviously worthy an organization — which included in its ranks three bishops, a rabbi, two ministers and a college president — should need defending was a reflection of the masterly demagoguery of Eugene Talmadge in creating a climate of fear and suspicion in all matters dealing with race.

As governor in 1941, he had purged the University of Georgia of a dean of the school of education on the grounds that he had advocated mixing white and Negro teachers in a practice school. This high-handed action against the university resulted in its loss of accreditation, which so enraged and alarmed many students and alumni that Talmadge was burned in effigy and was badly beaten in his race for governor the following year. The atmosphere of racial tension he had built up was so palpable, however, that the succeeding governor, Ellis Arnall, felt it and reacted to it in a surprising way.

A few days after he took office, Atlanta reporters attended a session of a practice school at West Georgia College, a branch of the university system. There was a discussion of blood transfusions, and one small boy in the back of the class jumped up and said, very excitedly, "I know one thing. I wouldn't let them put no nigger blood in me."

The teacher considered this statement calmly and then asked for the class to discuss it. Was there really any way that blood from different races could be identified, or that a transfusion could cause any genetic changes in the person receiving it? The conclusion was that blood is blood. It is a chemical, and though it might vary by type, it would be foolish to try to segregate it in the blood banks of the hospitals.

This story, when reported in the *Atlanta Journal*, caused a great furor, with former Governor Talmadge thundering that his worst fears had been realized — the university system *was* infested with teachers intent on mongrelizing the white race.

Governor Arnall, new in the office, was caught up in the excitement and there soon was a report from the capitol that he was going to fire the teacher at West Georgia and possibly call the president of the college on the carpet. McGill got on the phone to the capitol and asked for the governor.

"Is that you, Gene?" he asked, as Governor Arnall came on the line.

"This is Governor Arnall," replied the startled governor.

"Oh, excuse me," said McGill. "From what I've been hearing about the governor going to fire a teacher and discipline the president of West Georgia, I thought Gene Talmadge was still in the governor's chair. It didn't sound like something Ellis Arnall would do."

Arnall swore gently at his friend McGill, who had been his unofficial adviser throughout his campaign, and let the school matter drop.

Though McGill could privately stiffen the spine of a young and worried governor, he found it necessary for almost a decade during the late forties and early fifties to be extremely conservative in his public utterances on racial matters. He opposed a federal antilynch law and a fair employment practices act on the grounds that the states themselves must provide that protection to the Negro. He repeated over and over that neither he nor anybody else in Georgia, black or white, was advocating any form of social equality, or any breaking down of the old patterns of segregation in the schools. But, once having made this point, he would then go on to say that, even though the facilities could and should be separate, they in all fairness to the Negro must be equal. This had been promised, he pointed out, but it had not been carried out, and as a result, the matter of the separate schools had been given over to the Supreme Court to decide — a decision which could well destroy the traditional pattern of segregation in the South. "Someday," he warned solemnly, "it's going to be Monday" (the day on which the Supreme Court hands down its decision), and the South could well be in for a traumatic shock.

Looking back over McGill's public statements on civil rights in the period of the South's greatest trauma, it seems fair to say that, throughout nearly three decades, he was leading the thinking of his region, but only as far and as fast as his instincts told him he could go without losing his audience. From urging that facilities available to Negroes be truly equal, even though they might be separate, he moved one step further when he ventured the thought that in many fields the South simply could not afford the luxury of maintaining separate but equal facilities. A small, poor county might support two little one-room schoolhouses, equal in their shabbiness. It could not afford two big countywide consolidated schools with all the equipment they would require. Finally, with the handing down of the Supreme Court's decision, ordering an end to segregation in the schools, he stood on firmer ground. Though he did protest that "I have not said publicly or privately that I was happy over the Supreme Court decision," he did point out that, "nonetheless, it is the law."

Once the Court had spoken, separation in the schools because of race could no longer be defended on legal grounds. All that remained was for the states to begin the long agony of working out, with as little violence as possible, ways and means of obeying the Court order. In 1948, he was convinced that "there may be separation of the races and still equal justice before the law, equal opportunity to use one's skills and still not have to mix with other workers, equal opportunity for education without mixing in school." In 1966, he was writing: "Now . . . we see . . . clearly and painfully what a great weight and burden this policy of segregation put upon the southern people . . . when we chose out of heaven knows what disaster of decision to try to have two systems, when we couldn't really afford one good one."

McGill, in his private life, both believed in and practiced a far closer relationship between white and black than he could possibly advocate in public at that time. He invited Negroes to his home as dinner guests, and he went to their homes when invited, long before even the most liberal of his colleagues could bring themselves to make this violent break with southern tradition.

It was not, at first, an easy experience, even for McGill. Dr. Sam Cook, then a young Negro professor at Atlanta University, later on loan to the Ford Foundation from Duke, remembers one evening at McGill's home on Piedmont Road:

He seemed a little edgy and kept going to the window to look out toward the street. I thought he was expecting other guests who were late in arriving.

I found out later that this was the first time he had had a Negro as a dinner guest in his house, and he didn't quite know what to expect. If the Klan had gotten wind of it, he might *have* had other guests.

The caution with which McGill approached racial matters caused his old friend and fellow columnist Westbrook Pegler to describe him derisively as "the editor dimly seen" and a "Jim Crow liberal," and to even more ardent integrationists among the northern press he was no liberal at all. He took such criticism stoically, sending Pegler a soft answer and ignoring the others. He knew that he had to function in his own place and time, and he had to do it in his own way. In his more than thirty years in the business, he had built up an unerring instinct for survival, and whatever his deep-held personal convictions might be, he was not going to render himself voiceless by pushing either his readers or his bosses too far.

The merger of the papers actually had multiplied his problems in this respect. Unlike Major Howell, George C. Biggers, who ran the papers for Governor Cox, was not inclined to give his editors their head, nor was it his nature to spare their feelings. In his view, a newspaper was first of all a business, and he had a rough tongue for those editors whose policies he felt might offend any appreciable number of readers or advertisers.

One of Jack Tarver's main contributions to the task of "steadying the soapbox" for McGill was to dig up figures showing that McGill's political views were costing the paper only one or two percent in circulation at the most. Many readers who disagreed with McGill kept on reading him.

Even so, life was not tranquil under Biggers, and McGill in later years would look back upon the days just after the merger as a period of great travail of spirit. He couldn't write what he wanted to write without being called on the carpet by Biggers, and it was for him a most unhappy time.

This led to a number of divergent public utterances, causing one confused reader to write in plaintively: "To contradict yourself is normal. But you are now contradicting your contradictions. . . ."

McGill's liberal colleagues on the paper were occasionally less sympathetic than they might have been, knowing the pressure he was under from Biggers. At the Saturday poetry-reading and wine-bibbing sessions in Max Muldawer's delicatessen, somebody would ostentatiously start quoting Browning's "The Lost Leader" — "Just for a handful of silver he left us, just for a riband to wear in his coat." This would cause McGill to curse and thrash about in his chair. A young advertising copywriter named Paul Darcy Boles was sometimes present at these basement sessions; his first novel, *Deadline*, about an editor held down by his boss, purportedly had McGill as its central character.

In the belief that it would woo young readers to the papers, Biggers had committed his editors to the support of the state 4-H clubs, a promotional idea which McGill heartily approved of because of his fondness for young people and his love for all things having to do with the farm. Unhappily, the papers' main contribution was an annual dinner at the venerable Biltmore Hotel, where beaming teen-agers assembled to receive awards and to listen to interminable speeches. All top executives of the papers were under orders from Biggers to attend, with as many of their staff members as they could corral. McGill, who was usually called upon to distribute the awards, did not dare ignore this edict. To prepare himself for it, though, he would assemble his staff and take them to the Capital City Club bar, where all would anesthetize themselves with martinis until time to go to the dinner.

Occasionally, McGill found a martini helpful in mellowing the rough-tongued and heavy-handed Biggers. Once, after a run-in in which Biggers had left McGill cut and bleeding, he called Tarver. He'd had all he could take, he said. If Coca-Cola still wanted him, he was going to quit.

Tarver, who was leaving on a holiday, finally calmed him down, reminding him facetiously that Biggers could not be all bad since he, like McGill, was an old sportswriter. Two days later at his vacation retreat, Tarver got a special-delivery air mail letter from McGill.

"It's a shame you weren't here yesterday," he wrote Tarver. "Two gentlemen were seen staggering out of the Capital City Club arm in arm . . . two hearts that beat as one in the great brotherhood of ex-sportswriters."

Another one of Biggers's edicts was that his editors should not get involved in agencies or organizations that his Georgia readership might look upon with suspicion. Thus, when the Ford Foundation offered

McGill a place on the board of its Fund for the Advancement of Education, he was eager to take it, feeling that through it he could do great things for schools in Georgia and the South. Biggers didn't agree and implied that McGill should not accept the appointment, though he did not specifically forbid it. McGill didn't want to offend Biggers. At the same time, he was stubbornly determined to do what he thought was right. So he worried and fretted, postponing his answer until finally the foundation telephoned to ask for a decision. On impulse, he accepted and then sent Biggers a memo, innocently reporting what he had done.

Thereafter, when McGill would send down a memo politely asking Biggers whether he should accept membership on some board or make a speech before some controversial organization, Biggers would scrawl across it a grumpy "Do what you like." This would upset McGill, and he would ask Tarver, worriedly, "What do you think he meant by that?"

It meant that Biggers was not a stupid man. He soon realized that McGill, in just about everything he did, had the solid backing of Governor Cox, who owned the papers. The two had hit it off from the start, and this in large degree insulated McGill from Biggers's wrath. In many of McGill's bolder editorial stands, in fact, he was hied on by the governor, who did not always bother to consult Biggers. Knowing also that McGill was a worrier where his job was concerned, the governor went out of his way to give him reassurance. On McGill's fifty-fourth birthday, he sent him a telegram: "This is but the dawn of a new era in service to your time. As you enter the freshness of the morning, you take with you my congratulations and affectionate greeting."

"They were soul mates," said Tarver. "To the governor, McGill could do no wrong."

The old man, in turn, had been one of McGill's political heroes since 1920 when, despite Ralph's promise to his father that he would cast his first vote for a Republican, he had voted instead for the Democratic presidential and vice-presidential nominees, Governor James M. Cox and Franklin D. Roosevelt. The old governor's faith in the Democratic party had never wavered since, even in those years when it took considerable courage to throw the power of his papers behind a Democratic nominee.

The first year after the merger was one of those years. General

Eisenhower, who at that time was being very widely mentioned as a candidate for the presidency, with both Republicans and Democrats eager for him to serve as their standard-bearer, had come to Georgia to hunt quail at Bob Woodruff's Ichauway plantation. McGill was invited down to join the hunt. Years later, he told the story:

It was the autumn of 1951. In south Georgia in the late-autumn quail season, there still is a softness in the slowly cooling air. Early falling leaves cover the earth in the forests. But there is always the shining green beauty of pine leaf needles, the flaming leaves of sumac, and the varied colors of oak and hickory leaves. . . . It was the custom to hunt on horseback. A dog wagon, with automobile tires on its wheels, rolled easily through the woods and across fields, pulled by a sturdy mule. An extra pair of dogs was in a kennel on the wagon — always whining, eager to be let out to hunt.

The hunting was in pairs, with a rendezvous for lunch in some clearing in the trees. Then followed a continuation of the ritual of dog, man, bird and gun in the afternoon.

On one of these days General Eisenhower and I were paired together. . . . Politics and the offer from both Democratic and Republican parties for his participation as a candidate for the nomination in 1952 were discussed. We talked as we rode along or sat on our horses watching the dogs hunt out a field with that mysterious talent of mind, nose and instinct. . . .

I had asked him about politics and his assessment of what he might do. As I recall, his answer, interrupted by occasional covey shots and one hunting of singles, was as follows:

"I have never been a political man. I went to West Point when I was twenty-one. At the Point there is no talk of politics. We were taught that we were to serve our country and that the President, whoever he may have been, was our Commander in Chief. This was the essence of the Point — service to country.

"As a soldier I was moved from post to post. There was not much opportunity to register and vote. Somehow, I did not ever think in terms of parties, but of men. My first vote had been for a Democratic party candidate. I did not have any feeling against or for either party. I have been honored by being approached by both. I have thought much about it. My decision is to become a Republican. This is based on a belief that the Democratic party has been in for a number of years, through a depression and a great war. I think changes are needed. A candidate who runs as the representative of a party and wins is then committed, out of loyalty, to those who helped him win. He cannot make changes.

"I have," the general said, "a feeling that new men, the best minds available, should be brought into government. Business methods should be administered by men who are trained in them. This is the basis of the reasoning that led me to accept the opportunity to be the Republican candidate."

This was a secret at the moment, and it confronted McGill with a difficult decision. He was drawn to Ike as a fine and decent person of great integrity. He knew, too, that two men he admired greatly, Robert W. Woodruff and Robert Tyre Jones, the golfer, were much interested in Eisenhower's candidacy and would be highly pleased if McGill should swing the power of the *Constitution*'s editorial page behind him. Yet, deep in McGill's makeup was an instinctive faith in, and loyalty to, the Democratic party, which made it difficult for him seriously to consider supporting Eisenhower, now that he had decided to run as a Republican. Back in Atlanta, he was still pondering, in some agony of spirit, what he should do when a call came from the governor in Dayton, asking McGill to fly up to see him.

"Ralph," he said, "don't ever be ashamed of supporting a Democrat. Now and then, over the years, you may find yourself leaning toward a Republican. But don't be deceived. There are some good Republicans. But in the long run, the Republican party is no damn good for the country."

This was all McGill needed. As soon as the conventions ended in the summer of 1952, his eyes alight with the joy of battle, he threw all the editorial power he could muster behind the candidacy of Adlai Stevenson, the Democratic nominee. The race was a personal triumph for McGill and the *Constitution*, though a national disaster for the party. The Republicans put one hundred thousand dollars into Georgia, most of it into Fulton County, but Stevenson won handily, carrying the *Constitution*'s circulation area by three to one. The Republican county chairman told McGill that he had cost them fifteen thousand votes in Fulton County. "I hope so," said McGill cheerfully.

The morning after the election, McGill began to patch up fences and heal wounds opened by the fierce swordplay of the contest. He had traveled for two weeks on General Eisenhower's campaign train, and he had left it sadly disappointed and disillusioned with the Republican candidate. The general's very decency, his instinct for compromise, his inability to comprehend that there might be knaves in high places in politics had betrayed him, McGill believed, into the hands of men who could persuade him, in the interest of party unity, not to repudiate Senator Joseph McCarthy for his attack on General Marshall, who had been Eisenhower's friend and mentor.

The night he had left the campaign train, he sat down and poured out his anger and disappointment in a column he titled "Death of a Hero." He finished it at 2:00 A.M. and wired it to Atlanta. But, after sleeping on it, he decided it was too intemperate and phoned to order it killed.

"But I still believe the title was true," he later wrote to Barry Bingham, editor of the *Louisville Courier-Journal*, "and the saddest thing of all was that General Eisenhower did not seem to be aware of the many compromises he had made." This feeling of disillusionment and disappointment was strong in all the comments McGill made on the race thereafter.

But now the race was over, and Eisenhower had won by a landslide, and the time for rebuilding burned bridges had come. His telegram to the President-elect, already resting at the Augusta National Golf Club at Augusta, Georgia, was a graceful blending of pride and acquiescence:

> While as Democrats we are proud of our candidate, all of us here at the *Atlanta Constitution* send you sincere and hearty congratulations on a great victory and assure you that our admiration and respect for you never wavered and that you will have our support in anything you may ask of us if the opportunity for service ever arises.

To Bob Woodruff, he wired, on the day before the election:

> Once you put on a uniform and begin to fight, you have got to have integrity enough to fight on to the end. Regardless of who wins, I think we are going to have a good President in January. Next time I hope I am on your side, as I feel lonesome when I am not.

Woodruff's reply was indirect, through his secretary Joe Jones, who sent McGill a copy of a letter written to Stevenson by Ralph Hayes, a warm friend of McGill's and one of Woodruff's top executives. Hayes, a staunch Democrat in the past, praised the gallantry and lucidity of Stevenson's campaign and expressed comfort that the standard of the party would be in his keeping as the Democrats, the opposition party, revitalized itself "in preparation for a distinguished future worthy of its memorable past." However, Hayes said, he would be "one Democrat who tomorrow will be reluctantly voting Republican because of the feeling that infirmities born of long power dictate a transfer of responsibility."

McGill, in a pleasant note to his friend Ralph Hayes, praised his magnificent letter to Stevenson. Joe Jones had sent it, he said, "to heap coals of fire on my innocent head," but it had made him feel humble for another reason than its implied political rebuke. "Your letters," he told Hayes, "always make me wish I could write half so well as you do, and that makes me humble."

He felt as did Hayes about Stevenson — only so strongly it was not difficult to support him. As for Ike: "I guess I am a hero-worshiper at heart, and always will be, and it will take me a long time to get over the fact General Eisenhower felt it expedient to endorse certain persons, among them Jenner and McCarthy. . . . He did not need to be so extremely expedient.

"I never for a moment wavered in my respect and admiration for him. I was just disappointed, and I was never disappointed in anything Stevenson said or did."

With the Republican fences taken care of, he turned to the Democrats. To Adlai Stevenson, he wired that he and all at the *Constitution* were proud they had supported him and were happy that he had carried Georgia:

> It is our opinion that a really great American and the best Democratic nominee in our time was defeated by a combination of circumstances, some of them extremely unworthy, against which no candidate could have prevailed. We just wanted you to know that we are proud of you and proud to have fought by your side.

He followed this with a long letter to Stevenson, repeating his pride in having supported him and asking him if he would be good enough to drop a note to Governor Cox at his office at the *Dayton Daily News:*

I can tell you in confidence that it required considerable courage for Governor Cox to bring his papers strongly on the Democratic side, especially the one in Atlanta. He is really a great man, and unfortunately, the last of his kind in the newspaper business. He came up in the American tradition, and while he became a wealthy man, he somehow never had any awe of the country club, or banking set.

To Governor Cox at Dayton, he wired: "I am proud of you, proud of being a Democrat, proud of our candidate and proud we made the fight." Then to Harry Ashmore, editor of the *Arkansas Gazette*, he let his hair down: "Where was you when the egg hit the fan?" he wired Ashmore. "Is there a homestead that could be taken up in the Ozarks? I'm really ready." He followed this with a letter to Ashmore, still more lugubrious in tone. "You are so much younger than I am that I am depending on you to be around when I reach the sere and yellow leaf. I will depend on you to have a spot on the rim for me. . . ." McGill's forecast of a sudden decline into that company of aging and garrulous dotards on the rim of the copy desk was premature. The campaign of 1952 was the beginning of a lifelong friendship and affection for Stevenson, and four years later he again was girding himself with the armor of Democratic righteousness, happy at the prospect of drawing a sword and breaking a lance once more for Adlai Stevenson.

11

In 1946, McGill made his first visit to Palestine. Four years later he was invited back again by the young Israeli government, and out of this trip came a book comparing his findings, entitled *Israel Revisited*, a compilation of his columns brought out by Tupper and Love, a local publisher. It was a personal assessment whose mood is expressed in this paragraph:

> When I went there first, I came away with a feeling of having lived with great plans; of having been in currents strong and deep; and also of having dwelt for a time in the Leatherstocking tales in modern dress, as actors sometimes have done with *The Taming of the Shrew*. I felt, too, although I was too self-conscious to say so at the time, a sort of spiritual refurbishing from what I had seen and experienced. When I went back in the spring of 1950 to see in Israel the nation restored to life after 2,000 years, and witnessed every human and social problem being met with a mixture of mystic exaltation, sweaty toil and realism, I felt it once more. I was not unaware of the flaws, the failures, and the jarring contradictions, but I came away feeling as if I had left old friends with whom, in some distant past, I had worked and played and hoped. And I came away feeling strong, younger and surer about the eternal verities and the dignity of man.

McGill was never happier than when traveling. In late 1951 he jumped at the chance to visit India on a government-sponsored trip to report on how well our Point Four aid to Indian agriculture was working out. The year before, an Indian farmer, Amer Singh, had been brought to Carroll County, Georgia, by the *New York Herald Tribune* Forum to observe the way a small Georgia farm was operated. His host there had been Paul Patton, soil conservation supervisor; and now Patton and

McGill were repaying the visit at the invitation of Horace Holmes, one-time Tennessee county agent, serving as Point Four aid administrator in the United Provinces of north central India, where Amer Singh's village was located.

McGill left Atlanta with a ringing in his ears from the fourteen shots he had taken to ward off cholera, typhus and yellow fever, but "with a singing in my heart and blood" at the prospect of the trip. "There has always been," he wrote in a good-bye column, "a voice in me saying, 'there's something new beyond the horizon, go and find it.' "

Rome was a way station on his Indian journey, and there in the city that to him was lovely beyond compare, he went back again to the Spanish steps and the little house where John Keats had died. "The original wooden ceiling is yet there, being of carved painted medallions, some blue, some gold," he wrote. "The dying Keats must have looked at this many times in the long bitter weeks when life was slipping from him."

McGill stayed six weeks in India, spending most of that time in the little village of Makewa in the United Provinces, living the life of an Indian farmer and writing of it with vividness. As he had in Israel, he saw the Indian people in the first blush of their nationalism, optimistic of their future now that the British had departed. Even so early, Holmes recalls, McGill was speculating about the coming split between Russia and China, and the role which the new India would play. The question came to him as he drove along a rutted bullock-cart path to a place where sixty children sat on the ground before a schoolteacher's desk placed in the shade of a huge tree. On smooth boards rubbed with grease and soot, they were learning to write in an ink made of water and white clay.

McGill wrote:

This is a good illustration of what is going on in India. The people are learning to read and to write and their new freedom and the intoxication of political choice make their nationalism burn with a bright blue flame.

What does it mean to you and me? Well, it will certainly mean a lot to the boys and girls of this same school age in America what these millions of Indians will do some eighteen to twenty years from now. They will either grow up wanting to be one of the society of nations, or they will grow up on some "Asia for Asians" policy, hating all other races and turning to Russia for leadership. . . .

Just before he was to turn for home, he took a three-day holiday, went hunting with Amer Singh and his friends, and "knocked down three big partridges with wing shots, which pleased me, and missed five others, which did not." It was the open air and the comradeship that pleased him more than the hunting.

The sun was warm and the air smelled, because of the aromatic shrubs in it, like some exotic draught. It was good to be alive and to talk and laugh and feel the bond of friendship which comes, mysterious element that it is, out of too few meetings. I felt I had known these young men all my life and that perhaps the orthodox Hindu is right and that once before, in some former life, we had all been friends or brothers.

We rode back at dusk, the dust hanging in the still air, the narrow village paths, barely wide enough for the jeep, blue with the smoke from the cooking fires of dry dung cakes, which smell acridly like burning, mouldy straw but not yet offensively, as some might think. The tethered bullocks tugged at their homemade hempen ropes, children ran to see the jeep, and mothers clutched babies and stared at the mechanical monster, and dogs ran barking beside us.

At the house we bathed at the bathhouse, pouring a copper bowl of hot water over our heads, lathering and then pouring more and more bowls of steaming water until the body felt relaxed, soothed and warm. The night air was cold and sharp, the stars wonderful in the always cloudless winter skies. . . .

McGill came back to tell a committee of Congress how well our Point Four aid was working in India, limited as it was to the simple tools, the seeds and fertilizers that a primitive agricultural population could use. And he sharply put down those chauvinists who felt that the flag should be flaunted and the bands should play the "Star-Spangled Banner" every time an American truck, loaded with plows and plowpoints, rolled down an Indian road.

He left behind him pleasant memories. One Indian friend wrote from the village of Makewa:

I believe in reincarnation, and my conviction gets stronger every day that we come together for a few days by the desire of some Bigger Power due to our relations in the old life. You do not know what a trail of love and affection you have left here in this small period of a few days. . . .

McGill's admiration for the British, born of his knowledge of them in war, was diluted somewhat by what he had learned of them as empire builders in India. With his flair for epitomizing an era in one incident, he indicted the British as colonists forever for one act of brutality. The invention of the spinning jenny, the steam engine and the power loom in the late 1700s made Britain a producer and an exporter of textiles. Up until then, fine luxurious Indian cotton goods, all handmade, had been in worldwide demand. So, in India, he reported, the British overlords cut off the thumbs of the workers in the family industries so they could not operate the handlooms in competition with the machine-made textiles.

Conceding that the British were the most enlightened of imperialists, what he learned of British rule in India during his brief visit made him sympathetic ever thereafter to those countries which in the postwar years struggled to throw off the colonial yoke. As for the United States — "We can be glad we have no colonial regions, and we can hurry Hawaii and Alaska to statehood, and bring Puerto Rico along, or work out some other plan agreeable to her people."

A mannerism Ralph brought back from India was that of bowing to nearly everybody — a deep, almost oriental bow with which he greeted a new person. When a ribald colleague teased him for bowing to a local politician he was known to hold in low esteem, he cheerfully explained: in India, he had learned, one bows not to mortal man, but to God; but God is in every man, so the obeisance meant, "I bow to the God in you."

As he moved into his second half century, McGill found himself entering upon a period of searching for a testament and a faith. Often, in philosophical moments, he had written that he had learned not to try to define God or the meaning of faith for that would be to limit concepts that had no boundaries. He had come at last, he said, to know only this, "that chief among the virtues are stubbornness and humility." He was wary of the men "who speak with certitude from the pulpit, of the sure men who can cut out a faith for you and fit it to you as if it were a suit."

The stout armor of his boyhood faith, the stern Calvinism he had inherited from his parents, had long since been put off and he had not been an adherent of any formal religion since his college days. As his young son grew big enough to go to Sunday school, though, he, like many another father who was a fallen-away churchgoer, began to feel uncomfortable. Within a few blocks of the McGill house on Piedmont Road were congregations of Baptists, Methodists, Presbyterians and Episcopalians, and though McGill was not strongly drawn to any of these, he felt that he owed it to his son to at least expose him to the basic Christian concepts. So he and Mary Elizabeth, or more often, friends and neighbors who belonged to these churches, would pick up young Ralph and take him to Sunday school. After visiting them all, the one which he seemed to prefer was the church school at the Episcopal Cathedral of St. Philip. Here both Ralph, Jr., and his mother soon became involved in the formalities of the church, young Ralph as an acolyte, solemnly bearing the cross in the processional, Mary Elizabeth lecturing on herbs of the Bible before the women's organizations and raising flowers in her garden for the children's chapel. McGill himself began to take instruction, and on November 15, 1953, all three of them, on being presented by the dean of the cathedral, were confirmed in the Episcopal faith with the laying on of hands by the bishop. McGill began at once to take a busy part in the work of the church. He taught a Sunday school class of teen-agers, bringing them from his travels first-hand knowledge of the roads where Jesus walked as they look today, putting Bible stories in historical perspective out of his vast reading, and drawing moral lessons from the TV quiz-show scandals which then were shaking the country. He soon was made a member of the cathedral chapter, "the most curious appointment," he commented, "since the Emperor Caligula made his horse a consul." He became the friend and confidant of young ministers troubled about their commitment as priests, worried by what they felt to be the church's lack of relevance to the modern world.

For nearly a decade his life at the cathedral was happy and fulfilling.

Then in February of 1963, nine years after the Supreme Court's ruling on the schools, the Reverend Martin Luther King, Jr., asked that his son be admitted to Lovett School, a once-private institution that had placed itself under the financial and spiritual care of the diocese of Atlanta. He had been assured by a young Episcopal priest that there would be no problem, since the stated position of the Episcopal Church in America supported open schools and open churches. Dr. King's request was refused. Since Dr. King was a Baptist, the children of two black Episcopalians then sought admission to Lovett, on the theory that the school perhaps was only for the children of Episcopalians. They, too, were refused. The school, obviously, was for whites only. This, however, did not constitute a defiance of the church, its trustees argued. The school was not "officially" Episcopal and, therefore, was not subject to church discipline. To McGill this was hypocrisy. Fourteen of the school's twenty-one trustees were Episcopal communicants, the dean of the cathedral was, by law, their chairman, and the school's charter required religious teaching in accordance with the articles of the Episcopal faith as contained in the *Book of Common Prayer*.

McGill felt personally betrayed; he had been on the chapter at the meeting at which the school's charter was changed to bring it under the administrative control of the church. He had voted for the change, for it had not occurred to him that the school's new board would try to maintain Lovett as a segregated school after the Episcopal diocese in Atlanta had gone on record so strongly against segregation. Grieved and disillusioned, he moved his membership to downtown All Saints, whose rector, Frank Ross, said the things in the pulpit he thought needed saying, and whose congregation supported many projects in the inner city which interested McGill, including rehabilitation centers for skid-row alcoholics, a psychiatric counseling center for the mentally disturbed, and a room where the so-called latchkey kids, locked out of their houses while their mothers worked, could come after school to keep warm.

In the days when McGill was gun-shy of all churches and distrustful of most ministers, he had become the good friend of the Reverend Matthew Warren, who was then rector of All Saints, a cleric well known in Atlanta for his liberal attitudes toward labor unions and his strong views on racial justice. It was natural that McGill, in his disenchantment, should turn to his old friend's parish, even though Matt Warren had long since gone on to larger duties as headmaster at St. Paul's School in New Hampshire.

McGill was equally impatient with those in high political office whom he felt to be in error. Throughout the early fifties, during the heyday of Senator Joseph McCarthy, McGill was the implacable foe of the senator's methods and was one of the first to call upon Congress to censure him. At a time when some editors were handling Senator McCarthy with the delicacy of a cat poking at a hot coal, McGill wrote: "McCarthy's stuff reads as if it were lifted from *Mein Kampf*. . . . One of these days the nation is going to have to face up to the real meaning of McCarthy. . . . The reality is that Senator McCarthy has made the Star Chamber session a policy. He has intimidated and abused and challenged the basic rights of free individuals guaranteed in the Constitution. . . ." In a telegram sent to senators Russell, George, Douglas, and Fulbright, he said of McCarthy's attack upon the army:

> The White House cannot be another Pontius Pilate and wash its hands of this, nor can any American citizen wash his hands of it unless he wishes our army to degenerate into a political army which can be seized and used by some political opportunist. There is no reason I should worry you with this — except I get scared.

His attack on Senator McCarthy automatically made him a Communist in the eyes of many of his readers, and they did not spare him their opinions. One wrote, "It seems to me to be as inescapable as it is incredible that you are a Communist. I don't say you carry a card, but you employ every means at your command to support their declared purposes."

McGill was quick to answer such charges and equally quick to defend others whom he felt had been unjustly accused. He wrote "a personal friendly letter" to David Lawrence, editor of *U.S. News & World Report*, telling him how disturbed he had been by a Lawrence column referring to "anti-Communist senators."

This, he told Lawrence, implies that "you believe there are in the Senate and Congress pro-Communist senators and congressmen. This I find difficult to believe. It shocks me considerably," he said, "to think we have come to the point where in any defense of McCarthy we must assume he represents the anti-Communist force and any who do not believe in him must be labeled pro-Communist." He then gave Lawrence in detail the description of his own actions and attitudes which he gave in broad outline to his reader critics:

> I believe I would qualify as an anti-Communist, even under the McCarthy rules. For a good many years I have given the FBI what information I could obtain; I helped drive out of Atlanta the official Communist organization by a rather thorough job of keeping check on a fellow named Homer Chase, who was the southeastern Communist representative here; I ran down his family tree and printed the story of his New England father who had married a Russian woman and who had been converted to Communism. I published pictures of his father's grave under a stone in the New England cemetery with the hammer and sickle on it. I was attacked during the Progressive party campaign by Henry Wallace and in Atlanta by Paul Robeson, who announced me as a conservative reactionary. I have a good collection of Communist pamphlets in which I am one of their targets. I helped to drive out of existence what remained of the Southern Conference for Human Welfare, which for a number of years was a good organization but later in skeleton form became a Communist front. I never belonged to any of the organizations which were or later became Communist front organizations. I believe this would entitle me, by McCarthy's qualifications, to an anti-Communist status. Yet, I say to you frankly that McCarthy frightens me, and I am also frightened by the move of persons unfriendly to President Eisenhower to exploit McCarthy. I have never confused his insatiable ambition with Americanism.
>
> But what I chiefly wanted to write about was to ask you if you really have divided the Congress into the pro and anti factions as your column today would indicate. If so, this frightens me all the more. Maybe I am getting to be a timorous person, but I hope not.

In the spring of 1954 McGill was in London after a trip to Germany when he got portentous news from home. Eugene Patterson, bureau chief of the United Press in London, called him at his hotel there to tell him that the Supreme Court at last had handed down its school decision.

McGill and Patterson had first met in the winter of 1948 in the courthouse of the little town of Lyons, in Toombs County, Georgia. A mob of masked men had lynched a Negro there as he left a church with his wife and children. A few days earlier, in Montgomery County, Alabama, two white men had been freed after killing a Negro who had been bold enough to vote in the September primary. No arrests had been made in the Lyons case, and McGill had spoken out, editorially and in his column, in harsh and bitter criticism of the "murdering morons" responsible for the killing and of the law-enforcement officers who had made no arrests, even though the dead man's widow had recognized the man who killed her husband. His criticism had stirred the grand jury to summon McGill to testify.

Patterson, then a young UPI reporter and a veteran of Patton's Third Army, remembers McGill's arrival in the county seat, accompanied by Tarver, and how Ralph paced like a caged bear as he waited to be called into the jury room. He was wary and suspicious, anticipating a hostile reception. But his statement to the jury was an eloquent and reasoned plea for equal protection for the Negro before the law and a warning that if the South should fail in this, the federal government had no alternative but to step in:

Gentlemen, all of us, I take it, are working for what we believe to be the best interests of our state and region. My own idea is that we must present to the nation arrests, indictments and convictions in all cases of violence, lynching or otherwise, so as to demonstrate that we are people who believe in supremacy of law. Certainly there would be no agitation for antilynching legislation by the federal government if we in the South promptly had applied the full strength of the law in all such cases.

It does us no good to point out that the North too has violence. The records show that when there is violence in other sections, the law goes promptly to work and brings about arrests, indictments and many convictions. Rare indeed is the gang murder in the North that has gone unsolved and unpunished.

We cannot compare a killing in which the man is killed because he is a Negro with an ordinary murder. There is a great difference. The fact that very frequently killing of Negroes goes unpunished and the law uses little effort to bring about the full end of justice has made us vulnerable to federal legislation. . . .

I attended the Nuremberg trials in Germany, and I saw there men who had killed thousands of persons because they were Jews, Poles, Lithuanians, or other peoples to whom the German Nazis objected. I went to the concentration camps and to the gas chambers and saw there the pitiful bundles of those who had been killed because the German Nazis did not consider them proper people. Most eloquent of all were the bundles of little children's clothes and shoes. I came away more convinced than ever before that violence and prejudice are not ways of solving our problems at any time or anywhere.

It seems to me that Georgia needs what Negro farm labor she has. It seems to me that the merchants of Lyons and other cities accept trade and money from Negro customers. It seems to me that the Negro is an integral part of our economy. I can see no reason why this grand jury cannot assist the good Christian people in this community in setting a pattern which would allow the two races to live and work together in a community, separated socially but united in the rights which our Constitution guarantees to all citizens.

These strong words had no immediate effect. A white man was arrested for the killing, tried, and acquitted by a Toombs County jury. But Ralph would repeat them. Over the years that followed, in many aspects of the civil rights fight McGill sounded that same note, pleading with the states themselves to guarantee justice and fair treatment to the Negro and warning of the alternatives.

Only a few weeks before the United States Supreme Court ruling, writing of the pending school decision, he had said:

I personally hope the Supreme Court will not disturb segregation in the common schools, but I do not think it is my duty as a newspaper editor to deceive the people. On the contrary, I think it my duty to express what I think to be the truth, and I believe that truth to be that world sentiment and feeling run so strongly against segregation on the basis of color that legal support of it soon will be ended.

Now it was ended, as he had predicted, and in the UPI office in London, Patterson waited, pencil poised for McGill's reaction. When it came, it was curiously noncommittal. All McGill said was: "I am surprised that the vote was unanimous."

Patterson waited — "Yes?"

"I think that is all I want to say at this time," said McGill. "Thank you for calling me." He hung up the phone.

Patterson had no way of knowing what was racing through McGill's mind — that the Supreme Court decision was not the end but the beginning of a long battle in which an agonized and truculent South would turn to every legal means to circumvent the carrying out of the Court's order. The separate-but-equal doctrine which he believed had been best for the South and its people had failed because the South itself had failed. It had not been honest enough to provide the equal facilities it had promised.

Editorially he faced a delicate task of persuasion — to convince his readers that the answer lay not in defiance of the courts but in honest acquiescence.

Back home, writing of the sordid incidents of violence which would inevitably follow the school decision and pleading that they be held in check, he said: "If to the fears and suspicions created among the Americans by whát has come to be called McCarthyism is added racial hatred and violence, the load will indeed be hard to bear."

Firmly,, but courteously, he fired off admonishing telegrams to President Eisenhower, who, he feared had an impulse to compromise with the forces of reaction in the South. Only when the region finally accepted the inevitability of the Court's ruling could there be an end to violent resistance, he told the President. Any compromise would only encourage more resistance.

"There is only one alternative," he wrote in his column, "and that is secession by armed force." The South, he suggested, had tried that once before and it had not worked out so well. There was, of course, no armed secession this time. Instead there was a scattered campaign of guerrilla action in which angry citizens by armed intimidation sought to avoid the carrying out of the Court's orders. There were shameful and terrible incidents — riots and murders in Oxford, Mississippi, the dynamiting of schoolchildren and the use of police dogs in Birmingham. Yet the reaction was not, McGill noted, as bad as had been threatened by those who had sworn that not one Negro child would ever darken the door of a southern school. But it was bad enough.

The Klan, fragmented and unmasked in the mid-forties, took on new life in the wake of the school decision and McGill soon found himself again locked in combat with an organization with which he never had pulled his punches. The White Citizens' Councils organized to fight the

Court's decision, and he took them on, too. On the whole, McGill, with incredible optimism, felt that the violence and the murders had one good effect — they forced the apathetic to make a choice, the issue could no longer be ignored.

Under federal pressure there was token integration at many places in the South, mainly in the border states, until finally the hard core of resistance centered in the Deep South: Georgia, South Carolina, Alabama, Mississippi and Louisiana. And even here the despairing cry of a Little Rock, Arkansas, woman could be heard, echoing the death wail of resistance. She had taken her place in the schoolhouse yard to turn back Negro children as they arrived. Suddenly she saw black faces peering at her from behind a classroom window. "Oh, Lord God a' mercy," she moaned, "the niggers is already in the schoolhouse."

McGill was largely blamed for whatever integration had taken place. The angry and abusive phone calls to his home increased, with the callers frequently asking to speak to "Rastus" McGill.

In a whimsical moment he had taught a small dog, which he named "Rastus," to bark loudly at the sight of a telephone receiver. Rastus would sleep beside his chair as he sat in the den, reading in the evenings, and when the phone on the table beside him rang and a voice would say, "Is that you, Rastus?" McGill would answer amiably, "You want to speak to Rastus?" Then he would hold the phone down in front of the little dog. "Speak, Rastus," he would command, and the dog would bark shrilly and piercingly into the telephone.

Though McGill's answers to private individuals who criticized him were usually soft-spoken and placating, his patience did not extend to lawyers and judges, who, he thought, should know better than to attack the Supreme Court for its civil rights decisions. To an angry Alabama circuit judge he wrote: "Sir, I am delighted I do not have to appear for justice in your court." To other lawyer critics, he would recommend the poem by Carl Sandburg which contained the line: "Why does a hearse horse snicker, hauling a lawyer's bones." "Henceforth," he would tell them, "When I read this poem I will think of you."

His impatience with lawyers extended to his onetime friend, Charles Bloch, an "eminent constitutional authority" hired by the state to find a way to circumvent the Supreme Court decision. (Any barrister, he said, above the level of police court lawyer, was automatically dubbed an "eminent constitutional authority" if he opposed the school decision.) Though piqued with Bloch, he wrote him a friendly letter with no hearse-horse overtones.

Dear Charlie,

First, let me say I think a great deal of you personally. I hope you will always remember that.

Secondly, I am sorry we can't agree. Here is where I see our basic difference: My first and complete loyalty is to the United States of America and its government. It simply would never occur to me to have my primary loyalty in a region or a state. I, of course, have affection and pride in region and state, but my first loyalty is, and always will be, to my country and its government. I realize that other people do not feel that way. I do not understand how they can take that attitude, but then that certainly is their business. . . .

Anyhow, certainly I would much have preferred for things to have stayed like they were. It was more comfortable; there was less tension; and it was less trouble. And certainly I was not, and am not, for desegregation. I did not promote it or endorse it, and I do not now. But that is my personal feeling. As an American, it seems to me that we are either citizens or we are not, and while I may not like it, and while I may wish it another way, I cannot in conscience or in Christian belief accept the suggestion that some other citizen should be treated differently than I under the law of my country. So, however much I personally may feel about it, I am not going to advocate any position other than that prescribed by law. Therefore, I do not consider the Supreme Court has violated the Constitution. To me, that is a contradiction in terms. So long as the Supreme Court interprets the Constitution, it can't violate it.

Also, again, despite personal feelings, I do not think that we can say that any citizen of the United States has more rights than another citizen. I also think it ridiculous to assume or say that the states are sovereign. They haven't been sovereign since the Constitution was adopted in 1789. . . .

Certainly, I know the Confederacy had a Constitutional argument, but let's don't try to argue that the South did not commit itself on the wrong side of a moral question. No less a person than the vice-president of the Confederacy, Alexander Stephens, publicly acclaimed that slavery was the keystone of the arch of the Confederacy. The Confederacy officially proclaimed its belief and determination to maintain the institution of slavery. If that was not committing itself on the wrong side of the moral question, then I just don't know anything at all. Had they not done this, the constitutional argument would have been given a much more receptive hearing, but when the South committed itself to slavery, it was doomed before the bar of moral opinion.

I answer this in some detail because I have a great liking for you and want you to understand my position. Basically, I guess it is that first of all I consider myself an American citizen.

McGill had always held to the view that an editor should sail either with the wind or against it, but that he should never drift or lie at anchor, and this policy of tacking back and forth could at times confuse his readers. Before the school decision, he often had expressed the strong belief that the schools should remain segregated. And long after the decision had been handed down, he could write: "If we had had the good sense to have put a mere sprinkling or handful of Negro children in schools, we would have been given ten or fifteen years, at least, to move ahead without trouble." A half-dozen children in two or three schools would have been enough to bring this relief, he felt. He could at the same time argue that the Supreme Court's decision, once handed down, must be complied with in full, with no attempt at evasion or delay of its "all deliberate speed" provisions.

McGill finally received support from an unexpected quarter. In January of 1959, Senator Herman Talmadge, to whom all Georgians defiant of the school decision turned for comfort, said publicly that the Supreme Court decision on the schools was an accomplished fact and would remain so until reversed by the Court itself or nullified by Congress and the people. There was a faint cockcrow of triumph in McGill's language as he congratulated Senator Talmadge for pointing out this truth, which had caused him — and others who had taken the same position — to be abused and smeared and vilified. The title of his column was "Truth at Last from a Southern Senator."

McGill's friend and strong supporter, Governor Cox, died in the spring of 1957, leaving him feeling forlorn and vulnerable. On the paper, however, his season of anxiety was brief. In the fall of that year, George C. Biggers suffered a stroke and retired to Florida, where he died soon after, and the direction of the paper fell upon James M. Cox, Jr., the governor's son, who turned the running of the papers to McGill's protégé and friend, Jack Tarver, who became president.

There is no doubt that Governor Cox, by his support, saved McGill's career in a precarious and shaky time. Yet it is also true that he delayed its complete fulfillment. Since McGill's first short story had been published in *Harper's* in 1947 — a poignant vignette of a young cub reporter riding with the cops to investigate a "nigger killing" in a small southern town — he had been writing for a larger and larger audience. In book reviews and lead articles in the *Saturday Review, Survey Graphic,* the *New Republic,* and articles in *The Atlantic Monthly* and the *Saturday Evening Post,* he had spoken out frankly on the South's problems to a national readership.

His columns were made available to the Cox papers in Dayton, Springfield and Miami, and the *Jacksonville Journal* was picking them up. He was, therefore, coming to be a national figure, but in a haphazard and scattershot way. To Tarver, this was regrettable: McGill, as a syndicated columnist, would attract national attention to Atlanta Newspapers, Inc. He would also earn for himself a great deal of money, which he needed, for he had not only a family of his own to support, but there were aspiring young journalists who turned to him for help and a wide variety of bums and moochers who knew he was a soft touch.

Whenever Tarver would approach the governor to suggest that McGill's column be offered to one of the better syndicates, he would be turned down flat. McGill's strength, the governor argued, lay in the fact that he was a southerner, speaking for and to the South. It would be a mistake for him to start writing for a national audience.

But after the governor's death, Tarver took up with George Biggers the question of syndicating McGill, and Biggers, who believed that McGill's views were more acceptable to a national than to a Georgia audience, was happy at the prospect. So was John Wheeler of the North American Newspaper Alliance, with the result that McGill joined his stable of writers. Thus, Biggers, who for nearly a decade had sought to restrain McGill editorially, in one of his last acts before retirement assisted McGill to obtain, in his sixtieth year, a national readership.

In papers all over the country — sixty at first, over three hundred in time — readers began to discover Ralph's rambling, sometimes awkward and prolix prose in which anger, pity, nostalgia, deep compassion and broad humor were used to reveal sharp truths. They soon discovered what McGill's Atlanta readers had long known — that his instincts were gentle, but he would write with wrath and thunder when the subject moved him.

On an October Sunday afternoon in 1958, soon after his column had been syndicated, he came home late from a speaking trip in the Georgia mountains. His wife, Mary Elizabeth, met him at the door and told the driver of the company car to wait. The office, she told McGill, had been trying to reach him all day. The Temple, seat of Atlanta's biggest Jewish congregation, had been bombed.

Soon after, in his office, in twenty minutes of furious, uninterrupted writing, he produced three typewritten pages that smoked with anger and with shame. Under the heading, "A Church, a School," he said:

> Dynamite in great quantity ripped a beautiful temple of worship in Atlanta. It followed hard on the heels of a like destruction of a handsome high school at Clinton, Tennessee.
>
> The same rabid, mad-dog minds were, without question, behind both. They are also the source of previous bombings in Florida, Alabama, and South Carolina. The schoolhouse and the church were the targets of diseased, hate-filled minds.
>
> Let us face the facts. This is a harvest. It is the crop of things sown.
>
> It is the harvest of defiance of courts and the encouragement of citizens to defy law on the part of many southern politicians. It will be the acme of irony . . . if any of four or five southern governors deplore this bombing. It will be grimly humorous if certain state attorneys general issue statements of regret. And it will be quite a job for some editors, columnists, and commentators, who have been saying that our courts have no jurisdiction and that the people should refuse to accept their authority, now to deplore.
>
> It is not possible to preach lawlessness and restrict it. . . .
>
> When leadership in high places . . . fails to support constituted authority, it opens the gates to all those who wish to take law into their hands. . . . The extremists of the citizens' councils, the political leaders who in terms violent and inflammatory have repudiated their oaths and stood against due process of law have helped unloose this flood of hate and bombing.

This too is a harvest of those so-called Christian ministers who have chosen to preach hate instead of compassion. Let them now find pious words and raise their hands in deploring the bombing of a synagogue.

You do not preach and encourage hatred for the Negro and hope to restrict it to that field. It is an old, old story. It is one repeated over and over again in history. When the wolves of hate are loosed on one people, then no one is safe. . . .

This series of bombings is the harvest, too, of something else.

One of those connected with the bombing telephoned a news service early Sunday morning to say the job would be done. It was to be committed, he said, by the Confederate Underground.

The Confederacy and the men who led it are revered by millions. Its leaders returned to the Union and urged that the future be committed to building a stronger America. This was particularly true of General Robert E. Lee. Time after time he urged his students at Washington University to forget the War Between the States and to help build a greater and stronger union.

For too many years now we have seen the Confederate flag and the emotions of that great war become the property of men not fit to tie the shoes of those who fought for it. Some of these have been merely childish and immature. Others have perverted and commercialized the flag by making the Stars and Bars, and the Confederacy itself, a symbol of hate and bombings.

For a long time now it has been needful for all Americans to stand up and be counted on the side of law and the due process of law — even when to do so goes against personal beliefs and emotions. It is late. But there is yet time.

The next day he came on again in a different mood, with a poignant, personal "Memo to a Dynamiter," beginning:

It was too dark at the time of the blast to see what it did to the inside of the temple. This is what it did.

It buried the little sky-blue robes of the children's choir under glass and plaster dust. The white collars lay gray and torn in water from broken pipes.

It blew from the vestibule wall and buried a bronze plaque commemorating men of the congregation who were killed in the military service of the United States flag.

It shattered a little display case set up by the sisterhood of the congregation and spilled its contents onto the wet rubble. The contents lying there consisted of Bathinette covers and fuzzy little baby bibs sewn by the women.

It toppled menorahs from a broken shelf and left those symbolic candle holders lying bent and tarnished under wreckage. . . .

Nearly ten months later, on a sunny afternoon in May, his phone rang. It was Reb Gershon, calling to congratulate him. The radio was carrying the news of a Pulitzer Prize, won for McGill's editorials on the Temple bombing.

"You're kidding!" he said. Then his office door opened and Grace Lundy, his secretary, came in carrying a telegram. Her bright smile told the story. The message read:

I HAVE THE HONOR TO ADVISE THAT COLUMBIA UNIVERSITY TRUSTEES HAVE AWARDED YOU PULITZER PRIZE FOR EDITORIAL WRITING

It was signed by Grayson Kirk, president of Columbia.

With a sigh that rustled the papers on his cluttered desk, McGill sat down and reached for his coffee cup.

"I never thought I'd make it," he said.

12

April 2, 1959, marked the end of the thirtieth year since Ralph McGill, wearing a green-striped suit shiny of seat and elbow and carrying a suitcase full of books, had stepped off the Nashville train to go to work for the *Atlanta Constitution.* In that thirty years, he had written for the newspaper and for magazines more than fourteen million words on every subject under the sun. Many had been on the tortured relationship of the white and black man in the South, and these had made him the most loved and most bitterly discussed journalist of his time and region.

In an article printed in *The Atlantic*, McGill had told of his first job as a boy in Chattanooga. He had worked for an old Negro named Charlie, the boss of a roofing crew, and between the old man and the boy there had grown up a deep and mutual affection. This short paper stirred clamorous comment, typical of the pro- and anti-McGill sentiment throughout the South.

Two editorials illustrate the differing reactions; one by Hamner Cobb of the Greensboro (Alabama) *Watchman* attacked McGill as a carpetbagger; the other, by Neil Davis of the Lee County (Alabama) *Bulletin*, defended him.

Said Cobb: "We had just naturally assumed that McGill was a southern man by birth and had gone into the turncoat business on his own. But this *Atlantic Monthly* article gives his true background. He was born and raised on an east Tennessee farm, and he confessed, 'I did not see a Negro until I was six years old.' "

East Tennessee, Cobb pointed out, had statues of northern soldiers in its town squares, and during the War Between the States was "about as southern as the southern part of New Hampshire." This, he alleged, made McGill "a plain carpetbagger" instead of a scalawag, or apostate southerner, as Cobb had assumed. "He is no turncoat," said Cobb. "He just never was southern in the first place."

The remarkable thing about McGill's article, said Cobb, is that he seemed to consider it remarkable that a warm friendship could grow up between black and white:

> Whether Northerners or carpetbaggers such as McGill know it or not, the same thing has been repeated thousands of times in the South. . . .
>
> The real tragedy is that people of his stripe and the scalawags and carpetbaggers, the turncoats and apostates and the northern meddlers, are doing everything in their power to drive the races apart, rather than to bring them together in a peaceful civilization. These people . . . are the breeders of hate. They are breaking up the real friendships between the races, and driving Negroes such as Charlie out of jobs.

Davis, in his defense of McGill, pointed out that:

> . . . "the tissue-thin liberals, in and out of the South . . . whine that Ralph McGill . . . is too timid about speaking out on the issues of the day. They taunt him with every epithet from pussyfoot to scared. In recent months the frenetic right has joined the fuzzy-minded left to make the pack baying at Mr. McGill's heels so shrill and excited, the man is being victimized by a hysteria which seldom attacks the daily stint of so able an editor. . . .

After rebuking Cobb for his "ill-mannered piece," Davis continued:

> Of course, the real trouble with McGill, in the eyes of intemperate accusers at both extremes, is that he doesn't travel with either pack. His perceptive columns and editorials about the travail which followed in the wake of the 1954 U.S. Supreme Court school decision are not designed to give comfort to the hell-bent-for-leather integrationists-at-all-costs or the pull-down-the-house-atop us segregationists. He is paying the price for seeing our situation as it is. His critics do not want to be told the truth. He is pictured as a scalawag and turncoat because he insists upon dealing with realities.
>
> We say McGill has told the truth. . . . He consistently has taken the position that, like it or not, the Supreme Court has said what the constitu-

tional law is, and we have no alternative to complying with the law save destroying our public schools. . . .

When the history of these times come to be written, Editor McGill will be credited with having shed light and reason and having provided constructive leadership even though the safe and popular course dictated the opposite approach. The political hacks and other bitter-enders who have lost their bearings and played on the emotions and hatred of our people will not fare as well.

Ralph, who had been wounded by the charge that he was no southerner, was surprised and touched when his friend, Eugene Patterson, wrote an affectionately irreverent column signalizing McGill's three decades on the *Constitution.* It said in part:

There may have been more widely loved men in Georgia, and it is possible there may even have been somewhere a more generously cussed one, but seldom anywhere has the Lord wrapped a tougher hide around a gentler heart. . . .

But you have to know Pappy to judge him. If you have never met him you would be surprised.

The first thing that strikes you is that he does not have horns. He was born a butthead.

He does not have a forked tail. He has more the beam of a barge.

He has none of the cold-eyed arrogance you might associate with authority. He could use a little. He is so full of the wonder of perpetual youth that he's Pappy confessor to the human race, and that gets wearing.

How can a man be full of wonder after thirty years in the cockpit? Maybe it's his reading habits.

He tears knowledge from books like Henry the Eighth stripping a hambone. . . .

And always, he writes. He is full of words. They come up fresh like clear drops from a spring and get flung on paper with a velocity that won't always wait on spelling and punctuation, but with a grace that brings fan mail from such other journeymen as Carl Sandburg and Ernest Hemingway.

And always prevailing under the rock-hardened hide is that remarkable gentleness of heart. Before you tear the shirt off the editor you really ought to meet the man. He'll give you his own shirt.

More accolades awaited him in this climax year: Duke University gave him an honorary degree; his Pulitzer Prize–winning editorials were published in book form; and most important of all to his son, Ralph, Jr., Walt Kelly named a rowboat the "Ole Rafe McGill" in his comic strip "Pogo."

McGill's long years of hard work and hard travel in no sense slowed him down as he plunged joyously into his thirty-first year on the paper. In June at a small dinner at the White House, at which the vice-president was also present, he first learned of Nixon's plans to go to Russia. He immediately asked permission to go along.

The trip proved highly productive of good copy. Leaving the "summit" reporting to the wire services, McGill roamed Moscow and its environs with an interpreter like a wide-ranging bird dog casting for quail. He talked to Russians in the streets and restaurants and in the subways. He went to the courts, hospitals and the schools. He attended a Russian wedding. Yet, with a newsman's luck that seemed uncanny, he was tucked up close against Nixon's coattails at the American Exhibition when the vice-president got into his famous "Kitchen Cabinet" debate with Khrushchev. His lead that day began: "In a fantastic day, in which I stepped on General Klementi Voroshilov's foot and shook hands vigorously with Mr. Khrushchev, who thought I was on Mr. Nixon's staff. . . ."

McGill, when traveling, always was a worrier about how things were going at home, and how his columns were being received. Knowing this, Grace Lundy kept glowing cables flowing to him. One read: "Glorious columns through Friday. Quote Winship, *Boston Globe,* if anyone communicating with McGill, tell him we think is doing a hell of a job. End quote. All agree."

Not quite all. Westbrook Pegler, in a column vilifying the Russian people in general, said, "Ralph McGill wrote that he liked the Russian food. McGill is peculiar. He likes everyone and everything that Eleanor Roosevelt likes. He even likes Eleanor. Also bear in mind that Ralph has been eating in Atlanta restaurants for sixty-five years. Have you ever eaten in a restaurant in Atlanta?"

Pegler was wrong. McGill was still four years away from sixty-five. But the thought that the milestone year was even that close was a nagging worry at the back of his mind. For Atlanta Newspapers, Inc., had a supposedly ironclad rule. It retired its editors at sixty-five. The thought of it terrified McGill. The old line from "Ulysses" — "To rust unburnished, not to shine in use," began to haunt him. But out of his vast memory of poetry he had read, four other lines came back to comfort him:

Will shall be the sterner
Heart the bolder
Spirit the greater
As our strength lessens.

On February 12, 1960, Abraham Lincoln's birthday, Ralph was asked to speak at Cooper Union in New York City in commemoration of the address Lincoln had made there one hundred years before.

"As I recall it," McGill wrote to Harry Ashmore, "this was the speech which led to Lincoln's election, and thence to the Civil War. Naturally, I do not expect to match this, although there will be some minor reverberations, as I expect to speak plainly."

McGill, with a rasping voice entirely lacking in timbre and resonance, was not an infallible platform orator. Like Lincoln, it was the content of what he said which held his audiences spellbound. Sometimes, though, when he was tired and speaking without notes, he would lose the thread of his thought, grope desperately for it, and start all over again. Once in Dayton, Ohio, speaking before the annual meeting of the YWCA after an exhausting day, this happened to him. The hall was stifling, the introduction fulsome, and when he got up to speak he was sweating copiously and seemed groggy. His newspaper host remembered Ralph's distress: "He would swing from conditions in Scandinavia to the starving millions in India, and then he would look about him desperately, as if wondering where he was, and announce with great vehemence, 'And that's why you have to have a YWCA.' "

The Cooper Union speech posed a different challenge. Here the audience would be quiet — and critical. A sense of history was upon him as he wrote to an old friend, Colonel John M. Virden, sending him a copy of the speech. Virden, an amateur historian of the Civil War, was impressed by both the speech and by the selection of a southern editor to make it. He wrote to a friend, Mel Ryder: "This is quite an honor for ol' Peerless. I can't recall a Democrat, and a southerner to boot, ever having been so honored before."

McGill began by conjuring up the image of Lincoln standing at the same podium, delivering the speech which was "the pivot point of his life and the nation's." All his love and understanding of the man Lincoln, "the mystery of him, the humanity of him," he poured into this speech; and as his harsh, cracked voice came over the microphone, his audience could indeed "see him here a century ago, tall and gaunt in his new ill-fitting suit of black broadcloth, wrinkled from having been folded in the valise. . . . See him, too, on that damp and snowy night as he quit this auditorium to go back to his hotel, limping because one of his new boots pinched."

The subject of McGill's talk was "The Meaning of Lincoln Today." His argument was that it had little changed from that day to this. In 1860 Lincoln had pleaded for a national dialogue on slavery, which, if it had taken place, might have calmed hot tempers and deep fears and prevented the incredible folly of civil war.

"Even though the southern people will not so much as listen to us," Lincoln had said, "let us calmly consider their demands and give in to them, if in our deliberate view of our duty we possibly can."

"Lincoln's plea was rejected, and is still being rejected a hundred years later," McGill said, "as both political parties dodged an honest national dialogue on the subject of simple, legitimate civil rights."

McGill concluded his speech with a paraphrase of Carl Sandburg's quotation on Lincoln, which revealed that McGill, unconsciously perhaps, saw in his own trials a shadow of Lincoln's severer testing.

Sandburg had said of Lincoln that "in the chaos of clashing ideas and pressures, Lincoln almost never had a choice between right on one hand and wrong on the other." Most of the time, said Sandburg, Lincoln had to choose between what was partly right and partly wrong. As a result of his choices, "he was the target of slander, lies, half-truths, insinuations, lampoons, and a flood of criticism from much of a free press which hated him. But he went ahead, trying to do each day what seemed best."

Through the telescope of the years, McGill saw Lincoln as what he himself had tried to be, the man of moderation at work — "a harassed, troubled man . . . seeking for the answers he did not know, pleading with reasonable men to talk out their problems, their angers, their fears." He then called for a similar dialogue on civil rights, with all levels of leadership joining in, not only the politicians and the lawyers, but the men of business, the teachers and the churchmen.

The Lincoln speech was well received, and McGill came home feeling an uplift of the spirit. He found awaiting him a copy of a memo that Tarver had sent to a number of Cox editors throughout the circuit, warning them facetiously against any profligate spending at the upcoming convention of the American Society of Newspaper Editors. Linage, he added, is down.

This gave McGill a chance to reply, in feigned indignation, that there had been no reason to send him and William Baggs, editor of the *Miami Daily News*, a copy of this letter. "We have never participated in the Saturnalia of the so-called summit conferences," he pointed out. "We plan to continue our serious attention to duty and the higher things of life. We have already worked out a schedule which will keep us in touch with the best people. Therefore, we will have no time for participating in these extravagant, wasteful sessions which do so much to downgrade the image of the working newspaperman."

McGill, of course, was indulging in the persiflage which delighted him when he was in a good mood. He did not then, or thereafter, adhere to the austere life, and some of his extracurricular exploits, both at ASNE meetings, which he considered abysmally boring, and at political conventions, which he attended with the gleeful eagerness of a small boy at a circus, became minor legends in the trade.

Not long afterward, McGill's anxiety about his job had been assuaged. In late May, Tarver had dropped into McGill's office to tell him that he would not be forced by corporate rules to retire at sixty-five. Major Howell was stepping down as publisher to become vice-chairman of the board of Atlanta Newspapers, Inc. McGill, at sixty-two, would assume the publisher's role, which was not under the age-sixty-five retirement regulation. Eugene Patterson would move up to the editor's post, taking over the onerous chore of running the editorial page. Publishers of newspapers concern themselves with such matters as the cost of newsprint, the durability of delivery trucks, advertising linage, and circulation revenues. McGill knew nothing of such matters, and he would not be expected to learn. Tarver would continue to handle them as in the past.

McGill, therefore, would be free to devote his time to familiar pursuits — traveling, and advising presidents, and bailing old drunks out of jail, and helping high school kids go on to college, and writing his columns seven days a week, and putting his shoulder to whatever wheel needed a push.

The appointment of Patterson to succeed him as editor could not have pleased him more. George Biggers, shortly before he died, had met Patterson in London and hired him for the Atlanta newspapers. Since then he had become the closest thing to a soul-brother McGill had in the business. He had that quality which Ralph admired above all else — courage, both physical and moral. He could not be bullied or bought and he wrote like an angel.

Joseph Cumming, Atlanta correspondent for *Newsweek*, reported the change in his magazine:

> McGill, that grave, vexed, playful, wheezy-voiced, square-faced, weight-plagued and rumpled old editor who for thirty years was like a tabernacle, destined to carry forward the simple and unradical message that black people, too, are human beings . . . continues his column and is given the title of publisher. Patterson, who succeeds him as editor, is just right for the image; a young man, thirty-six, a native Georgian, a liberal on race with compassion for the white agony, a tough, jaunty figure with a do-right jut to his jaw and a tight prose style that shone like a suit of armor.

McGill wore his new dignity as publisher with diffidence, but Harry Ashmore, who had left the Little Rock (Arkansas) *Gazette* for the Center for the Study of Democratic Institutions at Santa Barbara, California, commented rudely on his new title.

"You might as well face it, McGill. You've got the build, but unlike Tarver, there just ain't enough sonofabitch in you; you're still a widows and orphans man at heart."

Also, he was still a political reporter and both conventions that year found him in attendance. He denounced prospective Republican presidential aspirant Barry Goldwater for what he called his "bumbling vagueness on vital matters," yet once he found himself, with his friend

Harry Golden, marching in a Goldwater demonstration shouting "We want Barry" along with the rest. His motive, he said, was to get a close-up of the kind of people who favored Goldwater.

One of his happy memories was of Golden addressing a gathering of Jewish delegates and urging them to write in the name of Adlai Stevenson when the time came to cast their ballots. Of the Republican convention he wrote to Carl Sandburg saying, "It was a pleasure to see the Republicans kicking and screaming and then finally doing what Mr. Rockefeller told them they must do."

With Adlai Stevenson reluctant to try for a third time, McGill went to the Democratic convention in Los Angeles hopeful for the chances of his friend Hubert Humphrey — to whom he had written, "You are the only one who has been saying anything which makes sense." He was nervous about Kennedy, whose fantastic spending in the West Virginia primary distressed him and he confessed in a letter to Adlai Stevenson that he was much disturbed by the cynicism of Senator Lyndon Johnson.

Before the Los Angeles convention he went up to Santa Barbara to spend a few days with his friend Ashmore. There, in a letter to a friend, he reported:

> The scenery was beautiful, the air was healing and there was a certain tranquilizing lotuslike quality to it all. Nobody rang up and called me an s.o.b.; nobody telephoned my home and threatened to kidnap my boy or blow up the house. All in all, I felt like the tranquil victims in Mr. Tennyson's poem about the lotus-eaters, and once or twice heard myself saying under my breath: "There is sweet music here that softer falls, than petals from blown roses on the grass. . . . Oh rest ye, brother mariners, we will not wander more. . . ."

He also found occasion while there to speak to Ashmore about his immortal soul. Earlier, in a letter, Ashmore had reported getting in a somewhat confused and alcoholic theological argument with an Episcopal priest, who had sought to convert him. "In the background," he wrote McGill, "I could distinctly see you flanked by bishops with their crosses clanking on the bar . . . so I happily informed the father that this was a mission reserved exclusively for McGill."

McGill wrote back:

I can see that you are still troubled with the images of childhood and don't yet understand that in the Episcopal fold you don't have to be converted; you simply have to believe.

I have a friend in Honolulu who is an Episcopalian. Recently a number of Buddhists came to the rector of his church and wanted to know if people who weren't Christians could be received into the Episcopal church. "Why not?" said the rector, "a great many already have."

Episcopalians, McGill pointed out, were very resilient, and Ashmore, for all his frailties, would no doubt be welcomed into the fold. He promised to discuss the matter further at a later date. Unhappily, the subject did not soon come up again, the pressures of events turning the attention of both men to more mundane matters. He noted in a letter to Ashmore that the Reverend Martin Luther King, Jr., the nonviolent Negro leader who could stir southerners to such paroxysms of rage that they committed violent acts, was leaving Montgomery, Alabama, to take a pulpit in Atlanta.

Wrote McGill:

I view this in much the same manner as the citizens of medieval cities who heard that the great plague was coming. I have the highest esteem for the reverend, but he could not have come at a worse time. The legislature will have just reached high gear by February 1, and the district court yesterday notified city officials that what the legislature did with the school placement plan will determine whether or not they have schools. . . .

It was a busy year for him. In April, taking Mary Elizabeth and young Ralph with him, he was in New York to receive the Lauterbach Award "for distinguished service in the field of civil liberties." A contrasting point of view was expressed by the Jackson, Mississippi, *Register*, whose columnist, Tom Ethridge, called him "Ralph McGill, renegade, who edits the mix-minded *Constitution*. Nothing could be more irrational or visionary than McGill's dream of an integrated South blindly obedient to political charlatans, and brotherhood fanatics of his own stripe."

A month later he appeared with his old political friend-turned-foe Roy Harris on an Ed Murrow documentary, *Who Speaks for the South?* He congratulated Murrow for giving Harris so much time on the program.

"He is such a caricature," McGill told Murrow, "we are all delighted for the country to see him as he is." (Harris had once dismissed the integration issue with the observation, "There ain't nobody for it but a few preachers and Ralph McGill.")

A little news story gave him the idea for a classic column. "My old mule is gone. I am drowned in this pond," was a note left by an old Negro sharecropper before committing suicide. McGill used it as a text for an editorial telling the whole story of the little farmer in the South, of the mule and the man whose day is over.

Now and then his recurring melancholy depressed him. He wrote to Ashmore: "Since you departed, I feel naked and alone." And to Demaree Bess of the *Saturday Evening Post:* "I feel blue, but I try to keep working." His blue mood arose from the fact that he felt that only an act of God could keep Nixon from the presidency. He had wired Nixon congratulations on the way he had handled himself in the face of hostile crowds in Latin America. He thought the vice-president had come off well in his confrontation with Khrushchev. But he had not changed his earlier opinion, formed in 1952. "Mr. Nixon," he had then written a friend, "is the type who would like to jail anybody who does not agree with him." Eight years later he was asking Adlai Stevenson: "Do you think the Lord has decided we deserve to have Nixon, much as he sent Attila the Hun and other well-known scourges?"

A brief visit by Carl Sandburg in mid-July brought a momentary light into the gloom he felt about the fate of the Democrats. Carrying a flagon of goat's milk to sustain him on his journey to the West Coast, where he was an adviser in Hollywood on a picture called *The Greatest Story Ever Told,* Sandburg left behind a memorable comment on the current state of the cinematic art. "Too many movies today," he said, "seem like reflections in the mirrors of a bawdy house."

The election of John Kennedy by the narrowest of margins (He received only 112,702 more popular votes than Richard Nixon, out of sixty-eight million cast.) took McGill by surprise. His private comment was that "the victory of this rich young man, a Catholic, with an unpopular father and a wife who was known as a society figure, was nothing short of a miracle."

Miraculous or not, the return of the Democrats to power after eight years seemed to him worthy of a special celebration. Gathering his cohorts of the *Constitution* city room around him, he went off to Henry Grady Square a block from his office, tugging on its carriage the *Constitution*'s little brass cannon which Henry Grady had first fired in 1884 to celebrate the victory of Democrat Grover Cleveland. Old tank commander Eugene Patterson loaded the cannon with black powder. McGill applied a match to the touchhole. There was a thunderous roar, a flash of flame, a billowing of smoke. The little cannon kicked back, climbing halfway up McGill's leg and peeling the skin from his shins and singeing off his eyebrows.

Bruised but triumphant, he returned to the office to start firing off a congratulatory telegram to President-elect Kennedy and a consoling message to Nixon.

"It was my hope things could work out so that we might be on your side," he wrote Nixon, "but that turned out not to be possible. . . . I want you to know, however, that I will always entertain for you a great admiration, respect and affection . . . and if I can in any way be of help to you, I will be happy to respond. . . . I have never really liked partisan conflicts, but once in them, I don't know anything else to do but go ahead. I'm sure you understand this."

The only way McGill could have supported Nixon was for him to have been running against Count Dracula. And to Ralph partisan conflicts were the breath of life. But once a political battle was over, it was not his nature to gloat.

So all that now remained was to say a melancholy farewell to Adlai Stevenson as a presidential possibility, and to welcome John Kennedy.

Of Stevenson he said in a column after the election: "He is the only American who could restore almost unanimous confidence in the United States around the world. But . . . he came along at a time when the Korean War had made the nation very weary and depressed. There was the loss of life, the wounded, and the great cost of it. He came along just at the beginning of the McCarthy era. His two campaigns coincided with the effect of it. He inherited the opposition of all those who were antiintellectual. It is a tragedy for our country that we were unable to use his talents as President."

Nor could he serve as secretary of state, another post for which he was admirably suited, McGill pointed out, for the opposition to him had spilled over into Congress.

McGill wrote:

> The Stevenson chapter in the 1960 election was very sad. The convention . . . knew Stevenson was the best-qualified candidate. The world crisis seemed to call for him, but Stevenson himself must bear some of the responsibility for failure. He had insisted he was not a candidate. He assisted none of those who worked for him. So it was that one of the most able men in the world, and one of the best qualified for the presidency, ended with 79½ votes. Somehow this should have been avoided.

"Meanwhile," he said, building a fence, "it will be well to study Kennedy. Almost everyone underestimated him." Not long after the election McGill had the opportunity to study young Kennedy at close range and in person. With Mary Elizabeth and Ralph, Jr., he called upon the President-elect at his vacation spot in Florida.

"Kennedy," he wrote later, "is a happy combination of the intellectual and the politician . . . a fellow who in a relaxed conversation will quote from a poem or from a bit of Greek philosophy, and do it naturally, not like putting raisins in a pie. They are a natural part of his articulateness."

In the brief time left to them, both the President and Robert Kennedy were to lean heavily on McGill. So did Stevenson as he went on to become ambassador to the United Nations under President Kennedy. He was not entirely happy in this job. The Bay of Pigs fiasco left him embarrassed before the world. By late 1962, there were rumors that Kennedy was none too happy with his representative at the U.N. and this was disturbing to McGill. Learning that Stevenson had been invited to make a speech at Notre Dame University, he called upon John Popham, editor of the *Chattanooga Times,* and the two of them did a great deal of research in the history, sentiment and lore of Catholicism in America — and at Notre Dame particularly — and sent up to Stevenson a half-dozen ideas which he could touch with his own genius and turn into a speech of such grace, warmth, humor and depth that it would be memorable to a Catholic audience. The idea, they told Stevenson, was to "use this occasion to give some oblique answers to his detractors, to get his captive Catholic audience warm and make them laugh and cry, which you can do so well. Thus, they will come away saying, 'Who says there's anything wrong with this guy? What the hell does Kennedy or anybody else mean by picking on him?' "

13

THE Christmas season was always a time of sadness for McGill as he remembered Miss Virginia and her bright laughter. Christmas of 1960 was made more melancholy by an act of brutal violence in Atlanta. On the morning after Christmas Day, he had gone sleepily into the pine-paneled kitchen of his little red-brick house to make a pot of coffee for himself and Mary Elizabeth. The phone rang, and as he picked it up, he heard a cackle of insane laughter. Such calls were not unusual, and he hung up and thought no more about it, until a few minutes later when he snapped on the radio to hear the news. Not far from his own house, during the night, a Negro public school had been destroyed by dynamite.

In his office later that morning he again poured out onto paper the rage he felt in his heart in a column couched in the language that two years earlier, after the temple bombing, had earned him the Pulitzer Prize:

The big brave men who tossed the explosive in the darkness of the night, and in the deeper darkness of their own minds and souls, have not stopped the processes of education. Their kind have appeared often in history. . . . Their soul-kin were among those who tended Hitler's gas furnaces. Their kind are related to those who scream filth in the New Orleans demonstrations.

Here again we have the essence of the Greek tragedy. In the end the decent civilized people will prevail. In the end there will be education for all children. Bombers prove nothing by bombing, or destroying a school or a church. God still lives. Learning remains. The tragedy is that even though the end of the play is known, there must be needless suffering, violence, and ugly lawlessness on the loose.

McGill, age four, with Grandmother Skillern on left, his mother on right

McGill, sixteen, at camp in Tennessee

In his senior year at McCallie Prep, McGill (front right) played the lead role in *What Happened to Jones?*

As a guard on Vanderbilt University's football team

Interviewing a farmer on the tour that won him the Rosenwald Fellowship

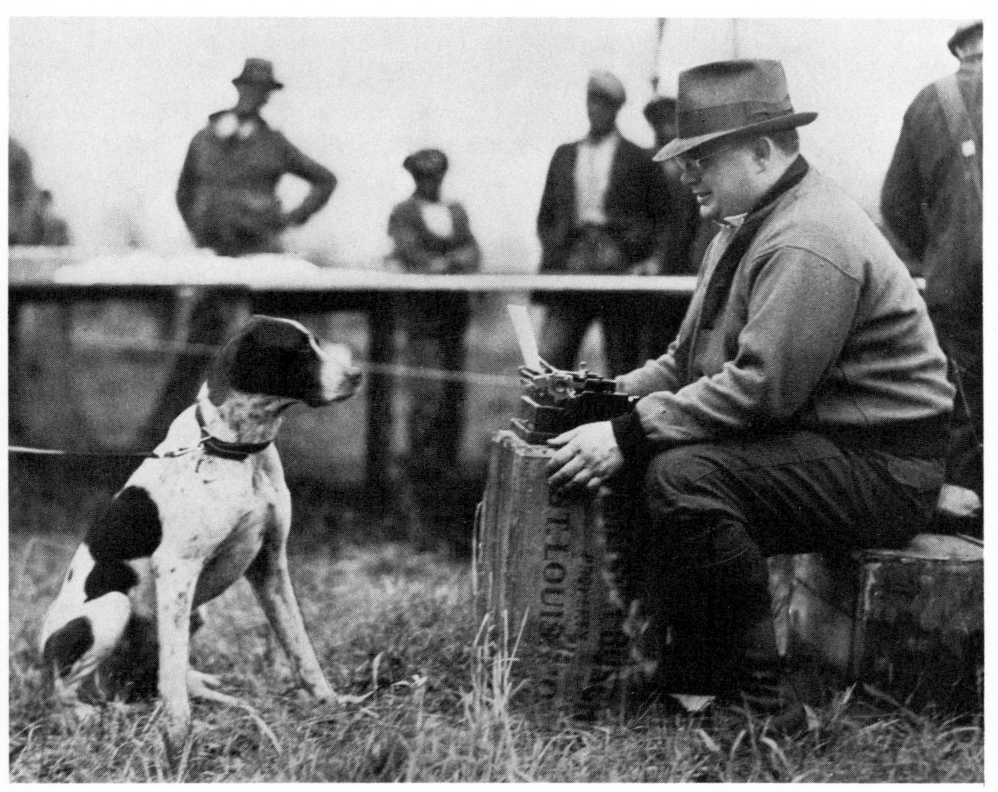

"Interviewing" Tom Chubb's pointer, Springwood Spider, Albany Field Trials, 1938 (*Photo by William Waddell*)

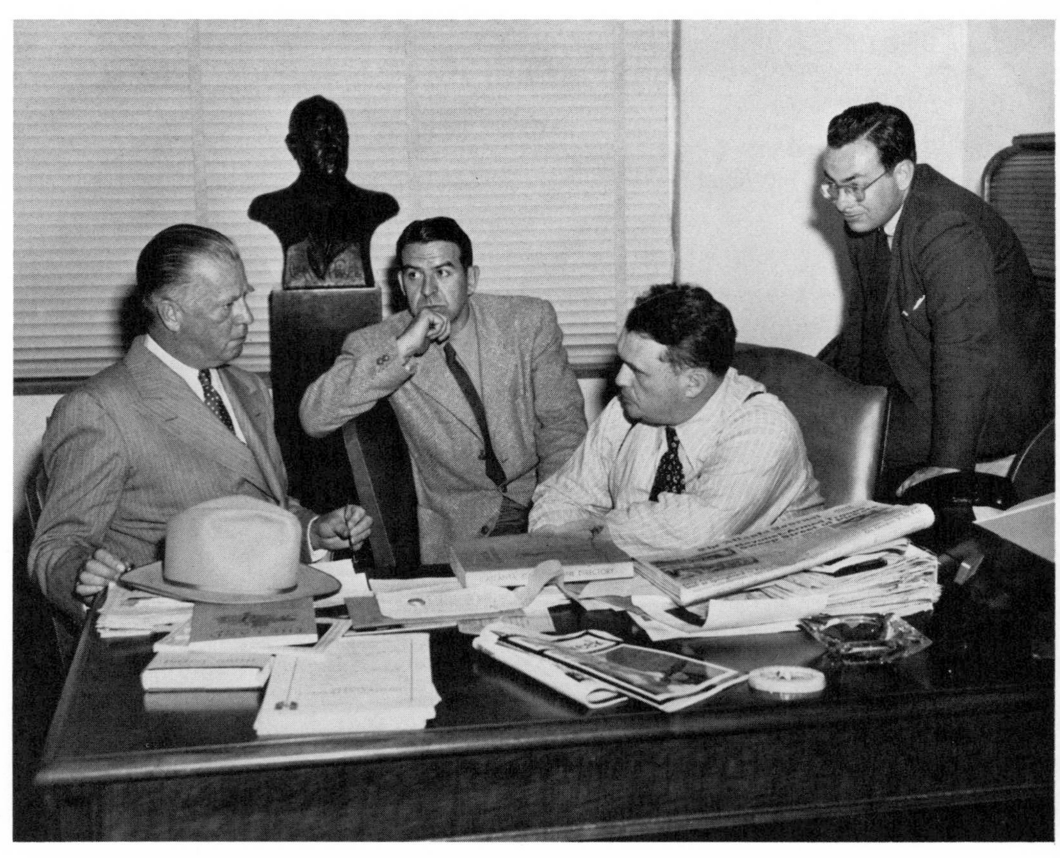

Westbrook Pegler visits the *Constitution*'s editorial offices early in 1943. Left to right: Pegler, Harold Martin, news staff; McGill, editor; Jack Tarver, associate editor

Washington, November 1947. After a European tour with a group of editors under the auspices of the secretary of the army. McGill at President Truman's left

Connemara Farm, 1953. Left to right: Carl Sandburg, Ralph, Jr., Ralph McGill

McGill visits one of the Negro playgrounds with Laura Demery, supervisor of the recreation division of the Atlanta Parks Department (*Photo by Larry Keighley*)

The McGills and Ralph, Jr. Composing room Labor Day picnic, 1959

Left to right: John F. Kennedy, Ralph McGill, Jr., Mary Elizabeth McGill, Ralph McGill, William Lawrence. The McGills were vacationing in south Florida in December 1960 and were given an audience with the President-elect at his West Palm Beach house

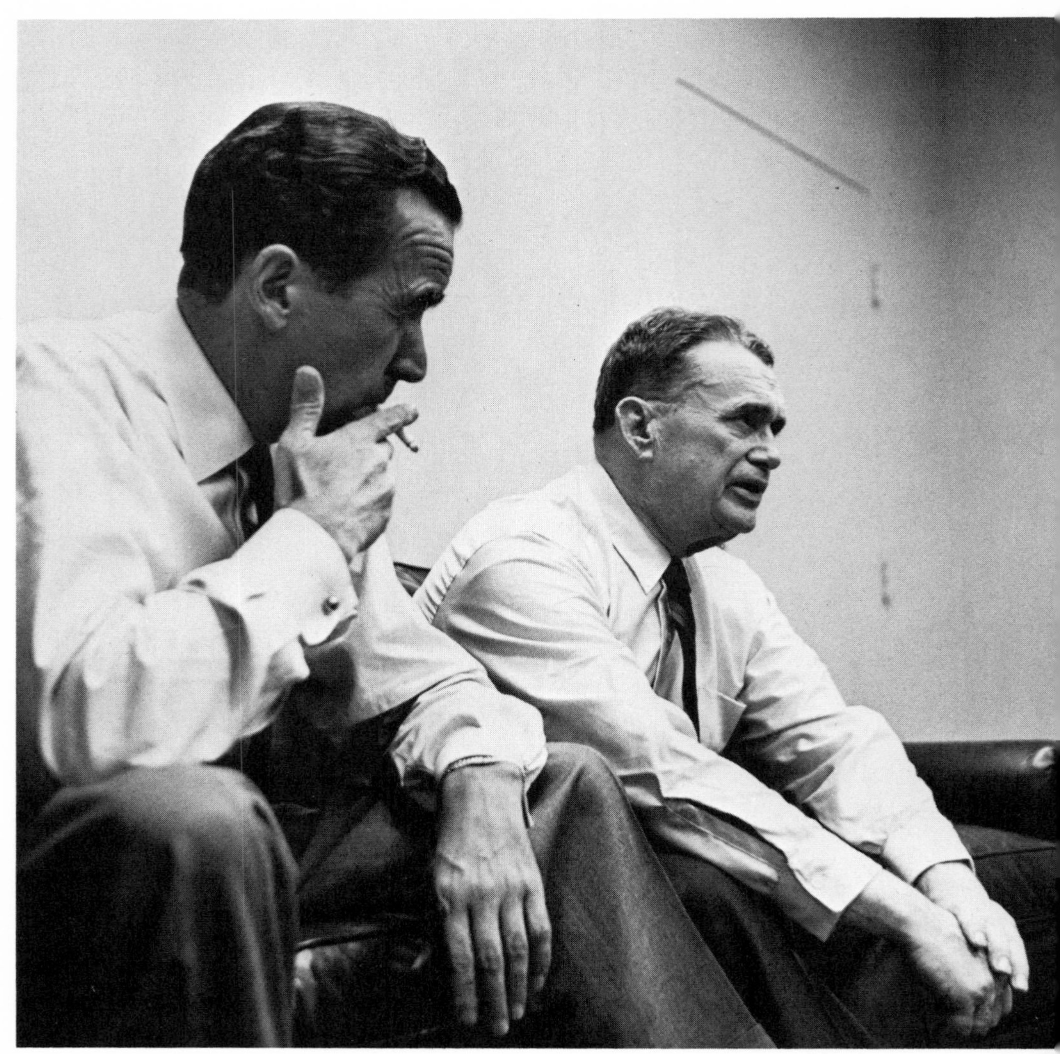

McGill is interviewed in his office by Ed Murrow, May 11, 1960, for a documentary on school desegregation for CBS (*Photo by Jerome Drown*)

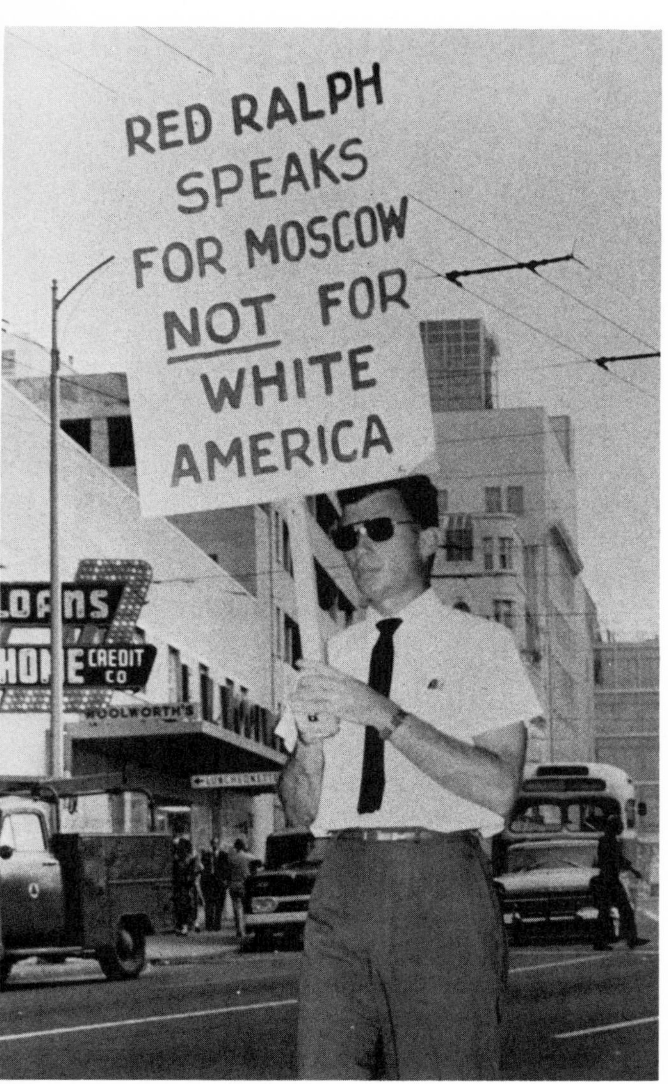

2 Pickets Blast Atlanta Papers, Publisher McGill

Two men picketed the offices of the *Atlanta Journal* and the *Atlanta Constitution* with signs accusing the papers and Publisher Ralph McGill of the *Constitution* of aiding communism.

The men said they were affiliated with the National White Americans Party. They carried placards reading "Red Ralph Speaks for Moscow, Not For White America" and "Atlanta Newspapers, Inc. aids Communism."

A third man passed out copies of a four-page publication, "The White American."

One of the pickets, Robert A. Bowling of Atlanta, charged that the Atlanta papers had given aid to the Communists by publishing reports of Russian Maj. Herman Titov orbiting the earth last weekend. "We have no proof, and we don't believe it's true," he said.

Police picked up one of the picketers when he refused to identify himself, but he later identified himself and was released without charge. He returned to the picket line.

Associated Press

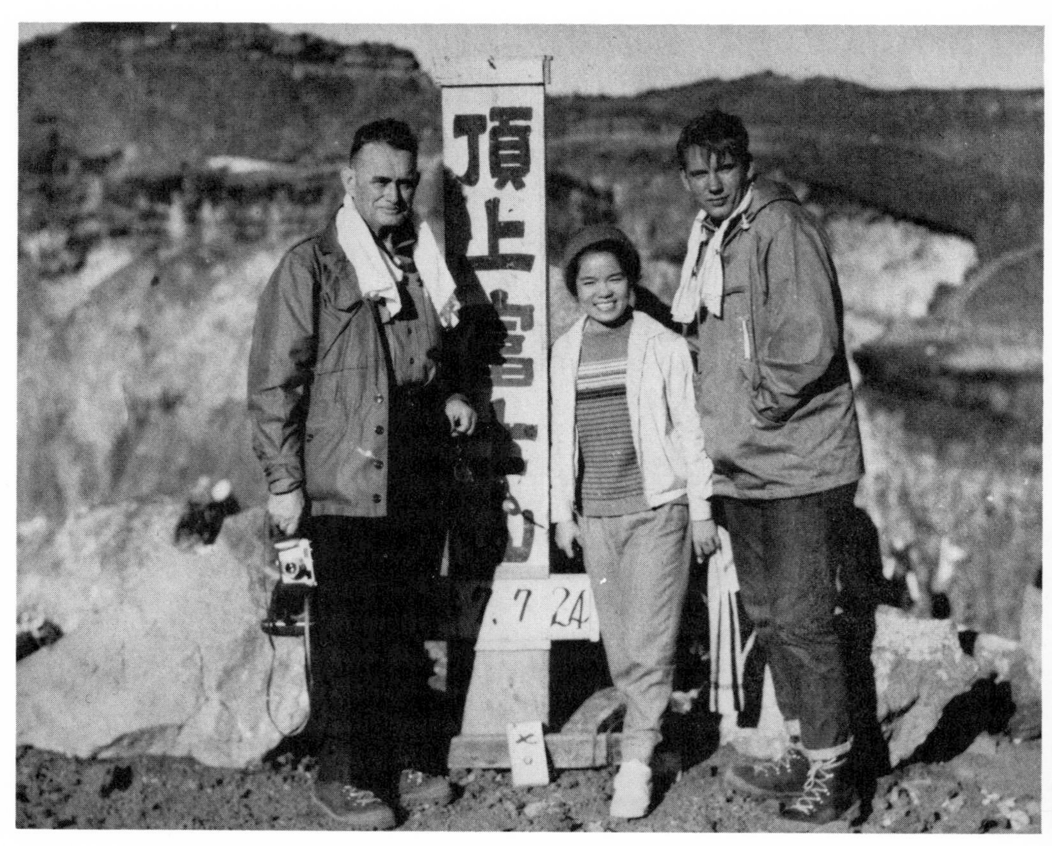

Top of Mt. Fuji, July 1962. Kimiko Kawata center, Ralph, Jr., right

Conferring with university students on a trip to West Africa, February 1963

Ralph and Mary Lynn McGill following their wedding, All Saints Church, Atlanta, April 20, 1967 (*Photo by Reeves*)

October 27, 1967. With President Johnson at the White House

With Grace Lundy – and hornet's nest (*Photo by Larry Keighley*)

Ralph McGill chatting with Spelman seniors following the commencement, at which Edward Weeks delivered the address. Judy Tillman, one of McGill's protégées, stands to his right (*Photo by Reeves*)

Early in December one new recognition came to lighten the gloom with which he usually greeted the holiday season. His Pulitzer Prize had been slow in coming, but in the year after its award, he was paid the honor of being named a member of the Pulitzer Prize Advisory Board, a committee of distinguished editors to whom the Pulitzer Prize juries submitted their choices for final approval. He brought to this task the breadth of his interest in the literary prizes, in the plays, books, and poems which the advisory board had to pass on in addition to journalism.

McGill, according to Barry Bingham, a fellow member of the committee, not only had read the many books recommended by the juries, he had read the reviews, both pro and con, and was able to give a balanced evaluation of the merits of a book. Once, Bingham remembered, a controversial novel was under discussion, and some board members were giving much weight to the less than flattering comments of a few of the reviewers. McGill gave a little talk in which he pointed out the particular sociological point of view from which most of the adverse criticism had come. He knew what other critics had said in favor of the book, and he balanced the hostile comments with these. The book won the Pulitzer.

In Bingham's view, this "beautiful sense of balance which rules his nature" was McGill's great virtue and the source of his strength, which made him hard to classify. He was neither "the wild-eyed radical betraying his homeland to the destroyer," as the KKK depicted him, nor "an Old Testament prophet scourging the South for its sins, as he was looked upon by his northern admirers." He was, said Bingham, "the reasoning, persuasive, unembittered son of the South, steeped in the traditions of his region, but never their prisoner. He was a free spirit."

McGill strove for a similar balance in his column, a change of pace that would not type him as a specialist in any particular field. In the spring of 1961 he was negotiating to have his column transferred to the Hall syndicate and he made a special effort to broaden his audience by shifting back and forth from serious to lighter matters. He wrote that President Kennedy's victory was due, no doubt, to his "consumption of generous portions of New England fish chowder, which kept him lively as a cricket, bright as a penny [McGill was not one to disdain the useful cliche], and seemingly ready for any emergency, physical and mental." Then followed a hard-hitting column decrying the idiocy of law and custom that would permit a clerk in a variety store to sell a Negro anything he wished to buy, but not to serve him a cup of coffee at a lunch counter. "A shoe store employee who can put a pair of shoes on a Negro's feet . . . would object to sitting beside him on a bus." After a humorous column about having a foxhound named for him he would speak of the sudden light that had dawned in the soul of Grand Dragon Bill Hendrix of the Southern Knights of the Ku Klux Klan, who after the dynamiting of the Atlanta school had told his followers: "I see no way to stop racial integration in the schools and it looks to me like the best thing to do is accept it. I cannot agree to go outside the law to maintain segregation. I can't agree to such things as bombing and burning schools." This, said McGill, was an honest statement and if adhered to, merited sincere recognition and commendation. "If Bill Hendrix, a relatively poor man whose opportunities for education and experience were somewhat limited, can find the courage to announce he is quitting the Klan because segregation has been held unconstitutional, what about the rest of us? What about governors, senators, legislators, tycoons of business, industry and the professions?"

The year of 1961 began with the kind of battle in which he took great delight. All over the South sentimentalists about the Confederacy were laying plans to celebrate the centennial of the Civil War. McGill, a sentimental man himself, thought that this was fine, provided that whatever was done taught one clear lesson — that the war was a piece of idiocy brought upon the nation by hotheaded extremists on both sides, and that it never should have been fought in the first place.

There is, he wrote, "ample reason to commemorate the conflict which brought an end to chattel slavery and made us a union in fact, beyond the power of legalistic, hairsplitting sophistry to destroy."

Articles, books, discussion groups and actions of commemoration which have purpose and dignity are excellent, he added.

Unhappily, though, "what we have now are increasing numbers of persons wandering about the South wearing sleazy imitations of Confederate uniforms, growing beards, renewing old hatreds, making ancient wounds bleed again, reviving Ku Klux Klans, working themselves into immature fits of emotionalism, re-creating old battles and otherwise doing a great disservice to the memory of those who died in the war of 1861–1865."

We do not need to refurbish old myths, he said, and he was particularly sardonic in his discussion of a contemplated replay of the Battle of Bull Run. He wondered, for example, "Will they show the carriages filled with congressmen and some of the more fancy ladies of pleasure who drove out from Washington in 1861 with hampers of picnic food and iced champagne to watch men die?"

It would, he said, add a touch of humor to report their pell-mell flight along the dusty roads with the rout of the federal army spilling along behind them.

> Some of the more than four thousand troops who died there that day, looking down from the ramparts of that Valhalla to which all good soldiers go, may be able to smile at this 1961 version of that hog-killing-like contact.
>
> But they will hardly laugh out loud.
>
> Most of those who fought there on that day were untrained youngsters in new, ill-fitting uniforms, and with new and little-understood muskets in their hand.
>
> What dignity or reward will there be in a schoolboy charade with popguns. . . . Once was enough.

Early in February McGill spent a week at Yale as a Chubb Fellow of Timothy Dwight College, a fellowship established by the family of his old friend Tom Chubb. His activities there were of such pace and variety that he reported feeling like a trained seal: he barked willingly, however, and at such length that he became hoarse. Thomas G. Bergen, master of Timothy Dwight, remembered that he kept apologizing for his loquacity. "We would not have it any other way," said the master, "for we fell in love with him at first sight." At Yale Ralph made candid acknowledgment of the fact that he at one time had held out firmly for segregation in the schools. "I finally had to be honest with myself. I had to admit that Negroes have not been allowed to participate in their developing country. They have been deprived so long . . . and we are paying the price for the continued denial of their rights."

Already, however, McGill was beginning to warn of the danger in seeking to secure their rights by violent means. Quiet sit-ins, marches and demonstrations had his full approval. But violence from the left could no more be condoned than that from the right. Here too, though, he could understand the emotions of the violent. Speaking at De Paul University in Chicago he struck out at the extremists in the civil rights movement, the Carmichaels and the fomenters of riots. Then he added, "The civil rights movement is not Communist directed or controlled, but when 'good people' remain aloof from the great issues of the day, when they fail to speak out against human suffering and injustice, they invite and make possible the participation of the radical left."

Later in the spring, when the Freedom Rides in Alabama were met with a declaration of martial law and one thousand white Alabamians rioted around a church where Martin Luther King, Jr., was trying to speak, McGill wrote:

> The Christian church may not be comfortable if it notes one aspect of the story that not a single white church congregation has held a protest meeting at this obvious and flagrant interference with public worship.
>
> Let the South — and the nation — look well. There are just two paths to take. One is that of law. The other is that of mobs, brutality, attempted murder, tear gas and troops. There is no way to pass by, like the Pharisee, on the other side.
>
> The Freedom Rides, like the sit-ins, dramatized a simple moral issue — the right of a citizen to buy a ticket on a bus or train and ride freely from state to state, sitting in any seat he pleases. The South must ask itself — are its states foreign nations? Do not the laws of the United States apply?

Ever since the Supreme Court decision, Georgia and the South had been fighting stubborn rearguard actions to protect the all-white school. Court cases backed by sit-ins, marches, Freedom Rides and boycotts had slowly chipped away at segregation in the trains and buses and trolleys, in waiting rooms, on the golf courses, and at the lunch counters of restaurants. But Georgia's schools still stood, white and unsullied, behind their ancient walls of segregation.

The year after the school decision, candidate Ernest Vandiver, in his campaign for lieutenant governor, had sworn to go to jail before bowing to the edicts from the courts. Elected governor four years later, he had sworn that "no, not one" Negro would be allowed to enter a Georgia school. Then, on January 11, 1961, two young, attractive, intelligent and courageous Negroes, Hamilton Holmes and Charlayne Hunter, armed with a court order, showed up at the University of Georgia requesting admission.

Later that summer, as he received an honorary Doctor of Laws degree from Harvard, McGill, in an address before the Harvard Law School and Graduate School alumni, described in detail that landmark event in Georgia's legal and social history.

At first there was a comic-opera quality about the whole episode, with lawyers in fast automobiles, representing both the students and the state, racing at high speed over the highways from Athens to the Federal District Court one hundred miles south in Macon, Georgia, seeking a stay of the court's order, and racing at equal speed from there to the Appellate Court, an equal distance away in Atlanta. While this old-time movie chase was going on, there was one night of violence on the university campus in which a thousand students, led by outsiders, rioted outside Miss Hunter's dormitory.

The Negro students were formally admitted, and there were some students who did make them welcome. Governor Vandiver, who had once sworn to go to jail before compliance, now announced painfully, "I will not defy the law."

The only alternative to admitting the students was to close the university, and by now phone calls and telegrams were pouring into the governor's office, and into the state legislature, urging that this not be done. If this had been some county school, the reaction might have been different. But the university occupied a special place in the hearts of all Georgians. The gist of the messages was resigned acceptance. "We don't like what has happened. But above all, don't close the school."

The floor leader of the Georgia House announced that the voice of the people had been heard. Of six hundred letters he had received, only twelve wanted the university closed. Quietly, the general assembly began abolishing all the laws designed to maintain segregation that had been so hastily passed in the last few years on the advice of the state's "constitutional experts."

That summer three black students, without protest, were accepted at the Georgia Institute of Technology. In the Atlanta public school system that fall, ten black students entered high school. There was no violence. A half-dozen young would-be agitators showed up at one school, but were quickly arrested, tried, and given thirty days.

This was a beginning. In years to come there would be conflict over busing and pupil placement and teacher assignments in schools making the traumatic shift to black and white, but the start had been made.

McGill, in his Harvard address, pointed out that the action of the governor and of the Georgia legislature marked a turning point, not only for Georgia, but in the Deep South pattern of pledged total defiance. The days of saying "never" and "no, not one" were over:

> There is reason for feeling that the racial climate of the South is changing. The most encouraging moment was watching the great play of the American process when the umbrella of the Constitution was raised over those two students . . . and when the forces seeking to deny them were cut down by orderly processes of law, when the state legislature reversed itself and admitted defeat on its position and the governor accepted it, it was a high moment.

McGill was speaking to many lawyers, and in his speech he took the lawyers of the South and their bar associations to the woodshed for having advised southern governors and political leaders that segregation could be maintained in defiance of the Supreme Court.

It was not necessary, he pointed out — lecturing them as he had lectured his old friend Charles Bloch — that the lawyers should agree with the Court's decision. But it was necessary, if the nation was to avoid anarchy and chaos, for them to defend the integrity of the federal judiciary and the right and duty of the Supreme Court to interpret the Constitution. The failure of southern lawyers to do so had resulted in the long years of fruitless legal maneuvering that had ended when Governor Vandiver had announced, "I will not defy the law."

McGill's award of the Doctor of Law from Harvard inspired his old friend Laurence Winship of the *Boston Globe* to send his star reporter, Charles Whipple, to Atlanta to do a capsule biography of McGill. It ran a full page and a half in the Sunday *Globe*, a perceptive, warmly written and friendly piece which caused McGill to write Whipple: "Dear Charlie: It was the smoothest whitewash job since Tom Sawyer's back fence."

Gene Patterson disagreed. In a memo to McGill he said, "Whipple didn't overstate it a bit. Seeing it all put down together makes me realize what a hell of a guy you are. It also reminded me of just how good Babe Ruth was." McGill's answer, scribbled at the bottom of the memo, was "While we Harvard men do not indulge in slang, permit me to say NUTS. You have taken hold in a hell of a fine way. You are further along at your age than I ever thought of being. Don't forget, I'm getting along. You are accepted and known in a fine manner, much better than I was at a comparable time."

At the commencement exercises Ralph was much interested in the solemn protocol of the ceremony: "Mr. Sheriff, pray give us order," and the archaic phrasing by which the degrees were awarded. Bachelors degrees in the arts and sciences, he noted, "admit you to the fellowship of educated men and women." The doctorates in philosophy and science "welcome you to the ancient and universal company of scholars." In medicine the doctorate indicates the recipient "ready to engage in an honorable and merciful calling." In theology: "You are well prepared to help men to know and love God." To graduates in law: "You are ready to aid in the shaping of those restraints which make men free."

The Harvard citation for him said simply: "In a troubled time his steady voice of reason champions a New South."

Arthur Schlesinger, Jr., told McGill, "Harvard has honored you and honored itself by placing its brand on you."

McGill, mindful of the trek of Harvard graduates to White House jobs, answered amiably, "I am now eligible for federal employment."

McGill always referred to his Harvard honors with humorous deprecation — noting the citation received from the Cooks, Waiters and Bartenders Union was longer and more flowery. But when the notice of the Harvard award arrived some months before the event, with the stern admonition that it be kept in strictest secrecy until publicly announced, he felt a pride he found hard to conceal at being accepted in such an honorable company of scholars — and after the event, it was noted that he always wore the black and crimson tie and drank his office coffee out of a huge cup bearing the Harvard seal.

A few days after the graduation Winship wrote to Grace Lundy in Atlanta:

As you would know, Ralph and Mary Elizabeth warmed the hearts of everyone who came near them in Cambridge. With all the ponderous scholars and their wives, Mrs. McGill was a breath of warm charm, and Dr. McGill, the unknown character from way down South, got the heartiest hand of all from the thousands who saw him get his honorary degree.

Mary Elizabeth was frozen most of the time, and went around with a heavy coat that looked like a horse blanket, loaned by a professor's wife, and with a shawl, and sitting in our backyard last night with a steamer robe wrapped around her legs. But she won them all.

What Winship could not know, for nobody knew except McGill and his wife's doctor, was that Mary Elizabeth McGill was dying. This trip to the Harvard commencement was the last journey for "The Lady Who Travels With Me" of McGill's columns. A little more than a year earlier, in the parking lot at Emory University Hospital late at night, Dr. Joseph Wilber, a big, soft-spoken Irishman, had told Ralph the bad news. The long battle against kidney disease she had so bravely fought all her life — her first attack was at the age of three — had been lost. The malignant hypertension so often associated with chronic kidney disease now had her in its grip. With the best of care, she could live for perhaps two years. Untreated, she would die within a month or two.

The treatment was begun — powerful doses of ganglionic blocking drugs which left the patient weak and subject to fainting spells. Her kidney function improved, her inner eye, which had shown the white patches that are the mark of malignant hypertension, began to clear up. She went home and took up again the church work that made her happiest. She fainted now and then, but would get up laughing and go on.

McGill did everything to help. She was on a no-salt diet, so, to share her misery, he refused to take salt on his food at home. To put a gourmet cook on a no-salt diet, he held, was cruel and inhuman punishment, and every time he took a trip he came back with some new kind of vegetable substitute for salt.

For almost two years she stayed on, going hard, enjoying life, drawing, her doctor felt, on some inner resources of spiritual strength that were more powerful than his medicine. But increasing slowly was the uremic poisoning, bringing with it the weakness, the anemia, the cold slowing of the life processes that had caused her to bundle herself in coat and shawl on a mild June night in Cambridge.

In December 1961, she went into Piedmont Hospital. On the early morning of March 21, 1962, a little more than two years after Dr. Joe Wilber first told McGill there was no hope, she died, quietly and without pain.

For all these last months, McGill was with her day and night, sitting in a corner of her room, reading, or writing his columns in longhand on a yellow pad and putting together the last chapters of the book that was to be published a year later, the prizewinning *The South and the Southerner.*

14

Ralph McGill, Jr., was seventeen when his mother died. McGill himself was sixty-four. For the first months after her passing his main thought was how to ease the blow for the boy; it was as if he felt a sense of guilt at having so often left his family alone as he made his long journeys overseas. The afternoon of Mary Elizabeth's funeral, he and young Ralph boarded a plane for Miami. There, as guests of Bill Baggs, editor of the *Miami Daily News,* they walked on the beach, lay in the sun, fished, and managed for a little while to forget the long, drawn-out anguish of Mary Elizabeth's dying.

Later, back in Atlanta, McGill would get up and fix breakfast for both of them, and to keep the youngster from coming home to an empty house, he would leave the office early. Some evenings Julia, the cook, would serve their dinner. More often, she would leave it on the stove, needing only to be heated and served. Father and son would eat together, with awkward silences at first, but afterward talking more easily, about school and books and how to write haiku and the virtues of football as a character builder. Now and then young Ralph would take down his guitar and play for his dad, who would try to sing in his harsh, rasping and unmusical voice. After dinner they would do the dishes; then, in the pleasant, book-lined room that was kitchen, dining room and den, McGill in his easy chair would read or write and Ralph, at the kitchen table, would study until bedtime.

Unfortunately, such nights were rare. Young Ralph was courting a girl in a town some twenty miles away, and he much preferred going to her house each night to play the guitar and study. Often he did not come in until two A.M. and McGill would toss restlessly, staying awake until he heard the car tires crunch on the gravel of the turnaround. The worst times were the weekends, when sometimes the boy did not come home at all, telephoning to say that he was spending the night with a friend. McGill, seeking counsel from friends who were also the parents of love-struck teen-agers, would thrash about in his chair and clear his throat and say, "Look, I know I'm behaving like an old hen with one chick, but what do you do? . . ." It was particularly troubling to him that he who could so quickly establish rapport with other youngsters could not reach the same level of understanding with his own.

Young Ralph, too, was sensitive. "Julia," he recalled, "was like a second mother to me. She was there before I was born; she looked after me all during my growing up, when my father was away and my mother was ill. So, Dad turned to her for help. She'd say, as if it were her own idea, that I ought to stay home with him more. And I would try. But I was seventeen, and much in love. So he tried another tack. He'd lay on little dinners at the house for my girl and me. Julia was a great cook and on weekends, he'd insist I have friends over to eat and play guitars and listen to records.

"But nothing did much good. Except for a few evenings my dad and I, then and for a few years thereafter, were strangers. No matter how we tried, we could not break through that barrier of years, of shyness, whatever it was, that kept us apart."

Young Ralph, taller and heavier than his dad, but not an athlete, was little like him in temperament. Bright enough, he found books boring and his lack of interest in the things of the mind kept his father in a perpetual state of anxiety during his last year at Westminster for fear he would not graduate. This would have been particularly embarrassing, since the senior McGill was to deliver the commencement address. Happily, though, despite McGill's fears, young Ralph made it and at the urging of the headmaster planned to go on to Wesleyan in the autumn

Said young Ralph:

I remember sitting there feeling proud that it was my dad up there making the commencement speech, because over the years I'd had to punch up a lot of those kids for calling him a Communist, and other things. But it was warm and I dozed off and didn't wake up again until he got to "Ulysses." I'd heard him speak at other graduations, and he always ended with the line about seeking a newer world and following knowledge like a sinking star, and seeking, striving and not yielding.

The graduation exercises were on Saturday and as they proceeded, the thought drifted into McGill's mind that on Sunday he'd do a humorous column about the father of a teen-age son who was in love and flunking Latin and scaring his Dad to death for fear he'd not graduate from prep school. The title would be "Don't Sweat It, Dad."

The column was never written. Early on Sunday morning his phone rang, bringing news of a cruel tragedy. A few hours earlier, at Orly Airfield outside of Paris, a heavily laden Air France charter plane, bearing one hundred and twenty-one Atlantans who had been in Europe on a tour of the art galleries and museums, had crashed and burned with no survivors. He had known nearly all of those aboard the plane, and six of them had been close friends. Out of his grief and faith he composed one of the most difficult statements of his career; he and the staff worked on the memorial edition until 2:30 A.M. Monday morning, he was up again at 6:30 to fly to Chapel Hill to deliver the commencement address at the University of North Carolina. The exercises were held in the stadium, and as the solemn processional filed in a gentle rain began to fall. By the time McGill rose to speak it had increased to a downpour.

The water dripped from his head, ran down his face, soaked his manuscript. Now and then he would ad lib a bit of humor. The rain at last had demonstrated a practical use for the mortarboard, he said, and it was too bad that custom demanded that the speaker doff his. This got a laugh. He also reminded the audience that the speech would not be as dry as it might have been. When, in the inevitable quote from "Ulysses," he got to the line, "It may be the gulfs will wash us down," he had to restrain an impulse to break the mood of Tennyson's poem by adding — "It seems they have already."

After it was over McGill went back to the chancellor's house, changed to dry clothes, and was driven one hundred and sixty-five miles to Charlotte to catch a plane for Atlanta. A young reporter for the *Charlotte Observer* rode with him. Ralph's voice was hoarse and rasping, his hair still wet from the downpour. His eyes were deep-sunken and he was hugely tired. Four hours sleep last night and tonight he would get only four hours more. His talk to the reporter on the long ride was of the plane crash: "There's a great sense of unreality about it. Your mind won't take it in. It's not like watching somebody who's been sick a long time slowly die. . . . It's a new sort of death. It does not fit the image of death."

His column had spoken of faith as the only comforting answer to the "Why?" of so great a tragedy. His thoughts in the night and the rain were more pragmatic.

"People are saying, 'Why did God let such a thing happen?' Others are saying, 'It's God's will. I will accept it.'

"I don't agree with either one of these viewpoints. . . . I don't think the theologians do, except the sterner fundamentalists. I don't think it was God's will. It was just a violation of natural laws . . . of the laws of aerial dynamics."

Damp, hollow-eyed and rumpled, at 2 A.M. he fell in bed in a motel across from the airport in Charlotte. At 5:45 he was up again, and flying to Atlanta, where at Morehouse College that morning he and President Pusey of Harvard were to be given honorary degrees.

During Mary Elizabeth McGill's last illness Ralph's friend, Dr. Benjamin Mays, the distinguished president of Morehouse, had written Ralph asking permission to put his name before the board. McGill suspected there might be reverberations if he accepted honors from a Negro university — but the hell with it. He and Benny Mays had fought the wars together, since the founding of the Southern Regional Council nearly two decades before.

The citation for his degree of Doctor of Humanities was eloquent, its theme — "You told the people the truth" — ending, "at the risk of losing social prestige, friends and even life . . . you revealed to the world what America is, at its best. . . ."

As he stood up to receive the honor, the cheering, clapping and stomping from the crowd was thunderous, and it went on and on. President Pusey, a veteran of many commencements, told McGill he had never in all his experience seen such a demonstration.

Not long before the Morehouse commencement McGill had had a letter from the Asian Foundation, asking him if he would go to Japan for a series of seminars with Japanese newspaper and university people.

He turned them down politely, explaining that his son would be leaving for college in the fall, and he wanted to spend these last few months with him.

The secretary of the Asian Foundation was pleasant, but insistent. Why not take young Ralph along? If finances were a consideration, he could turn in the first-class plane ticket the foundation would provide, exchanging it for two economy-fare seats. The difference would easily be covered by his honorarium, and in Japan the twenty-five-dollar-a-day expense allowance would be ample for them both.

To McGill, this idea had great appeal. He could see a part of the world he had never seen before. He would have a month alone with his son, and by juggling the tickets around, the expense would not be too great.

(Actually, McGill, who always assumed that because he was a newspaperman he would always live just one jump ahead of the sheriff, was better off financially than he realized. At Tarver's insistence he had changed syndicates, his columns were now appearing in fifty-four papers, and his income from the syndicate, plus his publisher's salary and fees for speaking was in excess of fifty thousand dollars a year.) Shortly before his takeoff for Japan, he wrote to Larry Winship:

> Young Ralph now has his first passport, which he took rather casually. This always astonishes me. Coming, as I did, from a farm and out of a background of childhood dreams about one day seeing the ocean, and traveling, I find myself continually nonplussed about this rather sophisticated acceptance of things. As a matter of fact, though, two or three of my friends have told me that he has talked to them and is really very excited about the trip. I suppose he just doesn't want his father to think he is very excited. He is now in a period of wanting to be very grown-up. . . .
>
> He's courting a very nice sixteen-year-old-girl quite heavily, and I will be relieved when he gets off for Wesleyan. President Pusey tells me Wesleyan is a very fine school, where President Butterfield has assembled about the finest lot of teachers to be found in any of the liberal arts colleges. He told me: "Your son will get unusually fine teaching." My only hope is that my son can take it.

As for his own situation, McGill reported, he was keeping himself busier than usual. "The adjustment continues difficult, but we are making progress." Already he had received one piece of news that had done much to lift his spirits. The manuscript he had been writing, in longhand, as he sat with Mary Elizabeth in her hospital room had won the five-thousand-dollar *Atlantic* Nonfiction Prize. The book — *The South and the Southerner* — would be published in the spring, and he expressed the hope that it would not fall on its face.

He hadn't had any real hope of winning the *Atlantic* prize, he said, but "I felt something like the story told of Lincoln when somebody asked him if he thought he'd receive the nomination in 1860. He replied, 'I don't have much hope, but I have the taste of it in my mouth.' "

Into this book he had poured heart and spirit, writing and rewriting to find the exact phrase to express the anger and compassion, the hope and understanding, the wisdom he had gained in a lifetime of more than six decades.

The trip to Japan marked the end of the sad, troubled period of restless half-mourning. It became one of the exciting experiences of his long career, the climax of it a climb with young Ralph to the top of Mt. Fuji, accompanied by a guide, a onetime Japanese submariner whose two-man suicide torpedo craft ran aground at the Battle of Midway, where he was captured. Also along was a tiny and personable young Japanese lady named Kimiko Kawato, known as Kim, "sent along by the Japanese newspaper publishers and editors association to summon medical aid in case I should collapse," McGill explained.

At the rest station after the first day's climb the young submariner, being aglow with Asahi beer, asked McGill, seemingly in all seriousness, to please postpone any heart attack he was thinking of having until he had left the mountain. It would be very bad for his reputation as a Fuji guide to have McGill expire on him. McGill was not sure whether this was a joke, or *in vino veritas*, until the next day.

The young man was not joking. The last five hundred feet to Fuji's peak is a bare rocky slope, very steep, up which the climbers toil by a zigzag path. Even young legs buckle on this last agonizing push to the top, and McGill's legs were no longer young. The last few steps Kim actually pushed him from behind, urging "Please, Papa, just one more step," until he finally stood at the crest, sweating, freezing, his breath coming in great gasps in the twelve-thousand-foot altitude. He was utterly exhausted, but feeling a great sense of exaltation.

He wrote afterward:

> One stands there, legs trembling, lungs laboring, and turns to wait for the sun. The dark awesome slopes of the old mountain already are softening in the growing light. The eastern sky suddenly blurs crimson. The flaming edge of the sun appears, causing the whole sky to turn rosy, then a deeper vermilion, as the round disc of day rises above the horizon. . . . It's a scene worth the climb. Shouts go up. Tired, grimy faces, streaked with the dark volcanic dust, are rapt.

The news that McGill was in Japan climbing mountains with a young Japanese lady caused a great flurry of correspondence between Harry Golden, Bill Baggs, Harry Ashmore and Adlai Stevenson, who was now the United States ambassador to the United Nations. Golden started it, with a communiqué to Ambassador Stevenson, with copies to Ashmore and Baggs, and of course, to McGill. It informed Stevenson that Sander Vanocur had reported from Tokyo that McGill not only had climbed Mt. Fuji with a lady, he had been spending a great deal of time in the steam baths being laved by giggling Japanese maidens.

McGill, in a letter to Stevenson, pointed out that he had had similar letters from Baggs and Ashmore, as well as Golden, and they were all canards.

"All three of them seem disturbed because my son and I climbed Mt. Fuji," he told Stevenson. "This is very easy for me to understand. These critics could never do better than lift one foot as high as a barroom rail. Naturally, it disturbs them to read about someone climbing Mt. Fuji."

He admitted that a young Japanese lady, age twenty-three, had made the journey with them. "She is a very attractive young lady and caused me to wish that I were twenty-five again, and caused my son of seventeen to wish that he were twenty-three."

Ambassador Stevenson replied graciously that he was greatly relieved to know that Golden was misinformed and misinforming about McGill's alleged exploits with Japanese ladies. However, he added, whatever services the ladies had performed for McGill — "I wonder if you think they would do it again? I think I am leaving for Japan presently . . ."

McGill answered with a picture of himself, Ralph, Jr., and Kim, standing on the edge of Fuji's crater. "I chose this position," he wrote, "because I seem to have spent most of my life standing on the edge of craters. There were no 'young ladies' involved, there was only one charming young lady who accompanied us. She does not scrub backs. She is a graduate of the University of Tokyo, and her hobby is translating Japanese haiku poems into French."

He came home from Japan feeling a great affection for Masaaki Kasagi, his newspaperman host there, and especially for Kim. The American male has proved particularly susceptible to the bright charm of Japanese women, and McGill was no exception.

As he was leaving, he told her: "If I were thirty years younger, Kimiko, I would ask you to marry me."

"If you should ask me, Papa," she said, "I would say yes."

Both were smiling and it was, of course, idle banter. But neither ever forgot . . .

With Mary Elizabeth gone and young Ralph away at Wesleyan, McGill's mood was one of restlessness. A prolonged stretch of dieting and abstinence had brought his weight down from his normal two hundred twenty-five to one hundred eighty-seven, and he was beginning to look drawn and bony. With the loss of weight had come a growing tension. In the lonely little house sleep would not come, and though his annual physical checkup continued to show the pattern that was normal for him — a slower pulse beat and a slightly lower blood pressure than was normal for other men — he told his doctor that, though he was on no medication of any kind, he felt more and more as if he was under the influence of some stimulating drug.

McGill's friends, who had always looked upon him, the trencherman and tippler, with mingled feelings of admiration, amusement and anxiety, now began to worry about the tense, sober and dieting McGill. "Don't lay in any booze for me," he wrote friends in Hawaii on the eve of a visit there. "I've reached the point where even one drink makes me feel bad for twenty-four hours."

Noting his new mood, Harry Ashmore wrote a friend: "His nerves are twanging like plucked harp strings, and he seems to feel things are crawling on him." One observer remarked that McGill looked exhausted. "Hell," said Jim Fain of the *Dayton News*. "McGill always looks exhausted."

His restlessness was reflected in an almost frenetic travel schedule, and one which, incidentally, got him in trouble with the Department of Internal Revenue. He was moving so far, so fast, throughout the first seven months of 1963 he found no time in which to file his tax returns.

In January, he was speaking in Michigan, attending a dinner for Carl Sandburg in New York, and sitting in on meetings of the Fund for the Advancement of Education. All of February and early March he was in Africa on a mission for the State Department, speaking before student groups in Senegal, Guinea, Mali, Ghana, Nigeria, Togo, Dahomey and the Congo. His mission was to put into perspective, for nations feeling the first strong stirrings of independence — and rapidly becoming infected with Communism — the new pattern of race relations in America, particularly in the American South. Ignoring the heat, and the occasional hostility, he worked tirelessly, talking with students and journalists and cabinet ministers.

Marx B. Lewis, his State Department host in Ghana, wrote:

> He never complained. He always asked what more he could do. He was exuberant and enthusiastic every minute of the day and night, and more importantly, perhaps, his honesty, integrity, sincerity and professionalism came through in all of his remarks. This had an effect on Ghanaians and even the virulent and polemic anti-American editors . . . acknowledged to me privately, "He is a good man."

McGill held a news conference which he shared with Cozy Cole, a Negro jazz drummer then performing in Ghana. "The Ghana press threw every question imaginable at them, mainly about race relations," Lewis recalled, "and the southern newspaper editor and the black jazz drummer carried the day with their straightforwardness and humor." Years afterward, McGill always brought up this press conference whenever he saw Lewis. "Wasn't that a hell of an exciting day? Cozy was wonderful."

Ralph was not one to load himself down with tourist knickknacks as mementos of far places, but one thing he brought home from Africa held for him a repulsive fascination. It was an antique necklace made up of porcelain segments like bits of broken, many-colored pipestems. It was given to him by United States Ambassador William Attwood at the embassy residence in Conakry, Guinea, and the curator of the National Museum certified that it was used in the West African slave trade. McGill had it mounted for display, with a note that "at one time, these beads were the full or part purchase price of a human being."

Travel always made him feel better, and he came home from his African trip in mellow mood, writing to Ashmore and Baggs in facetious vein, accusing them of apostasy to the southern cause and chiding them for their failure to cling to the faith of their fathers, the conviction that the African is an inferior race. One night in the remote, lonely old city of Zarin, he said, he had heard the talking drums speaking to him. They told him that in the tropical regions of California and Florida, where men and morals decay, there were two men who had deserted their southern heritage. The message recommended that he buy some sort of African robes which would hide the black hearts of these traitors to the Old South. This was done in the market at Accra and in due time, he said, the robes would be forwarded. A little later, he was writing that the robes, or smocks, were on the way, explaining that they were "the only raiment worn by the virile, untutored men of the northern tribes of Nigeria and Ghana. To see them striding along the road carrying a spear or a rifle is to see one of nature's noblemen, unconfined by conformity — or anything else."

Ashmore's thank-you note was ribald. The smock would cover his heart well enough, he indicated, but it was so short it would cover little else. "It may be all right for you who are handicapped," he wrote McGill, "but it clearly is not for us sash-weight types. The sentiment, however, is deeply appreciated, and I am sure it will come in handy sooner or later — say the next time I am guest of honor at a castration."

The publication of *The South and the Southerner* a few days after his return from Africa and meetings of President Kennedy's Committee on Labor and Management policy and of the President's Advisory Committee of the Arms Control and Disarmament Agency, set him off on another session of hard travel.

He had expressed the hope that *The South and the Southerner* "would not fall on its face." It did not. It was well received, especially in the

South, Atlanta alone purchasing over four thousand copies. "I kept nodding in agreement and recognition," a reader wrote. Edward Weeks called it "the most telling and noble book I have read about the South in my time." Harry Ashmore, in an article for the *Virginia Quarterly*, skeched a deft portrait of his old friend:

> McGill is more a preacher than anything else. Through the long season of the South's travail, his eloquent appeal to the conscience of his readers, well larded with hellfire-and-brimstone denunciation of their prejudice, has provided one of the noblest chapters in the history of American journalism. But he is also a troubadour, a social historian, and, when the occasion demands, a political fixer. His age is that of the century, but the scars of his many battles have not diminished the sense of wonder he brought with him from the hills of east Tennessee. . . ."

Promoting the book kept McGill traveling hard throughout the summer. Day after day he kept grinding out the columns — lap columns, he called them, written in longhand on yellow pads as he sat in planes or in airport waiting rooms and mailed wherever he touched ground, or dictated without notes to Grace Lundy over the telephone. They continued, as always, to be of infinite variety.

James C. Townsend, in a profile on McGill for *Atlanta Magazine*, said of him, "He is an emotional writer, and he writes most beautifully on those things which move him deeply. The fact is, however, that about everything moves McGill."

One thing that moved McGill to feelings of both anxiety and compassion was the stubborn campaign of nonviolent protest by Dr. Martin Luther King. The news that Dr. King was changing his headquarters to Atlanta had caused McGill concern, for fear Dr. King would stir up the Georgia legislature, then in session. In the spring of 1963, King moved on Birmingham with prayer meetings and sit-ins and peaceful demonstrations, to which Police Commissioner Bull Connor responded with police dogs, cattle prods and mass arrests.

McGill was in New York, attending a meeting of the Carnegie Foundation, at which methods of alleviating world tensions were under discussion, when the trouble started in Birmingham. In a special story for the *New York Herald Tribune*, he wrote that he "felt an occasional, near compulsive wish to break suddenly into loud despairing laughter.

Birmingham was smoking with hate . . . and the tensions there . . . were as real as those in Vienna or Berlin." Now and then, he said, he would leave his Carnegie meeting and its world problems and go to the phone, call his office in Atlanta, and ask, "In God's name, what is happening now?"

He then went on to trace the history of Birmingham. It was, he said, never an Old South city wrapped in crinoline and lace, but a brawling industrial town born of coal, iron ore and limestone. Its working population consisted of white and black sharecroppers transferred from farm to mine and mill, and all their fears and prejudices were transferred with them. Here in this fiercely combative city the unions had won their place, and the Negro, by CIO demand, had won his place in the unions — but it was a place in the back row of the hiring hall, where he never raised his voice. Birmingham, McGill said, was Bull Connor's town, and George Wallace's town, the white man's town all the way — and the Birmingham newspapers and the churches and the politicians and industrialists were content that this was so.

Now, the Reverend Dr. King had challenged this control. Not with guns, not with dynamite, not with violence, but with prayer. There were those Negroes who did not like this. They felt that Dr. King should have waited.

"There has been enough of waiting," said McGill.

The Black Muslims, an extremist group pledged to destroy the white man, hated Dr. King, McGill said, for his preaching love instead of hate, passive resistance instead of fire and sword.

"One of these days," McGill wrote, "the South, even Birmingham, will be grateful to Dr. King. Had a real hater — a Black Muslim — come along with Dr. King's power of speech and personality, the South long ago would have been bloodstained. The South is lucky to have Dr. King."

He touched on the same theme in later columns, when television and the press were beginning to present the fulminations of the more militant Negroes:

> The . . . Southerner knows that historically Negroes have been the kindest, the most generous, grateful and patient subjected group the world has ever seen. The American Negroes are trying for a chance to be

Americans and to live like Americans. . . . Even the younger, more driven and excited ones who gave the interrogating reporter some quotes neither he nor the average Southerner has ever heard before from "Negroes," is basically so very decent and nice and cooperative when you play fair with him. . . . This is the big picture. They don't want the Black Muslims any more than they want George Wallace or Bull Connor.

Birmingham, McGill said, was a special, ugly roadblock in the Negro's drive to be more, not less an American. It grew uglier still. In September 1963, a Negro Baptist Church was dynamited at the Sunday school hour. Four children were killed and twenty injured.

From then on the word "southern moderate," which McGill had once considered himself, took on for him a new and bitter meaning. Stirred by the killing of the children, a Trappist monk from the monastery at nearby Conyers sent him a Latin phrase which he took as a text for a column in which he revealed, though not in so many words, that he no longer thought of himself as a "moderate" in the new meaning the word had acquired. The phrase the monk had sent him — *Qui tacet consentire videtur* — meant "He who is silent is understood to consent." This, he declared, had destroyed the orginal meaning of the word "moderate" as applied to a southerner and his attitudes on racial matters. Silence had become the mark of the southern moderate.

"The word no longer has its former validity," he wrote. "Moderate now means to remain silent, to avoid controversy, to make no commitment, to avoid affirming belief in principle."

Here and there, he pointed out, in the days since the Supreme Court decision there were a few persons, acting as "moderates" in the true meaning of the word, who had moved from the sidelines into action, trying to save the schools, obey the law, and prevent violence.

They found themselves cursed by phone and letter and looked at askance by many of their church congregations and friends. . . . By acting as moderates, in the deep meaning of the word, they found themselves labeled as immoderates. By and large, the so-called moderates in business, in professions, in editorial offices, in education, have remained carefully silent and aloof.

In this column, which was a powerful attack on the Black Muslims as well as the White Citizens' Councils, he spoke out harshly:

So now, after the bombing of schools, temples, churches, homes and motels, comes the dynamiting of a crowded Sunday school where Negro children reading the lesson of the forgiveness of love were killed or maimed. . . . A few resolutions have been adopted. Expressions of horror and regret have been made. And silence falls again.

But tomorrow and tomorrow and tomorrow will creep into our petty pace. . . .

And until the "moderates" and the great body of Christianity make up their minds whether by their silence they give consent to the White Citizens' Councils or the dynamiters, we shall continue to trample out the bitter vintage where the grapes of wrath are stored.

Hereafter, McGill struck out harder and harder. Two libel suits, one for ten million dollars directed against him and the *Constitution*, caused him many sleepless nights before they were thrown out of court. They taught him to be extremely wary of accusing any individual in his column, for he knew well a southern jury would like nothing better than to clobber him with a heavy judgment. But his campaign against the hatemongers on both sides of the fence grew in intensity.

Whether Ralph was flaying the Citizens' Councils and the Black Muslims (the Klan as an organization was moribund and the Black Panthers had not yet come along) or drawing on the memory of his boyhood, surveys showed that his column was the best liked, the least liked and the best read in the paper. He paid no attention to formal surveys. His mail told him how the public pulse was beating, pro and con. He was particularly happy to hear from young people, and he answered their letters patiently — a patience derived perhaps from the problems that sometimes arose when dealing with his own son.

Ralph, Jr., had not done well at Wesleyan and had been asked to drop out after the spring quarter and apply again a year later. His precocity at reading had led to his starting prep school at Westminster a year earlier than his fellows, and at Wesleyan, he had found this lack of maturity a handicap. The plan for going back to Wesleyan after a year did not materialize. He came home in April and went to work for a construction company owned by a McGill neighbor. McGill, with his profound respect for education, and for a New England education in particular, was deeply disappointed but was careful not to show it. He waited for a week after young Ralph had come home before he mentioned the subject, and then, he recalled in a letter to Laurence Winship, "I was careful not to berate him, or yell at him. I said to him . . . that all I wanted him to do was try and not have any sense of guilt of having let me down. . . . It would be wrong to think he had failed, the only failure would be in not having learned anything about himself . . . but if he had learned anything about himself, the year was a valuable one."

It might be well, his father suggested, that young Ralph do his maturing in the army, navy or marines, or if he preferred, he could go back to school.

"I let him know that I had no recommendations, except for him to understand he couldn't repeat another year such as the last. He answered up at once, and said he wanted to go back to school and thought he could get down to work."

To his father's pleased surprise, he then expressed the view that, if he could get in, he'd like to go to McGill's alma mater, Vanderbilt. Always a sentimentalist about his old school, even though his own time there had been cut short by faculty edict, McGill immediately went into action. He told Larry Winship:

> I wrote a very candid letter to Vanderbilt, where I am no longer acquainted with any of the administration, and spared none of the facts. I told them I was asking for no favors, but if it was possible to consider him, I would appreciate it. They wrote back and said that their list was complete, but that they had made exceptions in the past and they hoped they would never run an IBM operation, but one which would contain some compassion and the willingness to give a second opportunity to young men who, in their judgment, merited it. They asked Ralph to go up and see them, and he spent a couple of hours talking with the dean and vice-chancellor. The dean of admissions talked with Wesleyan and the prep-school people. They got all the records, and last Friday Ralph was notified he had been admitted on a nonclassified basis. So that is a burden off my back, and I will now begin to concern myself with the others still there.

McGill was more closely acquainted with the Vanderbilt administration than his letter indicated. Some two years earlier, Dr. Harvie Branscomb, chancellor of Vanderbilt, had written McGill that "we have an important problem at Vanderbilt on which I think you can help us." He continued:

> The university is moving up to a level of activity and service which is different from that which we have known. This is in part due to the larger number of problems which the country is asking the universities to solve and partly to the growing strength and scope of the work on the campus. We have an important and difficult problem, however, one which, frankly, we do not know how to go about solving, in changing the popular view of Vanderbilt as a good southern college, and, except perhaps in medicine, little more. While a great deal is happening on the campus which would be of wider interest than merely in Nashville, we do not succeed, for example, in getting much publicity outside of our own community.
>
> The problem, thus, is a dual one. First, it is what kind of staff ought Vanderbilt try to develop in this broad area of public relations and communications? That leads to the second problem: what counsel and advice could you give us as to how we go about seeing that the materials that might be suggested or prepared are given attention?

In reply, McGill wrote the chancellor:

> In my opinion, there is one fundamental rule to keep in mind about publicity. It is that you must make your own publicity. The worst thing anyone can do is to spend time and money straining to get trivia in the papers or on television.
>
> The other thing I think is wrong is to tie up the football and basketball publicity man with the university's publicity and public relations staff. I would be sure that this latter group put away childish things and devoted energy and presentation to the real meaning and progress of the university. I had a couple of your braying alumni tell me that they were very hopeful the union with Peabody (a college for women) would be effective so they could have an education program for dumb football players at Vanderbilt. This would be the worst thing that could happen. . . .

He added that he "would earnestly hope that Vanderbilt, Tulane, and any other school that might be interested would soon form a new athletic conference to include those members which have sensible regulations concerning football and basketball" — a statement his old sports-writing companions, for whom a college existed only to serve its athletic teams, would have considered rankest heresy.

McGill then proceeded to a further heresy when he suggested that "If you are looking for something dramatic to attract attention regionally, I would suggest you turn to television. New York University had spectacular success with an early morning course in English and American literature. . . . You might even consider putting some of your stronger departments on regular television instruction in adult education. This is one of the crying needs of the whole South."

To McGill, as to millions of other Americans, the killing of President Kennedy in November of 1963 and the later murders of Robert Kennedy and Martin Luther King brought a terrible new defiance into American politics. This cold-blooded stalking of a public figure by a political assassin was beyond his comprehension.

He was on a plane bound from Washington to Nashville when the word came over the loudspeaker that President Kennedy had been shot. Through the feeling of shock came the remembrance of their first good talk, in the spring of 1953 — Jack Kennedy's first year in the Senate. Laurence Winship had a small luncheon in Washington to which he had invited Senator Kennedy and Senator Saltonstall. It was at a time when southern states, desperate for new industry, were offering all sorts of inducements to New England textile mills — rent-free buildings, years of tax-free operation — seeking to bring them to the South. Kennedy had spoken out strongly in the Senate against these practices, which were costing many of his constituents their jobs. But gruff old Larry Winship took a different view. Let them go, he argued. Textile mills, in the long run, are a blight on a community. It would be far better for New England to turn to other industries that could use the higher skills of its trained labor force. McGill remembered that after this lecture by Winship, Kennedy toned down his criticism of the southern tactics. It may well have been a key decision. If Kennedy had kept on, he could have built up an image of himself as an antisouthern Yankee. And without the support of the South, he would never have been elected President.

Victory or defeat in politics could so often turn on little, unpredictable things. It might well have been, McGill reflected, that Mayor William B. Hartsfield, of Atlanta was responsible for the sixty-odd thousand votes that constituted Kennedy's slim margin of victory over Nixon in 1960. Late in the campaign, the Reverend Martin Luther King, Jr., had been arrested and put in jail by a judge in De Kalb County, near Atlanta. It had been a distortion of legal process and a misuse of legal power that had outraged blacks and reasonable whites alike. But nobody had done anything — until Mayor Hartsfield, though unable to reach Kennedy, who was flying on the campaign trail, issued a statement saying that he knew that Kennedy was much concerned about the arrest of Dr. King. Later, when Kennedy did get the word, he reacted just as Hartsfield had predicted. He phoned Mrs. Martin Luther King, expressing his grave concern and offering the hope the injustice would be soon corrected. Nixon, on the other hand, took the advice of those who counseled silence, fearing that to speak out for Martin Luther King would cost him the segregationist vote. And all over the South and the nation, Negroes, undecided in their loyalty until then, made up their minds for Kennedy.

He remembered Kennedy telling him, after the first of the debates with Nixon, that he knew that whatever happened in the campaign thereafter, he could cope with it. Nothing he would have to face would be more difficult than this lonely confrontation with his opponent in an empty room with invisible millions watching, and weighing the two men in their minds.

There was one poignant memory, a courtesy extended by the young President for which McGill would ever be grateful. It was shortly before Christmas of 1960. The President-elect was at the Kennedy estate in Palm Beach. The McGills — young Ralph and Mary Elizabeth, now so ill that she could hardly walk — were driving through Florida on their way to a vacation in Key West. McGill had phoned ahead to Bill Lawrence of the *New York Times*, with the press corps at Palm Beach, asking him to set up, if the President-elect would agree to it, a little surprise for Mary Elizabeth.

On the pretext of just driving by "to see where the Kennedys lived," they had driven to the Kennedy estate — and right on past the guards. Kennedy couldn't have been more gracious. They walked in the gardens and chatted in the sun by the sea wall, looking at the sea, and the President had escorted Mary Elizabeth over the grounds and into the house, showing her everything. They had met and talked with Bobby Kennedy, and with Ethel, and here had begun a friendship that had endured.

Ralph, for several reasons, was to be grateful to President Kennedy. He named McGill to the President's Committee on Labor and Management Policy — which gave him a chance to hear what was going on in the minds of Henry Ford, of Tom Watson of IBM, and of Walter Reuther and George Meany. He also put him on the Advisory Committee of the United States Arms Control and Disarmament Agency. It was, on the whole, an impotent group — but it gave him a look at the inner, secret workings of our global nuclear policy.

His sharpest memory, though, was of a young President trying, through McGill, to get an insight into the working of the southern mind. It was early 1963, and McGill, just back from a State Department tour of West Africa, had been invited to the White House to talk about what he had learned. He had talked, in Ghana, to President Nkrumah, who had spent twelve years in the United States and had come away angry, embittered, and an implacable foe of this country. He had turned for support to Russia, and there, too, he had received a bitter shock, for Ghanaian students in Moscow had been attacked and brutally beaten in the streets. So now, McGill told the President, Nkrumah was turning toward the Chinese. He told the President also of the hostile crowds who had tried to interrupt him by reading aloud our pledge to the flag — "with liberty and justice for all" — and excerpts from the Bill of Rights. This line of talk led on to a discussion of civil rights legislation, and then the talk turned to Senator Richard B. Russell of Georgia, one of the most powerful and influential men in the Senate. And McGill remembered that the President's face grew puzzled as he talked of Senator Russell and his great talent for government, his great capacity for friendship and loyalty, his great gift for leadership. And yet this gifted man remained adamant and defiant in his opposition to any measure which would change the old pattern of race relations.

He was in his rocking chair as he talked, rocking gently — and McGill remembered thinking, this is an odd thing. Here is a troubled President, an overworked President, filled with concern and wonder, talking now not politics but philosophy, talking of man and his deepest motivations, and the mystery and absurdity and the paradoxical quality of life.

And that was his main memory of John F. Kennedy, dead now by an assassin's hand in Dallas. He reached under the seat for his stuffed, scuffed, underarm briefcase, pulled out a yellow pad and a pencil, and began to write.

In the stunned and horror-struck first hours after the murder of the President, he leaped immediately to the conclusion that it had been a right-wing deed. The column he wrote on the plane reflected that view, and it was with some difficulty that Eugene Patterson, tracking McGill down later in his hotel room in Nashville, persuaded him that the column should be killed. Lee Harvey Oswald, if not a pure psychopath, was more of the left than right, more a Communist than a conservative.

McGill reluctantly killed the column and sent a substitute, but he returned to the same theme in a "Speaking Out" article for the *Saturday Evening Post* three weeks later.

Writing under the title "Hate Knows No Direction," he pointed out that, "whether it came from the left or right, hate that is a blind killer and relentless already is a poison in our national life." He traced, briefly, Oswald's background as a neophyte Communist and added: "But he was not alone in his hate. His deed brought out the glee of the right-wing extremists." When news of the shooting and later the death of the President became known, he pointed out, some southern newspapers received anonymous jeering telephone calls: "So they shot the nigger lover. Good for whoever did it. . . . He asked for it, and I'm damned glad he got it . . . trying to ram the damn niggers down our throats."

Throughout the article he was careful to blast both "Communist-oriented and right-wing extremist groups," but the examples cited were all of right-wing violence — the school riots in Little Rock six years earlier, the rioting at the University of Mississippi in which two men were killed when James Meredith, a Negro, was enrolled, and the killing by a sniper of Medgar Evers of the NAACP.

The article, in effect, laid the blame for all violence, whether of the left or right, at the door of the "segregationist forces [who] for more than a year have openly condemned their country, its government and its leaders, and declared their hatred for it . . . extremists [who] have for six years directly or indirectly encouraged violence and defiance of federal authority":

> The list of these includes politicians, evangelists, spokesmen for organizations dedicated to defying the Supreme Court ruling against racial discrimination, the more rabid anti-Semitic and outright anti-Negro groups, and those of the more outspoken Birch Society mentalities who called Dwight D. Eisenhower a Communist stooge and the late Secretary of State John Foster Dulles a traitor and a Communist.

The response to his *Post* article poured in, letters couched in language that even he, as a connoisseur of hate mail, found exceptionally high in vitriol. His answers were restrained. In many of them he wrote "thanks for reminding me of the axiom: 'Listen to the fool's reproof. It is a kingly title.' "

15

McGill kept a bottle of analgesic pills in his desk — "The Big Fix," he called it. And for all his great bulk and his seeming calm, he seethed inwardly, as restless as a captive elephant stamping and swaying in his chains. He read late and was up early and he tossed restlessly at night. He drank too much, on occasion, but it was a matter of pride to him that in the years of his greatest pressures, "I didn't crawl in the jug."

One scene that all who knew him will remember is that of coming into his office to find him sitting in his chair, bent over in his old bucket-seat crouch, his broad, stubby hands clutching his head. Waiting for an elevator, he would cup his hands over the shoulders of the nearest friend and lean all his weight upon him, sighing gustily, eyes closed.

One thing which seemed to sustain him was the irreverent affection in which he was held by his colleagues. Whenever a new citation — in June 1963, he received seven honorary degrees — couched in words of fulsome praise, was hung upon his office wall, Grace Lundy could be sure that for a day or two associates would be calling in, asking innocently if they might speak to the "Conscience of the South," or "He who fearlessly mans the ramparts of righteousness."

Only once did Grace Lundy fail to respond in kind to this tomfoolery. A friend, unable to think of the latest accolade, asked, "Is he who is without sin among us today?"

"Nobody here answers that description," she said primly.

Tarver, in a note to Adlai Stevenson following a publishers' meeting in New York at which Stevenson had been the speaker, wrote: "I enjoyed being with you the other evening, though I am sorry McGill did not materialize. I called his hotel early the next morning, but from the way the phone rang, it was obvious his bed had not been slept in. . . ." He then explained that "Dr. McGill, now that he has our racial problems pretty well solved, has taken on the cause of underprivileged widows, North and South. . . ."

McGill, who hated all conventions except those put on by the Democrats and Republicans, wrote Stevenson: "I regretted not seeing you in New York, but it so happens that at the conclusion of the dinner and your excellent speech, I had had, as we say, a bellyful of publishers. I really had been through an experience which was almost more than I could endure. It did not reflect the entire audience, of course, but only a couple of those at my table. It was really pretty bad." (Ralph was referring to the fact that two publishers at his table had been rudely outspoken in their opinions of Stevenson.)

Then, in self-defense: "As for Mr. Tarver being able to determine, without the aid of telephone-television, that my bed had not been slept in, this was libel of the grossest sort. I was out early at CBS, working on a documentary film on the Ku Klux Klan."

Stevenson replied that he was glad that McGill had "slain that libelous Tarver with such swift arrows of truth and virtue. All the same, if you feel the cause of underprivileged widows, North and South, too burdensome, you can always turn to me for help. Although my time is meager and my credentials modest, my respect for the cause, and concern for your health, is great."

This bantering exchange was the last communication between McGill and the man he admired most above all others in public life. Less than three months later, Adlai Stevenson dropped dead on a London street. He was sixty-five.

Of his death McGill, who was two years older, said to Gene Patterson: "What a good way to go. Quickly, on a pleasant street in London, on a walk with a beautiful woman."

The passing of Stevenson brought to an end, too, a correspondence both men had found comforting and stimulating. Much of it was in facetious vein, as above, for each used bantering irony to conceal deep feeling. After the 1952 campaign, when then Governor Stevenson was still addressing his letters "Dear Mr. McGill," he was writing: "I have no regrets about the campaign and my conscience is comfortable, but I am afraid I have been a disappointment to some of my valiant supporters — yourself among the foremost. . . . There is work to be done in this country as you know, and I hope we can share a little of it along the way."

A year later, to "Dear Ralph," he was writing: "I have wanted to tell you that one of the few satisfactions I have found in my exposed life of late is your confidence and goodwill, so often and so eloquently expressed. I wish to heaven I had you for a ghost. . . ." In the summer of 1955 he was asking McGill to visit him in Chicago. "There is much I should like to talk about, of which politics is not more than ninety-five percent."

McGill's columns of support were a constant source of strength to Stevenson. "Your columns on the segregation business give me heart," he wrote in June of 1956, "and your patience and understanding in the emotional clatter to which I seem to be constantly exposed gives me a reassurance that I sometimes need. Bless you!"

His letters often were designed to revive McGill's flagging spirits. In an undated longhand note found in McGill's papers he said, "More and more sensible people in the South are accepting the inevitability of racial equality while more and more sensible people in the North better understand the problem in some areas of the South, where coeducation of adolescents of both races, for example, is not immediately possible or even desirable for either race."

McGill was not only one of the hardest-working journalists in the business, he was a masterly brain-picker, and his colleagues soon learned to clam up when he would clear his throat and ask innocently, "What do you know that I ought to know?"

Said Claude Sitton of the *New York Times:*

> I soon found out that if I had done a think-piece for the Sunday paper, I'd damn well better not tell McGill about it on Friday or it would be in his column in ninety-odd papers all over the United States on Saturday morning. He'd put it through his own verbal thing, and it would take you a minute or two, reading it, to realize that this was your idea that he had wormed out of you the day before. What worried me was the plagiarism. I knew nobody would ever accuse McGill of plagiarizing *me* — so that left me vulnerable when my piece came along a day after his column, expressing the same views.

McGill's habit of brain-picking his fellow journalists — frequently by long-distance phone — sometimes gave rise to wicked glee in the editorial rooms of the *Atlanta Journal.* He was a friend of Ralph Ingersoll, editor of the now defunct liberal New York tabloid, *PM.* Once a McGill column appeared side by side with an Ingersoll column from *PM* on the *Journal* bulletin board. Beneath them, somebody had written: "Two Ralphs with but a single thought."

Though McGill was unabashed in his gathering of other men's flowers, he was also most generous with his own knowledge when a fellow journalist needed briefing. He was on the State Department flyway, patiently trying to interpret the South to the visiting journalists from other lands as they passed through, and he was the first port-of-call for any national newsman, either from a paper or a magazine, who had an assignment in the South.

It was a grievous embarrassment to McGill that his paper, during the cataclysmic years of the civil rights struggle, chose to play down the news of the great confrontations, leaving the coverage of such events as Martin Luther King's Birmingham sit-ins and the Selma march to the wire services and the national press. It pointed up the fact that, though McGill had the title of publisher and had held the title of editor, neither rank carried with it command of the coverage or play of the news. The chain of command here ran from Tarver through his assistants, William H. Fields and William I. Ray, both dour and solid men, not given to taking stands that might cost the papers money or circulation.

Tarver usually rode with a loose rein, but in his decisions regarding coverage of civil rights stories, he was largely guided by the *Constitution*'s lawyers. These, a cautious lot by nature, were counseling that, in view of the libel suits McGill had already gotten them into, the papers should keep a very low profile when black and white were confronting each other on the streets.

McGill and Patterson were free to thunder editorially with rage and eloquence on any subject, and presumably were equally as free to move about as their news and editorial judgment dictated. (Patterson flew to Paris, for instance, to cover the Orly crash.) After the Meredith incident at Oxford gave rise to the libel suits, though, neither was allowed to take the forty-minute flight to Birmingham, where black school kids were facing police dogs and cattle prods. (The libel suits, incidentally, were settled out of court in 1968 following the Supreme Court's landmark decision in the case of *Sullivan* v. *the New York Times.*)

McGill was outraged when, on the advice of the lawyers, the decision was made not to staff the Selma march. His reaction was angry and impulsive. He went into Patterson's office to announce that even if the paper's decision was not to send reporters, nobody had said that he and Gene couldn't climb on a bus and go over there to join the march as participants. Patterson gently dissuaded him. It would be a grandstand play, he pointed out, a showboat gesture. They would not be demonstrating for Martin Luther King, but against the management of the papers. It would have been an insult to management, an affront that would tear some fabric that Patterson, at that time, was not yet ready to tear.

Actually, McGill was never out of touch; he had a wide acquaintance among the black leaders, who had confidence in him and would talk to him. And when they were in jail or on the picket lines and unavailable, he had the willing help of some of the top civil rights reporters in the country. John Popham of the *Chattanooga Times;* Claude Sitton of the *New York Times;* Karl Fleming, Bill Emerson and Joe Cumming of *Newsweek* were out there where the rocks were flying and the firehoses going, carrying the little chopped-off "chicken" notebooks that hid in their pockets and did not reveal their identity as reporters. As each crisis came and passed, they covered it for their papers or magazines — and then when it was over, phoned Pappy from the scene to give him the little insights, the shades and nuances that filled out the panoramic and continuing picture. Thus he kept abreast of events as they happened, not only in the streets where the action was, but in what Joe Cumming called "the stale, littered, little naked light-bulb headquarters of SNCC, CORE, COFO, etc.," where the early doctrine of nonviolence was giving way to a new, more belligerent policy, feeding on the rhetoric of Black Power.

In addition to his journalist friends, McGill often turned to other men of knowledge and wisdom in the field of race relations. Harold Fleming of the Southern Regional Council was an unfailing source who saw the great battle not only in terms of its hot skirmishes, but in its southwide panorama. Harry Golden, in North Carolina, and Harry Ashmore, at the Center for the Study of Democratic Institutions in

Santa Barbara, California, had their own special expertise, and from all these sources, plus his own contacts, McGill would distill the recommendations which he would pass along to presidents Eisenhower, Kennedy, or Johnson. John Griffin played a special role in this process of keeping McGill and his companions posted. First at Florida State University, later at the Southern Educational Foundation in Atlanta, Griffin would bring together at his home the group named above to spend a weekend talking over what was happening.

One such gathering took place in April of 1964 at Griffin's house in Tallahassee, where the group assembled to cut a tape for Griffin's educational radio program. The subject was: "Is There a New South?"

Griffin, Fleming and Ashmore all remember McGill's curiously antic mood on this occasion. A kind of rambunctious weltschmerz seemed to possess him. The great believer took on the role of iconoclast. He was the last to speak, and after Ashmore, Popham, Emerson, Sitton and Fleming had advanced their ideas, he proceeded to denounce them all for what he called their "pious hedging." There was no "New South," he argued. All the old shibboleths — "nigger," "white supremacy" — still held their potency. All the old hags still bestrode the shoulders of the southerner. He was still deep-mired in the swamp of racial prejudice.

That night, after the formal taping, the old friends sat around, drinking and talking, and McGill's mood was one of sentimental reminiscence. Soon, though, he excused himself and went to bed, after telling a story about a countryman from Arkansas in a big city hotel who ordered up a brown paper bag, "so he could leave a message." When they awoke the next morning, McGill was gone. But there on the kitchen table was a brown paper bag. On it McGill had scrawled:

> Dearly Beloved, at the dawning of a new day in the New South, I leave these greetings and apologies. I regret that a feeling of malmania [he seems to have invented a new word here], weakness and sweating came over me. I do not think it was caused by the conversation. Perhaps by my own frustrations. It was a fine weekend, and as I feel blood brother to you, an improvement for the time being in the human condition. I lean on each of you. Affectionately, R.M.

There was a curiously Last Supper-ish flavor about it, a mood of farewell. To John Griffin "it was a loving and penitent message in that, by bowing out early, he had failed us in affection." To Ashmore — "His old black Welsh mood was upon him. He was fleeing that Hound of Heaven."

What McGill had not told them was that he had had disquieting news from his doctor. The tough old heart that had been beating strong and slow for sixty-six years had started acting up in a most curious way. After a frightening pause, it would go suddenly into a flurry of rapid, shallow, vibrating beats. "Atrial fibrillation," the doctor had called it, and from then on, until he died, McGill had to carry with him a bottle of digitalis.

He didn't mention it. He kept on, as he had always done, coming into the office after his annual physical, announcing blandly that, if all his corpulent colleagues would imitate him in leading the clean and austere life, drinking only an occasional bottle of wine, eating no fattening foods, and taking a brief nap in the afternoons, they, too, would earn the praise of their doctors.

On the advice of a heart specialist, he gave up alcohol, tea and coffee, and under medication, the heart, which had been jumping to 140–150 beats a minute, slowed down to a far less dangerous 88. Though he looked gaunt and somewhat hollow-eyed, his mood was tranquil, even blithe, as reflected in his correspondence with his old friends.

As is natural for one who has won his own battle against obesity and ardent spirits, he began to counsel others less stout of will. He wrote his old friend Baggs of the *Miami Daily News*, who had begun to put on weight, congratulating him on taking up jogging and giving up smoking cigars, the latter act being especially pleasing, McGill said, since Baggs's cigars always had the aroma of burning straw from old flophouse mattresses. He warned Baggs solemnly that the chemistry involved in the mixing of vodka and tomato juice had a deleterious effect on the kidneys, especially when taken before noon. (Baggs, who had a chronic kidney problem which required daily medication, complained that, when rooming with McGill at hotels, he had to hide his medicine under the mattress. Otherwise, McGill would drink it, on the theory that if it was good for Baggs it also would help him.) He also recommended to Baggs that he might emulate Bishop W. R. (Bill) Rogers of Missouri, a candidate for President on the Theocratic party ticket.

"Bishop Rogers, for two years," McGill told Baggs, "has been running seven times around the courthouses in American counties with a Bible in his hand, in the belief that the wicked ones will fall down in the manner of the walls at Jericho. One has not really fallen, although the walls of a great many have weakened and cracks have appeared in some."

He suggested that Baggs take a Bible in his hand in his trots around the block, or if the full-sized Bible proved too heavy, he could carry a small pocket Testament.

Perhaps Ralph's greatest pleasure derived from this ironic banter that went on between him, Ashmore, Griffin, Golden, and to a lesser degree, Tarver, Baggs and Popham. Their correspondence, even throughout their carefree years, abounded with solemn admonitions to give up drink, to practice Christian charity, to lose weight, to adopt sounder political views, all couched in jesting terms. Ashmore, for example, rebuked McGill for what he called his "scabrous conduct" at both the Republican and Democratic conventions. At the Republican convention in Chicago in 1960, McGill allegedly had to be restrained during an evening of merriment at the 606 Club from punching a surly Mafioso type who had refused to allow his date to dance with him. McGill had fallen into a crouch, fists extended, announcing to the surrounding company that he had learned from Jack Dempsey himself that it was always best to fight from a crouch. He had also gained a certain renown for gallantry when the club's stripper, who finished her act by lighting the tassels attached to her breasts and revolving them in a clockwise direction, had trouble getting them to ignite. McGill, borrowing a cigarette lighter, leaped to her assistance and lit them for her.

The 1964 convention year was remembered, joyfully, around the office for an implied rebuke administered to Tarver by McGill for alleged parsimony. By Tarver's edict, executives of the paper, when flying commercial aircraft, were required to go tourist. Discovering that Mr. and Mrs. Tarver (in order to take advantage of family-plan rates) were planning to fly first-class to San Francisco for the Republican convention, McGill arranged for himself, Baggs and Eugene Patterson to get tourist seats on the same plane. He then asked Delta's president, C. E. Woolman, for permission to bring their own food and drinks aboard. This was granted, and McGill boarded the plane bearing several bottles of Moselle, which the stewardesses chilled for him, and a huge picnic basket of fried chicken which Julia had prepared. McGill, Patterson and Baggs sat three abreast in the tourist seats, drinking wine, eating chicken, and sending irreverent notes and an occasional drumstick up to the Tarvers as evidence of the high quality of the fare being served in the tourist section.

Later at the convention, McGill, forgetting his vows to practice abstinence, had become weary early in the evening and had gone pleasantly to sleep while reading the menu at an elegant French restaurant. Jim Fain and Patterson had left the dinner and taken him back to his hotel, where he got a good night's rest. The next morning, McGill was up early, bright-eyed and alert. A young journalist from *Life* recognized him in the elevator and spoke to him. "I enjoy your column in the *Washington Star*," he told McGill. "Are you carried locally?" Baggs, who had not gotten a good night's sleep, growled wearily from the back of the elevator, "Only at night," he said.

Despite earnest efforts to fight off such lapses, McGill was not always able to cling to the abstemious life he so strongly recommended to others. In September of 1964, he was called to Washington as one of the thirty distinguished Americans who had been awarded the Medal of Freedom by President Johnson, the highest honor the President can bestow upon a civilian. It was a proud moment for him, and McGill asked four of his oldest and closest friends — Jack and Margaret Tarver, Grace Lundy and Reb Gershon, his prep-school sweetheart — to share it with him. All went well at the presentation, and his citation was eloquent and apt. It read: "You have courageously sounded the voice of reason, moderation and progress during a period of contemporary revolution."

At the reception that evening at the State Department, McGill was chosen to make a brief impromptu speech in response to remarks by the host, Under Secretary of State George Ball. This in itself was an honor, for he was speaking on behalf of all the award winners, including John Steinbeck, Walter Lippmann, Carl Sandburg, Ed Murrow and Walt Disney.

Afterward, the McGill group moved on to dinner at Sander Vanocur's house, where he seemed to be in an exceptionally gay and lighthearted mood, spending a considerable time telling stories with a presidential aide, Dan Moynihan. Later, though, a friend remembers, a brooding sadness seemed to come upon him. Despite the friends around him, a feeling of being alone possessed him, for there was no one who truly belonged to him who was there to share the moment with him — Mary Elizabeth so recently dead; his mother ill at her home in Chattanooga; young Ralph unable to be there because he had to register at Vanderbilt on this day. It seemed particularly to trouble him that his son was not there.

After the dinner, he delivered Reb Gershon to the apartment where she was staying. Then he disappeared. The next morning, wearing an unexplained black eye, dreadfully hung over, and in a contrite mood, he called Reb, who was catching an early plane. He was "in sackcloth and ashes," he said. The feeling, she consoled him, was one soon to be shared by many. The date, she gently pointed out, was the eve of the Day of Atonement.

McGill's occasional departures from the path of righteousness were not always so somber. There was, for example, the evening of April 14, 1965, as remembered by Ann Landers:

> It was a spectacular party at the home of Senator Gaylord Nelson and Carrie Lee. Dozens of people were lapping up martinis, eating hors d'oeuvres, and swapping stories. The crowd was a happy mix of Washington types and newspaper folks who had descended on the nation's capital for the annual bash known as ASNE (American Society of Newspaper Editors).
>
> At about 1 A.M. it occurred to me that someone should start moving toward the door. Since I was one of the few guests who could still read a clock, I made the effort. It failed.
>
> At approximately 2 A.M. I enlisted the aid of Dr. Robert Stolar, a Washington dermatologist. I felt he was the logical one to start the exodus since a group of us had come in his car. By 2:30 A.M. Bob finally succeeded in getting most of his passengers out the door — Ralph McGill, Bill Baggs,

Larry Fanning and Yours Truly. So the five of us piled into Bob Stolar's Cadillac Coupe de Ville and headed toward the Washington Hilton.

As we neared Massachusetts Avenue, Larry Fanning said to Dr. Stolar, "Look at this thing on my face, Doc. Should it come off?"

Bob took a look under the spotlight and replied, "Yes it should."

Larry asked, "When can you do it, Doc?"

Bob answered, "Anytime."

"Where is your office, Doc?" piped Ralph McGill.

"About four blocks from here," Bob replied.

"Well, why don't we go there now and get it over with?" suggested Ralph.

"Sounds like a great idea," I added. "In Larry's present condition he won't need an anesthetic."

"I'll assist the surgeon," chirped Ralph. "I always wanted to be a doctor."

Everyone applauded, and the matter was settled.

The scene was one I'll never forget. The group of us — really quite respectable citizens — tromping into the elevator of the medical building at 3:00 A.M. to perform "emergency surgery." The laughter was uproarious. We could have been arrested for disorderly conduct.

Bob ushered us into his suite of offices and scrubbed up for surgery. McGill not only scrubbed up, but put on Dr. Stolar's white gown, surgical mask, and rubber gloves. Bill Baggs wanted to play doctor, too, and insisted on holding a scalpel and sponge.

No one had ever seen a happier patient. Larry was convulsed with laughter and came dangerously close to falling off the table. My job as "nurse" was to mop the patient's brow with a cloth and keep him horizontal. The surgical procedure lasted for approximately ten minutes. Although novocain was applied, Dr. Stolar did not wait for it to take effect since he agreed that Larry wouldn't feel a thing.

The doctor declared the operation a success, a bandage was taped over the wound, and we all helped Larry off the table.

Ralph's first comment was, "Doc, the assisting surgeon needs a drink. Where do you keep the alcohol?" The doctor replied, "Sorry, the bar is closed."

The next morning the story was the talk of the convention. By the time I heard it at 3:00 P.M., someone said, "Did you hear that McGill took out Larry Fanning's appendix last night?"

"Really?" I replied.

"Oh yes," was the response. "Ralph went to medical school, you know."

McGill's published utterances on the subject of drink varied with his mood. When penitent, he would write a column which Carrie Nation could have approved but not when he was nostalgic. One of his delightful columns, titled "Starting the Blood," was a reminiscence of Dover Hall and the legendary character who owned it known as Uncle Wilbert Robinson, who "was one of the original Old Orioles, of Baltimore, and who later became a legend as manager of Brooklyn's Daffiness Boys." The column read:

Visitors to Dover Hall, the baseball winter retreat near Darien, Georgia, were familiar with the need to start the blood. Dover Hall was the nearest thing to an earthly Valhalla that baseball has ever had. It was a modest, unadorned place. There was a small but adequate clubhouse of cypress planks. An artesian well flowed from a tall pipe near the front porch and ducks made merry in the clear pool formed by the generous spill of water. There was also a nearby long plank "dormitory" somewhat on the order of the straight-line motel.

On mornings that had a chill in them, the guests would be wakened by an ancient colored man who carried with him a tray on which sat tall glasses of steaming toddies, made in those days with strong nontaxed corn whiskey. The tray bearer would kick gently on the door with the toe of a heavy brogan-type shoe. When the guest came sleepily to the door, the tray would be extended and the old man would say, "Uncle Robbie say to take one of these to start the blood."

These toddies were sweetened with honey instead of sugar. It was Uncle Robbie's theory that the blood took more kindly to stimulation from a toddy so sweetened than one mixed with processed sugar. It seemed to him that a natural sour mash corn did better by man with a natural sweetener — "straight from the bees to man."

A man with his stagnant blood thus started would arrive at the clubhouse in a benign frame of mind.

A heavy breakfast of venison, sausage, pork sausage, bacon, ham, grits, fried and scrambled eggs, and "flannel cakes" with sorghum comforted the inner man.

Uncle Robbie, McGill pointed out, was "a generation ahead of medical science, which just now is learning that a man's blood needs 'starting' to wash away the dangerous accumulations of nighttime stagnation. Uncle Robbie's prescription of hot corn-whiskey toddy, sweetened with honey, horrifies doctors who prescribe exercise. Not being a scientist, I cannot say."

In July of 1967 he attended the funeral of Carl Sandburg, who died at Connemara, his home near Flat Rock, North Carolina, and wrote of it touchingly in his column. The two men had been close friends since Sandburg had first come to North Carolina in 1945. Often, over the years, McGill, alone or with young Ralph, had gone to call upon him at his mountaintop home, and the two would sit on the front porch in their shirt-sleeves talking until the dusk grew chill and the stars came out. Frequently, Sandburg, bringing a flagon of goat's milk and a bag of goat's-cheese sandwiches, would stop off in Atlanta while traveling and spend a night with McGill.

Sandburg was twenty years older than McGill, and as long as he was there on his mountaintop, vigorous and vital, full of song and laughter and deep folk wisdom, McGill himself felt reassured that he too could go on, working and producing until he was old. The snowfall of little memos which Sandburg sent to McGill over the years contributed to this confidence. "Life has taste and tang for you. May this ever be so with you," he wrote. "You have sagacity and serenity. People respond to you whether you are reporter or preacher." Once he wrote, "I think we are brother psalmists."

In his book, *The Sandburg Range*, the poet wrote "For Ralph McGill," under the title of the poem "Journey." "In proof," he added, "that you are a friend and cherished."

Now Sandburg was gone and McGill's sorrow was eloquent in the columns he wrote from North Carolina. He described the service in the little Episcopal church called St. John in the Wilderness and told how Edward Steichen, brother-in-law of Carl Sandburg, had walked alone to the coffin and placed upon it a green bough of Connemara pine. He quoted the poems read from the pulpit, poems by Whitman and by Sandburg himself. One, "Finish," by Sandburg:

Death comes but once, let it be easy. . . .
Sing one song if I die.
Sing John Brown's Body or shout all over God's Heaven.
Or sing nothing at all better yet.

"There was no eulogy," McGill wrote. "The poems were eulogy enough. He was a man for all the world, and so it seemed here today in the quaint little church tucked away among the trees and flowering shrubs of western North Carolina."

Curiously, as if to conceal his own deep sense of loss, his letter to Ashmore, Baggs and others describing the service sounded almost flippant: "The church, a small one," he wrote, "was built about 1836 and financed largely by Christopher Gustavus Memminger, a Charleston lawyer who later became treasurer of the Confederate States and broke his heart trying to contend with the inflationary spiral of that currency. You will recall the Confederate money stabilized itself very neatly — you needed a barrel full of hundred-dollar bills for a barrel full of flour. . . . At one point the organist played 'John Brown's Body' and Dr. Golden and I led the singing of it. I thought you would like to know that Dr. Golden and I have the distinction of having sung 'John Brown's Body' in a church built by a former treasurer of the Confederate States of America. . . ."

Helga Sandburg Crile, the poet's daughter, was well aware of how her father's death had affected McGill, and she made a gesture two days after the funeral that deeply touched him. She found her father's old green eyeshade and his small pearl-handled penknife and a color picture of the two old friends sitting on the porch together, and sent them on, "With Love," to McGill. He framed them together and hung them by his desk.

Now and then McGill could be sharp with his old friends and they with him when one felt the other to be in grievous error. The war in Vietnam, for example, placed a great strain upon the cordial and affectionate relationship between them. McGill was a strongly vocal advocate of our policy in Vietnam, and Baggs and Ashmore felt that his great prestige as a journalist was being cynically used by President Johnson. They were particularly wounded by what they considered his intemperate attacks on Senator Fulbright for his opposition to Johnson's policies. He, in turn, was much dismayed by their dovishness, and when the two of them went off to Hanoi in January of 1967 (without letting him know that they were going) to sound out Ho Chi Minh on the possibility of beginning peace talks, there developed a rift between them that never entirely healed. Their letters, though couched in terms of irony and humor, could not quite conceal a smoldering antagonism. In a memo to Jack Tarver, with copies to Baggs, Ashmore and John Popham — who sought in vain to heal the break — McGill summed up his views on Baggs and Ashmore's peace mission:

"I do disassociate myself from these doves. . . . I am a belligerent dove. . . . I insist, in the Coolidge manner, that peace would result if Dr. Ho would try removing his forces out of South Vietnam. . . ."

Baggs's reply was cheerful. "Dr. McGill has got on his old wrap-around puttees again, and is charging up San Juan Hill." Ashmore's observation was that McGill was looking at the war from the Marine Corps's squad level. Of course he was, McGill answered. As an old acting corporal of the 1917 war, where else could he view it from?

McGill's views on the war were summed up in a letter to Mrs. Herbert Bruckner, sister of Dr. Spock, who, with great eloquence and earnestness, had written him defending her brother. He simply could not understand, McGill answered, "those people who declare it is possible for us to halt the war and get out. It seems to me the stakes are too big for us to remove ourselves. The great struggle for world power has shifted from Europe to Southeast Asia. I admire Dr. Spock," he added, "but I do think, if you will pardon me, that he oversimplifies too much and is a little too glibly assured. Maybe I have the same faults."

No doubts about the wisdom and the virtue of our policy in Vietnam ever assailed him, however, and he never missed an opportunity to rebuke his dovish friends.

In 1967, Baggs was awarded the Eleanor Roosevelt Humanities Award, which McGill had received two years earlier. He wrote to congratulate Baggs, asking innocently:

There is one puzzling little matter and you will forgive me if I bring it up. I, too, was one of the ardent supporters of Israel in the war of Israel against the Arab states. I was not in favor of peace at that moment, but of victory in war by the valiant forces of Israel. But . . . I am a little puzzled by those who are for war in one part of the world and insistent on peace in another.

Baggs, ignoring McGill's half-angry, half-jesting criticism, plowed doggedly ahead with his unofficial efforts to find a road to peace in a war that he, an old bomber pilot twice shot down in World War II, did not believe in. In the spring of 1968, he and Ashmore were back in Hanoi. They came out to write a bitter book, *Mission to Hanoi: A Chronicle of Double-Dealing in High Places.* Within a year, Baggs was dead, at forty-eight.

In his tribute, "Bill Baggs: In Memory," McGill forgot all the times that Baggs had angered, wounded or annoyed him. Only the love shone through:

> Life sang in him, though he had no voice for singing. He was widely read. He wrote a strong, fearless column when there was need for it. He was compassionate and kind. He enjoyed fools, but did not always suffer them easily. He enjoyed poetry and good writing. He had a way with children and was devoted to his own.
>
> There is not room here to put down all the memories, all the laughter, fun and serious talks we had, or the experiences we shared. It was sad to see him begin to lose health and strength. Two exhausting trips to Hanoi sapped much of his stamina. He was, like many persons, greatly taken with Jack and Robert Kennedy. Their deaths further eroded his spirit. But he kept working, planning, telephoning his friends. Keeping in touch until the last illness and the terrible finality of death. He was not a conventional man.

McGill's own health, a shadow over his spirit since 1964, seemingly had improved greatly under medical supervision. Checkups in 1965 and 1966 showed him in good shape for a man of sixty-eight, and he mentioned to his doctor, Joe Wilber, a matter that was much on his mind. What would Dr. Wilber think of a man of his age getting married?

"Ralph," said Joe Wilber, "nobody can ever be sure about these things. But I think I can promise you ten more good years."

"I'll settle for that," said McGill.

16

Early in April of 1967 there appeared on the bulletin board of the *Constitution* newsroom a genial come-all-ye, addressed to "valued co-workers and friends" and bearing the scrawled initials "R.M." It advised the city room staff that at 2 P.M. on the afternoon of the twentieth, at All Saints Episcopal Church, he would, Deo volente, be married to Dr. Mary Lynn Morgan. All were invited to attend both the wedding and the reception which would follow in the church social hall, where, he warned, "the punch will not (repeat not) be spiked."

For some two years before this, McGill and Dr. Morgan, a children's dentist, had, in the high school phrase, been "going steady," and for McGill at least their romance was one of tremulous joy. Whenever they were at a party, his eyes followed her across the room, and whenever they were alone, his mood was tender and solicitous.

To Dr. Morgan, a slender, blue-eyed ash-blonde, direct and matter-of-fact in speech and manner, what later became a feeling of adoration began as an emotion no more poignant than admiration and respect. There was nearly a quarter-century difference in their ages — he was sixty-seven and she was forty-four when they started going together — and early in their courtship she told him frankly that her feeling for him was that of a daughter for a kindly, wise and doting father. Her instinct was to say "sir" to him, and she found it difficult to call him Ralph.

They had known each other casually for many years. They had met at Christmas parties at the home of a mutual friend, Dr. James Steele, specialist in zoonosis at the National Center for Disease Control. They had been founding members of a county pistol club, and when he had moved his membership from the Cathedral of St. Philip to All Saints

Church, he had seen her there, singing in the choir. To her, though, he was of another generation. She had read his column for a long time before she knew him as a person, and she was aware that his thinking had strongly influenced her own. Once, seeing him at the airport, tired and rumpled after a trip, and knowing he didn't drive, she had asked if she could take him home. She knew he had a terrible memory for names and she was flattered when he remembered having talked with her at Jim Steele's. So she drove him home, and they chatted, freely and easily, "about everything under the sun."

Soon he was calling her to join him for lunch downtown on Saturdays. Max Muldawer's Delicatessen, the old basement hangout of McGill's poetry-reading and wine-drinking friends, had been converted into a grocery store, and McGill, with Mary Lynn as his only companion, transferred his allegiance to the more elegant though less exclusive Capital City Club.

With young Ralph off at Parris Island — where McGill himself had survived boot training forty-seven years before — doing his six-months' basic before starting a five-year hitch in the Marine Corps Reserve, there was no reason for McGill to hurry home at the end of the day. He would take a taxi from the office to Mary Lynn's apartment, have a Dubonnet, or a Campari, or a sherry-on-the-rocks with her, and then the two would go out for dinner. Then they would go back to her apartment for a nightcap, after which she would drive him home.

It was a happy time for a lonely man and for a woman now moving gracefully into her middle years who had never married and who long since had put the thought of marriage out of mind. Her dental practice was her life — the children who came to her, wide-eyed and scared, and who, under her quiet voice and gentle touch, soon were not frightened any more.

So, though her relationship with McGill was a close and happy one, it was for her no more than a cherished friendship. When she first realized that he, on the other hand, was deeply in love with her, her innate honesty came to the fore.

"I told him that I loved going out to dinner with him, I loved talking to him, I loved just sitting with him at home not talking, or driving him somewhere in the car, but I didn't love him. I just looked up to him as a father figure. And we couldn't build a marriage on that."

McGill took this rebuff with patience, neither arguing nor begging, and their relationship went on as before.

And then, somehow, her feelings changed. He was no longer a father figure to Mary Lynn, but her contemporary. The change in attitude came while she was on vacation. When she was away, the cliché that absence *does* make the heart grow fonder proved true. She began to realize that he did mean far more to her than she had understood. And when she came home, she called him and frankly told him so.

This, he told her, was happy news, and he suggested that they meet for lunch at the Midnight Sun, a Danish restaurant he had come to favor. There, over aquavit, they talked it over. She explained that somehow, she did not understand quite how, her consciousness of the difference in their ages and intellectual interests had disappeared. She no longer felt in awe of him. She would marry him if he still wanted her.

He had mentioned marriage several times, though he had always expressed the feeling that he had no right to ask a woman so much younger than he to be his wife. Privately, too, he worried that he would not be able to satisfy the sexual needs of an active and healthy woman in her mid-forties. He also worried about his heart, and in this connection Joe Wilber, his doctor, was able to allay his fears.

It had been a curious courtship in that it was conducted partly through a third party — Mary Lynn's sister-in-law, Helen, living in Boston. To her, McGill wrote long and confiding letters, pouring out his love for Mary Lynn, whom he referred to amiably as "the Paragon," and expressing his doubts that a man of his years and peripatetic habits would make a satisfying husband.

By now, though, Mary Lynn's mind was made up. She loved him, and she told him so.

"From now on," she said, "the responsibility is mine . . . if it doesn't turn out the way you want it to, it's not your fault. . . ." She went to a young craftsman in gold and gave him the design for a wedding ring.

Nothing that had happened to McGill in many years had given him a deeper sense of happiness and fulfillment than this promise. It had been a very good year in many ways. He, along with a Catholic archbishop and a rabbi had arranged for the city of Atlanta to honor Dr. Martin Luther King, winner of the Nobel Prize for Peace, at an official dinner. Ten years, even two years, earlier, it would have been inconceivable that the white power structure would sponsor such a tribute to a black man, particularly one so controversial as King.

Young McGill, after causing his father much distress by three times failing in college, had come out of his marine training lean, bronzed, and self-assured, and with a sharpshooter's medal won on the rifle range. The rough-tongued DI's of Parris Island and Camp Lejeune, it seems, had matured him in a way the scholarly professors at Wesleyan, Vanderbilt and Georgia State had not been able to do. He still had no yearning for scholarship, but he had gone to work at an advertising agency, where he had begun to show ability as a fledgling copywriter.

Pride in his city, pride in his son, joy in his own good fortune at having won, so late in life, the love of an attractive and intelligent woman, made McGill's mood almost euphoric. His letters to friends were blithe and full of humor, his answers to hostile critics took on a more tolerant, tone, and he went out of his way to do small and unexpected kindnesses for folk he met in his travels. It was clear that life at last for him was good.

McGill's joy in his prospects of marital happiness in no way dimmed his feeling of sympathy for friends whose marriages had been ended by divorce or death.

To the wife of a friend who was spending days and nights at the bedside of her dying husband, he wrote of the emotional and physical exhaustion which he knew she was going through:

> You are sharing something that will stay with you all your life, and it will not always be a sadness; it is a mysterious sort of sharing of life in trouble and of the sufferings of a body, and the most frustrating agony of all is the inability to do anything about it. Nevertheless, there is . . . a strength in this sharing. You come to have a comprehension of a sort of immortality of the spirit. You learn, out of this strong sharing, that there is a spiritual something in life, which is a mystery. I don't know how much religion I have. I did not find the usual trappings of religion to be of much help. But I believe one comes to feel a sort of confidence in the existence of a Supreme Being, and in some sort of immortality, be it the Spirit or the Soul, or whatever you want to call it. One of the great strengths of a belief in the Supreme Being is the mystery of it . . . the not knowing of it. . . . It seems to me the spirit of man is so obvious that one cannot deny

it, nor do I believe it ends when a person passes into the mystery of after-life.

This was one of McGill's great talents — his understanding of the human heart. With very little formal knowledge of psychology or psychiatry, without even knowing the terms to use, he was able through some innate instinct to give strength and comfort to those who needed help.

In August of 1966, McGill's mother died in Chattanooga at the age of eighty-eight. Throughout that year, Mary Lynn had driven him once a month to see her, a matriarch of such fierce presence she dominated the room even from her sickbed. Though they had not specifically told her of their plans, the wise old woman could read their purpose in their faces. A few weeks before she died, she called Mary Lynn to her bed-side.

"Young lady," she said, "bend down close to me. I want to say some-thing to you."

Mary Lynn leaned near. "I just want you to know that we all love you very much," the older woman whispered.

For three days and nights McGill kept vigil beside his mother's bed as she lay dying. When it was over and the body lay, as was the country custom, in an open casket, Ralph asked if Mary Lynn could this once overcome her expressed reluctance to look on the face of death.

"I want you to see how pretty she looks — the way she looked when I was a little boy and she was young," he told Mary Lynn. She did as he asked.

His mother's Presbyterian conviction that God disposed all was reflected in McGill's own unshaken belief in predestination. He never spoke of any future plan without adding the provisional "God willing."

With his mother's passing, McGill, who for nearly a year had stayed close to home, began to travel again, and Mary Lynn soon understood what life would be like with him once they were married — a few weeks of happiness followed by long periods of separation. His mother died in August. In September he left for the Far East. In Vietnam, he called on all the higher authorities, rode helicopters and patrol boats into the combat zones, and spent one raucous evening in a frontline bunker with his godson, PFC John P. Martin of the First Cavalry, plying the platoon's pet monkey with beer. He moved on to Japan, where *The South and the Southerner* was being published in Japanese, translated from the English by Miss Kimiko Kawato — Kim, his tiny companion of the Fuji climb.

Just before leaving Saigon, he learned that the arch-segregationist, Lester Maddox, had trounced McGill's gubernatorial choice, Ellis Arnall, in the Georgia Democratic primary. This dismal news, he wrote to Harry Ashmore, so distressed him that he had an almost overwhelming impulse to get a job and remain forever thereafter an expatriate in Japan.

Two things called him home. One was his love for Mary Lynn; the other a promise made to his son.

Young Ralph, like his father, had fallen desperately in love and after a number of other romances had become engaged to Miss Adelaide Martin, known as Lady. On December 17 they were to be married, and to McGill's great delight young Ralph had asked his father to serve as his best man.

McGill and Mary Lynn had agreed to hold their own plans in abeyance until Ralph and Lady were wed and on their way. Now, only one obstacle remained — a promise to the State Department to make one more trip to Africa to talk to students and ministers of government in the emerging countries where the Soviet Union was making so strong a bid for power.

On leaving, he had asked Mary Lynn what she would like from Africa. Her answer surprised him. "I'd like a love letter," she said.

He laughed and shook his head. That, he said, was a literary form he had never mastered.

He left for his African trip on Sunday, February 26, 1967. Three hours out from Kennedy in a Pan Am jet high over the Atlantic, he took out a yellow pad and began to write in longhand the letter she had asked for. He began by explaining why he preferred the simple salutation, "My Dear Mary Lynn," as the beginning of a love letter — instead of the more ardent "My Dearest," or "My Precious," though they, too, were accurate. "Somehow, it sounds, to me at least, more meaningful," he said.

He then continued with a quote from Adlai Stevenson which he had come upon in a book by William Attwood, *The Reds and the Blacks*, which he had been reading on the flight. It was from a speech by Stevenson, made at Princeton in 1954:

"What a man knows at fifty he did not know at twenty is for the most part incommunicable . . . the knowledge he had acquired with age is not the knowledge of formulas, or forms of words, but of people, places, actions — a knowledge not gained by words, but by touch, sight, sound, victories, failures, sleeplessness, devotion, love — the human experiences of this earth, and of oneself and other men."

This I think is applicable in some undetermined measure to you and me — the love I have for you is for the most part incommunicable in words — it is not knowledge of why, or how, but a knowledge gained by touch, sight, sound, devotion, love — human experiences. As I have told you, I think the first knowledge, or coming, of being drawn to you, was one of sight — of liking the way you looked, standing, walking, of a certain style in your movements that appealed to me and made images in my mind. Other experiences, small and large, have been added until there now exists a composite of love and affection. Neither you nor I constructed it consciously. It came out of human experiences and out of oneself — ourselves, separately and together. So, I do not know in all its details why or how I love you, but I do.

This surely is an odd love letter if we take the common pattern of them.

So ended the formal love note, but the remainder of the three-page letter grew out of the same tenderness, the same deep concern for her happiness. He concluded his letter with his usual report on food and drink and weather and the speed of flight, which never ceased to amaze a man who remembered the buggy and the steamboat. He reported that drinks aboard were only twenty-five cents, but he had taken nothing, planning to have a split of red wine with his lunch. Unfortunately — "they ran out before they got to me, so I had tea."

He broke his journey in London, staying at Brown's Hotel, the famous old caravansary much favored by Lord Byron. He had tea at the House of Commons with the speaker, his good friend Horace King, and afterward, after a wonderful dinner at which the wine did not run out before it got to him, he had an evening of good talk with King and the journalists who cover Parliament. He moved off the next evening on an all-night flight to Accra, Ghana, and the beginning of the punishing but exhilarating African trip.

His letters and cards to Mary Lynn, and columns to the paper, reflected his excitement. He flew in a single-engine plane along the slopes of Kilimanjaro and swooped almost at antler height above the great herds of wildebeestes, zebras and giraffes on the plains of Kenya. He spoke many times before audiences hostile to America, and some of the questions were angry. But he kept his temper and answered coolly, and always some black man or woman who had been to the States and knew something of the Americans rose up to speak in his defense. He tried to go into South Africa but was denied a visa to that country of apartheid, and after a restless wait of three and a half hours, he finally caught a tourist plane out, never having seen more of Johannesburg than its airport lounge. This was vastly annoying to an old reporter, but it added much to his stature when he spoke thereafter in the black nations.

When he was not speaking, he was traveling, and every day he had to write a column. He would send them in batches of two or three at a time and wait in fretful nervousness until Grace would cable him that they had arrived.

"I don't know how I do it," he wrote Mary Lynn. "I only know it is at the expense of rest. But as Mr. Truman said, 'If you don't like the heat, get out of the kitchen.' "

In late March he was back home, writing to his friend, Robert Sommerville, the president of the Atlanta Transit Company, and sending him a bus token which he had carried halfway around the world. "I thought," he wrote, "that you would like to have such a well-traveled bus token."

There was something symbolic in McGill's returning it. For nearly forty years, when not hitching a ride with friends or neighbors, he had been battling the morning and evening crush on the Peachtree-Buckhead trolley. Now his straphanging days were over. In the months preceding their marriage Mary Lynn picked him up at home and drove him to the *Constitution* before doubling back to her own office in the Doctors' Building a dozen blocks away. Every afternoon, when her chores were done, she would phone him and he would set out walking to meet her, and somewhere along Peachtree she would see him, stocky, solid, hatless usually, with his hair blowing in the wind, the huge stuffed briefcase under his arm, limping a little on an old football knee, but plowing ahead.

This became one of the good times of the day for her. She used to tell him that it was almost indecent for a woman of her age to feel this strange excitement, this eager quickening of the breath, as with expectant delight she watched for the first sight of him, plunging toward her through the crowd. It was silly, she would tell him. It was embarrassing for her to feel that way.

It pleased him vastly, of course, for her to say such things, and he'd laugh and say he hoped he would always be able to cause her such pleasant embarrassment. Then he would settle back in the seat with a huge and windy sigh, and go through the routine of telling her "all the horrible things that had happened that day, what a terrible fix the world was in, and how unreasonable everybody was, and how stupid." Then with all this off his chest, he would settle back happily, and she would drive him to the grocery store, where he would take over the shopping and buy everything in sight.

Later, after he was gone, this was the most miserable part of the day for Mary Lynn, a time of ineffable sadness. She could not bear the sight of the empty seat beside her. She grew to hate the car and finally she gave it to her father, unable to bring herself to drive it any longer.

What Mary Lynn meant to him in the brief years they were married was reflected in the way he spoke of her to others. In his letters she was simply "the Paragon." In speech she was "MaryLynnGodblessher," spoken in one word.

What he meant to her was evidenced by her radiance when they were together. She had been a serious-minded little girl who studied all the time, had never learned to dance, had few boyfriends, and never felt that she was beautiful or even particularly attractive. McGill, somehow, had made her feel both beautiful and desirable. Another thing he had done for her was to make it possible for her to reveal her feelings. She had always been the strong one. She had never been able to show emotion, or to feel small and dependent on someone else. And now, with him to comfort her, she could break down and bawl like any other woman if she felt like it when she was tired or tense at the end of the day. He didn't quite understand this, of course, and was dismayed by it.

He would think he had somehow wounded her and would try to apologize. But she would tell him, dammit, not to worry. It was marvelous, it was wonderful, it was release of tension, it was the best of therapy.

They honeymooned in New England, a place to which McGill always went as to a second home. His heart was in the South, and he could never leave it, but the intellectual stimulus he felt when he was in Boston, the good talk with old friends, the sharp challenge of the questing minds he encountered when he spoke to the Nieman Fellows at Harvard, or at seminars at New England universities, never failed to excite him. It was only natural then that he should bring his bride to this place which had opened up to him adventures of the mind which he had rarely met with elsewhere.

He particularly wanted Mary Lynn to see Salem, where they once burned witches. It was fortunate that the custom no longer prevailed, he pointed out, or she, who had bewitched him, would be unsafe.

It was cold in New England that April, and at Boston, Salem, Concord, they walked in the snow until weary, visiting all the shrines of freedom where the nation had been born and having their picture taken at each one. At Sudbury, they stayed at the Wayside Inn, made famous by Longfellow, where Mary Lynn took a picture of McGill in bed, placidly reading the *Tales*. They stayed in the older portion, dating back to 1686, and she recalls that, in the mornings when both lay on the floor doing their setting-up exercises to start the blood, the timbers shook.

It was colder still in New York, where they stopped on their way home, and McGill, who hated hats, walked bareheaded in a bitter wind, feeling with unusual sharpness the hard bite of the cold. At her urging, he bought a beret which he wore with great aplomb thereafter, though there were those who felt it made him look like a Basque sheepherder.

They came home and for a few days he felt fine. The Met was in town and, for two evenings, the McGills went to the opera. Then the strain of the hard travel on the African trip, the emotional and physical drain of the wedding and honeymoon, the walks bareheaded in the cold, began to take their toll. He became hoarse and feverish and Mary Lynn put him to bed at home with viral pneumonia. He had been scheduled to speak at the University of Oklahoma Law School on May 4. He sent out his speech to be read. It was titled "Law — Giant Rock in a Weary

World," and its theme was that in every generation there are great social changes in progress and only the law — firm enough to hold fast the concept that individual liberty must be served, flexible enough to bend with the winds of change — can prevent the world from shattering into chaos and anarchy and the abandonment of all legal process.

It was during this illness that Mary Lynn, knowing about his arrhythmic heart, bought a stethoscope. She put it against his chest and listened, hearing only a faint thumping. When Dr. Wilber came, she told him that she feared she had bought an inferior instrument. She could hardly hear McGill's heartbeat.

Wilber looked at her strangely.

"Listen to mine," he said. He adjusted the stethoscope and put it against his chest. The heartbeat was loud and clear.

McGill, he explained, had a huge and muscular chest in which the beat could only be faintly heard by a trained ear. As for her, he pointed out gently, she had had the earpiece upside down. After that, Mary Lynn did not bother with the stethoscope. When they'd wake in the morning, she would put her head against McGill's chest, listening. She quickly discovered what Dr. Wilber had learned. Sometime during the past few weeks the old irregular pulse, under control for nearly three years, had come back. Listening, she would hear "bump-bump, bump-bump," a strong and steady double beat. Then there would follow a long and terrifying pause in which she heard no beat at all, and then would come the flurry of fast, shallow, close-together beats, more a fluttering than a rhythmic pumping.

He would ask casually, "Well, how does it sound this morning, Doctor," and if it were bad she'd answer, "Never mind!" and he would laugh. It never seemed to worry him.

It worried her, though, and without letting him know it, she bought bottles of oxygen and respirators for the house and car.

Medication soon brought the flutter under control, though an annoying cough hung on that caused Dr. Wilber to wonder about pulmonary embolisms. To the digitalis McGill had been taking, he added an anticoagulant.

Once out of bed, McGill, fiercely determined not to let illness slow him down, resumed a schedule of hard and unremitting travel. He flew to New Orleans to speak at Xavier University, to Detroit to address the historical society, to Chicago to catch a plane to Kansas City, where he would charter a light plane to take him to Topeka, and from there by car to Manhattan and Kansas State to deliver the Alf Landon lecture.

The Kansas trip was a memorable one. He stayed overnight with Governor Landon, Republican candidate for President in 1932, and was fascinated by the old man, still bright and alert of mind and able to ride a jumping horse at seventy-nine. He was one of the few Republicans McGill ever admired, and on his return he wrote in his column: "Alf Landon is a rare man, wise, philosophic and understanding. . . . The nation could have used his intelligence and common sense."

McGill's speech at Kansas State was a review of the changing politics in the South and the problems facing the Republicans there in their struggle to establish a two-party system. In it he strongly attacked the system of segregation which he once, in an earlier day, had reluctantly accepted:

> The creation of a system of segregation was an evil, the effects of which were deep and widespread beyond the easy assumption that it merely separated the races in travel, education and in housing. It subjected the Negro to a separation which made it impossible for him to know anything of participation in citizenship, much less the responsibilities of it.

He was not kind in his evaluation of the Republican party in the South: "Its leadership," he said, "is all too often those who have deserted the Democratic party because of opposition to civil rights legislation. Too much of the Republican effort in the South has been, and is, an attempt to win votes by adopting programs more racist than those of the southern Democrats. . . ."

He was no more gentle with the Democrats, whom he found to be "not without trauma and dilemma":

> The divisive efforts of racism and the determination of rural leaders to maintain segregated schools no matter what the cost to educational standards . . . have contributed to a substantial split in what used to be called the solid Democratic South. We now know we have no Democratic party such as existed in states outside the South. In the southern one-party state, the Democratic party was what the governor made it. There were factions, each calling itself Democratic, that contended for the governorship.

McGill felt that his talk at Kansas State went very well. In it, as in all his speeches, he had outlined the plight of all the deprived population, the black, the Puerto Ricans and Mexican-Americans, the aged and the poor. He analyzed and condemned the extremists of both persuasions, the Wallaces and the Maddoxes of the right, the Carmichaels and Rap Browns of the militant left. It should be obvious, he concluded, that the immediate and longtime needs of thirty-eight million Americans should not be abandoned because of the stupid, reckless, irrational protests and deliberately provocative acts of such governors as were symbolized in Wallace and Maddox, or by those of the New Left who were hostile to the existing society. "We are," he summed up, "in a period, complex, emotional and defiant, when common sense, understanding and patience are required of us."

Governor Landon, in a note to McGill a week after his speech, gave a good description of McGill's awkward but highly effective speaking style:

> I have delayed writing you on the reaction to your talk here. All last week I've run into favorable comment. I . . . never watched a more intent audience. There was hardly a wiggle or a scratch.
>
> I must confess for the first three or four minutes I thought, "It's too bad he isn't a better speaker." Then I found myself straining forward to catch every word. Mrs. Landon asked me afterwards, "Are you all right?" I said, "Yes, why?" She said, "I noticed your face became so flushed." This is my reaction to the drama you pictured so effectively through the power of understatement. A polished orator could never have gripped the audience as you did. . . .

McGill returned from Kansas to fill a speaking engagement which, a few years earlier, would have been inconceivable. A friend named Cecil Roberts, a woman of redoubtable faith in the final triumph of integration as a moral issue, persuaded the Young Businessmen's Club of Birmingham not only to invite McGill to speak, but to give him a plaque citing his great contribution to progress in the South. His talk there also brought comment on his speaking style. Dr. Alston Callahan, a strong supporter of McGill's, wrote him that "I hate those well-rounded, sharply oriented talks that have been worked over and prettied up into unity, coherence, and emphasis. It is better to hear a man just talk on something he knows about and is thinking about. . . ."

McGill, while traveling hard and speaking often, was also engaged in a running fight through the mails with critics, both of the right and left. A young liberal journalist named Gerald Lukenow was enraged by McGill's criticism of the black militants of the New Left. He wrote him that "you never could grasp the real meaning of Black Power, so you destroyed it and drove SNCC into a more extreme position." He also was disenchanted with McGill's stand on Vietnam and was made irate by McGill's columns criticizing the participants in the Washington peace march. McGill's reply was blunt:

> It might interest you to know I went out after the peace march and had a look at things. I saw the debris left behind and its contents. I saw what was scrawled on the walls of the Pentagon. I heard a tape of the little act put on by those clad in hippie costumes, and even in my old Marine Corps ears it was some of the worst filth I ever heard. . . . You really astound me when you say I destroyed the Black Power movement and drove SNCC [the Students' Nonviolent Coordinating Committee] into a more extreme position. Surely, Mr. Lukenow, you know this is absurd. SNCC was once a brave, wonderful organization which has now ceased to exist in its original form. Surely, you would not insist that SNCC is now comprised of students, that it is nonviolent, or that it is coordinated. Those who have it in charge have coordinated it with the other militant groups.
>
> You asked me to stop writing because I didn't know what I was writing about. I regret that I lack your omniscience, Mr. Lukenow, but admittedly I have never known all the answers. I promise to keep trying to seek for them.

By the end of summer the hard travel and the almost daily forensic jousting with his critics had begun to take their toll of the laboring heart. There was now a murmur, which worried Dr. Wilber, and the fibrillation had returned. On the advice of Dr. Bruce Logue, a heart specialist, McGill went into Emory University Hospital. The technique which was to be tried on him was a procedure designed to restore the regular rhythm of the heartbeat by means of electric shock, applied to the heart's pacemaker, a little muscular node at the top of the big heart muscle. The first shock worked perfectly. The fibrillation stopped, and the rhythmic beat was restored. Tarver, calling on McGill, found him in euphoric mood, which was reflected in a report from Tarver to Ashmore, Popham, Golden and John Griffin. Twenty physicians, he said, had gone over McGill and were staring at each other in amazement.

"Not only his heart, lungs and legs, but also his reactions, pituitary and libido, are those of an eighteen-year-old youth. Indeed, one gets the impression, listening to him, that a culture from his blood might be made into a serum which would eliminate the cost of Medicare."

Their jubilation was premature. For forty-eight hours after the first shock the heartbeat was strong and regular. Then the old erratic pulse came back again. Two more electric treatments were tried, one so severe it burned his chest. Both failed. McGill was tremendously disappointed, but after a period of deepest worry, he resolved not to let the failure slow him down. He was a great admirer of Dr. Paul Dudley White, who was an advocate of exercise to strengthen the heart. With the resolution of an athlete training for the Olympics, he and Mary Lynn would walk two miles together every afternoon. He would work in his garden, digging and bending and planting until the sweat poured from him, and he would swing a maul, splitting logs until he seemed ready to drop, a procedure he continued until his doctors found out about it and made him stop.

In December, in Capetown, South Africa, Dr. Christiaan Barnard performed the first successful heart transplant on a patient who lived for eighteen days. Both McGill and Mary Lynn read this story with fascination. They decided that if Dr. Wilber could keep him going for five more years, until the technique could be perfected, Ralph would be willing to risk a transplant. He ruled out an electric pacemaker carried in the pocket. The idea of being wired to an electronic gadget that would keep his heart beating rhythmically did not appeal to him. Mary Lynn also knew that with his incredible ineptitude with mechanical things, he would break it in five minutes.

Meanwhile, he went on driving himself hard. Mary Lynn did not try to stop him, nor did the doctors forbid him anything but the most strenuous physical labor. Each knew that to a man of his restless temperament the fret and worry of enforced idleness would be more harmful than work and travel.

17

McGill's memory was incredible, and when it failed him, as it did once in a great while, and he permitted an error of fact to creep into his columns, his embarrassment was painful to witness. When an editor in Palo Alto, California, pointed out that he had confused old Ibn Saud, who died in 1953, with his son, Saud, who was pushed off the throne by his half brother, Faisal, in 1964, McGill wrote: "It was a well-deserved rebuke. . . . I can't tell you how depressed I was about the error. I went around for days feeling low. . . ."

This was no exaggeration. Always, when some small fact, a date, a name, a line of verse, would not spring instantly to memory, he would beat his head and moan, "I am losing my mind."

This concern seemed to increase as he grew older. Deeper than his fear of physical disability was his fear of failing mental powers, indicating that the time for his retirement might be drawing near. Only serious illness could keep him away from the office when he was in Atlanta. When he came in, weary from the road, Mary Lynn would try to persuade him to write his column at home and send it in by messenger. He would refuse. "You've got to let them see you down there, or they'll forget you," he said.

Always inordinately fearful of being put out to pasture, his foreboding about this unlikely prospect became more pronounced as the result of one unhappy incident late in 1967.

For some years, the older Negro ministers of the community had sponsored a project called Operation Breadbasket, in which they sought to place black men and women in jobs in business and industry. McGill and Gene Patterson had supported them in this effort, and the *Consti-*

tution, with the backing of Tarver, had tried to find qualified Negroes for all its departments, or to upgrade those already there. Sometimes they succeeded, ofttimes they didn't — causing Tarver on one occasion to write a sardonic letter to editors McGill and Baggs:

"While you gentlemen are involved in the integration process on the philosophical and ethereal level, those of us who have to work out such matters in the field occasionally come across some problems which I am not sure either you or the drafters of the civil rights act envisioned."

He then cited the case of a black jumper who worked for a white driver on one of the newspaper delivery trucks. When promoted to driver and given a route and a jumper of his own, he found the new responsibilities too heavy and asked for his old job back. Tarver had also made clear to his department heads in the circulation, advertising and business offices that they should hire qualified blacks whenever they could be found and train others who showed promise. Under this program, more than thirty blacks had been hired, but about half of them, once they acquired new skills, had moved on to other jobs at better pay. McGill and Patterson, with Tarver's blessing, had made an earnest effort to find black reporters, who were almost nonexistent in the Atlanta area, a result of years of segregated education in which no Negroes were enrolled in journalism schools. Two, after some difficulty, had been found, and one had departed, after borrowing a comfortable sum from the credit union. Fortunately, the credit union did not lose on this deal, for the reporter had foresightedly gotten McGill as co-signer on his note.

Furthermore, Tarver had made a journey to the headquarters of the International Typographical Union at Colorado Springs, Colorado, where he sought to persuade union leaders to permit their locals in the South to start training black apprentices. He had met with little success.

He was, therefore, in a touchy mood one afternoon just after Thanksgiving when the Breadbasket committee came to call on him and his executives in the paneled board room of Atlanta Newspapers, Inc. Its spokesmen on this occasion was Dr. Martin Luther King, Sr. — "Daddy" King, father of the controversial young Negro leader.

Daddy King, like Tarver, was a man of ample girth and an almost Buddha-like serenity of countenance. He also, like Tarver, had a short temper and a sharp tongue when aroused. Tarver was particularly sensitive to any criticism, real or implied, of the way he ran Atlanta Newspapers. Daddy King was equally quick to take offense at any act or utterance he interpreted as a slur upon his race.

Once, for example, when driving with his son, Martin Luther King, Jr., then a small boy, a cop had pulled him over to the curb for some minor traffic infraction. "What's your name, boy?" the officer asked. "Tell him your name, son," King said to the boy. "I was talking to you," the cop said, looking at King. "This is a boy," said King, indicating his son. "I am a man. If you want to know my name, speak to me like a man."

King, in the Breadbasket meeting, started out quietly enough. For several years, he said, he and his minister friends had been calling upon the papers, asking them to hire more Negroes. The black community in Atlanta, he said, made up about a third of the *Constitution*'s circulation. The black people believed in the paper and supported it. They were proud of both the papers, he added, for giving McGill and Patterson the freedom to speak out boldly for fair treatment and equal economic opportunity for Negroes.

But, the Reverend King went on, the Negro community had been disappointed in the actual hiring record of the papers. There were still far too few black faces behind the ad and circulation counters, and in the newsroom, the composing room and the mechanical departments.

Tarver's eyes got narrow as he listened, and those who knew him realized he was about to blow. He stood up.

"That's enough, Reverend," he said, interrupting King.

Then, face white, voice trembling with anger, he outlined the efforts the paper had made to find and hire qualified Negroes and the efforts, not always successful, to train and keep them once hired.

This was in the days before the word "Negro" had been replaced by "black," and in his haste and anger, Tarver inadvertently slipped into the southernism "Nigra." King was on his feet at once.

"Just a minute, Mis-tah Tah-vah," he said in his own r-less speech. "Can you say 'Nee-grow'?"

Tarver, who was not used to being spoken to so brusquely in his own board room, looked at him in amazement.

"Yes," he said, "I can say 'Nee-grow.' "

"Then let me hear you say it, Mr. Tarver. Let me hear you say 'Nee-grow.' "

"Nee-grow," said Tarver.

"Thank you, Mr. Tarver," said King.

He walked to the door, turned, and delivered his ultimatum. Either there would be more black faces behind the counters and desks and in the composing room of the *Atlanta Constitution* or there would be a black picket line around the building. He went out. Tarver, still white with anger, went back to his own office. McGill and Patterson remained with the other Negro leaders, trying to salvage what goodwill and understanding they could out of the wreckage. These were not violent and militant young blacks, but sad and gentle old preachers, and the meeting ended peacefully.

Back in Patterson's office, which had been McGill's old office before he took on the title of publisher, the two of them glumly talked over the events of the afternoon. It had been a bad show all around. Both Tarver and Daddy King had lost their cool, as McGill put it, and both McGill and Patterson knew that in time they would bear the brunt of it. McGill, particularly, was disturbed. That evening he and Mary Lynn were to go to a small dinner party. The Tarvers also would be there, and McGill's instinct for trouble told him he would be wise to phone and make his excuses. Patterson dissuaded him. "Go on, Pappy," he said. "Nothing will happen. That's a social thing. . . ."

Early the next morning, hollow-eyed from lack of sleep, McGill came into Patterson's office. He slumped into the green leather chair — the same worn, rump-sprung chair where in years gone by so many men and women had sat as they poured out their troubles to him.

He looked thunderstruck. He had been right, he said, in thinking he should not go. The evening had been a catastrophe. And as he said this, he put his head down in his arms on Patterson's desk and began sobbing.

Patterson got up quickly and went around the desk, put his arms around him, and held him close. "Pappy, what in the world!" he said.

McGill got hold of himself then and began to tell the story. The evening had been an agony. Tarver, still angry, again and again had brought the table conversation back to the unhappy episode of the afternoon. He made it clear that he considered it McGill's fault that he had been exposed to the humiliating confrontation with King.

As Tarver remembered it afterward, the talk had been no more abrasive than the usual half-kidding, half-serious needling that went on between him and McGill when matters dealing with racial policies came up.

Perhaps it hadn't. But to McGill, growing increasingly sensitive as he grew older, the tone of Tarver's remarks had had an ominous ring. Particularly his last comment. As they were putting on their coats to leave, he had said, "McGill, maybe you'd better start filling out your retirement papers." Mary Lynn, who was standing nearby, had taken it as a joke, remembering that Tarver also had added that "we wouldn't want you to be embarrassed, having to cross the picket line your Negro friends are going to put around us." But McGill hadn't heard this half-facetious qualifier. One word only had burned itself into his mind: "retirement."

That night he could not sleep, and though Mary Lynn did her best to calm him, there was no way she could persuade him that Tarver had not been speaking seriously.

Even the thought that at some distant day he might have to retire always caused McGill to fret and brood, and now the prospect that it might be imminent seemed to terrify him. All his life, work had been his anodyne. No grief, no anxiety about the future, was ever so obsessive he could not put it out of mind when he sat down at a typewriter. If that shield was taken away from him, if he was suddenly forced into the limbo of retirement, it would destroy him.

Patterson tried to reassure him.

"You'll be here, Pappy, long after the rest of us are gone."

To Patterson, seeing McGill, the bravest and gentlest of men, brought to such a state of despair, was like seeing his own father in such straits.

"I loved the man the first day I met him," Patterson said. "I was fascinated with him, with the great range of his mind, the depth of his understanding, the utter charity in his heart. There was a human warmth about him that drew me to him — as it drew all men. When I was made executive editor, I'd go up to his office, and make big executive talk. But I was actually there as a supplicant for his wisdom, for his friendship. I wanted to learn from listening to him tell stories and read poetry what he, over the years, had learned from living — the song in the language, the music and the mystery of life, the cadence of the passing days and seasons, a reverence for the lasting things."

Patterson's proudest moment came when he was chosen to take over as McGill's successor, in the editor's office where Henry Grady's old rolltop desk still stood in the corner. It was Tarver who had engineered this change, and Patterson had been grateful, for he was happy, then, to spend the rest of his career "keeping Pappy's flag flying and walking the road he taught me to walk, and training whoever came after me to go down that same road."

But there was one thing that Patterson knew, as an old combat soldier who had commanded men in battle. You give orders, and you discipline men if you must, but no matter what stress you are under, you do not take away from a man his pride and self-respect. McGill was a man impregnable to his enemies. But there was in him, too, a curious innocence, a naïveté, that made him completely vulnerable to those he loved and trusted. And it was this childlike quality that stirred in Patterson a strong compulsion to shield and protect him, and a deep resentment against anyone who would willfully hurt him.

Patterson had sensed, after seeing McGill break down and weep, that his own days on the paper were numbered. Already there had been a growing tension between him and Tarver over the handling of staff. Inevitably, things would come to a head. There would be a clash, and Tarver would turn on him with the same mordant wit and biting tongue he had used on McGill. And for Patterson, that would be the end.

It came in September of 1968 on the night of the Democratic primary in Georgia. Patterson, staying late at the office to watch the election returns, got a telephone call. Tarver, at home, had read the first edition and had not been pleased with a column written by a bright young Patterson protégée named B. J. Phillips. Miss Phillips, coming along rapidly as the *Constitution*'s editorial voice of the younger generation, had written a satirical column attacking the Georgia Power Company, which was seeking a rate increase to compensate for a recently imposed federal surtax. This had put Tarver in an awkward position. The papers themselves were planning a rate increase, and in view of this, he had assured the power company executives there would be no editorial criticism of their move toward higher rates. He called Patterson and suggested, with considerable asperity, that Miss Phillips should confine herself to matters within her field of competence. Patterson responded that he had no intention of telling his columnists what they should or should not write, so long as they stayed within the boundaries of the libel laws and the canons of good taste. The conversation ended in mutual acrimony.

After this exchange, Patterson sat for a long time, thinking. The editorship of the *Constitution* carried with it great prestige. It carried with it also great responsibilities and opportunities, and he had made the most of these. In 1967, in his seventh year as editor, his editorials had won a Pulitzer Prize. There were also tangible rewards: his salary was adequate and his stock options, though paid for laboriously out of the grocery money, in time would make him rich. But against all this was the somber fact that he could not erase from his mind the memory of McGill with his head down on his arms, sobbing until his shoulders shook. Patterson turned to his typewriter, rolled in a sheet of paper, and began to write his resignation.

Nothing that had happened in all his professional career caused McGill such distress as the clash between Patterson and Tarver. He had a deep and genuine affection for both men. Tarver, bright, caustic, cynical, irreverent, though ambitious and mature in judgment, had been his discovery and had come to Atlanta at his urging. The two had supported each other through the uncertain years of changing management, and McGill's obligation to Tarver was deep. It had been Tarver, risen to executive rank, who had protected McGill against the cold malevolence of George C. Biggers, the wrath of outraged politicians and angry readers, the choleric complaints of advertisers with strong Republican leanings. He had pushed him up to publisher, a meaningless title in his case, so he would not have to worry about retirement at sixty-five. Knowing McGill's ineptitude with money, Tarver had, in effect, taken over the management of his income. He had put McGill into a Cox Enterprises paper mill deal and got him out with a ninety-six-thousand-dollar profit. He had urged him to change from one syndicate to another that would push his column harder. And he had set up for him a company stock-option arrangement that at the time of his death was worth over a million dollars — making him one of that wealthy class he had always innately distrusted. (Postscript: two of the witnesses to McGill's will, signed one Saturday morning and conveying his estate in equal parts to his wife and son, were B. J. Phillips and Eugene Patterson.)

McGill well knew what Tarver had meant to him in protecting him against his enemies. It is entirely possible that he did not know how much Tarver had done for him financially. Until he died he looked upon himself as a man of meager resources, and this seemingly was no pose. He frequently mentioned dolefully that he would have very little to leave his son. In letters to young Ralph he recalled those years of the depression when a reporter's pay might be ten dollars cash and twenty dollars in scrip, good at the grocery store, and he confided to friends that he had not had a salary increase since he became publisher. He worried about Mary Lynn in case he should die, and he took out a forty-thousand-dollar life insurance policy when they married, an indication that he had no idea what resources in ANI stock were at his command. He always moaned at the cost of new clothes and was aghast when Mary Lynn bought him a pair of slacks for thirty dollars. He wore them to church, and during the service he leaned over to her and whispered, "I'll bet I'm the only man here wearing a thirty-dollar pair of pants." He would, though, pay twelve dollars for a bottle of wine without blinking, and his usual donation to a panhandler was ten dollars. Nobody could pick up a luncheon check when he was at the table, and he was extremely generous when tipping waitresses, rewarding them not only for good service but good morals. "They could so easily have been whores," he would explain.

Though he might not have been fully aware of his debt to Tarver, he knew what Patterson meant to him, as colleague, counselor and friend. When Patterson finally decided to leave, McGill did not try to dissuade him, for he knew instinctively how Patterson felt. He got on the phone instead to newspaper owners whose professionalism he respected, telling them that Patterson was available and what a tremendous man he was. Patterson's choice was the *Washington Post*, where the managing editor's job was open.

The day Patterson left the *Constitution* was a dark one for McGill, and both his sorrow and affection came through in his column, "An Essay on Separation," in which he said good-bye to his friend:

> Gene and I, despite the gap of years between us, had the rare gift of being able to talk with one another in the full meaning of that word. We could talk philosophy, ethics, morality, books, poetry, history, men and meanings. . . . He and I often would talk about ourselves and how we had put our feet in paths that brought us together in affection and mutual respect. We enjoyed this. Sometimes we wondered about it as we worked, as we said, to keep the light burning in editorial windows so that all wandering sinners might return and the Philistines be more able to see. . . .

Patterson's last column in the *Constitution* was, by coincidence, a tribute to McGill. It was a book review of a collection of Carl Sandburg's letters. In one of them, commenting on a McGill column, Sandburg had written:

> I have read aloud on three or four occasions your short, short story, "My Mule is Dead. I am Drowned in this Pond." It is a history woven with contemplations you didn't know you had till you started to write that piece. Your health and your humor and your analytical insights keep going on. Sometime I may try to figure out who are the ten richest men in the country. You would be one of them. . . .

"The 1960 column was a classic," Patterson commented, "rich with the wisdom of McGill at his best, loving the South and its past more than angry clingers to the past can know, but striving to explain to them the tidal flow toward a future they will not credit. . . ."

Patterson's departure, though it grieved McGill, caused no rift between him and Tarver. They openly went back to their old give and take of friendly raillery, and soon McGill was stoutly defending Tarver against those who blamed him for Patterson's leaving. These critics were many, for liberal Atlantans had come to look upon Patterson as a civic asset approaching the stature of McGill himself.

Soon McGill was writing a soothing letter to Tarver's young daughter, Margaret, known as Sissy: "There are times, as Lyndon Johnson once said, when a man is caught like a jackass in a hailstorm — all he can do is hunker up and take it. That is what your daddy and the rest of us are doing. Most of the hail has been hitting him, but he seems to hunker up pretty well, so don't worry. . . ."

Nor did Patterson's departure weaken the strong ties of affection between him and McGill. One night in late 1968, when Patterson was still new in his job at the *Washington Post*, and a little unsure of himself, he looked up from his desk in the managing editor's glass cage to see Pappy, "his wise-old-owl face breaking into a big laugh," coming toward him, arms outstretched. They gave each other the big embrazo, the back-pounding bear hug with which McGill loved to greet his closest friends.

"Introduce me around, Gene," he said. And Patterson knew then why he had come. Instinctively, McGill had understood that on this paper, a new and still untested editor from the Deep South could use some moral support from a colleague whose liberal credentials were unassailable. They moved out through the newsroom and the young black staffers crowded around McGill, and the knowledgeable old pros of both races came up to speak to the man who for so long had been a legend in their trade.

"You've got a good managing editor here," he told them, his hand on Patterson's shoulder, and to Patterson it was like winning another Pulitzer Prize.

That night over a brandy after dinner at Duke Zeibert's, Patterson told McGill how much he appreciated what McGill had done. Not only had his visit given him status with his staff — more important, it had given him the reassurance he had needed that McGill was not hurt with him and disappointed at his leaving.

McGill looked at him.

"Gene," he said, "I never blamed you. I understood how you felt. If I had been your age, I think I would have done the same thing. But now, I am getting old. I am just playing out my string. . . ."

18

For a man "just playing out my string," McGill showed an enormous drive and vigor. His fascination with the "adagios and arabesques" of the politicians remained unabated, his zest for forensic battle with his enemies was as keen as ever, and he kept up a travel schedule that would have exhausted a circus elephant.

The action of the Georgia legislature in choosing Lester Maddox as governor after a general election in which a write-in vote for Ellis Arnall, defeated in the primary, prevented either Maddox or the Republican candidate from getting a majority, was one of the arabesques of politics which fascinated but did not please him. "The election of Maddox," he wrote to a young friend, Diane Love, "was a grotesque disgrace, but understandable. We are caught up in many traumas in which the race problem is a part. . . . Presently a great many persons with some sense are trying to control and direct him and are having little success . . . the man remains, in my opinion, a psychotic person."

At the same time, so great was McGill's sympathy for a father with a wayward son that he wrote Maddox a letter when his boy got in trouble with the law for the alleged theft of a TV set. He had heard, he said, that the governor was going to renounce his son and cast him out. He urged Maddox not to do this, but to stand by the boy and support him. "He needs you now more than ever," he wrote.

The morning after he mailed the letter, Maddox showed up unannounced at McGill's office. He put out his hand.

"Mr. Ralph," he said, "some of my friends gave me bad advice. You gave me good advice, and I appreciate it." He was crying. He later went on the air, not to renounce his son, but to ask the electorate to pray for him.

Certain developments in the civil rights controversy during the hot summer of 1967 troubled McGill deeply. Over the years he had been preaching that the Negro was the most patient and gentle of men, who had endured with superhuman stoicism the generations of insult and discrimination that had been his lot. Now he discovered that the modern young black was neither patient nor gentle but angrily, militantly aggressive, demanding his rights instanter, and sometimes was rashly irresponsible and unreasoning in his pursuit of them. This disturbed McGill. In a letter to McGeorge Bundy, congratulating the Ford Foundation on making a grant to CORE, one of the more conservative of the Negro organizations, he outlined what he believed to be the dilemma of Martin Luther King, Jr., — who, he said, was being forced to go part of the way with the violent wing, the Black Panthers, while at the same time opposing their methods.

After a visit to a little Negro church, once the haven and refuge of the gentlest and meekest of the blacks, he had come away convinced that King's days as a leader of his people were coming to an end. King, he felt, was rapidly losing the following of the Negroes under thirty-five. What was needed, he believed, was a responsible Negro leader, younger than King, who could stand off the challenge of the violent men, Stokeley Carmichael and Rap Brown.

At the same time, he could defend Carmichael against an enraged white citizen who had written the President and Justice Department, urging some special action against him:

> Our modern courts are a little better than the older courts, which used to hang children and condemn people for witchcraft. A dangerous person like Carmichael is protected by the Constitution and its guarantees of individual rights. If you start trying to take them away from Carmichael because you are angry at something he has done, somebody will come along to use this as a precedent to take them away from you.

McGill had supported peaceful sit-ins, but the growing violence in the streets, evidenced by the riots in Newark and Detroit, worried him. They also brought increased fusillades from his critics. One of these, a visitor from Maryland who spent his summers at Sea Island, a posh resort on the Georgia coast, sent McGill a picture of a Detroit Negro pushing a grocery cart full of loot. "This is the kind of guy you want on the American team," he had written. He went on to say that he read McGill's editorials religiously and "found them uniformly poor. They almost persuade me not to vacation in Georgia each July, and would, except for the fact that Georgians I meet have a uniformly low opinion of you." Then, incongruously, he signed himself "Cordially, William W. Werber."

McGill's reply was tart. "By all means, keep coming back to Georgia. It is always refreshing to have sociological comments on the poor and underprivileged from the rarefied air of Sea Island. I am complimented if you do find disagreement with my comments. At any rate we need you in Georgia, Mr. Werber. You assist us with the balance of payments."

W. H. Duckworth, crusty old chief justice of the Georgia Supreme Court, wrote that he did not believe McGill realized how much comfort, even encouragement, he had given the rioters by enumerating repeatedly the injustices done to Negroes which presumably set off the riots: "Since you have established by a long, brilliant and courageous record that you are a friend of the poor Negro race, you are now in position to blister the kooks and criminals for their conduct in defense of the law. And I believe you have a public duty to do so."

And blister them he did. Using material based on FBI data, McGill kept up a ceaseless attack upon the more militant Negro leaders and their organizations, particularly SNCC, which, he said, had long since abandoned the idea of nonviolence. However, he told Judge Duckworth, he "felt it important the public should know that the moderate Negroes are the targets of these same people." He also told the judge that he was wary of raising the "law and order" cry, knowing it meant white man's law keeping the black man in order.

It was six months after their marriage before McGill found opportunity to take Mary Lynn to Washington to show her off to his friends in high places there. They stayed in the owner's suite of the Jefferson with its own little kitchen, which McGill kept stocked with grapefruit, yogurt, skimmed milk, cereal and apples, food which he fondly believed to be good for his ailing heart.

They had tea at the White House, with President and Mrs. Johnson, luncheon with Chief Justice Warren, visits with J. Edgar Hoover and Dean Rusk. "I am exposed to much secret information," Mary Lynn wrote to her sister-in-law, Helen, in mid-visit. "For my own comfort, I just don't let it reach me."

She, in turn, had shown off her new husband to the National Academy of Pedodontists, holding their convention in Washington. At her suggestion, in his luncheon speech he had given her dentist friends — whose main preoccupation with government in the past had been with avoiding too great a bite from the I.R.S. — a walk through history. He described the terrible burden a President must bear, from Lincoln wandering through the White House in his carpet slippers, to Lyndon Johnson, pondering the terrible decisions of the Vietnam war.

McGill described this trip in a deadpan letter to his sister-in-law, Helen Morgan, in which he referred to Mary Lynn throughout as "the Paragon" and referred to himself in the third person, as he was listed on the luncheon program of the pedodontists — simply as "the husband of Dr. Mary Lynn Morgan":

On the day following this luncheon, the President of the United States received the Paragon. He personally showed her through the White House — the family rooms, the room where the two daughters had had their dates, the Lincoln room, where Winston Churchill also was a guest, the room where four queens have visited, and so on. He then escorted the Paragon through the Rose Garden and the exquisite Jacqueline Kennedy garden, which Mrs. Johnson created and named for Mrs. Kennedy. [The husband of Dr. Morgan also was along.] We then returned to the White House family living room and then outside to a corner of the corridor where we sat about a coffee table and had, of course, coffee and conversation.

The President then said to the Paragon and her husband that he, the President, was going out to dedicate, or assist in dedicating, the new memorial to Teddy Roosevelt. He said he would like to have us go along. So we did. The Paragon sat on one side of the President and her husband on the other. Crowds along the way waved to the Paragon and her President. The dedication was really moving. Secretary Udall, Chief Justice Warren, who also spoke, Mrs. Longworth, Teddy's daughter, and other notables were present. We then returned to the White House where the President showed the Paragon various items of interest and presented her with an autographed picture of the family — including the new grandchild and the son-in-law to be. He then called a White House car and had the Paragon and her husband sent back to their hotel. . . .

In other letters he described Mary Lynn as a gardener and dog-breeder. Though she had never so much as potted a geranium before their marriage, under his tutelage she was learning fast.

"The Mary Lynn daffodil garden was a great success," he reported:

Rich golden masses . . . they are all gone by now. But the Mary Lynn rose garden is blooming — the dozen roses she and I set out — the yellow roses blooming first with the red and other colors budding. The Mary Lynn lily garden is up and will be blooming by June. . . . We now have twenty-four tomato plants out in the Mary Lynn vegetable garden, plus twenty-four Bibb lettuce plants. The rabbits are eating these. We are so pleased to have wild rabbits we are going to plant more lettuce, hoping to have some for ourselves.

The most active member of the McGill household was a miniature dachshund named Carol, who in the course of time had puppies, with McGill and Mary Lynn in attendance; four of the five pups survived, which McGill passed out to carefully selected colleagues in the newspaper business, giving advice on their feeding and training.

Whatever concern he might have felt about his own health, he rarely mentioned it, and when he did, he spoke of it lightly. In a letter to a friend he wrote, "The rhythm of my heart is permanently interrupted, but I am told that if I must have a heart problem, this is the best one I can have."

Editorially and in private conversation and correspondence, McGill's stand on the Vietnam war remained unshakably that of Lyndon Johnson's, though many old friends whose opinions he respected now sharply criticized him. Dow Kirkpatrick, a minister friend in Evanston, Illinois, whose pulpit he once filled, had written him regretfully:

I have delayed and debated many weeks, and finally find I must write and register my objections and disappointment over the manner in which you have handled the Vietnam situation. . . . I find it difficult to understand your hundred percent defense of administration policy. . . . It is a great disappointment that you are not playing your usual role of stimulating critic. . . . I wish you were asking crucial questions now, rather than making defensive statements.

McGill was unmoved. He appreciated his old friend's candor, he said, but was deeply grieved at his position. "We are in Southeast Asia because our national interest requires us to be there, and I am unwilling to water that down," he wrote.

A young admirer, Don Rhodes, once a city-room intern on the *Constitution*, later a police reporter on the Savannah papers, had been drafted into the army and was on his way to Vietnam. He wrote McGill a warm and affectionate letter, and then added his views on the war. "Pappy," he wrote, "I think we shouldn't be there. I think it is a needless war that is bankrupting the country and I feel very bad in thinking I will probably die in a conflict I don't even advocate. I'm not a hippie, but I've thought a lot about this war. . . ."

McGill's reply was a patriotic pep talk, followed by a short course in world history and a fast look at points of threat and danger around the world. "You have taken the oath of service and I know you will obey it. But you can cause yourself a lot of grief and psychological trauma by getting involved in the great complexity of Vietnam. . . ."

Now and then, in letters to those close to him, he took off his armor of omnipotence and poured out his concerns. In a letter to Reb Gershon, on her way to England, he wrote:

I get melancholia at times, trying to adjust my thinking to changes. I guess one has to go back to the eighteenth century when the great European powers were struggling with each other to find anything comparable to today. Britain is a sad place. France has about destroyed the NATO alliance and is trying to destroy Euratom, which is an international organization designed to regulate and keep an eye on the peaceful uses of atomic reactors in Europe. As you know, I serve on a rather impotent and wholly frustrated congressionally created agency — the Arms Control and Disarmament Agency — and a nonproliferation treaty has been agreed to by the Soviets and three or four other European nations, but all of a sudden the French violently oppose it, and a group of smaller nations, largely in Latin America and Africa but including India and Pakistan, [have begun to] object. I now doubt if the nonproliferation treaty goes through. The small nations take the highly nationalistic but somewhat understandable attitude of why should the small nations be excluded from something the big ones have? This indicates a complete lack of awareness of the real and terrible meaning of nuclear energy. . . .

When global problems troubled him, or the hate mail became particularly venomous, as it did when he advocated a gun-regulation law or opposed the playing of "Dixie" in the schools, he turned for relief to his garden or his kitchen. Serenely he spaded and planted and pruned, counseling Mary Lynn solemnly on how to prepare a proper mulch. Knowing that her dexterity with her hands did not apply to kitchen utensils, he would now and then surprise her by demonstrating his prowess as a cook. Once, on Julia's day off, she came home to find that he had prepared a rack of venison, which he served with a sturdy red Spanish wine, Sangre de Toro. He kept up a steady flow of affectionate letters to Ralph and Lady in Richmond. He had been appointed to a national committee of the Episcopal church to conduct a three-year study leading to a revision of the prayer book. There would, of course, be fierce opposition from traditionalists, he said, but he had already found himself in agreement with some of the suggested changes. For instance, the sentence "Thou who takest away the sins of the world" had been changed to "Thou who takest away the *sin* of the world." His rector, the Reverend Frank Ross, had explained that the plural use of "sins" included all sorts of little petty things, the kind of sins that Governor Maddox worried about, whereas "sin" meant the rejection of Christ and his teaching.

There was another change of which he approved. This was "On the third day He rose again, according to the Scriptures, and ascended into heaven." "This always had a weaseling sound to me, as if there was some doubt. So now it reads, 'On the third day He rose again in accordance with the Scriptures. . . .' "

McGill loved the thunderous music of the King James Bible, and the stately cadence of the Psalms were often heard in his own writing, but his flexibility of mind and thought would not permit him to defend the old phrases merely because they were majestic and familiar.

"The King James Version," he wrote, "was and is the most totally magnificent piece of writing there ever was, but I must say that, when all our communication is in today's English, I do not feel the church should stick to seventeenth-century English, beautiful and poetic though it is."

Most of those who objected to the new wording, and to the translation of the Bible into modern English, were the older parishioners, and although he had quietly passed his seventieth birthday, he obviously did not number himself as one of these.

Shortly after his birthday he got a note from Whitney North Seymour, telling him that he was being elevated to an honorary, nonvoting trusteeship on the Carnegie Foundation Board since, at seventy, he could no longer function as a voting trustee. Seymour said that this biblical concept of man's useful span now seemed ridiculous in light of modern scientific developments, "and particularly in the case of one as lively and useful as you always seem to us to be."

McGill gracefully accepted his new role: "It is good of Mr. Carnegie's ghost to keep check on my age. I must say I don't feel seventy, even though I am sure I must look it. I am delighted to be getting older, because I consider the alternative to be much less pleasant. . . ."

He did express some mild regret at being "excluded from the company of the young and virile. But it is spring, and here the dogwoods are blooming. Who knows, I may take a little juniper juice and turn myself loose."

In August of 1967, about the time he was having his first session with the heart shock at Emory, Ralph and Lady confided to him that they were expecting a baby sometime in the next April. No news could have made Ralph happier. Thereafter, on his journeys north he would make a point to stop off in Richmond to check on Lady's progress. He gave her only a modicum of advice; he did, however, admonish her to continue her efforts to keep her weight down. He quoted Dr. Paul Dudley White's aphorism — "the better the legs, the clearer the brain." In Lady's case, of course, he felt that walking, not jogging, would probably be best for the baby.

He then recalled his first decision to take off weight "and try to give myself all possible odds to have a reasonably long life. It came about one day when Ralph was just a few months old. I was on a plane going to New York and looking through the ads in a magazine. I came across one by Metropolitan Life Insurance Company, which dealt with the bad health effects of overweight, and as I was already a somewhat middle-aged father [he was forty-seven and weighed about two hundred twenty pounds], I tried to adopt a program of moderation in eating, alcohol, and all other attractive habits which might cut years off my life."

In the last weeks before Lady's accouchement, McGill was in a state of nerves, worried that the baby might come at a time when he was so involved in other matters that he could not be there to welcome it. A telegram to the "Social Secretary, White House, Washington, D.C.," dated April 10, 1968, was evidence of his determination to keep himself available. It said: "Mr. and Mrs. Ralph McGill deeply regret irresolvable conflict will prevent their accepting President and Mrs. Johnson's invitation for April 16." The child arrived on April 23. McGill, alerted in time, caught a plane to Richmond that got him there at 1:45 P.M., and at 6:13 P.M., Ralph Emerson McGill, III, was born. It was McGill Senior who outran his son down the hall, arms outstretched to take the baby from the nurse bringing it from the delivery room. But she did not let him have it. It went first to the father. As the third McGill to bear the name, the baby was immediately nicknamed Trip. McGill's pride was boundless.

Despite his gloomy predictions that the nuclear proliferation treaty would never be signed, due to the stubborn oppositon of the smaller nations, McGill on March 31, 1968, was in Mexico City with Vice-President Hubert Humphrey for the ceremony at which Mexico would become the first signatory. He went down as a member of the Advisory Committee of the United States Arms Control and Disarmament Agency, but soon found himself reverting to his old character as a phone-grabbing competitive reporter working one of the hottest news stories of the decade. With the vice-president's party he had gone on to the American ambassador's residence several miles out of town for dinner. Cocktails and hors d'oeuvres had been served and a small orchestra was playing as the company awaited the arrival of the

President of Mexico. It was then announced that the President, along with the ambassador and Humphrey, was in the ambassador's study listening to President Johnson's speech.

McGill's old newspaper instincts told him something big was brewing. With the other newspapermen and Humphrey's staffers, he gathered around a small radio in one corner of the reception room and there, through the squeal and squawk of static caused by a sudden heat-lightning storm, he heard Mr. Johnson announce that he would not run again.

A Humphrey aide came out to say that the vice-president would soon make a statement but would answer no questions, and the party would immediately go in to dinner.

The vice-president's statement was brief. Standing in the glare of the television lights, tears glistening in his eyes, he told the furiously scribbling newsmen that the President had come by his house a few hours before he had left for Mexico City to tell him of his decision. He was saddened by it and had tried to dissuade him, but without success. He then praised Johnson for having accomplished more in the field of civil rights, voting rights, federal aid to education and the general welfare than all four presidents who had preceded him.

Not since Edward VIII of England had abdicated his throne had a chief of state of such stature renounced all future claim to office. And the man who with warm partisanship appraised Johnson's achievements might himself become his successor. He did not say so. In fact, he left McGill convinced that he would not try. But the possibility was there.

As Humphrey finished, they all went in to dinner, McGill's journalistic instincts fighting with his sense of what was socially permissible. Squirming in his chair, he lasted until the first course was served. Then, hastily excusing himself, he went in search of a telephone. He found four of them in the ambassador's office upstairs — with twelve reporters in loud and angry battle over who was to use them first. The connections were bad, due to the lightning storm, and the men on the phones were yelling and cursing as they tried to make themselves understood in New York, Chicago, and Washington.

McGill fell in line at a phone, with three men ahead of him. He looked at his watch. It was moving on toward midnight in Atlanta, and the deadline for the *Constitution*'s last edition was 12:40 A.M.

As a Mexican reporter hung up, the phone rang. Atlanta was calling Mr. McGill, the embassy operator said. Back in her apartment in Atlanta, Grace Lundy had heard President Johnson make his announcement. With the prescience that made her almost an extension of McGill's own thought processes, she knew that, somewhere, he was trying to get through to her. She reached for the phone, her mind running back over the hour-by-hour schedule she tried to keep for him when he was on the road. Two minutes later her call was being received in the ambassador's residence. "Excuse me, gentlemen," said McGill blandly, moving ahead of two men. Then half-heard, fading and crackling over the miles, his croaky voice began dictating a substitute column to Grace.

"I think if I were a young teen-age reporter," he began, "I would have said, 'This is a moment you will never forget. . . .' "

The Johnson announcement left many stunned, McGill among them, and his bewilderment was reflected in his comments. For all that he had accomplished, he said, Johnson had not been able to end the war — and it was this that was driving him into retirement. For McGill, who had supported Johnson all the way, it was easy to place the blame:

> President Johnson had inherited a war and had guided it with energy and necessary escalation. . . . For that, the liberals, who do not care what reality is, had damned him. The President had accomplished what generations of liberals had sought and failed to gain. Yet they are those who illustrate the kind of support that destroyed Adlai Stevenson and reduced the late Jack Kennedy to such a state of unpopularity and legislative failure that his advisers sent him to Texas in search of lost popularity.

Though he did not say so in his column, one of the liberals whose opposition had helped Johnson to his decision was McGill's own minister and good friend, the Reverend Frank Ross, rector of All Saints. A week before Johnson's announcement, McGill was writing Ross:

> You distressed me Sunday by your attack on Johnson. The Democratic party is pretty well shot; there is going to be blood on the moon. Mr. Kennedy and Mr. McCarthy have not merely assured us of a split in the party, they have assured us of a really tremendously hot summer — and unless I miss my guess, a tremendous swing to the right in the whole country. It

will be more of a swing to the right than going to Mr. Nixon — a harsh right swing such as the country has not before experienced. It will give us several years of violence. The only light I can see is that all of you people who don't like Lyndon Johnson will then be happy having got rid of him. Otherwise I'm very fond of you. Especially Kitty.

Two days after he had come home, weary of body and still puzzled and saddened by Johnson's decision to lay down the burdens of the presidency, McGill was suddenly stunned, enraged, and far more deeply saddened by the murder of Martin Luther King. His column on the morning after King's death poured out his anger and his hurt:

At the moment the triggerman fired, Martin Luther King was the free man. The white killer (or killers) was a slave to fear, a slave to his own sense of inferiority, a slave to hatred, a slave to all the bloody instincts that surge in a brain when a human being decides to become a beast.

In the wake of this disaster in Memphis, a great many such slaves must consider if they wish to continue serving their masters of fear, hate, inferiority, and beastliness. It is something of an irony that Dr. King was free and was hated by so many slaves. It is perhaps too much to hope, but much of the violent reaction to this bloody murder could be blunted if in every city and town there would now be a resolve to remove what remains of injustice and racial prejudice from schools, from training and job opportunities, from housing, and community life in general. . . .

The white South — the white population in all the country — must now give answer. If injustice and inequity, if racist prejudices and discriminations now become the targets of all decent men and women, Dr. King's death may bring about what he sought for himself, his people and country.

If this does not happen, then slaves who serve masters of hatred, fear and evil will have to be put down mercilessly and immediately.

Out of martyrdom must come the right answer.

For more than a week before he turned to other things, McGill's column assayed the King killing. He traced the King legend, from the evening in 1955 when an aged Negro woman, her feet hurting, her spirit seized by a great weariness, refused to move to a back seat on a Montgomery bus when the driver ordered her to. She was arrested, and out of that incident grew the Montgomery bus boycott, and the rise of the charismatic young minister, Dr. King, to fame and danger in Birmingham, and Selma thirteen years later, and finally to death in Memphis. McGill wrote of the hate mail and the calls he received. The overwhelming response was one of grief and regret, but there were those — "spiritual brothers to the killer in madness and hate" — who called or wrote him with "the stew of hate bubbling in their skulls."

He pointed out that nearly every act of progress in civil rights legislation had come after some act of violence. The civil rights bill that Lyndon Johnson pushed through was known to journalists as the "Bull Connor Memorial Civil Rights Act," its passage given impetus by the sight on TV screens of Connor's snarling police dogs and fire hoses. The assassination of King, he predicted, would end the opposition in Congress to an open housing act. "Must it always be so," he asked, "that some act of horror must shock the country into doing what is right and fit?"

Violence flared in more than one hundred cities throughout the United States in the wake of King's murder. Riots in Washington caused President Johnson to call out troops, and in Atlanta there was a growing tension as the day of the funeral approached. President Johnson, on the phone to McGill, told him that his security forces had strongly advised him not to attend. In the presence of massed crowds, in the possibility not only of violence but of a mass hysteria, they could not guarantee the safety of the President. McGill told Johnson he was wise to follow the counsel of his security staff. The mood of the city was one of sorrow, not of anger, but no one could anticipate what might happen if some spark should set off an emotional explosion in a hundred thousand black mourners.

Not long afterward, former Vice-President Nixon, candidate for the Republican nomination for the presidency, called. He was coming to the funeral, he said, and would be grateful if McGill could arrange for him to call on the widow, Coretta King, at her home. McGill told him what he had told the President — that Atlanta's Mayor Ivan Allen and Police Chief Herbert Jenkins had pledged that the city would do its utmost to insure that the King funeral was carried out safely, with due reverence. But nobody could guarantee this. And if Nixon should come, and there was a riot, he might be hurt. There was a pause. Then Nixon said: "Well, I think I shall come down anyway. My advisers tell me I need the television exposure."

Feeling a sense of mild outrage, but admiring, ruefully, the unselfconscious audacity with which Nixon followed his political instincts, McGill arranged for the meeting with Coretta King. He called Xernona Clayton, a rising young leader of the black community, who soon, under his quiet sponsorship, would begin the first television program presented by a black person in the South. Miss Clayton called her friend, Coretta King, and on Sunday afternoon, three days before the funeral, Nixon, accompanied only by an aide, called on Mrs. King at her home in Atlanta. There was no advance notice and no photographers were present.

Of the several presidential aspirants present for the funeral, neither Nixon, nor McCarthy, nor Rockefeller, nor even Vice-President Humphrey got the heaviest exposure. When Senator Robert F. Kennedy, accompanied by his wife, Ethel, and his brother, Edward, and his sister-in-law, Jacqueline, appeared at Ebenezer Baptist Church, where the private services were held, muted but excited comment ran through the vast crowd outside the church. When Robert Kennedy came out after the service to join the four-mile march behind the mule-drawn casket to the public services at Morehouse College, they cheered him.

"Wherever he went," reported the *Constitution*'s political editor, Remer Tyson, "people cheered him, rushed up to shake his hand, pushed close to touch his clothes, and at one point, thousands of them mobbed him."

Nixon and Vice-President Humphrey, Tyson reported, left the church unnoticed by a side door and left Atlanta soon thereafter.

The meaning of the great throng of black mourners, estimated at two hundred thousand, and the presence of a host of political figures in attendance was not lost on McGill:

> The funeral services of Dr. King revealed . . . not merely an immense outpouring of respect and affection for Dr. King, but also a great demonstration of guilt feeling on the part of America. There was revealed, too, many examples of the most pragmatic politics, lacking in any other quality save pragmatism. One does not need to question those men who were sincere and those who were not. But only the most naïve would fail to see in the tremendous attendance at Dr. King's services in Atlanta the evidence there of increased "black power" in the nation's politics. This is a healthy thing.

It was less than ten years ago that the Negro had very little voting power. One of the real phenomena of change brought about by law and the use of federal registrars has been the tremendous increase in Negro voting. Southern resistance to civil rights has motivated Negro migrants from the South, now gathered in the many cities about the country, to register and to take militant positions in behalf of equal rights for their people everywhere in the nation.

So it was not at all cynical, but a perfectly reasonable and practical bit of politics that political leaders from states with large numbers of Negro voters should have been present at the services. One does not have to assume they were there for any reason save to pay respects to a man who had stood against violence. But, also, their political pragmatism should not be overlooked.

On the other side of the coin is the fact that no southern-elected senator or congressman was visible at Dr. King's rites. Most of these men, of course, would have calculated their presence there as a political liability. Even those southern politicians who made polite statements of regret about his assassination included many who privately were relieved that Dr. King was no longer alive. He had badly upset the status quo in their region. That his death has opened the doors for even more severe problems does not seem to occur to them. . . .

19

THE arrival of his grandson, Trip, for his christening ceremony at All Saints Church in Atlanta two weeks after the King funeral did much to rally McGill's sagging spirits. Also in this period he had good news from the lawyers who had been defending him in a ten-million-dollar libel suit brought against the paper and him personally by Major General Edwin Walker. The case had been settled out of court and he was relieved at last of a worry that had nagged him since the University of Mississippi demonstrations at Oxford, Mississippi, in 1962. His new status as a grandfather had put him in a gently reminiscent mood. Grace Lundy gave him a set of giant diaper pins, and he recalled his early experience as a diaper-changer. "I once was pretty well adept at changing diapers, and I imagine my old skill will come back if needed."

After the christening he wrote a teasing note to one of those present, a frisky old lawyer named Henry Troutman, whose friends, on his eightieth birthday, had given him a cake decorated with seventy-nine miniature bottles of gin and one small bottle of vermouth. Troutman was photographed holding the baby, and McGill, tongue in cheek, had written: "It is somehow a little sad to see an innocent child of two months loking up so trustfully into the face of such an old sinner. However, innocence is frequently deceived." He added that the baby had seemed unusually sleepy after having been held by Troutman, and "a doctor present indicated that it had been made drowsy by martini fumes."

The baby's christening was the only happy highlight in a period made traumatic by the murder of Robert F. Kennedy. Hubert Humphrey, rather than Kennedy, was McGill's choice for the Democratic nomination, but Ralph and Senator Kennedy had been friends since first they met at Palm Beach after the election of John F. Kennedy. Watercolors, finger-painted by the Kennedy children, hung on the walls of McGill's office, and he felt a personal attachment to the whole family.

Once, while in Robert Kennedy's office in Washington, he had suggested that he would like to send Jacqueline Kennedy some flowers as a token of his respect. "Why don't you let me take you out and you can give them to her in person?" Robert Kennedy asked.

They had ridden out together in the attorney general's limousine, and McGill remembered the visit afterward as a wonderful and moving experience. Jacqueline Kennedy had been out with the children, playing in the snow. She came in dressed in boots and riding pants and a turtleneck sweater, and greeted him graciously. Soon the children came in to say good-night to their mother. They were dressed for bed, John in blue flannel pajamas that had feet in them, Caroline in pajamas and a blue silk robe. Soon John had climbed into McGill's lap, asking questions about his watch and about a black spot on his thumbnail, bruised when he mashed it pushing too hard on a sticky shirt drawer.

He told Caroline a story about her that he had heard from Dean Rusk. One morning during a Far East crisis Rusk had gone early to the White House to see the President, and while waiting in the Oval Room, Caroline had come in and said, "Good morning, Mr. Secretary, and how is everything in Laos this morning?" And Mrs. Kennedy had laughed, saying she remembered that morning, and how the President had coached Caroline for some ten minutes to be sure she would bring it off.

As the children went off to bed. Mrs. Kennedy talked of her husband and told McGill, without restraint, of their last morning together and of the terrible moment of the President's death. She had heard Governor Connally scream in pain and shock and had turned from him to the President at the exact moment when the bullet struck and the blood spurted and a piece of his skull came off.

Robert Kennedy was not in the room at the moment, and they talked of him and of the love with which he had served his brother. And then the talk turned to books and ballet and minor things. It was a footnote to history and McGill was grateful to Robert Kennedy for having made it possible.

And now Robert Kennedy himself was dead of an assassin's bullet. McGill's first column was quiet, matter of fact, a sigh of despairing acceptance of an ugly fact. The murder of Senator Kennedy, he wrote, "is but another exhibit of the steady growth of violence as part of the mosaic of our national culture":

> Violence has always been a part of our culture. We had almost a hundred years of the most horrible and brutal lynchings in which the bodies of the lynched were mutilated before or after death. Some of the lynched were burned alive. We have had men in recent years dynamite a church at the time it was crowded with Sunday school children, killing and wounding some of them. . . .

He wrote of the new leadership of the poor and black — violent men who had replaced the dead apostle of nonviolence, Martin Luther King. He pointed out that university students wishing to dissent now had begun to use the tactics of the street mob, burning and looting and destroying property.

"We continue," he concluded, "to pander to the environment of violence." And then he added, almost helplessly, "Until we can change the climate, we will have more and more violence. Pray God the horror in Los Angeles will move us to careful, intelligent action."

In his column of the next day, all of his sorrow and raging anger burst forth. "Flaming death out of a gun barrel — mindless, senseless, violent death — has taken another man from the ranks of those who believed in human rights and justice."

He called the roll of these men: John F. Kennedy, Medgar Evers, Martin Luther King . . . and now Robert F. Kennedy. He remembered lines from Edna St. Vincent Millay's "Dirge Without Music":

> *Down, down, down into the darkness of the grave*
> *Gently they go, the beautiful, the tender, the kind.*
> *Quietly they go, the intelligent, the witty, the brave.*
> *I know. But I do not approve and I am not resigned.*

He turned then on "the jackals, the cowards, the traitors, the failures, the yapping feist pack that tries to drive out truth; those who dislike Jews, Negroes, Catholics and liberals; the bitter and evil persons who organize themselves and send out hate literature; the Klan types, the States' Rights diehards; those who dynamite churches, synagogues and homes — they are the abscesses in America's society."

He quoted a letter received, rejoicing in the killing of Robert Kennedy as others had come in exulting in the killing of President Kennedy and Martin Luther King.

"America," he thundered, "is sick — sick with its haters, sick with its cowards, sick with its do-nothing 'good people.' "

Sirhan Sirhan, killer of Robert Kennedy, was captured at once. On the day that Robert Kennedy was buried beside his brother on the green slopes at Arlington, James Earl Ray, looking like any tourist in sports jacket, slacks and sunglasses, was arrested at London Airport and charged with the murder of Martin Luther King.

On McGill's office wall hung a framed note, bearing the date of April 1963. It said, "Dear Ralph, Where are you? Put President Kennedy's picture up a little higher on the wall or I will come down and get you. I enjoyed Confederate Memorial Day — even without you. Best regards, A Yankee from Boston."

The Yankee from Boston, of course, was Robert Kennedy, the attorney general, in Atlanta on a mission for his brother. He had come into Georgia from Alabama, where he had passed on to the governor and state officials the earnest hope that they would accept the civil rights laws, so that there would be no need to send federal troops into the South again.

"He was," McGill recalled, "offering his brother's plan to send only U.S. marshals in the event mobs sought to prevent the carrying out of court orders in the field of human rights. He was trying to persuade state officials to use their own police forces to enforce federal laws so that there would be no need for troops and marshals. He got little encouragement."

The memory of the dead President's efforts to keep the peace while enforcing the law reminded McGill of the utter uselessness and futility of the violent resistance of the past. He asked in his column:

Why was it necessary for southern leadership to have brought out mobs when Arthurine Lucy sought to enter the University of Alabama? There are now perhaps two hundred Negroes in the university. They do as well as white students. The football team, which for many seems to be the university's *raison d'être*, continues to go to bowls. The social prestige of the white students seems not to have declined. In other words, admission of qualified Negro students made no difference at all. The ugly anarchy of the mobs, the violence, the hate, all these were unnecessary.

The same story could be told from state to state, from city to city. He asked bitterly:

Who were those who lied to us and deceived many of us? Who were the governors, the senators, the congressmen, the mayors, the police commissioners and police chiefs, the managers of aldermanic boards and commissions, the preachers, the editors — who were all these who lied and influenced and excited resistance and mobs?

The politicians who lied and incited riots are now seeking Negro votes. Negroes are in the schools, in offices, and increasingly in jobs.

Why all the stupid, costly resistance of the past?

Why now are there school boards, churches, editors, mayors, politicians who still encourage lawlessness and resistance to law?

It is impossible not to think about that — meditating on the two Kennedy brothers who sleep side by side in Arlington, Virginia.

In mid-June of 1968, the *Constitution* celebrated its one hundredth birthday, and McGill, in marking the centennial milestone, gave his own ideas of what had enabled the paper to survive and prosper. It had, he pointed out, never been content to be merely a local newspaper, provincial and narrow of view. It had, from the beginning, reported national and international events and had commented on them as they related to Georgia and the southern region. McGill himself had carried on this tradition. Wherever he was, his compass needle pointed south, specifically to Georgia, and specifically in Georgia to Atlanta.

By mid-July he was on the first commercial jet flight between the United States and Moscow. He found a grain of hope for peace in the fact that all that was needed now to fly from Atlanta to Moscow was "a visa, a smallpox vaccination card, and the price of a ticket." His columns out of Russia had in them the recurring note of reassurance that the cold war might be thawing.

"Somehow," he wrote from Moscow, "I felt better about the future. The people of the USSR are as good and friendly as any people. They may be even more disinclined to war than any other power because they have a closer knowledge of what war means. They lost in combat and civilian deaths about twenty-five million people in the Second World War."

He approached the Russian people with sympathy, noting that, since his last visit in 1959, there had been much new housing built, and the people, particularly the women, were dressing much better. The miniskirt had made its way to Moscow and the girls, he said, "look as cute as ours." But, he added, "Fat Russian girls seem to have the wisdom not to wear the brief skirts."

Remembering how the czars and the Orthodox church had worked together to keep the Russian peasant in serfdom, he could not be overly critical of the modern Russian disdain for religion, though once, on a Russian plane it caused him mild embarrassment: On takeoff from Moscow he looked at his watch and announced to the man in the seat beside him that "God willing, we'll get to Sverdlovsk on time." The stewardess overheard him and took him up sharply. "We have a good plane and an experienced crew. We are leaving on time and we will arrive on time. God has nothing to do with it," she said. On his return home he cast about for some appropriate gift to send his Russian guides and interpreters. At the suggestion of his favorite bookseller, Margaret Goldstein, he sent four copies of Robert K. Massie's *Nicholas and Alexandra.* He got no answer.

In late July, McGill was packing his rumpled seersucker for a journey to Miami and the reporting he liked best — the coverage of that great quadrennial circus, a national political convention. He found on his arrival for the Republican convention there that the "palms, delegates, and the candidates are fretted, in both major meanings of that word." This was the first convention by either major party ever to be held in the Deep South and he was not made happy by the choice. "The humid heat," he wrote, "greets one in a manner reminiscent of an embrace by a wet, friendly sheep dog."

The mood of the nation he found equally sultry in this hot August of 1968. Many factors other than politics had diffused the national interest in the conventions and he ticked them off one by one: Vietnam, the assassinations of Jack and Robert Kennedy and Martin Luther King, the problem of correcting racial injustices accumulated over a century in which a rural nation became urban; "a Congress so concerned with its election problems that national needs have been irrelevant, the lack of empathy for the poor, the discontent of the poor whose attitude is perhaps accentuated by the affluence of goods and possessions they see on television" — all these, he said, have detracted from the national interest in politics and candidates.

The dilemma of the Republicans would also be the dilemma of the Democrats when they met later in the month in Chicago. "There are two parties," McGill pointed out, but "there are not two politically different ways of moving to solve the paradox of urban growth and decay, the problems of human neglect . . . of the poor, the untrained, and the uneducated, or the policies of the nation as a nuclear power. . . ." The Republican choice of Richard Nixon as their standard-bearer did little to lift the gloom that hung like a miasma over his spirit, nor was he made happy by the choice of Spiro Agnew as Nixon's running mate. At one point in the proceeding he wandered away to another convention recommended to him by Walter Cronkite, a gathering of Negro morticians. The morticians, McGill discovered, were concerned about a gross discrimination in freight rates. To transport a corpse, even though properly laid out and sealed in a boxed casket with handles, the railroads charged fifty cents a mile. This placed an especially heavy burden on the poor southern black whose family members often went off north to find work, died there, and had to be transported by rail. McGill found the morticians substantial people, and their conversation more interesting than the political talk he had been hearing around the great hall where the Republicans were convening.

Pausing only long enough in Atlanta to pack a clean shirt, McGill moved on to Chicago and the Democratic convention. It was the last great political conclave he would cover, and in many ways it was the most memorable.

It began under a troubling shadow, the movement of Communist troops into Czechoslovakia, so grimly reminiscent of those aggressions by which Adolf Hitler triggered World War II. It ended with savage fighting in the streets between police and disenchanted young people. McGill looked about him and was also disenchanted, not only with the young people, whom he found to be whining and petulant, but with many of the delegates. "The visitors crowded into this worried, almost besieged city talk about the harsh repression of the Czechs by the Soviets. But in the next breath, some of them — mostly, but not all southern — are cheering and hoping for the ugly and harshly vicious repressive measures proposed by George Wallace."

The motives of the Russians to McGill were obvious. The Soviets went into Prague because they believed they had to be there. "We," he said, "are in Vietnam because we believed it necessary to stop the expansionism of China and the Soviets in that area. Let us remember," he concluded, "the Great British Empire is now merely three major islands in economic difficulty. There are but three powers — the United States, the Soviet Union and upcoming China. It is dangerous to think in the old images."

New images in Chicago fascinated, and in the long run, dismayed McGill. A quote from John Milton came to his mind: "When night darkens the streets, then wander forth the sons of Belial, flown with insolence and wine."

"All the dissenters are here," he wrote, "including sweet maids going about in a demonstration titled, 'Baring Breasts for Peace.' "

McGill was more interested in the sons of Belial. "There are real revolutionaries here — men skilled in the arts of disruption, sabotage and killing," he wrote in his column. "They are disciples of Che Guevara, the Viet Cong and other guerrilla fighters." The militant and dangerous Students for a Democratic Society were present, he noted, and Black Panthers and other Negro militants who walked the streets shouting obscenities at the cops.

The rioting outraged McGill, and he felt that everybody — particularly TV — did a poor job of reporting it. His sympathy, obviously, was with the police and not the rioters — who were "not kids, at all," to him, but professional revolutionaries led by the same dangerous men who had struck before at Columbia University and the Pentagon.

He wrote Helen Morgan:

I detest brutality — all my instincts cry out against it, but all that day I had heard the cops cursed and insulted . . . subjected to insults such as "We've got your wife out tonight," and worse. Anyhow, before the wild, hysterical charge, there was a barrage of bottles, rocks and other debris — then the charge. Being attacked by near hysterical young men and a few frantic young women did not permit just standing there and being hit in the face or knocked down. Some of those arrested wore, for instance, wrist bands with heavy metal points — sharpened. It is difficult for us to believe that we now have a small movement led by those who aspire to be local Che Guevaras. . . .

Well, anyhow, it was rough. . . .

I love the Democratic party — it is all-American. It did not discipline as did the Republicans . . . every group was there, in the open, fighting, name-calling, damning, snarling, and revealing all the diversity of opinion. I consider the long debate on Vietnam to be one of the more magnificent examples of public debate since the Lincoln-Douglas meetings. Imagine a party being willing to let millions see and hear how divided it is. We may be defeated, but it was a historic convention for all its crudities and divisions. . . .

The nomination of Hubert Humphrey, "a kind, compassionate man, whose milk of human kindness has not been soured by the acids of pragmatic politics," and the choice of Edward Muskie as his running mate, gave McGill hope for the victory of the Democratic party in November. He did all he could to bring it about. Knowing that the strongest political force in the South was the surge toward the Wallace candidacy, he turned his heaviest guns on the snarling little Alabamian. About all it gained him was an outpouring of hate mail.

Though politics engrossed him, human beings and their specific problems took up much of his time. Troubled white teachers, faced with the prospect of teaching mixed classes, poured out their doubts and fears that integration in the schools would ever work. He wrote back urging them to have faith in the goodwill and sound sense of the children themselves. Patience and understanding and the passage of time, he counseled, would in time bring peace.

Negro mothers wrote him. One, a teacher in a small town in south Georgia, sent him a picture of her small daughter, who had won a history prize awarded by the DAR. She wrote: "I am a Negro in transition from lower class to middle class. . . . The law says I am a citizen with rights the same as every citizen, but I am not. That, in our town, must come later."

An Irish journalist wrote of McGill's "tremendously sympathetic understanding" and added: "To have been so constantly on the side of the angels and yet never to have come over as a prig seems to me to be the biggest achievement of all."

To one erudite nonadmirer, Eleanor Hutchins of Huntsville, Alabama, McGill represented "the classic image of the reformer so obsessed with zeal for his cause" that he is willing to "disregard fact . . . even to manufacture evidence for the sake of a moral crusade." She found in him, she said, "the link between zeal and hatred that Sterne insists upon in Tristram Shandy. . . . Beneath McGill's magisterial style, you can sense the cunning partisan determined to crush his enemy, and the same hostile calculation seems to underlie his idolatrous enthusiasms. Yet, he was on the generous, compassionate side in the major controversies. . . . It is a fascinating paradox, the diabolic aspect of reform. . . ."

McGill had no patience with an adversary who, he thought, should have known better, and he was intolerant with those who he thought were motivated by greed or meanness. He was particularly rough on friends who he felt had strayed from the true liberal path. Eugene Methvin, a *Reader's Digest* editor stationed in Washington, was a friend and warm admirer, but often crossed swords with McGill over what Methvin considered his ultraliberal views. "He was," said Methvin, "capable of being terribly unfair. He'd set up a straw man and destroy it with arguments that were not always so. Even when badly informed, he'd never advance the possibility he could be in error, though no one could be right seven days a week."

Actually, when the flow of angry mail slowed down, McGill was troubled. He felt this indicated that he was losing his grip, that he no longer had the old power to stir his readers one way or the other. In his last months, it seemed that he deliberately set out to enrage a broad segment of his readership. One touchy subject was anything that had to do with wearing the Confederate uniform, flying the Confederate flag, or playing the old war song, "Dixie." At the Republican convention in Miami, he had discovered that there was a great deal of resentment in the black community because the South Dade County High School athletic teams were called the Rebels, and the high school band paraded in gray Confederate uniforms and carried the Stars and Bars of the old Confederacy.

The young blacks had asked that the name of Rebel be changed to something else and the Confederate flag and uniforms not be used. Parents of white students, and many of the students themselves, sprang to the defense of what they had come to look upon as the sacred symbols of a tradition worthy of being preserved.

McGill pointed out that such an attitude in Dade County, Florida, was preposterous. Dade County was a wilderness, inhabited largely by alligators, and Miami did not exist when men in gray were fighting under these battle flags. There was no remote historical connection between South Dade County and the Civil War.

The Confederate flag and uniform worn at a school in its public parades could not fail to be an affront to the Negro student, he pointed out, for these were symbols associated in their minds with the degradation of human personality, reminders of slavery and a war fought to keep the black man in the status of a slave. Use of these symbols could not be defended on any reasonable ground. It was only one of many small affronts, said McGill, which the white man, often unnecessarily, imposed upon the Negro — and it was the repetition of these relatively "little" grievances that led to the outbursts of violence in the ghetto.

His comments on the uniform and the flag stirred up a most soul-satisfying row. No sooner had it begun to die down than McGill ignited another. In a column entitled "Pandering to a Myth," he stated that "Dixie," the war song of the Confederacy, was not southern after all. "The song," he wrote, "has no southern origin or tie whatever. . . . The product of a minstrel-show producer, performer and songwriter, Daniel Decatur Emmett, it was written in New York City . . . and was sung there for two years before being brought South in 1861."

It was heard in New Orleans immediately after the firing on Fort Sumter, and its catchy, exciting tune caught on. It was played at Jefferson Davis's inauguration at Montgomery, and from then on, it took on the mystical character of a "southern" song.

"Dixie," McGill explained, was one of a type greatly popular in the years immediately before the war. "It is wryly humorous," he said.

"that all the really famous 'darky songs' were written by northern composers for the minstrel shows which were enormously popular in the South.

"They were," he pointed out, "racist — and honestly so. They pandered to the myth that slavery was really a benign institution and that all the slaves were happy, dancing, singing, simple souls who dearly loved the old plantation and Ol' Massa and Ol' Missus. So the songwriters, with their eye on the cashbox, wrote for the myth."

He approved the fact that throughout the South, in answer to black students' protests, school and college bands were dropping the playing of "Dixie." "The reaction," he added, "is what one might expect. Governor Maddox . . . heatedly declared that if there is any more talk about abandoning the playing of 'Dixie,' he will have the tune played from the capitol dome every day at high noon. This might be an acceptable solution. School bands should give up the tune and leave it all to the governor. . . ."

McGill could hardly have stirred a greater hornet's nest if he had announced that Robert E. Lee was a Yankee and Traveler was a mule. By now, many readers who usually saw eye to eye with McGill began to feel that he was overdoing the "Dixie" issue. One correspondent, a lawyer, pointed out gently that though the song might conjure up visions of slavery, it in no way had offended Abraham Lincoln, who ended slavery. He quoted a statement by Lincoln, made on April 10, 1865, the day after the last Confederate forces had surrendered: "I have always thought 'Dixie' one of the best tunes I have ever heard. Our adversaries over the way attempted to appropriate it, but I insisted yesterday that we fairly captured it. I presented the question to the attorney general, and he gave it as his legal opinion that it is our lawful prize. I now request the band to favor me with its performance."

A letter from a lady began, "For years I have been one of your greatest admirers, but I find your attacks on the playing of 'Dixie' both tedious and irritating. . . . I asked a charming, intelligent Negro girl in my office what she thought of your campaign. She thought it too trivial for serious consideration. Please leave the windmill-tilting to lesser minds."

This was no angry red-neck blasting him as "a senile old goat" or a "putrid liberal," as several did, but an intelligent woman employed at the National Communicable Disease Center, whose staff of international experts on disease control McGill admired and respected. He quietly laid the anti-"Dixie" campaign to rest. It had served its purpose. By stirring up controversy, it had kept alive McGill's zest for combat; it had also given him one more chance to speak out for human dignity.

Late in December of 1968, McGill wrote for the *Encyclopaedia Britannica* a summing-up of all the failures and achievements of the civil rights movement in the fourteen years since the Supreme Court decision had outlawed segregation in the schools. It was also, in a way, a summing-up of all that he had fought for, and all that he had achieved in those years of struggle.

He began, as always in his talks and articles, by describing the South and its peculiar mystique, with a quick backward look at the landmark years of 1876–1877. He reiterated his charge that the political leadership of the East and North sold out to the South in the Hayes-Tilden presidential contest, and in so doing, handed the race problem back to the states'-rights dogmatists.

The heritage of this political knavery, he said, was the restoration of slavery without the name, the resubjugation of the Negro by violence and tyranny, practiced now not in the name of property rights but of white supremacy. Under the peonage of the sharecropper system, there was little else the white, illiterate rural southerner could boast of than the color of his skin, and it was this stiff pride, this arrogance, that led to the lynchings, the murders, the burning of Negro homes and churches with which the poor white segregationist sought to maintain his separation and his supremacy. It was an attitude, McGill pointed out with sorrow, against which only a few liberal voices were lifted. The southerner, in his instinctive opposition, had the support of not only his political leaders, but his preachers as well.

"The church," he said, "has been perhaps the greatest single failure as a force for reforming the social revolution.

"One cannot know," he wrote "what might have ensued had the political leaders of the South accepted the court ruling of 1954. For a few weeks it looked as if there was a chance. The more blatant and racially demagogic of the southern governors, senators, congressmen and local officials were for the moment silent."

Then with the Virginians leading, the storm of opposition broke. Riots in Little Rock and in Oxford, Mississippi, amounted to brief civil wars. Violence almost as fierce broke out in New Orleans, Tuscaloosa and Birmingham.

Against this white violence, the Negroes opposed with two nobly conceived and bravely supported organizations devoted to nonviolence — Martin Luther King's Southern Christian Leadership Conference and the Student Nonviolent Coordinating Committee, known as SNCC.

Dr. Martin Luther King, Jr., to McGill, was the one tremendous force of the early years, from the 1954 school decision to the final passage of the Civil Rights Act — "the essence of moral power in the movement" whose "superb courage and moral force," combined with his nonviolence, stirred Congress to action on the rights bills.

SNCC, in its early days, when it worked in the rural South, teaching and preaching of human rights, registering voters, sitting-in at bus stations and restaurants, drew its membership from young people, both white and black, throughout the nation.

"They were, I believe," wrote McGill for the *Britannica,* "the sweetest, gentlest, most courageous youngsters. . . . They were the Freedom Riders whose buses were burned and stoned. They endured the coarsest and most brutal treatment. . . . Some were murdered."

"The chapter written by the early biracial SNCC," said McGill, "was a fine and inspiring one." Then came the passage of the official civil rights legislation and the voting laws, making the crusading of the chanting, singing, dedicated young people "less necessary and less fruitful."

Yet, new laws and voting rights did not bring the millennium, and the militant black members, contemptuous of nonviolence, disillusioned with trying to work with white people, turned to the new and dangerous concept of Black Power —— of separatism — of two races living side by side.

"They despise the 'old-timers' who envisioned an America shared commonly by all, and see it as impossible and undesirable. They see everything before Watts [the riots of 1965] as only a class movement aimed at a sharing of white capitalism and white values. They insist there must be two Americas, black and white."

Their anger and frustration and their pride McGill could understand.

It grew out of the history of their movement through the struggling, tragic, despairing and finally triumphant years. And he agreed that civil rights laws on the books but not yet in the hearts of men are not the answer.

But the alienation and separation of the two-nation concept, he argued, is not the answer either to the problems of the millions who live in the ghettos of the great cities. These are both black and white, though mostly black, and they are desperately poor, and the challenge to the nation now is to find the answer to their poverty and despair.

"Civil rights, per se," wrote McGill, "cannot do much for the desperately poor. The rhetoric of revolution cannot feed or clothe them."

If the "second separate nation were instantly created, it would include most of the poverty and would be helpless to cope with it."

He expressed the fear that a "reactionary Congress in 1969 and a national will weakened by the racist elements of the 1968 campaign" might give aid and comfort to elements on both sides attracted by the concept of a black-white separatism.

He pleaded that it never come to pass:

> There is enough evidence of what we can do in the story of what we have done to make me hold fast to a faith in America commonly shared by all its people. . . . It is not mere rhetoric to say that any form of apartheid will be destructive of all things. It has been a relatively brief but tremendously exciting sweep of years since that May 17, 1954. Yet, we have come a long, long way. The political processes, so long denied, do work. There are laws on the books and they will not be ignored. There is already a common sharing of America undreamed of in 1954. The critical national problems are our poor and our unprepared.
>
> Apartheid is not the answer. We have tried that already.

So McGill's article, prepared for the *Britannica*, was his last long statement on civil rights, summing up the battle he so long had fought in the triple role of combat correspondent, strategist and common soldier. And as had been typical of all he had written over the years, it was a plea for peace and understanding.

The year, so full of tragedy and shock, was coming to a close, and now the small and quiet things commanded his attention. With Mary

Lynn he went to the theater and to the symphony. Old friends passed through, and he had long evenings with them and much laughter. Tom Chubb, the poet, his good companion of field-trial days, came to visit his married daughter. There was a cocktail party for him to which Mary Lynn and McGill were invited. The two old friends had not met for years, and it was a tremendous emotional experience for both. McGill greeted the slender, reserved, impeccably mannered Chubb with a joyous bear hug. Then their thoughts went back for nearly forty years, and while the babble of the cocktail party rose around them, they laughed and told again the old tales — of Springwood Spider, Chubb's champion pointer who failed his first All-Age Stakes test when he flushed a shoat and killed it, of the dog that pointed the whiskey jug, of the mule that was trained to point quail, and the mule whose owner claimed it could point fish.

Then McGill reached in his pocket and pulled out a slim volume and called for silence, and in the sudden startled hush he read aloud to all the party guests from Tom Chubb's book of poems, *Turkey Gobbler Land,* written years before about the south Georgia hunting country. The listeners were brokers, bankers, conservative financial types, Chubb remembered, most of whom thought of McGill as a wild-eyed liberal and a menace to the country. But they listened spellbound as he read Chubb's poems. As he finished, he put the book in his pocket and hugged Chubb again and said good-bye and quickly left, for above all things on earth, in his latter days, he hated cocktail parties.

As the holiday season came on, he sent off to his friends in the North his usual gifts of grits, country ham and water-ground corn meal. To friends in Atlanta, to whom such fare was not exotic, he carried bottles of wine, tied with red ribbon.

Two days before Christmas, with Mary Lynn driving, he left for Richmond to spend the holidays with Ralph, Jr., Lady, and his grandson, Trip, now eight months old. It was perhaps a period of the deepest contentment and undiluted happiness McGill had ever known. In letters to Tom Winship and to Mary Lynn's sister-in-law, Helen, he wrote at length of what he described modestly as "one of the nation's more superior grandsons." Trip liked McGill to carry him about on his shoulder, "yelling with glee as he gave my hair a pull," and McGill insisted that Mary Lynn take pictures of this.

The entire family went to the Richmond Museum to see a new exhibition of impressionists. Ralph wrote:

> I carried Trip through the new exhibition, and then to the Egyptian wing, the Russian wing, and the Japanese wing. I give you my word he did not fret or show any sign of impatience. I am well aware he did not know what he was looking at. But he was seeing something — lines, squares, parallelograms and colors. He was enchanted, for example, at some paintings, mostly red and yellow, of Mandarin emperors. He admired sculpted heads. He looked somberly at mummies. He waved his right hand at some bright-colored landscapes. In one Japanese painting I put my finger, the guard not being near, on Mount Fuji, snow clad and beautiful, and said to him that his Daddy and I had once climbed that mountain. He gave it his intent look. . . . There was a fountain in the lobby in the center of a large pool. He was enchanted with it.

Although Ralph's gourmandizing days were over, he described with relish the Christmas dinner Lady prepared. "No turkey, but instead a five-pound fillet done as beef Wellington . . . a magnificent sauce of mushrooms, scallions, parsley and celery leaves and a rich brown crust done to the proverbial turn. Ralph, Jr., had dug up two bottles of Château Neuf de Pape. . . . It was a great dinner."

On their return to Atlanta McGill prepared to attend the Nixon inauguration. On the rainy Saturday before the inauguration, he went to the courtyard of the Justice Department for the unveiling of a bust of Robert Kennedy. Ethel Kennedy was there, and the Kennedy children, and he felt again the strength and resolution that had always drawn him to the Kennedys. The chief justice was there and invited McGill to stay and have lunch with him on Tuesday.

It was almost as if he had come to say farewell to all the old friends he had known in Washington in years gone by. He called briefly on President Johnson and Hubert Humphrey, and on Sunday he went to Andrews Air Force Base with those welcoming Averell Harriman home. Henry Cabot Lodge was there, who had been kind to him in Vietnam. McGill had learned, through a friend, that Ambassador Lodge had been very fond of his father, a scholarly philosopher and poet who had died when his son was young, and that the son had always been sensitive about the fact that his father had been so little recognized. So he went up to the ambassador and told him that he had only recently discovered what a great man his father had been and that he had read his poems and intended, if the ambassador had no objection, to write a column about him. And Lodge's eyes grew misty, McGill remembered, as he told him this.

To McGill, the inauguration was low-key, matching his mood of concern over the country's future. In his column, he chanted again the litany of sorrows facing Nixon:

> The feuds and moods of the Congress, the constant competition for power between the two chambers of representatives and the White House, the increasing weight of poverty and unrest and the near bankruptcy of cities . . the militancy bred by hunger and joblessness, and the revolutionary commitments by the more extreme — all these will press upon him.
>
> So, today, the at times intolerable burden [of the presidency] passes . . . the checks and balances begin to function, and to gall and frustrate.
>
> So quietly is the transition of government being achieved that the Nixon administration seems to be, as one observer put it, "disappearing into government, not taking over." There is no "personality." The nation has had a long line of presidents with recognizable personality traits. FDR, the salty Truman, glamorous Ike and his beaming fatherly reassurance, Jack Kennedy with his dramatic "style," and Lyndon Johnson — all these were personalities. Mr. Nixon is taking charge almost like a corporation president with his board.

Though he found the inauguration less than exciting, he covered it with his usual zest and gusto, and when he came home to find that not all the sidebar stories he had sent in had made the paper, he bellowed like an anguished cub. In one of the last memos he was to address to the city staff, he chided them, kiddingly, but with an undertone of anger, for the way they had handled his copy:

> Now and then I hear echoes of pain from a reporter whose copy has been cut or eliminated. It just occurred to me that my Washington experience might be of minor interest.
>
> I sent in a short feature about meeting Chief Herbert Jenkins [Atlanta's Police Chief] at the inaugural ball in the Mayflower. He was clad in long tails, white tie, gloves, etc. In the copy I said he was more distinguished-looking than anyone I had seen that day, including Richard Nixon and

Spiro Agnew. Someone, undoubtedly a rascally Republican, eliminated the reference to Nixon and Agnew. I also sent in a short feature in which I said that of the five prayers offered at the inaugural ceremony, that of the Reverend Billy Graham was voted in fifth place by an overwhelming majority, while that of the rabbi was given first place. The other three were given fair to middling ratings. I had said that Dr. Graham's prayer was political and was directed entirely at a WASP audience. This feature was given pocket veto. I can only assume this was done by a fellow North Carolinian who was revealing his own Baptist fundamentalism.

At any rate — as I learned over forty years ago — it is hell to be cut.

20

Mary Lynn soon discovered that in marrying Ralph she was taking on a ready-made family — not only Ralph, Jr., Lady and young Trip, but a host of others who over the years had come to look upon McGill with filial affection.

One of the first of those he "adopted" in spirit if not officially was a tall, black-haired, beetle-browed Georgian with the gait and build of a prizefighter. Hyman Byzinski, the son of a Lithuanian immigrant settled on a Georgia cotton farm, came to Atlanta in the depressed thirties. There, he began to paint — raw, rude sketches of the red Georgia earth remembered from his boyhood on the farm and his hunting and camping expeditions along the Chattahoochee River. At about the same time, McGill was painting his own word pictures of backcountry Georgia, and Byzinski, on impulse, went to see him at his office, bringing with him an armload of sketches. Before he left that afternoon, he had a job on the *Constitution*, working as an apprentice in the engraving department at a salary that would pay him enough to buy paints and canvas but little more.

Byzinski cared for little more. He worked eight hours a day on the paper, and painted and studied painting four hours a night at the High Museum and School of Art, where McGill had arranged for him to enroll. There he caused his instructors to despair by proving himself almost unteachable. He cared little for technique, but continued to draw, with rude, fierce, untrammeled power, pictures which had a strangely compelling strength.

At McGill's urging, Byzinski, who had taken the name of Robert Byzinski, started drawing a daily cartoon for the paper. Its subject was "Georgia Oddities," which he signed "Biz."

"Biz," said McGill, "started in at art school with the cartoonist's bold approach. He drew an object as it looked to him. It didn't always look that way to his teachers. But that was all right. I never saw a fellow more excited about painting."

"Biz," was his first "discovery" and McGill followed his career as proudly as if he were his own son.

The war interrupted Byzinski's art training. He went off to fight as an armored trooper in the Italian and African campaigns and distinguished himself at Kasserine Pass. After the war, he settled down in Paris to take up his art studies at the University of Paris, supported by the G.I. Bill. There, during the late forties and early fifties, his studio in the Beaux Arts Academy and his table at the Café Dôme became a port of call for McGill whenever he was in Europe. His visits to Byzinski in Paris helped make up for the fact that he had missed the Paris of the twenties when Hemingway and Fitzgerald and Gertrude Stein were there. He immersed himself in the life around him, and though he was far older than they, the young expatriates of Biz's set welcomed him as one of themselves.

"They tell me that the Café Dôme is not what it was in the twenties," McGill wrote on his return from the Nuremberg trials in 1947. "I wouldn't know. But it is colorful enough — full of models, young and old, and with painters and poets and writers and Nymphes de Pavé." The tasks the young students had set for themselves fascinated him, and he sat long over *fines*, listening to their talk. There were nearly two thousand ex-G.I.'s studying in Paris in the first years after the war, and McGill, making discreet inquiry, was pleased to find that, along with Norman Mailer, his protégé, Byzinski, was among those who showed the greatest promise.

When McGill came home he made a point of calling up Byzinski's father, who was dying of cancer, to convince him that young Robert was not disgracing him; instead he was bringing honor to the family name. The old man responded by forgiving his son and inviting McGill and Mary Elizabeth to his family Seder, a ceremonial dinner held on the first night of Passover. Biz went on to justify McGill's faith in him by becoming a well-known artist and teacher of art, his paintings being shown in many of the better galleries, including Atlanta's High Museum, whose art teachers once had despaired of him.

Another young and creative person whose career McGill furthered with encouragement and understanding was Ruthanna Boris, the great ballerina. McGill had been a ballet buff since college days, when he covered a performance by Anna Pavlova and her company in Nashville and the magnificent dancer had called him to thank him for his review. He knew nothing of the dance then, but his love for it never dimmed and most of the ballerinas of his generation were his friends. He first met Miss Boris in 1939, when she was the twenty-one-year-old prima ballerina of the Metropolitan Opera Company. She had danced *Carmen* in Atlanta and was taking her makeup off, getting ready to leave the theater, when Edward Johnson, director of the company, told her that the editor of the *Constitution* was waiting to take her to the after-opera party. Miss Boris told Johnson she was far more interested in a hamburger than in the editor of the *Atlanta Constitution* and as for the party, she felt that that was an imposition and she had no intention of going.

Johnson was persuasive, and Miss Boris, muttering angrily, soon found herself being introduced to McGill. He charmed her completely by thanking her for curing his bursitis. It began to disappear during her second-act dance, he said, and by the fourth act, it was completely gone. She was startled and pleased to find that "in this wild forest of 'kulture' I had at last found someone who felt differently than the others and talked differently than the others."

In a taped memoir she sent to Edward Weeks after McGill's death, Miss Boris recalled the friendship that grew out of this meeting. For thirty years thereafter, wherever she was dancing, McGill would show up without warning to take her to supper after the performance. They might see each other only once or twice a year, but whenever he traveled in foreign countries he would pick up books on the ballet for her, and in this country, when feeling lonely, he would telephone her. Once he called her from Detroit — "roaring drunk and in a rollicking mood," to tell her he had discovered the secret of how Henry Ford made his millions. Ford's boyhood notebooks, in which he had kept a meticulous record of every penny he ever spent, had been released to public inspection.

They carried on a tender but spasmodic correspondence that was almost telepathic. Sometimes, when after months of silence he would write her, he would receive a letter from her written on the same day. Soon after they met she left the Metropolitan to become the premiere danseuse of the Ballet Russe de Monte Carlo, which appeared frequently in Atlanta. When the *Constitution* opened its new building, she went to see him at his office, carrying a potted plant. It was an old Russian custom, she said, to carry a live plant on the first visit to a new building. On another visit to Atlanta, McGill took her to a little Negro church in the country. As they sat through the service and the preacher became more and more emotional, the people in the pews began to chant and sway. Boris felt herself being carried away and "when the people rose and started really moving it, I had to get up and move it with them. And Ralph moved it too."

So the editor of the *Atlanta Constitution* and the prima ballerina of the Ballet Russe de Monte Carlo danced in the aisles of a little country church in the South, and to her it was a "wonderfully exciting, happy time and I had the feeling he felt absolutely at home and very comfortable. He loved them, and they loved him. . . ."

Miss Boris "came to see the South through the eyes of Ralph McGill and to understand it with his heart, and this was an indescribably precious thing. . . ."

Intermittent as were their meetings and sporadic as was their correspondence, each felt a great dependence on the other. In time of personal and professional discouragement she would pour out to him "all my troubles and my dreams and my hurts and my fears," and his answer always gave her courage. When he lost a hard-fought political battle and was feeling low, he would write to her. "I am tempted to leave the South. I do not think I will. But I still am thinking about it. I belong here and I suppose I will stay. But it isn't fun."

The correspondence that passed between them over three decades of platonic friendship was remembered by Miss Boris as "a very beautiful part of my life." "This man understood the world," she said. "Nothing was too small for him. Nothing was too big for him. . . . He was a man of beginnings; he hoped for things that seemed impossible and he worked for them, and a lot of them have happened, or are trying to happen."

Often the young people McGill sponsored had no other place to turn. One was William Gordon, an Arkansas sharecropper's son who, in the mid-forties, wrote McGill asking for a job on the *Atlanta Constitution.* It was too early then for a white Atlanta newspaper to put a black man on its staff, and McGill had to turn him down. He wrote a most encouraging letter, though, urging Gordon to keep in touch with him. Gordon finally went to work in New York on the now defunct newspaper, *PM.* He kept in touch with McGill, and in 1950, when Gordon came to Atlanta as managing editor of the Negro-owned and edited *Atlanta Daily World,* he and McGill became close friends. To Gordon, McGill was a symbol of hope and light in a dark time, stubbornly carrying on the fight for racial justice. To McGill, Gordon, as a reasonable man of judgment and sincere purpose, was living proof that he was right in his arguments — that the Negro, given equal opportunity, was in no way inferior to the white man. He was determined that Gordon, who possessed all the needed native talent, should be given his opportunity to reach his highest potential. His first move, two years after Gordon's arrival in Atlanta, was to urge his acceptance at Harvard as a Nieman Fellow. The owner of the *World,* a conservative, did not approve, and it was necessary, McGill found, to have several of the leading Negro businessmen and the presidents of the Negro universities bring pressure on the newspaper owner to get him to grant the necessary leave of absence. Even this did not suffice, and only after the head of the bank which held the *World*'s note had suggested that it would be a great thing for the paper for Gordon to have this opportunity was he able to go off for his year at Harvard.

Five years later, McGill pushed him one step further. Remembering how his own Rosenwald Fellowship had broadened his horizons, he put up Gordon's name for an Ogden Reid Foundation Traveling Fellowship in international journalism. Under it, Gordon traveled in western Europe and in some fourteen African countries and as McGill had anticipated, the experience opened new doors. Shortly after his tour was finished, the Eisenhower administration drafted him for the State Department and he was sent back to Africa as public affairs officer for the United States Information Agency in Nigeria. Superior officers filed glowing reports on him, causing McGill himself to beam as if his own son were being praised.

Gordon was in Africa in 1963, when McGill arrived on a tour sponsored by the State Department. It was a memorable occasion for both.

McGill was sixty-four at the time, but he worked with the insatiable curiosity of a cub reporter. His fascination with everything African caused Gordon some concern. He would stop while traveling along rural roads, for example, to talk with the people passing by, would eat from their bowls of chicken, rice and red peppers, and now and then would pluck a mango from a tree. Gordon, aware of the dysentry visitors could suffer from eating unwashed African fruits, shuddered, but McGill's insides, he finally assumed, were made of boiler plate. They traveled together, ate together, slept in the same rooms, and Gordon treasures the inscription McGill wrote in his copy of *The South and the Southerner:* "I will always remember our good days as roommates in Kaduna and Enugu."

They last met in 1968 when Gordon, on home leave, called on him in Atlanta. "I found him worried — about the trouble in the cities, poverty, school integration. He foresaw efforts to turn back the clock."

To Gordon, McGill seemed unduly pessimistic. When Gordon had left Atlanta ten years earlier, separation of the races was almost absolute. Now there were black faces behind the tellers' windows in the banks where a black man once could work only as a janitor. There were black clerks in the stores and black representatives in the legislature and black aldermen in city hall. These things could not be reversed.

They lunched together at a restaurant which a few years before would not have served a black man. After lunch, they walked back to McGill's office, where Gordon said good-bye:

> I thanked him and started to leave. We shook hands, and for a moment he stood looking away as though something were weighing heavily on his mind. And as he had done many times before, he embraced me as a father would his son. But this time there was a difference; there were tears in his eyes as he turned and walked back into his office. I didn't have to ask him if something was wrong. I could feel it in his handshake. I could see it in his face. That was the last time I saw him.

McGill's understanding of the problems besetting eager, ambitious, poetic, and sometimes puzzled and rebellious young people never diminished. Sometime in 1963, William H. Fields, the *Constitution*'s managing editor, read in the University of Mississippi student newspaper a short story which impressed him so favorably he got in touch with the author and asked her to serve as an intern in the *Constitution*'s summer training program for promising college students. She came, a tiny, black-haired, blue-eyed girl with a quick smile, a bright mind, an independent spirit — and a feeling of sympathy for the young blacks who were struggling still to break the barriers of segregation in southern colleges and schools.

Nancy Mason had been born in Chicago, daughter of a Mississippi machinist who had moved there during the depression. When she was fifteen, he brought his family back to Mississippi, to the little town of Pontotoc. There she finished high school and entered the University of Mississippi at Oxford. In 1962, her sophomore year, James Meredith integrated the school, and this was the beginning of her troubles. Feeling none of the prejudices that her parents and the majority of her fellow students felt toward the Negro, she and a companion, born and raised in New York, outraged the mores of Ole Miss by being nice to the Negro students. They would study with them in the library, walk with them on the campus, eat with them in the cafeteria.

It was an emotionally traumatic experience. When Nancy and her friend Carol would enter the cafeteria with their Negro friends, four hundred students would get up and walk out, leaving their trays on the tables. Daily, and sometimes twice a day, Nancy was called to the office of the dean of women, who first asked her, then ordered her, and then finally begged her, to give up her association with the black students. Why, the dean demanded, was Nancy doing these things that so greatly disturbed the peace and tranquility of Ole Miss? Who was paying her to do these things?

Working as a stringer for papers in Helena, Arkansas, and Memphis, Tennessee, Nancy covered sit-ins and other acts of racial confrontation in her area. She was told to give up this reporting, which also was "disturbing to the community." She refused, as she had refused to stop her friendly association with the Negro students.

A campaign of harassment began. The mother of her friend from New York, ill of cancer, received threatening telephone calls telling her that, unless her daughter left Mississippi, she would be killed. Calls were made to Nancy's parents, threatening harm to her if she did not give up her "nigger-loving ways."

Harassed and troubled, she headed west, to the University of California, hoping to finish her education there. When she requested her credits so that she could make the transfer, the University of Mississippi refused to send them. The reason given her when she returned, angry and despairing, was that she still owed the library for an overdue book. When she wrote McGill about it, he replied immediately to express his "indignation and sense of outrage at the way you have been treated."

Nancy began the fall term of her senior year at the University of Mississippi to find that the campaign to force her to mend her ways was taking on a new, more threatening form. In early November, the dean of women informed her that her case was to be taken up, not with the chancellor or any administrative official, but with the chief of campus police. In words that seemed curiously ominous to Nancy, the dean told her that "the time has come to decide your fate at the university."

Campus underground brought her the rumor that it had already been decided. Under pressure from the Klan and the White Citizens' Councils, the Mississippi authorities were to attempt to persuade Nancy's parents that their daughter was mentally unstable and should be committed to an institution.

That night Grace Lundy got a collect call at home from a very angry and frightened Nancy. The next morning, she laid on McGill's desk the notes she had made of the phone call. Immediately, he wired Nancy money to take a bus to Atlanta. Leaving was not easy. Wanting to make a clean break, she went to the dean and asked for final permission to withdraw. The dean refused. When Nancy stubbornly persisted, the dean became angry. She called Nancy's parents and told them that Nancy was having a breakdown. Nancy, now even more frightened, caught the northbound bus.

At Tupelo, the first stop on the bus route from Oxford to Atlanta, Terry Wooten and Jimmie, his wife, newspaper friends she had known since her high-school days in Pontotoc, boarded the bus, took her off, and took her to their home. A call had come from Nancy's friend Carol, in Oxford, they said, telling them that there would be an effort made to take Nancy off the bus before it crossed the Mississippi line. As they talked, Nancy's parents drove up. Nancy, hiding in a closet, heard them ask about her. Yes, the hostess admitted, she had been there, but she had gone. Afterwards, Nancy, trading her red coat for Jimmie's black one, lay on the floor of the back seat of the Wootens' car as they drove her to Memphis and safety.

The next day, Nancy arrived in Atlanta, where Grace Lundy put her up. The second day, her incredible story was confirmed. An FBI agent came by McGill's office to tell him that informers in the Mississippi Klan had reported there were plans afoot to do away with Nancy.

Sharing the apartment with Grace Lundy, Nancy immediately began to look for work, found it, and on Christmas Eve came by McGill's office to pay him the thirty-four dollars he had sent her for bus fare. After Christmas, she borrowed another fifty dollars and enrolled at Georgia State at night to finish earning her degree there. In early 1966, with the help of a phone call from McGill, she went to work at the Coca-Cola Company.

Working by day, going to school at night, it took her three years to finish her college education. In January of 1969, McGill was writing her, congratulating her on her graduation and a promotion in her job. "I am very proud of you," he wrote, "because of the way you have kept the faith and kept up your courage. Your graduation is wonderful. If I was any help, I am glad. . . ."

She is in no way bitter about her experiences in Mississippi. In Atlanta she continues to reach out a hand to the poor and the black. On weekends, she serves as "big sister" to two little ghetto girls. She picks them up at their homes, takes them to parks and the zoos and museums and children's concerts, and encourages them in their schoolwork.

Once McGill decided that a young person was worthy of his help, nothing could stop him from putting forth the utmost effort. In early June of 1965, there appeared in his office a slim, big-eyed, earnest young black girl whose simple, unaffected manner seemed to belie her high intelligence. Judy Tillman's father was no longer in contact with the family. Judy within a few days would graduate, second in her class, from Spelman, a Negro woman's college in Atlanta. Her record was such that she had been offered teaching scholarships at several good midwestern schools. To the despair of her counselor, she had turned them down, for she did not wish to teach. She wanted to take a master's in journalism at Columbia and go on to become a newspaperwoman. She had not been able to apply at Columbia, though, for she had no money for tuition. But she now had learned that, on the basis of her academic record, she had been awarded an all-expense scholarship, given by Mrs. Laurance Rockefeller, good at any school she might choose. She applied forthwith to Columbia — and was turned down on the grounds that her application had arrived too late.

This was a challenge McGill could not ignore and he wrote immediately to Dean Edward Barrett of the Columbia School of Journalism. He was aware that Miss Tillman's application had arrived late and he hoped that the school would be able to "stretch whatever points need to be stretched to give this young lady an opportunity. For a good many sound reasons, and for reasons of instinct, I am very high on this girl."

He wrote:

> I think that you know, and your board probably knows, that we may as well be honest and say that there isn't in the whole United States a really first-class Negro institution . . . if we compare them with Columbia, Harvard, Yale, Chicago, or any of the major state universities or private schools. This is one of the prices of the long system of segregation. Miss Tillman will not be as well prepared as would a girl graduating from Smith, Wellesley, or any one of the other private or state universities. But this youngster is ambitious — she has qualities for learning and her record of achievement sustains this belief. I urgently hope you can do this for this girl.

Columbia, evidently mulling the matter over, moved with annoying slowness, and McGill, in a follow-up letter, wrote:

> I don't want to be a nuisance, but I do suggest you consider, not only this year but for the years ahead, two points which I consider important.
>
> One, if we are to develop some first-rate Negro newspapermen in and from the South at the graduate level, it must be understood that they will not have had the educational opportunities . . . possessed by applicants from other areas.
>
> Second, the great need is to make a breakthrough, not only in graduate and undergraduate schools of journalism, but all other aspects of education which would train young Negroes for various occupations and professions. I know it is presumptuous of me, and I ask the pardon of the deans, assistant deans and staff, but I would suggest that in each class for the next several years room be found for at least one person who, even though he or she

may not measure up in educational preparation with other applicants, is a southern Negro student of promise. I hope that this year and for the next several years ahead you will find a place for the Judy Tillmans.

Late in July, McGill had a brief note from Dean Barrett.

"Dear Ralph: If you haven't heard by now, let me tell you that all your lobbying on behalf of Judy Tillman has paid off. She has been admitted."

McGill wrote Barrett: "I thank you and salute you."

McGill had already heard. Judy had called the day before in great excitement to tell him the good news. She had been much worried, she said, for the entrance tests had been administered in a white person's house in a section of town which McGill described to Barrett as "what Ed Rivers used to call the 'silk-stocking, gin-smelling, northside region.' " The unfamiliar surroundings had admittedly made her nervous.

Getting her enrolled was only the beginning of McGill's efforts on Judy's behalf. He wrote to John Hohenberg, professor of journalism, friend, and associate on the Pulitzer Prize Advisory Board, asking him to "be a sort of counselor for her and keep an eye on her work." He wrote to Mary Painter on *The New Yorker* and to Charlayne Hunter Stovall, the Negro girl who had integrated the University of Georgia, now a *New Yorker* staffer, asking them if they could seek out Judy and volunteer to be her "consultants and counselors," for though "Spelman is a good college in the context of southern education, neither it nor any other southern school prepares a young woman, or young man, for the sort of competition you get in the north, especially in graduate school."

At the end of the first month, John Hohenberg was writing McGill that Judy, with her lack of preparation, was indeed having a rough time of it. Fear of failure was driving her to concentrate on trying to read the school's whole reading list in a hurry, staying up late and exhausting herself. What she needed to do first, Hohenberg said, was to improve her typing, spelling and grammar.

On the plus side, Hohenberg pointed out, was the fact that Judy was a person of great potential, even though the youngest in the class. She was poised under pressure. So — "I think we can help Judy. Certainly I promise you to do my best."

McGill's letters to Judy were affectionate and paternal. Without telling her any of John Hohenberg's adverse comments, he told her of his confidence that she was going to make the grade. She shouldn't feel, he said, that she was competing against other people who were better prepared. She was competing only with the work itself. He then urged her to get at least an hour's more sleep each night. "Otherwise, you might get in what we call a run-down condition and catch flu or something." He advised her to take a flu shot, but to take it before a day when her schedule of work was light, for she might have a few hours of aches and fever.

In his letters to her, he always closed with some casual statement about scholarships not providing too much in the way of spending money, and he would often include a twenty-dollar bill.

She wrote:

> I don't think I ever will be able to express what your friendship means to me. When I went to my mailbox last Thursday and discovered your letter, I was so excited and happy to hear from you I couldn't even wait to get to my room. I just tore it open in the elevator with people standing around, and they must have wondered what was wrong because all I could say was, "Oh, no. Oh, no." Mr. McGill, it wasn't the monetary value of the twenty dollars that moved me to actual tears . . . it was the thought that kept running through my mind — that you really cared about Judy Tillman, as a person.
>
> I do hope you won't be offended, Mr. McGill, if I confide another reaction. For you to take such a personal and genuine interest in me gives me some idea of how it would be to have a real father. You see, my mother and father were divorced when I was very young. I never really experienced the interest and understanding that only a father could give. That is why . . . I respond to your actions with tears of joy and a deep humility.

Soon good word was coming back from Columbia. Judy had passed her first two examinations; and McGill wrote a long letter to Mrs. Laurance Rockefeller, telling the story of Judy, her family background, her ambitions, and her handicaps. Judy not only endured, she prevailed, with McGill fussing over her every step. He called on her in New York and took her to dinner and learned that she had stayed up all the night before working on a paper. He went by to see Dean Barrett and John Hohenberg at Columbia to check on her progress, and to offer to pay for any special tutoring she might need.

As winter came on, he wrote her:

> I don't want you to have to worry about anything that will distract you from your work. It gets colder up there than it does in Atlanta, so do not under any circumstances try to go into winter up there without warm shoes and clothing. You will certainly need a sweater or two, galoshes and fur-lined boots. Let me know what you need and I will see that you have the money for it. You can count it as a loan, to be paid back to me, or my son, or somebody, when you settle down to work, or you can use it to help someone else.

Her reaction both disturbed and pleased him. She took the money he sent her and used some of it for clothing. The rest she spent on a reference book, *Governing New York City*, and on a trip to the Metropolitan Museum of Art. She had sweaters, she wrote him, and a winter coat, and her boots weren't fur-lined but would do nicely if worn with warm socks.

He praised her for going to the Metropolitan Museum and told her she would also enjoy the Modern Museum and the Frick. He also told her that, if she could find the time, a trip to the U.N. would be wonderful. He sent along a little gift, "so that you can take a friend and have a good Thanksgiving dinner and see a movie." His letter, containing fifteen dollars, came as Judy faced a Thanksgiving weekend alone in her dormitory.

"I won't dwell on the point of how and why fate chose me for such a wonderful and dear relationship," she wrote. "I will only continue to thank God for Ralph McGill."

Worth far more than money to the frequently frightened and discouraged girl was his steady and unfailing encouragement. He had heard from her teacher that she was doing "reasonably well," he wrote. "That," he told her, "is good enough. So hang in there and keep your backbone straight."

Now and then keeping the backbone straight and the spirits up was more than Judy could muster. When the dark mood was upon her, she would pour out her fears to him.

He wrote back, bolstering her faltering ego. "Your professors tell me: 'Every member of the faculty likes Judy. We haven't had a girl here in a long time for whom the faculty had more respect.'" Her depression, he said, was a natural thing. All southerners, white or black, feel it when they go off East to school. His own son, he said, felt it when he went one year to Wesleyan. "All of us down here have a sense of not having had as good preparation as those in the eastern schools. . . . But, the great majority of those in the eastern schools don't take advantage of the opportunity, and it usually works out that a person from the South who works very hard ends up doing better than many of those who had superior opportunity."

He told her that the male student who told her she had "become a whore to western ways" because she had her hair straightened was "both rude and stupid." How any person wore her hair was strictly her own business:

> It is nobody's business what you do to your hair. I would simply write off the young man who chided you for "copying western ways" as a very rude young man and an unimportant one. I would continue to treat him with indifference. I would say the same about the one who is trying to get you to be more friendly with him. . . . You are up there to do a job, and in the course of that, you will make friends, but it isn't necessary for you to worry about being friends to people in whom you are not interested. You are courteous, and that is enough.

Once, in a low moment, she wrote that she felt she was a "poor example of her race." "Put that out of your mind," wrote McGill. "You are a fine representative of the human race . . . a fine young woman with more courage and talent than anybody I have met in a long time. So don't quit praying, and keep working. Feel free to write me or Miss Lundy and feel free to call me. (He gave her his unlisted home number.) By all means take up your personal problems with me. Getting this off your chest is good therapy."

He feared that her periods of depression might be a reflection of physical illness. Her blood pressure, she reported, was low. He urged her to have a checkup and send him the bill.

In mid-May he got a note from John Hohenberg. "Our girl, Judy Tillman, has made it and will have her MS in journalism come June 1. She's grown up in a year and handles herself very well now."

The news that Judy had indeed turned out as he had predicted caused McGill great satisfaction. He wrote to his friends in the newspaper business, telling them that she would be available for job interviews soon. (She had expressed a wish to work in the East before coming back South.)

To Judy he wrote: "I'm really proud of you. You've hoed a tough row, and you have done it well."

Believing that Judy's mother would like to share in the triumphant graduation, and assuming that a trip to New York would put a strain on a schoolteacher's budget, he wrote, "I will be glad to purchase a round-trip ticket for your mother if she needs it and will accept it. If you would feel better, we will consider it a loan which you can pay back after you have been working a while." As usual, he enclosed "a little contribution. It's not a loan to be paid back, but comes under the category of help you are going to pass on to someone else in the years to come."

In June she graduated — not last, but thirty-ninth out of a class of eighty-four. Three months later, in Sisters Chapel at Spelman College, she married a young Ethiopian journalist named Makonnen Gebre-Hiwet, whom she had met at Columbia. They went to live in Addis Ababa. They returned from there two years later so that Judy could have her baby in the States. She was at her mother's home in Atlanta, awaiting the arrival of Aklesian Florence Marian Gebre-Hiwet, to be known as Fu Fu, when the word came that McGill was dead. In the paper that reported his passing, a letter from Judy and Makonnen led all the other tributes. It read:

> Ralph McGill was always a source of light when all other ways seemed dark and closed. He was never too busy to help a young person's need. He always opened his office and heart to those in distress, and a whole new world of opportunity, truth, and beauty was opened to them. . . . Although we have lost the warmth of his physical presence, he has left us with much

more — a strong spirit of love and honesty that cannot die. A part of his legacy will be the thousands of children he had, both black and white, whom he discovered, encouraged and nurtured. We are but two of them.

There were many others. Dino Shorte, a young Negro actor, who got his chance on Broadway because of McGill. Marré Danger, who for ten years he guided and counseled in her search for a writing career. Kids without number, both black and white, who went on to become teachers and journalists. "You may not remember the day you came to my father's house," wrote Ruth Ayer Glover. "I was the little girl in the faded cotton dress, cooking dinner while my mother was hanging out the wash. But you took time to talk to me, and that talk changed my life, for with your help, I entered college. . . ."

21

On the first Sunday in February 1969, Ralph and Mary Lynn were sitting in the pine-paneled kitchen which also served as the living room of their little red-brick house on Piedmont Road. He, in a deep-seated armchair, was writing with a ballpoint pen on a yellow legal pad. She, on a bench that once had been an old church pew, was scraping paint off a metal medicine cabinet. It made a screeching noise, and concerned that she might be disturbing him, she asked, "Does this bother you?" He looked up. "What?" he said.

Later, talking to friends of McGill's who were also journalists, she said, "I've been told that Ralph could write anywhere, anytime, about anything. Can all of you do that?" John Popham of the *Chattanooga Times* answered for everybody there. "Not like him," he said.

The genius of McGill lay in the fact that everything turned him on, mentally or emotionally, and once the idea began to glow and shimmer in his mind, there was nothing that could throw his thoughts off track. He could write a paragraph, answer a phone, chat with a visitor — and then turn back to his typewriter and pick up the rhythm again. He could indeed write anywhere, anytime, on any subject.

Some of his best-remembered columns were born of some trivial incident that to most men would have gone unnoticed. One morning, for example, he woke up early, could not go back to sleep, got up to put the coffee on, and went out in his robe and slippers to get the morning paper out of his mailbox.

As he reached the street, an old Negro man in a ramshackle wagon drawn by a bony horse pulled up and stopped. There was a plow in the bed of the wagon, and the old man asked McGill if he could do some yard work or plow his garden for him. McGill was in no particular need of such services, but the old man obviously was in need of work. So a deal was made, and McGill went back in the house and sat down at the kitchen table to drink his coffee and read his paper, but in the back of his mind, pictures were beginning to form. From his Bible reading, he remembered the war-horse, sniffing the battle afar off. Out of his memories of the Victorian poets, he heard again Tennyson's lines he so often had recited as a boy in grammar school:

> *"Forward, the Light Brigade!*
> *Charge for the guns!" he said.*
> *Into the Valley of Death*
> *Rode the Six Hundred.*

He reached for a yellow pad and sat there for a minute, his brow furrowed, thinking of horses. Then in a plain, square-lettered hand he began to write. He recalled his Tennessee boyhood when he rode a horse to the mill with a sack of corn for grinding on the saddle in front of him. He remembered the smell of barnyards and of horse sweat, the creaking of harness and the sighing snort of a tired horse turning at the end of a plowed furrow.

In war and husbandry, he wrote, the tracks of horse and man have moved together down the centuries, though now men ride to battle and till the fields in iron monsters that scar the earth with a different track. Old stories came into his mind. He wondered what it must have been like when the chariots of Pharaoh went thundering through the city gates, the charioteers cursing, their whips cracking, the dust rising under the hoofs of the horses as they set out in pursuit of the children of Israel, fleeing from Egypt's land.

He remembered Xerxes, and how, when his chariots came to a stream, their numbers were so great that men and horses would swiftly drink it dry. He remembered Ben Hur, and the rumbling wheels of the Roman racing chariots, and he recalled the Spanish conquistadores, bringing the first horses to the New World, and how a tribe of Plains Indians called the Sioux captured the Spanish horses, and riding naked and bareback, became the continent's first and fiercest light cavalry.

The names of the great cavalry leaders of the Civil War came back to him — Stuart, Forrest, Phil Sheridan. And from the depths of his memory he dredged an obscure fact: In the Battle of New Orleans in the War of 1812, "Old Hickory" Jackson's men had stampeded their horses into the British lines. The beaten British had captured them and taken them aboard ship as they made sail for England. Thus, there were Tennessee horses in the charge of the British dragoons that broke the back of Napoleon at Waterloo. . . .

And so, long before the old man and his tired horse had finished plowing McGill's little garden plot, he had tracked horse and man through history from Pegasus to Citation, touching, in passing, on plowed fields and green pastures, knights jousting in armor, and fire engines rolling with clanging bells. And now, he finished moodily, the horse had about had his day and "somehow my coffee has lost its savor and the morning its bright charm."

It took very little to trigger his interest, intellectual or emotional. One morning in his office, he read a small news item buried deep inside the paper, which said that the rock fortress of Masada in Israel had been restored and would be open to tourists. The fort had been built by Herod, the story said, and it was the scene of the last fierce defense made by a Jewish force after the sacking of Jerusalem by the Romans in 70 A.D. That was all. But that was enough to light a spark in Pappy's memory. On a nearby shelf were the works of Flavius Josephus. Not many newspaper editors can reach out at will and lay their hands on a copy of Josephus, but McGill could, and he did. And out of his rereading of Josephus's report, written nearly two thousand years ago, came a memorable column in which the blood and horror and cruelty of the sack of Jerusalem all mingled in a grisly climax at Masada. Josephus, through McGill, told the story of the Sicarii, the "rough and violent fellows" who had sorely harassed the Romans and had finally been driven to bay — seven hundred of them — with all their wives and children, in the vast rock fortress by the Dead Sea. And there, under a leader named Eleazar, "a potent man," they held out until it was clear they could hold out no longer. So, knowing that only slavery and torture faced them if they were captured by the Romans, they chose ten men to slay all the rest. And they wept and embraced each other and the killing was done, and when it was over, each of the ten surviving men died by his own hand. Only a few lived to tell the story — two old women and five children who had hidden themselves. And the Romans, Josephus said, "could not but wonder at the resolution of the Jews, and the contempt of death which they had shown."

That little item in the paper had given McGill the opportunity to tell again a story he loved to repeat, of a race whose heroism he admired — and to whose religion all his life he was strongly drawn.

McGill was an emotional man, and all of his columns about people, whether born in anger or in sympathy, were written from the heart. Once there was a brief item in the paper which told the story of a ninety-year-old woman dying in the Georgia State Hospital for the insane at Milledgeville. She had been there since she was nineteen, and in all those seventy-one years, she had never had a visitor.

Why, wondered McGill. Who was she and who had sent her there to live forgotten? All the record that could be found was a few lines on a yellowed page: "Annie Lee. Lunatic. Age nineteen. Baptist. Violent toward mother."

From these few facts, McGill fashioned a savage indictment of the still-existing public cruelty to the mentally ill. How hostile was Annie Lee, he asked. What sort of a person was Mama? Did she deserve to be honored by her child, or did she herself drive a sensitive child to rebellion? One thing convinced him that the young girl had been simply put away. The fact that no relative had come to see her in all her long life in the asylum to him was a confession of a sense of guilt. Could she not by more kindness have been restored to useful life, he asked her doctor. McGill, in his anger, traced the whole history of the "lunatic asylum," from Bedlam to the present day, ending with the questions: "What about the mental health program in your own community? Are there buried there forgotten Annie Lees?"

McGill cared about anything and everything that people cared about. A mother wrote him asking him what to do about a left-handed son whose teachers were trying to break him of left-handedness. In a column titled "Glorify Your Southpaw," he wrote that "left-handers are protected by special fates. Leprechauns accompany them everywhere to give them aid and comfort." He then wrote of all the great southpaws of history, the warriors and athletes, and even twenty years later, readers were still asking for reprints of this column. Another was a gentle, philosophical discourse on man's relation to God and nature, an answer to a child's query, "Who Shakes the Trees?"

Pappy's columns rarely were reflections recollected in tranquility. They were scratched on pads held in his lap in planes and airport waiting rooms, beaten out on borrowed typewriters in newspaper offices, or most often, when he traveled, which was constantly, spoken into telephones without ever being put down on paper in ordered fashion at all. He would read over the hardly legible scribblings he had put down on the backs of envelopes, arrange his thoughts, and then proceed to dictate to Grace Lundy, the words pouring forth in a steady flow, until she, noting that she had reached the tenth page in her shorthand pad, warned him that he had to wrap it up — the twenty-six inches allowed him on the front page of the paper were nearly filled.

The product turned out in such haste was roughhewn, the sentences often awkward. He put down the words as they came tumbling helter-skelter into his mind — dictated more by emotion than by logic, and he rarely paused to polish a phrase. So great was his mastery of the language, though, his meaning was always clear, his phrases fresh, and often, in the pell-mell rush of the prose, there could be heard the rhythms of the poets and the stately cadence of the King James Testament.

After young Ralph's fifth birthday, he never changed his Christmas columns. On the day before Christmas Eve, he told the story of the caravan on the road to Bethlehem. On Christmas Eve, he told the story the early Christians told their children — of how the robin got its red breast and the lightning bug its green taillight. And on Christmas Day, he wrote of how the angels taught the nightingale to sing and what the animals say on Christmas morning. These became the most widely read and reprinted columns written by McGill in his nearly forty years with the *Constitution.*

John Popham of the *Chattanooga Times* was one of those who saw in McGill's choice of subjects a deliberate technique, like a canny old pitcher mixing in with his fast ball an assortment of curves and sliders:

> He'd write for two months about things that would make them mad enough to lynch him. Then he'd sit down and write a piece about a foxhound he used to know, or retell the story of that Georgia Tech bear that had the hangover. Or he'd write about the children in an orphanage in Vietnam, or a little boy asking "Who is God?" and pretty soon he would

have them laughing and crying and cutting out his column and putting it away in a scrapbook to grow yellow with the years.

For all the vast variety of his subject matter and his occasional inconsistency, in larger matters there was an amazing consistency of theme and point of view. He was instinctively *for* the quiet and humble and poor, and against the arrogant, the powerful, and in general, the rich — though he greatly admired the rich who used their wealth with wisdom and compassion and the powerful who used their authority with restraint. He was for the young and flexible of mind, and against the elderly whose thoughts had crystallized. He had the faculty of looking with amazing prescience at the shape of things to come, but he also could look back and with a Proustian genius conjure up a remembrance of things past that illuminated history. He was by instinct a preacher and a teacher, though gently so.

He wrote because he had to write, out of a compulsion as strong as hunger, as deep as the need for love. He began writing a daily column before he was twenty-one, and he kept it up for fifty years. He looked on vacations as a sign of weakness, and any lessening in his productive effort would have seemed to him a sign of sloth, a concession to the advancing years. When he started, a daily essay was all that was required of him. He continued it, seven days a week, long after an added burden of travel, speaking, teaching at seminars, sitting in committees of government, and outside writing took so much of his time that the column had to be written at odd or random moments snatched usually from hours needed desperately for sleep.

This first Sunday in February was a fine fair day of rare quietness. Somewhat penitent after sleeping late, Ralph had worked steadily all day on the outline of a book that had been stirring in his mind for several years — its theme the agony of the Christian church in a time of racial crisis.

The stern Calvinism into which McGill had been born had mellowed over the years into a gentler faith, but there was always in him some instinct that would not let him accept a less than complete commitment to the Christian commandment, "Love thy neighbor."

"McGill," Harry Ashmore once wrote, "knows that the world's great need is for love. And he stands ready to whip any man in Dixie who isn't prepared to offer it, without stint, to black and white alike."

McGill, up until his middle years, had shown no great enthusiasm for the church. His buoyant spirit had found the restrictions of his bluestocking ancestors burdensome, and to a degree, hypocritical. "An irreverent uncle," he said, "once assured me that Presbyterians sinned as frequently as did anyone else. They just did not enjoy it as much."

From his college days, therefore, up until the time, nearly forty years later, when young Ralph had grown to Sunday school age, he gave no time and little thought to formal religious matters. Though a man of deep and abiding faith in God, and in His Son, he had felt that the modern church in great degree was a failure. In its obsession with saving men's souls, it had abdicated whatever responsibility it might have felt for their mental and physical well-being, their health, education and general welfare. He recalled with bitterness the days of the depression, when the CIO organizers were moving into the South, asking for a living wage for the hungry and consumptive mill hands. The preachers in the little cotton-mill towns were spokesmen for the mill owners, equating a labor union organizer with Beelzebub himself.

In the forties and fifties, with the beginning of the movement toward civil rights, it was the ministers of the evangelical churches who gave aid and comfort to the Klansmen and the Columbians, and spiritual support to the White Citizens' Councils — offering scriptural "proof" that God Himself had decreed segregation and that the Bible abundantly condoned the separation of the races. Of these men and their delaying effect upon the segregation movement, he wrote in *The South and the Southerner:* "There is no blinking the fact that, in general, the Christian church has been either in retreat or standing afar off wringing its hands in an agony of spirit." This unhappy state, he said, was worsened by "the religious albinos who dressed God out in a Klan robe or put into His mouth the most extreme prejudices and shibboleths of the more fanatic and blindly defiant." The reluctance of the church to speak out in a time that called for commitment deeply troubled him. The active and aggressive antisegregationists speaking from the pulpit were in the minority, and were vulnerable to attack. His deeper concern was with the silent clergy, with their failure to "decry, deplore and condemn . . . the joblessness, illiteracy, frustration of spirit and body, lack of opportunity, squalor — the daily offering of the plate of humiliation and discrimination to the average Negro. . . ."

Speaking out for fair treatment for the Negro was rare enough from the pulpit. Welcoming him as a brother in Christ, sitting in a pew, was rarer still. The fact that this was so caused young ministers of sensitive heart and mind great agony of spirit. They were caught between the dictates of their own conscience and stated church policy on the one hand, and the prejudices of those members who "ran" the church on the other. So, they either fell silent, or they spoke out for brotherly love and an integrated church and were drummed out of the pulpit by their angry congregations. Young ministers of many denominations sought McGill's help and counsel. He urged them not to leave the ministry but to keep trying to find a place where they could speak out. For those who had lost their pulpits he became a sort of way station on an underground railway, passing young preachers on to freedom with more liberal congregations farther north.

All these things were in his mind as he sat, pad on knee, in the little book-lined den-kitchen with its open fire. At hand was a copy of a letter he had written Edward Weeks nearly three years before. "I have a vague idea about a book. I am interested in and disturbed by the church in the South and its attitude toward the great social changes of our day." He remembered his talk in Africa with W. E. B. Du Bois, the great Negro expatriate, and Du Bois's recent book on the church and the race problem. His article on Du Bois in *The Atlantic Monthly*, he felt, might set the theme for his own book on the agony and failure of the church. ". . . I don't know whether this idea is any good or not. . . ."

Weeks's reply was enthusiastic: "The answer is 'yes.' Damn the torpedoes! Full steam ahead!"

The head of steam had been slow in building up, but now at last he was ready to work. Around his chair were letters written in defense of Bishop Pike against those who had accused him of heresy. There were other letters accusing McGill of being anti-Christ for defending Pike. There was a letter to a leader of his own church in which he had called the Lovett School incident "The Little Rock of the Episcopal church." His book on the church, he realized, could not focus solely on beleaguered leaders such as Pike and their struggles over doctrine, nor with his conflicts with his own church for its failure to practice in the world what it preached from the pulpit. Nor could it, as first intended, deal only with the church in the South. The issue of civil rights was now nationwide and the book must stress the failure of the national church, not only of one denomination but of them all. The central theme was now clear in his mind — "The failure of the Christian church to speak out in all its authority in support of racial justice is the single most melancholy aspect of what has been called the moral decline of our time." But how to get into it? He thought a moment. Then in blue ink on a yellow pad, in a scrawl almost childlike in its clarity, he wrote:

"No southerner escapes an environment of religion and for most of us it is a rather grim and unrelenting experience. . . ." He went on for a page and part of another, describing his early religious training: "the sense of a hot hell and the wages of sin, the weekly verbal washings in the blood of the lamb. . . ."

There was a flicker of crimson at the window, and he put down his pen and yellow pad and got up. He looked out through the double doors into the little courtyard, whose wavering brick wall he had built himself — and which, his friends averred, was held up only by the climbing roses now growing upon it. At the bird feeder a cardinal, seeking sunflower seeds, was busily scratching the millet and other seeds out upon the brick terrace, which was wrinkling under a moving carpet of feeding doves. The doves, he noted, remembering crisp golden mornings in the hunting fields, were now becoming as urbanized as pigeons.

Dusk was coming on — the cold pearl-gray of a dying February day in Georgia — the time for their evening walk. He called to Mary Lynn, busy in the back of the house trying to sort out and classify a roomful of old scrapbooks, photographs, coins, paintings and random objects he had gathered in thirty years of wandering around the world.

On the stove near his chair, there simmered a pot of stew that filled the room with the smell of herbs and spices. Mary Lynn had no skill in the kitchen, and on Sundays when Julia was not there she gladly assigned to him the task of preparing their evening meal. So, early in the afternoon, before sitting down to work, he had chopped up the celery, the carrots, the onions and the good beef. In another hour it would be ready.

Mary Lynn came in, in blue jeans, sweater and walking shoes. Pulling on a sweater against the coming chill and yanking down over his ears the beret that made him look like a Basque sheepherder, McGill armed himself with a knobbed stick to fend off the neighborhood dogs. Then with Carol, the dachshund, wriggling happily ahead of them, he and Mary Lynn set out. They walked at a good pace for two miles along the tree-shaded sidewalks of the old residential neighborhood and came back, tired but happy and relaxed. The room was warm, and rich with the aroma of the supper stew. On the hearth a dying fire glowed under gray ash. Sitting at the rough wooden table on benches that had come from a pioneer church, they ate huge bowls of the stew, drinking with it a sturdy Burgundy. They went to bed early, well content, on this their last night together.

22

The next morning, Monday, February 3, dawned clear and crisply cold. Mary Lynn, an early riser, was up and off to her office while McGill, in robe and slippers, was still sipping his morning tea.

He dressed, with a certain sense of satisfaction, in a handsome camel's-hair jacket he had once given young Ralph, who now had outgrown it and given it back to him, and in the gray thirty-dollar slacks whose cost had once so horrified him. He put on also the new ankle-high boots, not laced but strapped and buckled, which he had bought in Washington during the Nixon inauguration. His conscience had pained him when he paid fifty dollars for them and had twinged again, though less sharply, when, not wishing to be teased for his extravagance, he had told Mary Lynn that they had cost only thirty-five dollars.

Only one cloud hung over the day as he waited for the taxi that would take him to his office. February 3 was the birthday of Virginia, the little girl he and Mary Elizabeth had adopted after their first child had died in infancy. If Virginia had lived, she would have been thirty-three years old today, and hardly a day had passed in all those years that he had not thought of her.

By the time he reached the office in mid-morning, this melancholy mood was gone. He was blithe and joking, seeming particularly pleased by the fact that he had his weight under such control he now could wear a jacket that was too small for his son. He had done a prodigious amount of dictating on Friday, and there was not much mail needing his attention. (He would let mail pile up for weeks, sometimes for months, and then answer it all in one great flurry.) He sat for an hour in the outer office where the secretaries had their desks, talking with Grace Lundy and Mary Murphy, whose boss, Reg Murphy, had taken over the editorship when Patterson left. Reporters and desk men, on their way to the city room, saw him through the big glass doors and stopped to chat, and he talked with them of politics and sports.

Being syndicated, he had to keep five or six columns ahead, and he checked on these to see if they still were on top of the news. The ones in type on this day showed his typical change of pace. One told of flying into Chicago and getting stacked for two hours in the fog over O'Hare, where he suffered in tortured silence while a boorish seatmate snarled in his ear the angry litany he had kept up all the way from Atlanta — "I get damned tired of hearing from social-worker do-gooders about all the hungry people. If they are hungry, it is because they are too shiftless to work. . . ." McGill quoted.

Whether there was such a garrulous bore beside him or not, it was typical of many similar utterances by rude and foolish men, and it gave him a peg on which to hang a few controverting facts. In this column, he quoted United States Public Health Service surveys which showed that out of twelve thousand poor in Texas and Louisiana, twelve to fifteen percent were in need of medical attention for ailments based on hunger. Old diseases of malnutrition, rickets and goiter, were coming back, he said, and stunted babies were being born. It was a column full of statistics and the thrust of it was that hunger and disease, not laziness, were the bane and burden of the poor, whom the man in the seat beside him had cursed for their shiftlessness. He quoted Harvard researchers who said that the multibillion-dollar farm subsidy programs were being foolishly spent. The money went to large landowners for reducing crops. It should go to small landowners to help them grow more food. . . .

There was another column on a serious theme. On a visit to Des Moines in January, he had seen a handsome new housing project, sponsored by the Des Moines Council of Ministers, who required that the construction unions who built it should open their ranks to workmen from the minority groups.

"Most councils of ministers," he pointed out, "do little more than adopt mild resolutions. They are not for . . . aggressive social work. But," he said, approvingly, "the Des Moines Council is different."

There was a political column, asking the heretical question whether or not it was good for the South for the more important committees of

Congress to be under control of southern reactionaries. It was such leadership, he said, that had kept the South poor in income, education, and jobs, and left her all the troubles growing out of the racial problem.

All these columns were good enough, designed to lead and enlighten. But none of them would spark his more volatile readers to controversy. So, he chose a subject he knew would set them to grinding their teeth in rage.

"Pro football," he wrote, "has been reading its mail, putting data into computers, feeling the ticket-buying pulse, and reportedly is about ready to reveal its decision to abolish one of sports' oldest bores — the football half-time marching bands."

Since the pros set the style for college football, he pointed out, this led to the hope that colleges would follow suit, thus sparing the football crowds the ennui of looking at a ceremony as rigid in form as a High Church ritual. He expressed the view that most of the drinking at football games "derives from persons fleeing the half-time spectacle and finding some corner where they can fortify themselves while waiting it out."

He suggested that the universities and colleges might convert their marching bands into symphony orchestras, chamber music groups, or brass ensembles. He also spoke disparagingly of baton twirlers. Baton twirling is an ephemeral skill at best, he said, lacking in practical application, and baton twirlers should be trained for some other work at which their dexterity could be more gainfully employed.

He then went on to praise the half-time entertainment he once witnessed at Wesleyan College in Connecticut. The band members, most of whom were bareheaded, strolled into the stadium in the usual campus garb of old sports jackets, slacks and a variety of footgear. They wore no uniforms nor did they march. They sat down and played several airs, all of which were unfamiliar to McGill, and he discovered later that they were original compositions. No baton twirlers were in evidence. "Those twenty minutes of good, creative music were rewarding. . . ."

He pulled the column from the typewriter and handed it to Grace Lundy, glanced at the big clock over the door — he rarely wore a watch — and noted that he had just enough time to go across the street to a café he called with rueful affection "The Dirty One." There he ate a trayful of salads and then caught a taxi to his speaking engagement at Booker T. Washington High School.

The auditorium was packed with the students of the junior and senior English classes as he walked in, the youngsters not noisy but quiet and expectant. The young girl student who introduced him was nervous and helped to break the tension between speaker and audience when she announced that "Mr. McGill was born in 1998." This made everybody laugh, including McGill. He put his hand on her shoulder as he stood up to speak. "I am glad you made that mistake," he told her, "for day after tomorrow happens to be my birthday, and I want birthdays to keep coming. I don't like to consider the alternative to birthdays ending. . . . I would like to start over in 1998 . . . maybe in some re-incarnation. . . .

"You have heard," he went on, "that this column of mine has appeared for thirty-nine years; that's true. In fact, if April comes around and I'm still with it, then I will have finished up forty years of newspaper work here in Atlanta.

"It was mentioned that I was from Soddy, Tennessee. People always ask me, 'Where in the world is Soddy?' and I tell them Soddy is just three miles from Daisy — and everybody knows where Daisy is."

This made them laugh again, and he went on establishing his rapport with his audience of workingmen's children by telling them of his father, who went to a little one-room schoolhouse which had one teacher who taught all seven grades.

"So you know," he said, "how much education my father had and how hard he had to work all his life."

Then he told them how he had worked, too, waiting tables and stoking furnaces to go to school, and how he had first wanted to be a doctor and then had just sort of drifted into the newspaper business — just as many men and women may not know at first what they want to do. He then went on to tell them about his son and about the fact that he was wearing his son's coat, which made him "feel kind of younger than I am."

It was a typical McGill speech, rambling, friendly, warmly humorous, philosophy brightened by whimsy, with nuggets of wisdom almost casually dropped in.

Young people, he said, get tired of hearing grown people tell them what to do, and he didn't want to give them any advice. "Only this — try to learn to like to read. For some people it comes easily. For others it is hard to do. But once you learn to read, you've got a tool nobody can take away from you."

Knowing that for many of these youngsters college would be out of the question, he explained that everybody should be able to go to college who really wanted to — but that a college education as it was known in the past wasn't absolutely essential anymore. There were so many useful skills that could be learned outside of college; not just the old vocational skills of carpentry and laying bricks, but new things, like computer processing and all the skills that serve the new technology.

"So," he told them, "don't think, 'If I don't go to college, I won't amount to anything.' But do learn to read, for that is the key that unlocks all doors."

He then asked if there were questions, and hands began to shoot up all over the hall. They asked him how he kept so well abreast of what was going on in the world, and he explained that he used the telephone a lot. If there was something he wanted to know about what was going on in the Vietnam peace talks, he'd call Ambassador Lodge or Harriman in Paris, or whoever was there, and ask what he wanted to know. He called people all over the world, he said — journalists or diplomats — asking them things. Sometimes, he said, when the business-office people saw his telephone bill, they got upset with him.

They asked him about black separatism, and he said it was wrong for the blacks to try to separate from the whites. The white man, he said, had tried to separate himself from his black neighbors, and it didn't work. "You can't separate yourself from life. You can't separate yourself from the world. You can't separate yourself from your fellowman. . . ."

He was on the platform talking and answering questions for more than two hours. Gloria Weaver, a teen-ager in the audience, said in her report in the school paper: "All the time he was standing there, I felt he was just so content. . . . He seemed so patient. If we got twisted up in our words, he'd say, 'Uh-huh, uh-huh,' and encourage us to continue, like he really understood what we were trying to say. . . . When it was over, everybody clapped a long time."

He was back in the office at mid-afternoon, physically tired but exhilarated, as he always was after talking to youngsters. Grace closed his office door and turned away visitors, and he lay down on the long red leather sofa in his office and slept for nearly an hour. He came out, yawning and blinking. "Who-ee," he said. "I slept like a log." Grace handed him the clean typed copy of the column he had written that morning on the boredom of the half-time ceremonies at football games. He read it over again, chuckling.

"That ought to stir them up," he said.

She showed him then the green galley proofs of the column that would appear in the next morning's paper. Its title was "Listen, Please, Sec. Finch," and it began: "Secretary Finch . . . if you have just a moment, sir, please lend an ear."

He then went on for six hundred words, urging the secretary of Health, Education and Welfare not to accept or support the freedom-of-choice school plan which many boards of education in the small-town rural South were asking the government to accept. The plan, he argued, "offers a segregationist, racist-dominated community . . . an opportunity to proclaim a free choice while they covertly employ 'persuasions' (meaning threats) to maintain segregation or meager tokenism."

The column, Grace Lundy told him, was fine so far as it went, but it lacked an inch going far enough. It needed five more lines to fill his front-page space.

McGill took the proof, read it over hastily, and then scribbled at the end the needed five lines: "You may be assured, sir, that the freedom-of-choice plan is in fact neither real freedom nor a choice. It is discrimination."

Thus, fittingly but almost by chance, the last words he ever wrote were an earnest and eloquent plea for justice and fairness, a rejection of the evil he had fought against all his life — discrimination.

A few minutes later, as dark came on and the rush of the home-going traffic began to ebb, Mary Lynn picked him up in front of the office to take him to John Lawhorn's house for dinner. It was to be in celebration of McGill's seventy-first birthday — two days early — and a celebration, too, of the deep friendship that had grown up between the two men.

John Lawhorn, young soft-spoken Ohio-born Negro, was a genius as a teacher of small children. A concert pianist with a master's degree from Columbia University, his specialty was the teaching of music by use of a technique that made music an instrument for teaching many other things, principally reading and the use of words and numbers.

In the spring of 1968, when the Summerhill section of Atlanta was threatening to explode under racial tension, Lawhorn had written to the President in Washington and had telephoned to the mayor and all the federal, state, county and city agencies, urging them to establish a series of music schools in the tense slum areas of Atlanta. His argument: the program would take the child off the streets and give him an interest in life more meaningful and useful than the usual ghetto recreation programs of Ping-Pong and volleyball.

"I called them all and got as far as their secretaries, from whom I received a polite brush-off," he recalled.

Then he called McGill and got Grace Lundy. She listened a moment and knew instinctively that here was something that would interest her boss. "Hold a minute," she told Lawhorn. "I know he'll want to talk to you."

Within an hour, the young teacher was in McGill's office, nervous and stammering at first, and then pouring out his theory of teaching music and its meaning to the slum-bred child.

Two months earlier, he said, he had started working with children in a ghetto section who showed all the symptoms of the disadvantaged child: the hopelessness born of repeated failures in school, the shy backwardness that comes from daily abuse for alleged ignorance, the complete disintegration of personality that derives from never being able to do anything right. He had seen them, through music, transformed into different people, their faces suffused with "the bright glare of happiness" as they stood up and sang and sang and sang, hitting a wrong note now and then but still going joyfully on. Music to these kids, he told McGill, had become a happy thing, a natural development of the innate rhythms that are part of the makeup of every human being. It was gleeful and spontaneous and fun, and they learned to sing and play simple instruments with all the zest that kids used to learn to play baseball before the Little Leagues turned play into a deadly serious thing.

That, he said, was what had happened to music teaching in the past. The emphasis was on the hunt for the star, the talented and dedicated, a search for the concert artist. This, he thought, was wrong. Every child's musical talent should be developed to the limit of its potential, but if the potential was low, so what? The child could still learn to sing and carry a simple tune and play a simple instrument, joyfully if not well.

The next day, at the Agnes Jones School in a black section of town, McGill, who could not carry a tune in his hat, found himself patting his foot and humming and beating time with his hands as John Lawhorn stood up before a class of children listed as slow learners and demonstrated what he had been trying to tell McGill.

In his column, he described Lawhorn at work:

Before him sat second-grade children, their faces eager with anticipation. There was love in their eyes for the young man who stood before them.

Their ages were seven through nine years.

"Now," he said, "put your left fingers on your right wrist. You feel that beat, that's what we call the pulse; put your right hand on the left side of your chest, feel that? That's the beat of your heart. There is a beat in all things.

"Remember what we had last time, beat with your hands: Hickory, dickory, dock, the mouse ran up the clock; the clock struck one, the mouse ran down, hickory, dickory dock."

Hands clapped in unison, giving the loudest slap at the end of each beat.

"That's fine, you didn't make a mistake.

"Now, let's go again. Want to do Mr. Foster?"

They did. Hands beating: "Mr. Foster went to Gloucester, in a shower of rain; stepped in a puddle, up to his middle; won't go there again."

Progress.

"Now, let's show our visitor how far we've gone. What words do you want to use?"

"M-words . . . P-words."

There were many requests. (Pupils learn words by taking each letter of the alphabet and selecting words beginning with a particular letter to chant.)

"A . . . map is a picture showing how to go. Many, many places that have sun and snow. A map always tells us how to find our way and a nice time to travel is the month of May."

The children beat their hands in rhythmic beat to chants featuring other words. After a while one realized that here were children who, for the second grade, had quite a vocabulary. And were using it. They were putting it together in sentences. Also, and equally important, the beat-chant was making them familiar with syllables, was promoting clearer enunciation.

Not merely were they learning, they were happy to be learning. Learning was fun, great fun. It gave one a sense of achieving, especially since the teacher was thoughtful enough to commend accuracy in enunciation and beat, and to correct the few errors with a smile. "Let's try that one again, we don't want to miss, do we?" . . .

It is grossly unfair, McGill concluded, to label any child as "unable to learn." Too often it is a teacher who hasn't learned to teach.

Even before he sat down to write the column, McGill had telephoned to Peter White, executive director of a small, alert and agile foundation called the Southern Council on International and Public Affairs. Founded and supported by a group of southern business and professional men with an interest in their region that went beyond the counting-house, it was flexible enough to get a good project going while larger and more muscle-bound agencies were trying to untangle their own red tape.

"Peter," said McGill, "I don't know how to describe what I saw today. But I want you to go see it for yourself. And I hope you can find this man some money."

Peter White went and saw, and then got on the telephone and called his wife, Julia, and told her to come down and bring the children, so that they too could see and experience this thing. Then, as a test, they went the next day to a strange neighborhood, and John Lawhorn picked up a bunch of kids he had never seen before, and within an hour, he had them singing and chanting and keeping time to music and learning new words. Here, Peter White noted, John Lawhorn could be tough as well as gentle. One of the larger boys was rude and boisterous at first. Lawhorn took him by the shoulder with one hand and doubled his other into a fist, which he held under the youngster's nose. "Sonny," he said, "how do you expect to sing with your teeth knocked down your throat?"

That was the beginning. Peter White found some money and an old house provided by a church was renovated as a pilot school. And now

John Lawhorn was a consultant to the state Board of Education, and in five slum areas of Atlanta teachers trained by him were at work.

One thing John Lawhorn remembered well, as he and Phyllis, his wife, checked the dinner table to make sure everything was in order as they waited for the McGills, was the way McGill had looked as the class ended that first afternoon. The children called Lawhorn "Daddy," and they rushed up to him and hugged him as they said good-bye. And then, without any prompting, they lined up and one by one hugged McGill. And as he hugged them back and told them good-bye, John Lawhorn could see that his eyes were wet.

It was a happy evening at Lawhorn's home, with McGill sharing the birthday honors with Michael, the Lawhorns' son, aged twelve. McGill was more silent than was his custom, and once or twice Mary Lynn thought she saw him surreptitiously feeling for his pulse. But he seemed to be feeling fine, and he listened with obvious delight as Mary Lynn, out of her own interest in children, talked with bright-eyed animation to Lawhorn about his work.

After dinner they went into the living room. McGill, sitting in a big easy chair facing the three of them, was talking about how to raise money for a new dream John Lawhorn had — a bus equipped as a traveling music school — when suddenly, in the middle of a sentence, he stopped.

As Lawhorn remembers it:

For just a moment, he seemed to lose control of his eyes. I looked at Mrs. McGill to see if this was something unusual, and I could tell by her expression, and by the tone of her voice, when she said, "Ralph, Ralph, are you all right?" that this was something bad, something she had never seen happen to him before.

He seemed to recover for a moment and he said, "Yes, I'm all right, but I think we should be going now." He stood up and then he began to fall, and I grabbed him and caught him and laid him down gently on the floor.

My wife is quick about doctors. We had a little baby die once because the doctor didn't get there in time, and she said as we laid him down, "Who's his doctor?" and Mrs. McGill told her "Joe Wilber" and gave her his telephone number. And my wife ran upstairs to the telephone.

Mrs. McGill was down on the floor beside him now, calling his name, making his collar loose, trying to help him get some air. But I think, even that quickly, he was gone . . . and I remember thinking how glad I was I'd been able to catch him as he fell. If he'd fallen down hard or off in a room by himself, it would always have bothered me.

Mary Lynn knew at once when McGill stopped speaking in mid-sentence that something was dreadfully wrong.

"I felt the fear come on, making my ears feel funny, feel full. I knew the time had come that I had told myself I someday would have to face. I knew that, statistically, it was almost inevitable that he would go and leave me. But I knew, too, that I was going to fight as hard as I could to save him."

On this night the oxygen bottle she always carried surreptitiously on the long trips had been left at home. But many times she had thought of what she would do in such an emergency as this. Lying on the floor, her mouth on his, she breathed into his lungs, seeing with rising hope the color come back to his lips and the pupils of his eyes remain contracted, indicating there had been no brain damage. But all this time, in the massive chest, she could feel no throb of a heartbeat. Calmly, steadily, without panic, pausing now and then to call his name, minute after minute, she kept on.

At his home far across town, Dr. Joseph Wilber took Mrs. Lawhorn's frightened call and left at once. It was nearly ten o'clock and traffic was light, and he ran the red lights and risked the cops as he raced to Lawhorn's house. For McGill was more than a patient to him. He was counselor, guide and friend.

An ambulance called by Mrs. Lawhorn had arrived, and the driver, kneeling beside Mary Lynn, was compressing McGill's chest, as she kept up her own desperate fight to start him breathing. She felt a great surge of hope as Dr. Wilber came in, hurriedly taking out his stethoscope. But he could find no pulse, no heartbeat, and to a massive dose of adrenalin injected directly into the heart there was no response.

In the back of the swaying ambulance as it raced to nearby Holy Family Hospital, Dr. Wilber and the ambulance attendant kept up their efforts, Wilber giving chest compressions, the aide working with a rubber breathing bag.

At the hospital, Joe Wilber for the first time in his life found himself praying to see on an EKG the jagged pattern of a fibrillating heart. There was nothing. Three more injections of adrenalin were made, and finally as a last resort, electric shock.

Mary Lynn was waiting, her lips bruised and tender, as Joe Wilber came out.

"There's nothing more anybody can do," he said. "Pappy is dead."

In her apartment in town, Grace Lundy turned on her television to watch the eleven o'clock news. As the tube flickered and grew bright, the telephone rang and she turned down the TV sound. Jack Tarver was on the phone.

"How are you, Grace?" he began, and she knew at once he had not called to ask about her health. "Fine," she said, and there was a long pause.

"Grace," he said, "Mr. McGill is dead."

Her reaction was an immediate rejection. "No, Mr. Tarver," she said. "That is not possible."

Then all at once she knew that it was possible, and that it had happened, and that deep down and subconsciously perhaps she, like Mary Lynn, had known that someday she would have to face this news. Years before, when first she knew about the bad heart, she had hidden in her desk, where he would never see them, the telephone numbers she would call in an emergency. . . .

Now, numb with shock but functioning calmly, she went out into the cold of the February night and got in her car and drove to Piedmont Road and spoke to Mary Lynn. Then she drove back downtown to her desk at the *Constitution* and stayed there, answering phones and digging things out of the files for the wire services and for the *Constitution* reporters who were writing the story, pawing at their typewriters half blind with tears. She stayed there, doing whatever needed doing, until nearly four o'clock in the morning, and then she went home. Before she left, she checked the engagement book in which she kept a record of where McGill was supposed to be, and what he was supposed to do, and whom he was supposed to see the next day, and the next, all through the year. The meeting next day with the young minister who was leaving the church, the trip next week to West Point to make a speech to the cadets, the monthly vestry meeting at All Saints — all of these would have to be canceled. And she remembered what he always said when he accepted an invitation: "Tell 'em, the Lord willing, I'll be there."

The nurse who followed Joe Wilber, bringing Ralph's spectacles and wallet to Mary Lynn, was small and young and shy.

"Mrs. McGill," she asked, "was Mr. McGill crippled in some way?"

"No, why?"

"Well, he was wearing funny-looking, high-topped shoes."

Deep as was her shock, Mary Lynn could not help laughing. Ralph had been so pleased with his new chukka boots.

The spectacles reminded her of another small vanity of his. His dentures were back at John Lawhorn's house. She had slipped them out as she began trying to revive him, and as she did so, the thought flashed through her mind that she was glad he didn't know what she was doing. He was sensitive about the fact that he wore false teeth. They were a symbol, to him, of childhood neglect, a reminder, too, that he had grown old. He would never let her see him without his teeth.

Her anger at her failure to save him, the bitter sense of frustration that had swept over her when Joe Wilber came out to tell her there was no hope, began to fade as John Lawhorn drove her home. If death had to come, it was better this way. Lines from a long-forgotten poem came to mind — "Let it be high noon, and let it then be night." So had his passing been: sudden, final, without struggle or pain. It was best for him that way. A stroke could have turned him into a mute and helpless vegetable, and she would have nursed and cared for him all his days. But that, she knew, would have been worse than death to a man so vital, so determined to make every living moment count. It could have been far worse for her, too, she thought. If it had happened in the car on a lonely road . . . or in the high-speed traffic on the expressway . . . or in a hotel room somewhere at night in a strange city. . . .

They drove up to the little house on Piedmont Road to find Jack and Margaret Tarver at the door, waiting to help her with the melancholy chores that faced her — the sad "bustle in the house the morning after death" of Emily Dickinson's poem, the "sweeping up the heart and putting love away . . . we will not need to use again until eternity."

Tarver, the next morning, went down to the funeral home to pick out the casket. Mary Lynn had admonished him not to choose anything fine or fancy. "He wouldn't like that," she said. "We'd been to a lot of funerals lately, and he'd always lean over to me and whisper, in a voice the people in the pews around us could hear: 'Look at that casket. I'll bet it cost ten thousand dollars. I want you to get a cheap one for me.' "

Tarver observed this whim of his old friend as he thought best, but he did make one last small gesture he knew would please McGill. He had taken to the funeral home the clothes that McGill was to be buried in, and just before the casket was to be closed, he made one last inspection. The tie, he noted, was right — the loosely knotted black and crimson stripe that McGill had adopted as his "old school" tie since Harvard gave him its honorary doctorate. One thing, though, was missing: The tie pin that McGill and Baggs and Tarver had been proud to wear — the tiny silver shoe sole with the hole in it that had been Adlai Stevenson's emblem. Tarver took off his own, and pinned it on McGill.

In a dozen years of peering over his spectacles from the pulpit of All Saints Episcopal Church, the Reverend Frank Ross, rector, had learned that one glance at the people who came to a funeral told more about the nature and character of the deceased than could any spoken eulogy. Never, though, had he seen such a mix of humanity gathered in his church as this crowd that had come to say good-bye to Ralph McGill. In the same pew with Hubert Humphrey sat Julia Johnson, gentle old Negro waitress, long retired, who for many years had served him lunch at a downtown tea room. Crunched together, back to belly in the line that pushed into the sanctuary, were Senator Herman Talmadge, a conservative on civil rights, and the *bête noire* of all conservatives, Charles "Chuck" Morgan, canny and combative lawyer for the American Civil Liberties Union. Crowded into the pews and standing along the walls were a cross section of Atlanta and the South, black and white, rich and poor, old winos sitting hip to hip with millionaires and all of them his friends. There were many there in whose lives he had been deeply involved: Marré Danger, Judy Tillman, Bill Gordon, Nancy Mason, Dino Shorte, youngsters he had helped and believed in. There were hundreds present, though, whom he had never met, had never spoken to, save through his writing. For this was his great gift — that he could change the lives of strangers, influencing men and women whom he never knew to become more gentle, compassionate, kind and understanding, turning them to a bolder, better way despite their fears, their ingrained prejudices.

One of those who was in his debt, and knew it, and freely acknowledged it, was his pastor, Frank Ross, who as a young minister had left the lowlands of Louisiana years before to come to Atlanta, partly because McGill was in the papers there and writing every day.

Sitting now in his study in the hour before the funeral, Ross ran over in his mind his memories of McGill. He recalled him in the vestry meetings, bored by the dull routine of administering a big church, yawning as the money-minded members wrangled over a budget. Sometimes, in the middle of such a session, he and two kindred souls, Elbert Tuttle, a federal judge, and Dr. William Kiser, a child psychiatrist, would break off into a discussion of their own — of the role of the church in a changing world, of the place of the church in the welfare picture, of the Head Start program and the children whose needs it served. The other yestrymen would fall silent, listening, and Ross, presiding, would let them talk, for to him these things, instead of the nickel-and-dime stuff, were what the living church was all about.

Ross, by his own self-understanding, knew that he was not by nature an aggressive liberal. He needed someone who would keep prodding him, reminding him of what he and his church should be saying, loud and clear and without equivocation, when he stood in the pulpit on Sunday morning.

McGill, for Ross, was that prod and reminder.

"He made you feel better about yourself and about the human race," Ross said. "He called out in you some strengths, some instincts for good you maybe hadn't paid much attention to before. And you found yourself wanting to do what he wanted done. He wasn't infallible. He wasn't God. He could be badly wrong about a lot of things and stubborn in his wrongness. Like the Vietnam war, for instance. But he did the job a hero had to do. He stood in a hero's place, and he stood firm. . . ."

Outside the old brownstone church, the police whistles were shrilling on North Avenue and West Peachtree Street. Ross looked at his watch. It was two P.M., a half-hour before the service, but already the sanctuary was beginning to fill. He thought of what was coming. It would be a sad walk for him, walking down that long center aisle ahead of the casket of his friend draped only with its damask pall. All men, high and low, were equal under that simple white cloth, adorned only with the crimson cross. And for all men, the majestic prayers and supplications were the same. But somehow, this was different; this was for McGill. . . .

Restless, he left his study and started for the church to make one last check to see that all was ready. A tense young man — one of former Vice-President Humphrey's security guards — stopped him. A call had just come in to the church office, he said. A male voice, sounding young, but harsh and rasping, had told Ellen Archer, the church secretary, "There's a bomb in the church. . . . It's set to go off at ——." He named the time.

Ross shook his head in angry disbelief. "My God," he thought. "Can't they even let him get out of this world without bugging him? Does he have to have an unlisted number at his own damn funeral?"

There was time for a search. Secret service men, moving unobtrusively among the arriving mourners, checked the pews in the sanctuary. Atlanta police swarmed through the rest of the church, searching the basement, the chapel, every hiding place that might conceal a bomb. While waiting for their report, Ross carried on in his mind an imagined conversation with the unknown caller, and all who felt like him: "Listen, you. Let the guy go. He's all right. Let him go. Leave him alone. Leave *us* alone. Go away. Talk about it tomorrow. Talk about it yesterday. But leave this day alone. . . ."

No bomb was found. At the appointed time, from the back of the church Frank Ross, in his white robes, started down the aisle, walking before the casket of his friend, intoning the majestic reassurance of the opening sentences: "I am the resurrection and the life, saith the Lord; he that believeth in me, though he were dead, yet shall he live; and whosoever liveth and believeth in me shall never die. . . ."

At the crossing before the altar where less than two years before McGill and Mary Lynn had said their marriage vows, the casket lay beneath its pall. In the service which followed, there was one departure from the traditional ritual of the Episcopal church. At the request of Mr. Ross, the Reverend Sam Williams, Negro chairman of the Community Relations Commission and pastor of the Friendship Baptist Church, spoke in eulogy of McGill.

"He lived among us as our teacher, loving us as Jesus taught us to do, yet shocking us, chiding us, as Socrates did his beloved Athens," said Sam Williams.

"He never tired trying to teach us what it means to be a civilized community, for the qualities of such a community were clear to him. They are truth, beauty, peace, adventure, art, justice and love. . . ."

The route of the funeral procession from All Saints to Westview Cemetery lay through the old part of town, now largely Negro in population. And at every intersection they were gathered — old cooks and maids and nurses with their strong, bent, blocky, wide-hipped bodies; grizzled old gardeners, yardmen, and janitors, lean and stooped; black-suited butlers and chauffeurs — all standing bareheaded in the cold, bright afternoon, wiping away tears and waving good-bye to the man who had done his utmost to open new doors for them and their children. The children were there, too, thronging one intersection, little fellows from the Agnes Jones school, where less than a year before, McGill had gone to hear John Lawhorn teaching them music and on leaving had told him, "John, you've got something here we must not let die."

Frank Ross had ridden many times before along this route, following a hearse from church to burying ground. But never before had it been like this, with the people weeping and calling their good-byes.

"To me," he said, "that summed it all up. That said all that needed saying about McGill and what his life had meant."

At the cemetery, a troop of black Boy Scouts from the Hope Lutheran Church, a storefront mission church in downtown Atlanta, waited in valiant but ragged line as an honor guard beside the grave. There was no official reason for their being there, their minister said. "They just wanted to come."

The graveside rites were brief. With Sam Williams beside him, Frank Ross took red earth into his hands, intoning the ancient commitment prayer: "Unto Almighty God we commend the soul of our brother departed, and we commit his body to the ground; earth to earth, ashes to ashes, dust to dust. . . ."

The sun went behind gray clouds, and a cold wind began to blow. Heads bowed in communal murmur of the Lord's Prayer and the shovels began to work as the closing prayers were spoken. Then over the raw mound of earth at last was laid a blanket of flowers.

The crowd turned away until only one mourner was left, an old Negro woman who stood, head bowed, beside the grave. "I come on the bus and got here late," she said. "I think I'll stay just a minute longer."

His grave lay beside that of Mary Elizabeth, at the foot of the two small stones which marked the place where their two little daughters had been buried more than thirty years before. Elizabeth, the first one, had lived four days, and McGill had brought the tiny casket to this place holding it on his lap. Virginia, who was his heart, had lived five years, but the carver had made an error on her stone, which showed that she died at four. His own temporary marker said simply, "Ralph Emerson McGill, 1898–1969."

After the funeral, a baker's dozen of old friends, among them Ashmore, Vanocur and Ann Landers, gathered at the house on Piedmont Road to drink to the memory of McGill and tell again the stories that had made him a legend — the rude and rowdy ones, the tender ones, the funny ones. There was much laughter, as there always is at such a time, for the human heart, when deeply hurt, stubbornly tries to shield itself from sorrow. They gathered, for the most part, in the narrow, fire-lit kitchen-dining room and den, where he used to sit and read and write.

In the shelves behind his chair were the books he liked to keep close at hand — books by or about people he knew and loved: *Angel Mo' and Her Son, Roland Hayes,* by MacKinley Helms, the story of the great Negro singer and his mother who was born a slave, Hemingway's *Old Man and the Sea,* Sandburg's poems and letters and his great biography of Lincoln, Carson McCullers's *The Heart Is a Lonely Hunter,* Flannery O'Connor's *Wise Blood,* and Nedra Tyre's *Red Wine First.* And Peggy Mitchell's *Gone With the Wind,* and the poems of the gaunt, consumptive Georgia mountaineer, Byron Herbert Reese. There were books there by John and Robert Kennedy and Adlai Stevenson and Martin Luther King, Jr. All were inscribed to him, with warmth and affection, and the inscriptions told much about him and the kind of man he was.

There was one book, though not inscribed, which had in it lines that sounded as if they were purposefully put together as an epitaph for him. It was a book of verse containing Robert Frost's "The Road Not Taken," which ends:

Two roads diverged in a wood, and I —
I took the one less traveled by,
And that has made all the difference.

McGill, like Frost's traveler, had seen his path diverge many times along the route he had followed from student to sportswriter to editor to publisher, from local celebrity to world figure. Each time, by some instinct, he had chosen the hard road, the lonely road, "the road less traveled by." And it had indeed, to him and to his region, made all the difference. For as the South he had loved moved out of its ancient thralldom to myth and legend, he who had led the way became himself a part of the lore and history of the new South that at last was coming to birth.

Epilogue

Journalists are by nature sentimentalists, and they never fail to mark the passing of one of their own, no matter how obscure he might have been. The death of Ralph McGill, who was in no sense obscure, stirred the brotherhood to reminiscence at home and around the world.

Jonathan Daniels of the *Raleigh News and Observer* struck the keynote of many another editorial comment when he said: "Ralph McGill is a man for remembering, not for sadness now. . . . He lived a life of joyousness as well as concern. His spirit still shines, a star for guidance . . . in a world which should — like Ralph McGill — never miss the beautiful while ministering to the damned."

In his raw copy for *Newsweek*, Joe Cumming wrote: "For all the uncommon dimension of his life, history will have to record him in his lonely role as the lightning rod that drew crackling whips of fire out of the stormy southern psyche. . . . Out of the deepest kind of love for his native land he stood fast, and in denouncing him the South was struggling within itself, in some unrealized way, to be free of its own inner demons. . . ."

To Celestine Sibley, fellow columnist on the *Constitution*, there was a simpler, less complicated McGill. In her farewell column to her old friend she wrote: "If he should have to be identified at heaven's gate, I think he will be happiest if St. Peter says, " 'Lord, this is Ralph McGill, newspaper reporter.' " There was an element of clairvoyance in this observation. Sibley and McGill had planned to cover the James Earl Ray trial together, and in November had gone up to Memphis to be mugged and fingerprinted. When the trial began the following March, McGill was dead and they gave her his identification card as a memento. On it, the editor, publisher and Pulitzer Prize–winning columnist was identified simply as "Ralph McGill, Reporter, *Atlanta Constitution*."

So, with a catch in its throat and a misty eye, the newspaper profession he had often rebuked and chided for its faults, but whose honest craftsmen — and the "men of wit and wonder" he loved and encouraged — said good-bye to the man who had in many ways epitomized its virtues.

There were many outside the profession who remembered him with tenderness. In New York, editor Mary Painter thought of him in Stephen Spender's words, as "one of those who were truly great" —

> . . . *who in their lives fought for life*
> *Who wore at their hearts the fire's centre.*
> *Born of the sun they travelled a short while towards the sun,*
> *And left the vivid air signed with their honour.*"

And from the little town of Butler, Georgia, Louise Suggs, a French war bride whose life in America was made bearable through McGill's writings and his friendship, wrote of him: "To me he was like Tolstoi, a man full of tenderness, full of humanity, loved by so many and by so many misunderstood."

Some of those who did not like him wrote in to express their pleasure at his death, though they were remarkably few. A typical excerpt from a scribbled card signed "A Reader": "He was a liar, a sneak, a plagiarist, a Red, a man of little learning and nebulous intellect. I'm frankly glad he's dead."

Another anonymous communication in a different vein was left in my mailbox the night after his death. There was no clue to the author. It was a poem, "On Ralph McGill, Who Fought for Those Denied a Place about the Common Table." In stately cadence it urged:

> *Waste not your tears in grief about his fate.*
> *He was a warrior happy in the fray. . . .*
> *He savored life and drank quite deep of it. . . .*
> *If tears are shed, then let them fall*
> *For this dear, sad, divided land he loved. . . .*
> *He loved this land, he held its people to his heart*

But kept uneasy watch upon
Its conscience; like a mother he reminded it
That being just is oft more difficult
Than being brave. . . .
Good men leave goodly gifts; kind men
Leave love behind, let his memorial be
A kinder heart, a truer sympathy.

He did leave love behind, and men of kinder hearts and truer sympathy, and goodly gifts from some of them soon made possible more tangible monuments to his memory. With a gift of ten thousand dollars from his old friend John Griffin's Southern Education Foundation, matched by another ten thousand dollars from the Atlanta Newspapers, a Ralph McGill Memorial Fund was set up at the Atlanta University Center — a consortium of predominately Negro Colleges. With a gift of fifty thousand dollars from the James M. Cox Foundation, matched by fifty thousand dollars from an anonymous "friend" — who was, of course, Robert W. Woodruff — the Ralph McGill Scholarship Fund was established to provide help to journalism students in southern colleges and universities. The Atlanta Board of Education named a new school the Ralph Emerson McGill Primary School. The Atlanta Gas Light Company and Radio Station WSB set up in front of the *Constitution*'s splendid new building a gas light to burn in his memory with an eternal flame. And at the downtown Commerce Club, haunt of the economic fat cats who used to glower at him when he lunched there, a room was named in his honor.

So, though he was the humblest of men, his finish was triumphant, as he found his final place in the annals of his profession, his city and his region.

Index